C Primer Plus

Related Titles

C Primer Plus

Revised Edition

Mitchell Waite, Stephen Prata
and Donald Martin

The Waite Group

HOWARD W. SAMS & COMPANY

A Division of Macmillan, Inc.
4300 West 62nd Street
Indianapolis, Indiana 46268 USA

REVISED EDITION
FIFTH PRINTING—1988

International Standard Book Number: 0-672-22582-4
Library of Congress Catalog Card Number: 87-60388

The Waite Group Developmental Editor: *Mitch Waite*
The Waite Group Managing Editor: *James Stockford*

Acquisitions Editor: *James S. Hill*
Copy and Production Editor: *Diana C. Francoeur*
Interior Designer: *T. R. Emrick*
Illustrators: *David Cripe, T. R. Emrick*
Cartoonist: *Bob Johnson*
Indexer: *Ted Laux*
Compositor: *Shepard Poorman Communications, Inc.*

Printed in the United States of America

Contents

About the Authors   xiv

Preface to the First Edition   xv

Preface to the Revised Edition   xvi

1 Getting Ready   1

Whence C?   3
Why C?   4
Whither C   5
Using C   5
    Using an Editor to Prepare Your Program   7
    Source Files and Executable Files   9
    Compiling C on a UNIX System   9
    Compiling a C Program on an IBM PC (Microsoft C)   10
    Another Strategy   12
    But Why?   12
Some Conventions   12
    Typeface   12
    Screen Output   12
    Input and Output Devices   13
    Keys   13
    Our System   13
Advice   13

2 Introducing C   15

A Simple Sample of C   17
The Explanation   18
    Pass 1: Quick Synopsis   18
    Pass 2: Details   20
The Structure of a Simple Program   26
Tips on Making Your Programs Readable   27
Taking Another Step   28
And While We're at It   29

What You Should Have Learned   30
Review Questions   30
    Answers   31
Exercises   32

3 Data, C, and You   33

Data: Variables and Constants   37
Data: Data Types   38
    The Integer   40
    The Floating-Point Number   40
C Data Types   42
    The *int* Type   43
    Other Integer Types   46
    Using Characters: Type *char*   49
    Types *float* and *double*   53
    Other Types   55
    Type Sizes   57
Using Data Types   59
What You Should Have Learned.   59
Review Questions   60
    Answers   61
Exercises   62

4 Character Strings, #define, printf( ), and scanf( )   63

Character Strings—An Introduction   66
    String Length—*strlen( )*   68
Constants and the C Preprocessor   70
    C—A Master of Disguise: Creating Aliases   73
Exploring and Exploiting *printf( )* and *scanf( )*   75
    Using *printf( )*   76
    Conversion Specification Modifiers for *printf( )*   79
    Using *printf( )* to Make Conversions   82
    Using *scanf( )*   83
    The * Modifier with *printf( )* and *scanf( )*   85
Usage Tips   86
What You Should Have Learned   87
Review Questions   88
    Answers   88
Exercises   89

5 Operators, Expressions, and Statements   91

Introducing Loops   93
Fundamental Operators   95
    Assignment Operator: =   96
    Addition Operator: +   97
    Subtraction Operator: −   98
    Sign Operator: −   98

Multiplication Operator: *   98
Division Operator: /   101
Operator Precedence   102
Some Additional Operators   104
Modulus Operator: %   105
Increment and Decrement Operators: ++ and --   106
Decrementing: --   109
Precedence   110
Don't Be Too Clever   111
Expressions and Statements   112
Expressions   112
Statements   113
Compound Statements (Blocks)   115
Type Conversions   117
Cast Operator   120
An Example Program   121
What You Should Have Learned   123
Review Questions   123
Answers   126
Exercises   129

6   Input/Output Functions and Redirection   **131**

Single-Character I/O: *getchar( )* and *putchar( )*   134
Buffers   136
Onward   137
Reading a Single Line   140
Reading a File   141
Redirection and Files   144
UNIX   145
Non-UNIX   149
System-Dependent I/O: 8086/8088 I/O Ports   152
Using a Port   155
Summary   156
Tapping the Hidden Horsepower of Your Computer   156
What You Should Have Learned   158
Review Questions   158
Answers   159
Exercises   160

7   Choosing Alternatives   **161**

The *if* Statement   163
Adding *else* to the *if* Statement   165
Choice: *if-else*   165
Multiple Choice: *else-if*   167
Pairing *else's* with *if's*   170
Which Is Bigger: Using Relational Operators and
Expressions   173

What Is Truth?   175
So What Else Is True?   176
Troubles with Truth   177
Priority of Relational Operators   178
Let's Get Logical   179
Priorities   181
Order of Evaluation   182
A Word-Count Program   182
Character Sketches   184
Analyzing the Program   186
The Conditional Operator: ?:   191
Multiple Choice: *switch* and *break*   192
What You Should Have Learned   197
Review Questions   198
Answers   199
Exercises   202

8   Loops and Other Control Aids   **203**

The *while* loop   205
Terminating a *while* loop   207
Algorithms and Pseudocode   208
The *for* Loop   212
Using *for* for Flexibility   213
The Comma Operator   217
Zeno Meets the *for* Loop   220
An Exit-Condition Loop: *do while*   222
Which Loop?   223
Nested Loops   225
Other Control Statements: *break, continue, goto*   227
The *break* Statement   227
The *continue* Statement   229
The *goto* Statement   229
Arrays   233
A Question of Input   237
Summary   241
What You Should Have Learned   241
Review Questions   242
Answers   245
Exercises   247

9   How to Function Properly   **249**

Creating and Using a Simple Function   252
Function Arguments   255
Defining a Function with an Argument: Formal
Arguments   257
Calling a Function with an Argument: Actual
Arguments   257

The Black Box Viewpoint   258
Multiple Arguments   259
Returning a Value from a Function: *return*   259
Local Variables   262
Finding Addresses: The & Operator   262
Altering Variables in the Calling Program   263
Pointers: A First Look   265
The Indirection Operator: *   266
Declaring Pointers   267
Using Pointers to Communicate between Functions   268
Putting Our Knowledge of Functions to Work   272
Specifying Function Types   275
The *void* Type   276
All C Functions Are Created Equal   278
Summary   280
What You Should Have Learned   280
Review Questions   281
Answers   281
Exercises   283

10   Storage Classes and Program Development   285

Storage Classes and Scope   287
Automatic Variables   289
External Variables   289
Definitions and Declarations   291
Static Variables   291
External Static Variables   292
Register Variables   293
Scope Summary   294
Which Storage Class?   294
A Random Number Function   294
Roll 'Em   298
An Integer-fetching Function: *getint( )*   301
A Plan   301
Information Flow for *getint( )*   302
Inside *getint( )*   303
String-to-Integer Conversion: *stoif( )*   305
Trying It Out   307
Sorting Numbers   308
Reading In Numeric Data   310
Choosing the Data Representation   310
Ending Input   310
Further Consideration   310
The Functions *main( )* and *getarray( )*   311
Explanation   312
Sorting the Data   314
Printing the Data   316

Results 316
Overview 317
What You Should Have Learned 319
Review Questions 319
Answers 320
Exercises 322

11 The C Preprocessor **323**

Symbolic Constants: *#define* 325
Using Arguments with *#define* 328
Macro or Function 331
File Inclusion: *#include* 333
Header Files: An Example 333
Other Directives: *#undef, #if, #ifdef, #ifndef, #else, #elif,*
and *#endif* 335
What You Should Have Learned 337
Review Questions 338
Answers 338
Exercises 338

12 Arrays and Pointers **341**

Arrays 343
Initialization and Storage Class 344
Pointers to Arrays 347
Functions, Arrays, and Pointers 349
Using Pointers to Do an Array's Work 351
Pointer Operations 353
Multidimensional Arrays 356
Initializing a Two-Dimensional Array 359
Pointers and Multidimensional Arrays 360
Functions and Multidimensional Arrays 362
What You Should Have Learned 367
Review Questions 367
Answers 369
Exercises 370

13 Character Strings and String Functions **373**

Defining Strings within a Program 377
Character String Constants 377
Character String Arrays and Initialization 378
Array versus Pointer 379
Specifying Storage Explicitly 380
Arrays of Character Strings 381
Pointers and Strings 382
String Input 384
Creating Space 384
The *gets( )* Function 385

The *scanf( )* Function   387
String Output   388
    The *puts( )* Function   388
    The *printf( )* Function   389
The Do-It-Yourself Option   390
String Functions   391
    The *strlen( )* Function   392
    The *strcat( )* Function   392
    The *strcmp( )* Function   393
    The *strcpy( )* Function   396
A String Example: Sorting Strings   398
Command-Line Arguments   400
What You Should Have Learned   404
Review Questions   404
    Answers   407
Exercises   408

14   Structures and Other Data Delights   411

Example Problem: Creating an Inventory of Books   413
Setting Up the Structure Template   415
Defining a Structure Variable   416
    Initializing a Structure   417
Gaining Access to Structure Members   418
Arrays of Structures   419
    Declaring an Array of Structures   420
    Identifying Members of a Structure Array   421
    Program Details   422
Nested Structures   422
Pointers to Structures   424
    Declaring and Initializing a Structure Pointer   426
    Member Access by Pointer   426
Telling Functions about Structures   428
    Using Structure Members   428
    Using the Structure Address   430
    Using an Array   431
Structures: What Next?   433
Unions—A Quick Look   433
typedef—A Quick Look   435
What You Should Have Learned   438
Review Questions   439
    Answers   441
Exercises   443

15   The C Library and File Input/Output   445

Gaining Access to the C Library   447
    Automatic Access   447
    File Inclusion   447

Library Inclusion   448
Library Functions We Have Used   448
Communicating with Files   448
    What Is a File?   449
A Simple File-reading Program: *fopen( )*, *fclose( )*, *getc( )*,
    and *putc( )*   449
    Opening a File: *fopen( )*   450
    Closing a File: *fclose( )*   451
    Buffered Text Files   451
    File I/O: *getc( )* and *putc( )*   452
A Simple File-condensing Program   452
File I/O: *fprintf( )*, *fscanf( )*, *fgets( )*, and *fputs( )*   454
    The *fprintf( )* and *fscanf( )* Functions   454
    The *fgets( )* Function   455
    The *fputs( )* Function   455
Random Access: *fseek( )*   456
Testing and Converting Characters   459
String Conversions: *atoi( )*, *atof( )*   462
Getting Out: *exit( )*   465
Memory Allocation: *malloc( )* and *calloc( )*   465
Other Library Functions   469
What You Should Have Learned   469
Review Questions   470
    Answers   471
Exercises   474

16   What Next?   **477**

The ANSI C Language Standard   479
    An Overview   480
    The *void* Function Type   481
    New, Improved Structure Status   482
    The C Library   485
    Function Prototypes   487
    Changes in Types   490
    Arithmetic   491
    Enumerated Types   491
    Other Types   492
C++   494
    C++ Goals   494
    Classes   494
    Operator Overloading   496
    Function Overloading   496
    Back to Classses   497
    C++ Philosophy   501
    C++ and C   501
Closing Words   502
What You Should Have Learned   502

Review Questions   503
    Answers   503

A   Additional Reading   **507**

The C Language   507
Programming   508
The UNIX Operating System   508

B   Keywords in C   **509**

Program Flow Keywords   509

C   C Operators   **511**

D   Data Types and Storage Classes   **517**

The Basic Data Types   517
How to Declare a Simple Variable   518
Storage Classes   519

E   Program Flow Control   **521**

The *while* Statement   521
The *for* Statement   522
The *do while* Statement   523
Using *if* Statements for Making Choices   523
Multiple Choice with *switch*   524
Program Jumps   525

F   Bit Fiddling: Operators and Fields   **527**

Operators   527
    Bitwise Logical Operators   527
    Bitwise Shift Operators   529
Fields   530

G   Binary Numbers and Others   **533**

Binary Numbers   533
    Binary Floating Point   534
Other Bases   535
    Octal   535
    Hexadecimal   535

H   IBM PC Music   **537**

The *tone( )* Function   537
    Tone Duration   538
    Tone Frequency   538
    Using the *tone( )* Function   540

I   ASCII Table   **543**

Index   **547**

About the Authors

Mitchell Waite, president of The Waite Group, is an experienced programmer, fluent in a variety of computer languages. He has studied nuclear engineering, built biofeedback machines, written poetry, and raced motorcycles. Mr. Waite is the coauthor of several Sams/Waite titles, including *UNIX Primer Plus, CP/M® Primer,* and *Soul of CP/M.*

Stephen Prata is a professor of physics and astronomy at the College of Marin in Kentfield, California, where he is involved with teaching UNIX and the C language. He received his B.S. from the California Institute of Technology and his Ph.D. from the University of California, Berkeley. His association with computers began with the computer modeling of star clusters. Dr. Prata is coauthor of *UNIX Primer Plus.*

Donald Martin is Director of the Computer Science Center at the College of Marin. He received his A.B. from the University of California, Berkeley, and his M.A. from San Jose State University. He has long been interested in the problems that students have in developing their reasoning and critical thinking skills. This interest has led him to the LOGO computer language, a course he now teaches on a UNIX-based system at the college. Mr. Martin is coauthor of *UNIX Primer Plus.*

Preface to the
First Edition

C is a simple, elegant programming language that is the choice of a rapidly increasing number of programmers. In *C Primer Plus,* you will find a friendly, easy-to-use guide to learning and using C.

The *Primer* in the book title indicates that our first goal is to guide you through the basics of C. Experience is the best teacher in programming, and you will find many examples to use, study, and play with. We've tried to use figures whenever we think they help clarify a point. The main features of C are summarized and highlighted with a screened background to make them easy to find. There are questions (and answers) to let you check your progress. We don't assume any great past computer language experience on your part, but we do make an occasional comparison with other languages to aid those readers who know them.

The *Plus* in the title represents several extras. One, already mentioned, is a question and answer section at the end of each chapter. A second plus is that we go a bit beyond the boundaries of a simple primer and discuss some of the more advanced topics, such as using structures, casts, file operations, the new C++ language and, in the appendix, C's handling of bits. A third plus is that the book covers both the UNIX and the microcomputer environment for C. For example, we discuss redirection of input and output in both environments, and we illustrate the use of ports for the 8086/8088 microprocessor. The cartoons provide another plus, a rather pleasant one.

We've tried to make this introduction to C instructive, clear, and helpful. To get the greatest benefit from this book, you should take as active a role as possible. Don't just read the examples. Enter them into your system and try them out. C is a very portable language, but perhaps you may find differences between how a program works on your system and how it works on ours. Experiment—change part of a program to see what effect that has. Modify a program to do something slightly different. Ignore our occasional warnings and see what happens. Try the questions and the exercises. The more you do yourself, the more you will learn.

We wish you good fortune in learning C. We've tried to make this book meet your needs, and we hope it helps you reach your goals.

Mitchell Waite   Stephen Prata   Donald Martin

Preface to the
Revised Edition

One nice thing about writing computer books as opposed to writing novels is that you can go back and improve the original book. And that is what we've tried to do in this Revised Edition of *C Primer Plus*. The improvements and changes occur mostly in four areas:

☐ *Coverage of the ANSI C Standard and of the C++ programming language.* The world of C is changing, so we have added a chapter to describe these important recent developments.

☐ *More questions and exercises.* The surest path to learning any programming language is to use the language. Therefore, we have added many new questions (with answers) and exercises to give you more experience in using C.

☐ *New or revised explanations.* We have rewritten explanations, as needed, to clarify the subject matter, and in many places you will find an additional sentence or two to further aid your understanding.

☐ *Fixed glitches and snags.* We've fixed many small inadvertent errors that our readers have been kind enough to point out. (Please keep up the good work.)

All in all, these changes make the Revised Edition more up-to-date, more informative, and easier to understand. We hope you enjoy using this edition.

With love to Vicky and Bill, my parents—S.P.

Acknowledgments

The authors would like to thank Robert Lafore of the Waite Group for his editorial advice and Bob Petersen for his technical assistance. We thank Lifeboat Associates (Joshua Allen and Todd Katz in particular) for providing and supporting the Lattice C and Advantage C++ Compiler. We also thank C-Systems, The Software Toolworks, Telecon Systems, and Supersoft for providing us with information about their C compilers, and special thanks go to Microsoft (and Marty Taucher) for providing the Microsoft 4.0 C Compiler used with this Revised Edition. Last but not least, we would like to state our appreciation to Nancy Lebed Berry and Douglas Adams for their editorial work on the Revised Edition.

1

Getting Ready

Concepts

- C history
- C virtues
- Compiled languages
- Running a C program

Welcome to the world of C. This chapter will prepare you for learning and using this powerful and increasingly popular language. Just what do you need to get ready? First, you need an interest in C. Most likely you already have that, but, to increase your interest even more, we will outline some of the more attractive aspects of C. Second, you need a guide to the C language. This book will serve you there. Next, you need access to a computing system with a C compiler. That you will have to arrange yourself. Finally, you need to learn how to run a C program on your system, and we will offer you some advice about that at the end of this chapter.

Whence C?

Dennis Ritchie of Bell Labs created C in 1972 as he and Ken Thompson worked on designing the UNIX™ operating system. C didn't spring full-grown from Ritchie's head, however. It came from Thompson's B language, which came from . . . . But that's another story. The important point is that C was created as a tool for working programmers. Thus, its chief goal is to be a *useful* language.

Most languages, we suppose, aim to be useful, but often they have other concerns. One of the main goals for Pascal, for instance, was to provide a sound basis for teaching programming principles. BASIC, on the other hand, was developed to resemble English so that it could be easily learned by students unfamiliar with computers. These are important goals, but they are not always compatible with pragmatic, workaday usefulness. C's background as a programming tool does, however, support its role as a programmer-friendly language.

Why C?

C is rapidly becoming one of the most important and popular programming languages. Its use is growing because people try it and like it. As you learn C, you, too, will recognize its many virtues. Let's mention a few of them now.

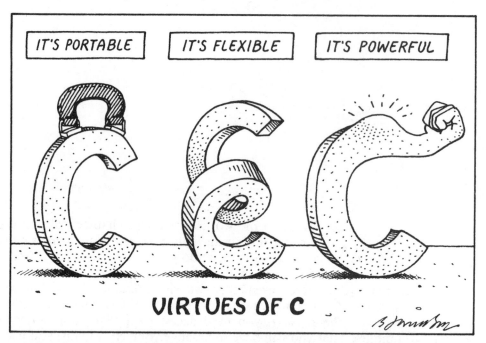

VIRTUES OF C

C is a modern language incorporating the control features that computer science theory and practice find desirable. The design of C makes it natural for users to use top-down planning, structured programming, and modular design. The result is a more reliable, understandable program.

C is an efficient language. Its design takes advantage of the abilities of current computers. C programs tend to be compact and to run quickly.

C is a portable language. This means that C programs written on one system can be run with little or no modification on other systems. If modifications are necessary, they can often be made just by changing a few entries in a "header" file accompanying the main program. Of course, most languages are meant to be portable, but anyone who has converted an IBM PC BASIC program to Apple® BASIC (and they are close cousins) or tried to run an IBM® mainframe FORTRAN program on a UNIX system will know that there can be many troublesome details. C is a leader in portability. C compilers are available for about 40 systems, running from 8-bit microprocessors to the world's current computer speed champ, the Cray 1.

C is powerful and flexible (two favorite words in computer literature). For example, most of the powerful, flexible (see!) UNIX operating system is written in C. This includes compilers and interpreters for other languages, such as FORTRAN, APL, Pascal, LISP, Logo, and BASIC. So when you use FORTRAN on a UNIX machine, ultimately a C program does the work of producing the final executable program. C programs have been used for solving physics and engineering problems and even for animating sequences in movies such as *The Return of the Jedi*.

C exhibits some of the fine control usually associated with assembly language. If you choose, you can fine-tune your programs for maximum efficiency.

C is friendly. It is sufficiently structured to encourage good programming habits, but it doesn't bind you in a straitjacket of restrictions.

There are more virtues, and, undoubtedly, a few faults. Rather than delve further into the matter, let's ask one more question.

Whither C?

C already is a dominant language in the minicomputer world of UNIX systems. Now it is spreading to personal computers. Many software houses are turning to C as the preferred language for producing word processing programs, spreadsheets, compilers, and other products. These companies know that C produces compact and efficient programs. More important, they know that these programs will be easy to modify and easy to adapt to new models of computers.

Another force helping to spread C to the personal computer environment is the desire of UNIX C users to take their C programs home. Several C compilers are available now to let them do just that.

What's good for the companies and the C veterans is good for other users, too. More and more computer users are turning to C to secure its advantages for themselves. You don't have to be a computer professional to use C.

In short, C is destined to be one of the most important languages of the 1980s and 1990s. It is used on minicomputers and on personal computers. It is used by software companies, by computer science students, and by enthusiasts of all sorts. And if you want a job writing software, one of the first questions you should be able to answer "yes" to is: "Oh say can you C?"

Using C

C is a *compiled language*. If that fails to ring a bell (or succeeds in ringing an alarm bell), don't worry because we will explain "compiling" as we describe the steps in producing a C program.

If you are accustomed to using a compiled language, such as Pascal or FORTRAN, you will be familiar with the basic steps in putting a C program together. But if your background is in an *interpreted* language, such as BASIC or Logo, or if you have no background at all, you may find the process a little strange at first. Fortunately, we are here to guide you through

Figure 1.1
The virtues of C

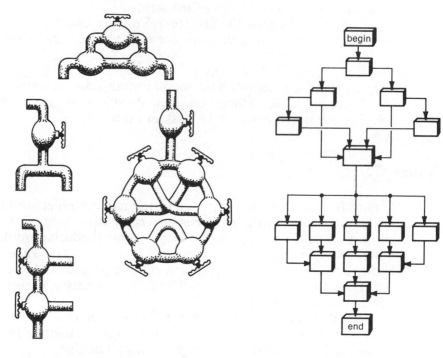

Flexible control structures *Structured format*

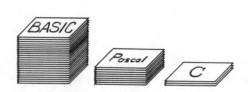

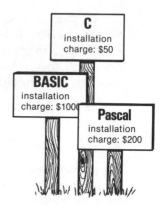

Compact code—small programs *Portable to other computers*

Figure 1.2
Where C is used

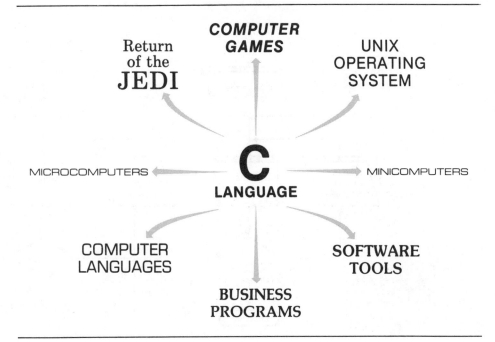

the process, and you'll see that it is actually pretty straightforward and sensible.

First, to give you an overview of the process, here is a simplified outline of what you do to go from writing a program to running it:

1. Use an editor to write your program in C.

2. Submit your program to your friendly compiler. It will check your program for errors and let you know if it finds any. If not, the compiler undertakes the task of translating your program to your computer's internal language, and it places this translation into a new file.

3. You can then make your program run by typing in the name of this new file.

On some systems, the second step may be subdivided into two or three substeps, but the idea is the same.

Let's take a longer look at each step now.

Using an Editor to Prepare Your Program

Unlike BASIC, C does not have its own editor. Instead, you use one of the general-purpose editors available for your system. On a UNIX system, that

Figure 1.3
Interpreter versus compiler

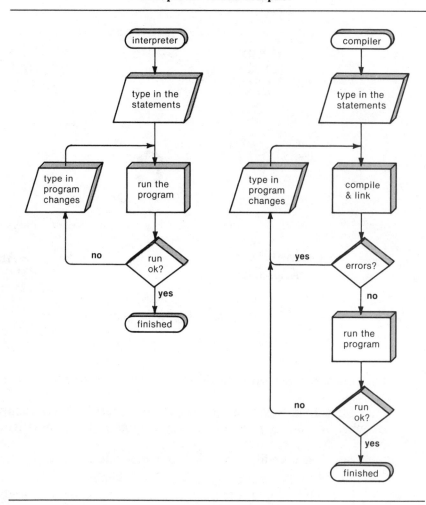

might be **ed, ex, edit, emacs,** or **vi.** On a personal system, it might be **ed, edlin,** WordStar®, WordPerfect®, or any other of a vast number of editors. With some editors you need to specify a particular option. On WordStar, for example, you would use the **N,** or nondocument, option.

Your two main responsibilities here are typing the program correctly and choosing a name for the file that will store the program. The rules for a name are simple: it must be a legal name for your system, and the name should end with **.c.** Here are two such names:

```
sort.c
add.c
```

Choose the first part of the name to remind you of what the program does. The second part **(.c)** identifies the file as a C program. In the wonderful world of computers, the part of a name following a period is called an *extension*. Extensions are used to inform you and the computer about the nature of a file.

Here is an example. Using an editor we prepared the following program and stored it in a file called **inform.c.**

```
#include <stdio.h>
main()
{
 printf("A .c is used to end a C program file name.\n");
}
```

The text we just typed is known as *source code,* and it is kept in a *source file.* The important point here is that our source file is the beginning of a process, not the end.

Source Files and Executable Files

Our program, although undeniably brilliant, is still gibberish to a computer. A computer doesn't understand things like **#include** or **printf.** It understands *machine code,* things like 10010101 and 01101001. If we want the computer's cooperation, we must translate *our* code (source code) to *its* code (machine code). The result of our efforts will be an *executable file,* which is a file filled with all the machine code the computer needs to get the job done.

If that sounds tedious, don't worry. We have managed to shift the burden of this translation to the machine itself! Clever programs called *compilers* do the brunt of the work. The details of the process depend on the particular system. We will outline a few approaches now.

Compiling C on a UNIX System

The UNIX C compiler is called **cc.** All we need to do to compile our program is to type:

```
cc inform.c
```

After a few seconds, the UNIX prompt will return, telling us the deed is done. (We may get warnings and error messages if we fail to write the program properly, but let's assume we do everything right.) If we use **ls** to list our files, we find that there is a new file called **a.out.** This is the executable file containing the translation (or "compilation") of our program. To run it, we just type:

```
a.out
```

Figure 1.4
Preparing a C program using UNIX

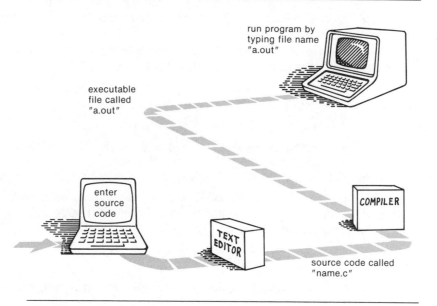

and our wisdom pours forth:

```
A .c is used to end a C program file name.
```

The **cc** program combines several steps into one. This becomes more obvious when we examine the same process on a personal computer.

Compiling a C Program on an IBM PC (Microsoft C)

The exact steps depend on the operating system and on the compiler. The example we give is the Microsoft® C Compiler running under PC-DOS 3.1. Again, we start with a file called **inform.c.** Our first command is:

```
msc inform;
```

(The compiler interprets **inform** as **inform.c**). If all goes well, this produces a file called **inform.obj,** which contains the *object code* (machine language code) for our code. Then we type:

```
link inform;
```

and this produces our goal, an executable file called **inform.exe.** (If you don't have a hard disk, you will probably have to change floppy disks when using Microsoft C. Check your compiler manual.) If we type:

    inform.exe

or, for short,

    inform

the program runs.

Figure 1.5
Preparing a C program in Microsoft C

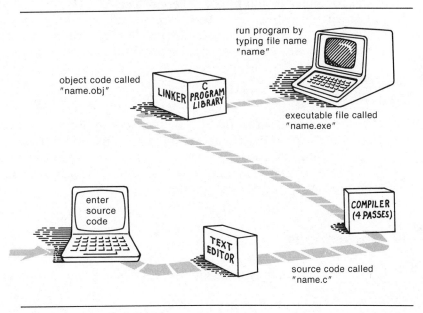

You don't really have to know what is going on to use this procedure, but here's a rundown if you are interested.

What's new here? For one thing, the file **inform.obj** is new. Since it is in machine code, why aren't we finished here? The answer is that the complete program includes parts that we didn't write. For example, we used the command **printf**, which is a program stored in the C library. A complete program needs to use some standard routines stored elsewhere. This is where the second new item, the **link** command, comes in.

Link comes with the IBM DOS operating system. It links our object code file (**inform.obj**) with a start-up file of some standard items and searches a library for functions. It then combines all the elements together into the final program.

The UNIX **cc** program goes through a similar sequence of steps; it just hides the fact from us, erasing the object file when it is done. (But if we ask nicely, it will give us the object file under the name **inform.o**).

Another Strategy

Several personal computer C compilers take a different route. The method we just discussed produces an object code file (extension **.obj**) and uses the system linker to produce an executable file (extension **.exe**). The alternative method is to produce an *assembly code* file (extension **.asm**) and then use the system *assembler* to produce an executable file.

Oh my! Yet another code! Assembler code is very closely related to machine code. Indeed, it is just a mnemonic representation. For example, JMP may represent 11101001, which is the part of the machine code telling the computer to jump to a different location. (If you visualize a computer headed towards a lake, be aware we are speaking of different *memory* locations.) Humans find assembler code much easier to remember than pure machine code, and the assembler program takes care of making the translation.

But Why?

Those of you used to BASIC may wonder about going through these steps to run a program. It may seem time-consuming. It may even *be* time-consuming. But once a program is compiled, it will run *much* faster than a standard BASIC program. You trade some inconvenience in getting a program running for a much swifter final product.

Some Conventions

We are almost ready to begin. We just need to mention some conventions we will use.

Typeface

For text representing programs, computer input and output, and the names of files, programs, and variables, we will use a type font that resembles what you might get on a screen or printed output. We already have used it a few times; in case it slipped by you, the font looks like this:

```
printf("Howdy!\n");
```

Screen Output

Output from the computer is indicated with a light gray screen. Where lines of output are interspersed with user input, only the screen output is highlighted. For example, here is a program run from Chapter 14:

```
Please enter the book title.
Press [enter] at the start of a line to stop.
My Life as a Budgie
Now enter the author.
Mack Zackles
```

Input and Output Devices

There are many ways that you and a computer can communicate with each other. However, we will assume that you type in commands using a keyboard and that you read the response on a screen.

Keys

Usually you send a line of instructions onward by pressing a key that is labeled "enter," "c/r," "Return," or some variation of these. We will refer to this key as the [enter] key. The brackets mean that you press a single key rather than type out the word "enter."

We also will refer to control characters such as [control-d]. This notation means to press the [d] key while you are depressing the key labeled "control."

Our System

Some aspects of C, such as the amount of space used to store a number, depend on the system. When we give examples and refer to "our system," we speak of an IBM PC running under PC-DOS 3.1 and using a Microsoft C compiler.

We also occasionally refer to running programs on a UNIX system. The one we use is Berkeley's BSD 4.1 version of UNIX running on a VAX® 11/750 computer.

Advice

You learn programming through doing, not just reading. We have included many examples. You should try running at least some of them on your system to get a better idea of how they work. Try making modifications to see what happens. Try working through the questions and exercises at the ends of the chapters. Be an active, experimenting learner. You will learn C more quickly, and your comprehension will be deeper.

Okay, you are ready and we are ready, so let's turn to Chapter 2.

2

Introducing C

Concepts
- Structure of a simple program
- Declaring variables
- Using comments
- Readable programs

Operators
- =

W   hat does a C program look like? Perhaps you have seen a
           sample in Chapter 1 or elsewhere and found it peculiar-look-
           ing, sprinkled with symbols like { and ***ptr++**. As you read
           through this book, you will find that the appearance of these
and of other characteristic C symbols grows less strange, more familiar,
perhaps even welcome! In this chapter we will begin by presenting a rather
simple example program and explaining what it does. At the same time we
will highlight some of the basic features of C. If you desire detailed elabora-
tions of these features, don't worry. They will come in the following chapters.

A Simple Sample of C

Let's take a look at a simple C program. We have to admit that the following
example is not very practical, but it will serve to point out some of the basic
features of a program in C. Before you read our line-by-line explanation of
the program, read through the program to see if you can figure out for
yourself what it will do.

```
#include <stdio.h>
main() /*a simple program */
{
 int num;

 num = 1;
 printf("I am a simple ");
 printf("computer.\n");
```

```
    printf("My favorite number is %d because it is first.\n",num);
}
```

If you think this program will print some things on the screen, you are right! But exactly what will be printed may not be clear, so let's run the program and see what comes out.

The first step is to use your editor to create a file containing these innocent lines. You will have to give the file a name; if you can't think one up, use **main.c** for a file name. Now compile the program. (Here we wait patiently while you consult the manual for your particular compiler.) Now run the program. If all went well, the output should look like this:

```
I am a simple computer.
My favorite number is 1 because it is first.
```

All in all, this result is not too surprising. But what happened to the **\n**'s and the **%d** in the program? And some of the lines in the program do look a bit strange. It must be time for an explanation.

The Explanation

We'll take two passes through the program. The first pass will highlight the meaning of each line, and the second pass will explore some of the implications and details.

Pass 1: Quick Synopsis

```
#include <stdio.h>    ←include another file
```

This line tells the computer to include information found in the file **stdio.h.**

```
main()   ←a function name
```

C programs consist of one or more *functions,* which are the basic modules of a C program. This program consists of one function called **main.** The parentheses identify **main( )** as a function name.

```
/* a simple program */   ←a comment
```

You can use the symbols /* and */ to enclose comments. Comments

Figure 2.1
Anatomy of a C program

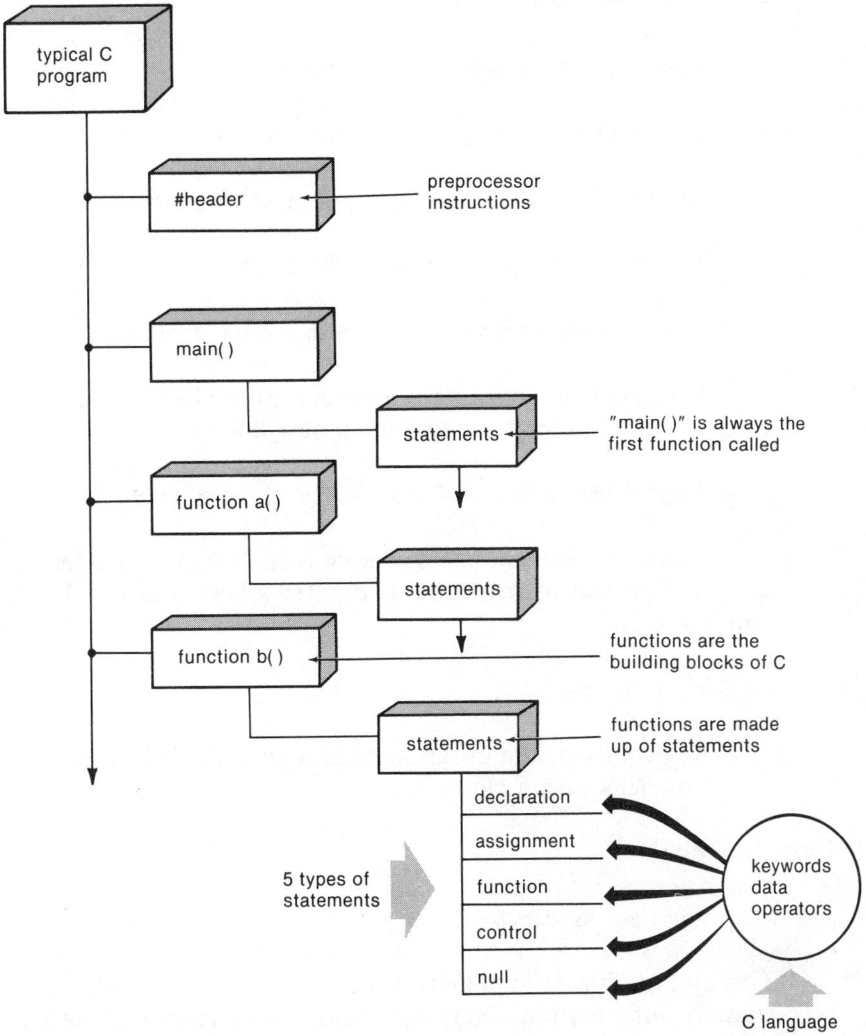

are remarks to help clarify a program. They are intended only for the reader and are ignored by the computer.

  {   ←beginning of the body of the function

This opening brace marks the start of the statements that make up the function. The function definition is ended with a closing brace, }.

```
int num;   ←a declaration statement
```

This statement announces that we will be using a variable called **num** and that **num** will be an **int**eger type.

```
num = 1;   ←an assignment statement
```

This statement assigns the value 1 to **num.**

```
printf("I am a simple ");   ←a print statement
```

This prints the phrase within the quotes: `I am a simple`

```
printf("computer.\n");   ←another print statement
```

This tacks on `computer` to the end of the last phrase printed. The **\n** is code telling the computer to start a new line.

```
printf("My favorite number is %d because it is first.\n", num);
```

This line prints the value of **num** (which is 1) embedded in the phrase in quotes. The **%d** instructs the computer where and in what form to print **num's** value.

```
}   ←the end
```

As promised, the program ends with a closing brace.
Now let's take a closer look.

Pass 2: Details

```
#include <stdio.h>
```

The **stdio.h** file is supplied as part of the C compiler package, and it contains information about input and output (communications between the program and your terminal, for example). The name stands for **standard input/output header.** (C people call a collection of information that goes at the top of a file a *header.*)

Sometimes you need this line; sometimes you don't. We can't give you a hard rule, for the answer depends on the program and on the system. On our system we don't need this line for *this* program, but you may need it for your system. The **stdio.h** file makes information available to the compiler; any information that it does not use does not become part of the program, so including an unnecessary file does not make the final program any longer. And, in any case, including the line won't hurt. From now on, we will show this line only when it is needed for our system.

Perhaps you are wondering why something as basic as input and output information isn't included automatically. One answer is that not all programs use this I/O (Input/Output) package, and part of the C philosophy is not to carry along unnecessary weight. Incidentally, this line is not even a C language statement! The # symbol identifies it as a line to be handled by the C *preprocessor*. As you might guess from the name, the preprocessor handles some tasks before the compiler takes over. We will come across more examples of preprocessor instructions later.

```
main( )
```

True, **main's** a rather plain name, but it is the only choice we have. A C program always begins execution with the function called **main( )**. We are free to choose names for other functions we may use, but **main( )** must be there to start things off. What about the parentheses? They identify **main( )** as being a function. We will learn more about functions later. For now, we will just repeat our earlier statement that functions are the basic modules of a C program.

The parentheses generally enclose information being passed along to the function. For our simple example, nothing is being passed along, so the parentheses remain empty. Don't leave them out, but don't worry about them yet.

Incidentally, the file containing the program can have any name we want to give it, as long as the name satisfies the system's conventions and ends in **.c**. For example, we could use **mighty.c** or **silly.c** rather than **main.c** as names for a file containing this program.

```
/* a simple program */
```

Using comments makes it easier for someone (including yourself) to understand your program. One nice feature of C comments is that they can be placed on the same line as the material they explain. A longer comment can be placed on its own line or even spread over more than one line. Everything between the opening /* and the closing */ is ignored by the compiler, which is just as well, since it wouldn't understand such un-C language, anyway.

```
{ and }
```

Braces mark the beginning as well as the end of the body of a function. Only braces { } work for this purpose, not parentheses ( ) and not brackets [ ].

Braces also can be used to gather together statements inside a program into a unit or "block." If you are familiar with Pascal or Algol, you will recognize the braces as being similar to **begin** and **end** in those languages.

```
int num;
```

The *declaration statement* is one of the most important features of C. As we said earlier, this particular example declares two things. First, somewhere in the function, we will be using a *variable* having the name **num.** Second, the **int** announces that **num** is an *integer,* that is, a whole number. The compiler uses this information to arrange for suitable storage space in memory for the **num** variable. The semicolon at the end of the line identifies the line as a C "statement" or instruction. The semicolon is *part of the statement,* not just a separator between statements as it is in Pascal.

The word **int** is a C *keyword* identifying one of the basic C data types. Keywords are the words used to express a language, and you can find a list of C keywords in Appendix B.

In C *all* variables must be declared. This means you have to provide lists of all the variables you use in a program, and that you have to show what "type" each variable is. Declaring variables is generally considered a good thing.

At this point, you may have three questions. First, what choices do you have in selecting a name? Second, what are data types? Third, why do you have to declare variables at all? We've prepared two boxes to answer the first and third questions.

We'll deal with the second question in Chapter 3, but here is a short summary. C deals with several kinds (or types) of data: integers, characters, and "floating point," for example. Declaring a variable to be an integer or a character type makes it possible for the computer to store, fetch, and interpret the data properly.

Name Choice

We suggest that you use meaningful names for variables. The number of characters you can use will vary among implementations, but the upper limit will be at least 8 characters. Microsoft C, for example, allows up to 31 characters. (Actually, you can use more than the maximum number of characters, but the compiler won't pay attention to the extra characters. Thus, on a system with an 8-character limit, **shakespeare** and **shakespencil** would be considered the same name since they have the same first 8 characters.) The characters at your disposal are the lowercase letters, the uppercase letters, the digits, and the underscore _, which is counted as a letter. The first character must be a letter.

Valid Names	Invalid Names
wiggly	$Z^**
cat1	1cat
Hot_Tub	Hot-Tub
_kcaB	don't

Library routines often use names beginning with the underscore symbol. The assumption is that users are unlikely to choose names beginning with this symbol; thus, there is little chance of a user accidentally using one of these names to mean something else. Resist the temptation to begin names with an underscore symbol, and you will avoid a clash with the library.

Four Good Reasons to Declare Variables

1. Gathering all the variables together in one place makes it easier for a reader to grasp what the program is about. This is particularly true if you give your variable meaningful names (such as **taxrate** instead of **r**) and if you use the comment facility to explain what the variables represent. Documenting a program in this manner is one of the basic techniques of good programming.

2. Thinking about what to put into the variable declaration section encourages you to do some planning before plunging into writing a program. What information will the program need to get started? What exactly do I want the program to produce as output?

3. Declaring variables helps prevent one of programming's more subtle and hard-to-find bugs, that of the misspelled variable name. For example, suppose that in some language that shall remain nameless, you made the statement:

```
ANS = 19.7*BOZO - 2.0
```

and that elsewhere in the program you mistyped:

```
BOZO = 32.4
```

thus unwittingly replacing the numeral 0 with the letter O. The program would create a new variable called **BOZO** and use whatever value it had (perhaps zero, perhaps garbage). **ANS** would be given the wrong value, and you could have a heck of a time trying to find out why. This can't happen in C (unless you were silly enough to declare two such similar variable names) because the compiler will complain when the undeclared **BOZO** shows up.

4. Your C program will not work if you don't declare your variables. If the other reasons discussed here fail to move you, you should give this one serious thought.

```
num = 1;
```

The *assignment statement* is one of the most basic operations. This particular example means "give the variable **num** the value of 1." The fourth line allotted computer space for the variable **num,** and this line gives it its value. We could assign **num** a different value later on if we wished; that's why we call **num** a variable. Note that the statement is completed with a semicolon.

```
printf("I am a simple ");
printf("computer.\n");
printf("My favorite number is %d because it is first.\n",num);
```

These lines all use a standard C function called **printf( )**. The parentheses tell us that we are, indeed, dealing with a function. The material enclosed in the parentheses is information passed from our function (**main( )**) to the **printf( )** function. Such information is called the *argument* of a function, and in the first case the argument is "I am a simple ". And what does the function **printf( )** do with this argument? Obviously, it looks at whatever lies between the double quotation marks and prints that on the terminal's screen.

Figure 2.2
The assignment statement is one of the most basic operations

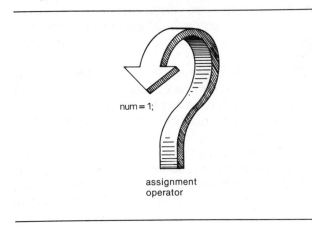

num = 1;

assignment
operator

This line provides an example of how we "call" or "invoke" a function in C. We need only type the name of the function and include the desired argument(s) in the parentheses. When your program reaches this line, control is turned over to the named function (**printf( )** in this case). When the function is finished with whatever it does, control is returned to the original (the "calling") program.

But what about this next line? It has the characters **\n** included in the quotes, and they didn't get printed! What's going on? The **\n** actually is an instruction to start a new line. The **\n** combination represents a single character called the "newline" character. Its meaning is "start a new line at the far left margin." In other words, this character performs the same function as the [enter] key of a typical keyboard. "But," you say, "**\n** looks like two characters, not one." Well, they are two characters, but they repre-

Figure 2.3
The function *printf( )* with an argument

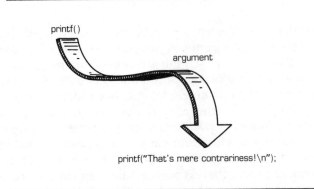

printf( )

argument

printf("That's mere contrariness!\n");

sent a single character for which there is no single-key representation. Why not just use the [enter] key? Because that would be interpreted as an immediate command to your editor, not as an instruction to be stored away. In other words, when you press the [enter] key, the editor quits the current line on which you are working and starts a new one, leaving your last line unfinished.

The newline character is an example of what is called an *escape sequence*. An escape sequence is used to represent difficult- or impossible-to-type characters. Other examples are \t for tab and \b for backspace. In each case the escape sequence begins with the backslash character, \. We'll return to this subject in Chapter 3.

Well, that explains why our three print statements produced only two lines; the first print instruction didn't have a newline character in it.

The final line brings up another oddity: what happened to the %d when the line was printed? As you will recall, the output for this line was:

```
My favorite number is 1 because it is first.
```

Aha! The digit **1** was substituted for the symbol group %d when the line was printed, and **1** was the value of the variable **num**. Apparently the %d is a kind of placeholder to show where the value of **num** is to be printed. This line is similar to the BASIC statement:

```
PRINT "My favorite number is "; num; " because it is first."
```

The C version does a little more than this, actually. The % alerts the program that a variable is to be printed at that location, and the **d** tells it to print the variable as a **digit.** The **printf( )** function allows several choices for the format of printed variables. Indeed, the **f** in **printf( )** is there to remind us that this is a formatted print statement.

The Structure of a Simple Program

Now that you've seen a specific example, you are ready for a few general rules about C programs. A *program* consists of a collection of one or more functions, one of which must be called **main( ).** The description of a *function* consists of a header and a body. The *header* contains any preprocessor statements, such as **#include,** and the function name. You can recognize a function name by the parentheses, which may be empty. The *body* is enclosed by braces { } and consists of a series of statements, each terminated by a semicolon. Our example had a *declaration statement,* announcing the name and type of variable that we were using. Then it had an *assignment statement* giving the variable a value. Finally, there were three *print statements;* each consisted of calling the **printf( )** function.

Figure 2.4
A function has a header and a body

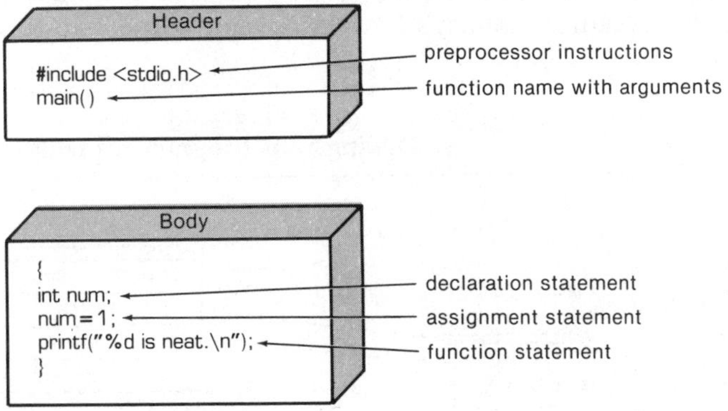

Tips on Making Your Programs Readable

Making your programs readable is good programming practice. It makes it much easier to understand the program, and that makes it easier to correct or modify the program, if necessary. The act of making a program readable also helps clarify your own concept of what the program does. We will point out useful techniques as we go along.

We've already mentioned two techniques: choose meaningful variable names and use comments. Note that these two techniques complement each other. If you give a variable the name **width,** you don't need a comment saying that this variable represents a width.

Another technique is to use blank lines to separate one conceptual section of a function from another. For example, in our simple program, we had a blank line separating the declaration section from the action section (assigning and printing). The blank line is not required by C, but it is part of the C tradition to use it as we did.

A fourth technique we followed was to use one line per statement. Again, this is a convention not required by C. C has a "free form format." You can place several statements on one line or spread one statement over several. The following is legitimate code:

```
main() { int four; four
=
4
;
printf(
        "%d\n",
four); }
```

The semicolons tell the compiler where one statement ends and the next begins, but the logic of a program is much clearer if you follow the conventions we used in our example. Of course, there wasn't much logic to follow in our example, but it's best to develop good habits at the beginning.

Figure 2.5
Making your program readable

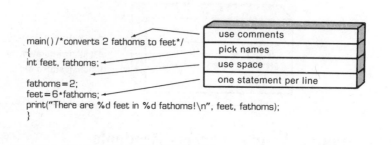

Taking Another Step

Our first example program was pretty easy, and our next example won't be much harder. Here it is:

```
main() /* Converts 2 fathoms to feet */
{
int feet, fathoms;

fathoms = 2;
feet = 6 * fathoms;
printf("There are %d feet in %d fathoms!\n", feet, fathoms);
}
```

What's new? First, we have declared two variables instead of just one. All that was necessary was to separate the two variables (**feet** and **fathoms**) by a comma in the declaration statement.

Second, we have made a calculation. We harnessed the tremendous computational power of our system to multiply 2 by 6. In C, as in many languages, the * is the symbol for multiplication. Thus the statement:

```
feet = 6 * fathoms;
```

means "look up the value of the variable **fathoms,** multiply it by 6, and assign the result of this calculation to the variable **feet.**" (Judging from this paraphrase, plain English is not as clear as plain C; that's one reason we have developed computer languages.)

Finally, we make fancier use of **printf( )**. If you run the example, the output should look like this:

```
There are 12 feet in 2 fathoms!
```

This time we have made *two* substitutions. The first %**d** in the quotes was replaced by the value of the first variable (**feet**) in the list following the quoted segment, and the second %**d** was replaced by the value of the second variable (**fathoms**) in the list. Note how the list of variables to be printed comes at the tail end of the statement.

This program is a bit limited in scope, but it could form the nucleus of a program to convert fathoms to feet. All we need is some way to assign other values to **feet**; we will learn to do that later.

And While We're at It . . .

Here is one more example. So far our programs have used the standard **printf( )** function. Here we show how to include and use a function of your own devising:

```
main()
{
    printf("I will summon the butler function.\n");
    butler();
    printf("Yes. Bring me some tea and floppy disks.\n");
}
butler()
{
    printf("You rang, sir?\n");
}
```

The output looks like this:

```
I will summon the butler function.
You rang, sir?
Yes. Bring me some tea and floppy disks.
```

The function **butler( )** is defined in the same manner as **main( )**, with the body enclosed in braces. The function is called simply by giving its name, including parentheses. We won't return to this important topic until

Chapter 9, but we wanted you to see how easy it is to include your own functions.

What You Should Have Learned

Here's a summary of some hard (but not cruel) facts we hope you have picked up. We've included short examples.

What to call the file containing your program: **eye.c** or **black.c** or **infan.c,** etc.

What name to use for a one-function program: **main( )**

The structure of a simple program: header, body, braces, statements

How to declare an integer variable: **int varname;**

How to assign a value to a variable: **varname = 1024;**

How to print a phrase: **printf("Wanna buy a duck?");**

How to print the value of an integer variable: **printf("%d",varname);**

The newline character: **\n**

How to include comments in a program: /* **cash flow analysis** */

Review Questions

Here are a few questions to help you check and extend your understanding of the material in this chapter.

1. Ichabod Bodie Marfoote has prepared the following program and brought it to you for approval. Please help him out.

```
include studio.h
main{} /* this program prints the number of weeks in a year /*
(
int s

s := 56;
print(There are s weeks in a year.);
```

2. Assuming that each of the following examples is part of a complete program, what will each one print?
   a. `printf("Baa Baa Black Sheep.");`
      `printf("Have you any wool?\n");`
   b. `printf("Begone!\n0 creature of lard!");`
   c. `printf("What?\nNo/nBonzo?\n");`

d. `int num;`

```
num = 2;
printf("%d + %d = %d", num, num, num + num);
```

3. Identify and correct the errors in the following C program.

```
MAIN[]
(
   print 'Welcome to error-free programing/n'
)
```

Answers

1. Line 1: Begin the line with a #; spell the file **stdio.h**; place the file name in angle brackets.
   Line 2: Use ( ), not { }; end comment with */, not /*.
   Line 3: Use {, not (.
   Line 4: Complete the statement with a semicolon.
   Line 5: Mr. IBM got this one (the blank line) right!
   Line 6: Use = and not := for assignment. (Apparently Mr. IBM knows a little Pascal.) Use 52, not 56, weeks per year.
   Line 7: Should be **printf("There are %d weeks in a year.\n",s);**.
   Line 8: There isn't a line 8, but there should be, and it should consist of the closing brace, }.

2. **a. Baa Baa Black Sheep.Have you any wool?**
      (Note that there is no space after the period. We could have had a space by using " **Have** instead of "**Have**.)
   b. Begone!
      O creature of lard!
      (Note that the cursor is left at the end of the second line.)
   c. What?
      No/nBonzo?
      (Note that the slash (/) does not have the same effect as the backslash (\ ).)
   d. 2 + 2 = 4
      (Note how each **%d** is replaced by the corresponding variable value from the list. Note, too, that + means addition, and that calculation can be done inside a **printf( )** statement.)

3. Line 1: Lowercase **main** and use ( ) instead of [ ].
   Line 2: Use { instead of (.
   Line 3: Should be **printf("Welcome to error-free programming\n");** i.e., use **printf** instead of **print**; use parentheses; use double quotes, not single; spell programming correctly; and end the statement with a semicolon.
   Line 5: Use }, not).

Exercises

Reading about C isn't enough. You should try writing a simple program or two and see if it goes as smoothly as it looks in this chapter. Here are a few suggestions, but you can use your own ideas if you prefer. (We'll never know.) *? Wow, Big brother is not watching*

1. Write a program using one **printf( )** call to print your first name and last name on one line, a second **printf( )** call to print your first and last name on two separate lines, and a pair of **printf( )** calls to print your first and last name on one line. The output should look like this:

   ```
   Mae West    ←first print statement
   Mae         ←second print statement
   West        ←still the second print statement
   Mae West    ←third and fourth print statements
   ```

2. Write a program to print your name and address, using three or more lines.

3. Write a program that converts your age in years to days. At this point, don't worry about fractional years and leap years.

3

Data, C, and You

Concepts
- Interactive programs
- Basic data types
- Variables and constants
- Declaring different types
- Words, bytes, and bits

Keywords
- *int, short, long, unsigned, char float, double*

Operators
- `sizeof`

P rograms work with data. We feed numbers, letters, and words to the computer, and we expect it to do something with the data. In the next two chapters we will concentrate on data concepts and properties. Following that, we will pounce on some data and see what we can do. But since it is not much fun just talking about data, we will do a little data manipulation in this chapter, too.

The main topic in this chapter will be the two great families of data types: integer and floating point. C offers several varieties of these types. We will learn what the types are, how to declare them, how to use them, and when to use them. Also, we will discuss the differences between constants and variables.

Once again it's time to look at a sample program. Also, once again, you'll find some unfamiliar wrinkles that we'll iron out for you in the main body of the chapter. The general intent should be clear, so try compiling and running this program. To save time, you can omit typing the comments. (For reference, we've included a program name as a comment. We will continue this practice with future programs.)

```
/* goldenyou */
/* a program to find the value of your weight in gold */
main()
{
    float weight, value; /* 2 floating-point variables */
    char beep;           /* a character variable */

    beep = '\007';       /* assigning a special character to beep */
    printf("Are you worth your weight in gold?\n");
    printf("Please enter your weight in pounds, and we'll see.\n");
```

```
    scanf("%f", &weight);        /* getting input from the user */
    value = 400.0*weight*14.5833;
            /* assumes gold is $400 per ounce */
            /* 14.5833 converts pounds to ounces troy */
    printf("%cYour weight in gold is worth $%2.2f%c.\n",beep,value,beep);
    printf("You are easily worth that! If gold prices drop, ");
    printf("eat more\nto maintain your value.\n");
}
```

When you type in this program, you may wish to change the **400.00** to the current price of gold. We suggest, however, that you don't fiddle with the **14.5833,** which represents the number of ounces in a pound. (That's ounces troy, used for precious metals, and pounds avoirdupois, used for people, precious and otherwise.) Note that "entering" your weight means to type in your weight and then press the "enter" or "return" key. (Don't just type your weight and wait.) Pressing [enter] informs the computer that you have finished typing your response. When we ran the program, the results looked like this:

```
Are you worth your weight in gold?
Please enter your weight in pounds, and we'll see.
175
Your weight in gold is worth $1020831.00.
You are easily worth that! If gold prices drop, eat more
to maintain your value.
```

The program also has a nonvisual aspect. You'll have to run the program yourself to find out what that is, but the name of one of the variables should provide a clue.

What's new in this program?

1. You probably noticed that we used two new kinds of variable declaration. Before, we used only an integer variable, but now we've added a floating-point variable and a character variable so that we can handle a wider variety of data. The **float** type can hold numbers with decimal points, and the **char** type can hold characters.

2. We've included some new ways of writing constants. We now have numbers with decimal points, and we have a rather peculiar-looking notation to represent the character named **beep.**

3. To print these new kinds of variables, we have used the %**f** and the %**c** codes of **printf( )** to handle floating-point and character variables, respectively. We used modifiers to the %**f** code to fine-tune the appearance of the output.

4. To provide keyboard input to the program, we use the **scanf( )**

function. The **%f** instructs the program to read a floating-point number, and the **&weight** tells **scanf( )** to assign the value to the **weight** variable. The **scanf( )** function uses the **&** notation to indicate where it can find the **weight** variable. We'll discuss **&** further in the next chapter; meanwhile, trust us that you need it here.

5. Perhaps the most outstanding new feature is that this program is *interactive*. The computer asks you for information and then uses the number you type in. An interactive program is more interesting to use than the noninteractive types we used earlier. More important, the interactive approach lets us make more flexible programs. For instance, our example program can be used for any reasonable weight, not just for 175 pounds. We don't have to rewrite the program every time we want to try it on a new person. The **scanf( )** and **printf( )** functions make this possible. The **scanf( )** function reads data from the keyboard and delivers that data to the program, and **printf( )** reads data from a program and delivers that data to your screen. Together, these two functions let you establish a two-way communication with your computer, and that makes using a computer much more fun.

This chapter will deal with the first two items in the preceding list: variables and constants of various data types. Chapter 4 will cover the last three items, but we will continue to make limited use of **scanf( )** and **printf( )** in this chapter.

Data: **Variables and Constants**

A computer, under the guidance of a program, can do many things. It can add numbers, sort names, command the obedience of a speaker or video screen, calculate cometary orbits, prepare a mailing list, draw stick figures, draw conclusions, or do whatever else your imagination can create. To do these tasks, the program needs to work with *data,* the numbers and characters that bear the information you use. Some data are preset before a program is used and keep their values unchanged. These are *constants*. Other data may change or be assigned values as the program runs; these are *variables*. (We've already used the term in the last chapter, but now you are formally introduced.) In our sample program, **weight** is a variable and **14.5833** is a constant. What about the **400.0?** True, the price of gold isn't a constant in real life, but our program treats it as a constant.

The difference between a variable and a constant is pretty obvious: a variable can have its value assigned or changed while the program is running, and a constant can't. This difference makes the variables a little tougher and more time-consuming for a computer to handle, but it can do the job.

Figure 3.1
The functions *scanf( )* and *printf( )* at work

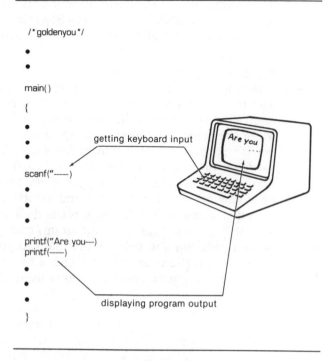

/* goldenyou */

main( )

{

scanf("-----)

getting keyboard input

printf("Are you---)
printf(-----)

displaying program output

}

Data: Data Types

Beyond the distinction between variable and constant is the distinction between different "types" of data. Some data are numbers. Some are letters, or, more generally, characters. The computer needs a way to identify and to use these different kinds. C does this by recognizing several fundamental *data types*. If a datum is a constant, the compiler usually can tell its type just by the way it looks. A variable, however, needs to have its type announced in a declaration statement. We'll fill you in on the details as we move along. First, though, let's look at the fundamental types recognized by standard C. C uses seven keywords to set up the types. Here are those keywords:

```
int
long
short

unsigned

char
```

```
float
double
```

(For a discussion of the new types **void, const,** and **volatile,** which are covered in the proposed ANSI standard for C, please see Chapter 16.)

The **int** keyword provides the basic class of integers used in C. The next three keywords (**long, short,** and **unsigned**) are used to provide variations of the basic type; we'll discuss their use soon. The next keyword, **char,** is for letters of the alphabet and for other characters, such as #, $, %, and &. The final two keywords are used to represent numbers with decimal points. The types created with these keywords can be divided into two families on the basis of how they are stored in the computer. The first five keywords create "integer" types, while the last two create "floating-point" types.

Integer types? Floating-point types? If you find these terms disturbingly unfamiliar, be assured that we are about to give you a brief rundown of their meanings. If you are unfamiliar with "bits," "bytes," and "words," you may wish to read the next box first. Do you *have* to learn all the details? Not really, not any more than you have to learn the principles of internal combustion engines to drive a car. But knowing a little about what goes on inside a computer or engine can occasionally help you out.

For a human, the difference between an integer and a floating-point number is reflected in the way they can be written. For a computer, the difference is reflected in the way they are stored. Let's look at each of the two classes in turn.

Bits, Bytes, and Words

The terms "bit," "byte," and "word" can be used to describe units of computer data or to describe units of computer memory. We'll concentrate on the second usage here.

The smallest unit of memory is called a *bit*. It can hold one of two values: 0 or 1. (Or we can say the bit is set to "off" or "on"; this is another way of saying the same thing.) You can't store much information in 1 bit, but a computer has hordes of them. The bit is the basic building block of computer memory.

The *byte* is a more useful unit of memory. For most machines a byte is 8 bits. Since each bit can be set to either 0 or 1, there are 256 (that's 2 times itself 8 times) possible bit patterns of 0s and 1s that can fit in a byte. These patterns can be used, for example, to represent the integers from 0 to 255 or to represent a set of characters. Representation can be accomplished using "binary code," which uses (conveniently enough) just 0s and 1s to represent numbers. We've included a discussion of binary code in Appendix G; please feel free to read it.

A *word* is the natural unit of memory for a given computer design. For "8-bit" microcomputers, such as the Sinclairs or the original Apples, a word is just 1 byte. Many newer systems, such as the IBM PC and its clones are "16-bit" machines. This means they have a word size of 16 bits, which is 2 bytes. Larger computers may have 32-bit words, 64-bit words, or even larger. Naturally, the larger a word is, the more information it can store. Computers usually can string two or more words together to store larger items, but this process does slow the computer down.

We will assume a word size of 16 bits for our examples, unless we tell you otherwise.

The Integer

An *integer* is a whole number. It never has a fractional part, and in C it never is written with a decimal point. Examples are 2, −23, and 2456. Numbers like 3.14 and 2/3 are not integers. Integers are stored pretty straightforwardly as binary numbers. The integer 7, for example, is written 111 in binary. Thus, to store this number in a 1-byte word, just set the first 5 bits to 0 and the last 3 bits to 1. See Figure 3.2.

The Floating-Point Number

A *floating-point* number more or less corresponds to what mathematicians call a "real number." Real numbers include the numbers between the integers. Here are some floating-point numbers: 2.75, 3.16E7, 7.00, and 2e-8. Obviously, there is more than one way to write a floating-point number. We

Figure 3.2
Storing the integer 7 using a binary code

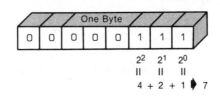

will discuss the "E"-notation more fully later. In brief, the notation "3.16E7" means to multiply 3.16 by 10 to the 7th power; that is, by 1 followed by 7 zeros. The 7 would be termed the "exponent" of 10.

The key point here is that the scheme used to store a floating-point number is different from the one used to store an integer. Floating-point representation involves breaking up a number into a fractional part and an exponent part and storing the parts separately. Thus, the 7.00 in this list would not be stored in the same manner as the integer 7, even though both have the same value. The decimal analogy would be to write "7.0" as "0.7E1". Here "0.7" is the fractional part, and the "1" is the exponent part. A computer, of course, would use binary numbers and powers of two instead of powers of ten for internal storage. You can find more information on this subject in Appendix G. Here, let's concentrate on the practical differences, which are these:

1. Integers are whole numbers, while floating-point numbers can represent both whole and fractional numbers.
2. Floating-point numbers can represent a much larger range of values than integers can. See Table 3.1 near the end of this chapter.
3. For some arithmetic operations, such as subtracting one large number from another, floating-point numbers are subject to greater loss of precision.
4. Floating-point operations normally are slower than integer

Figure 3.3
Storing the number *pi* (π) in floating-point (decimal version)

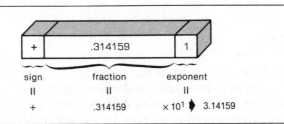

operations. However, microprocessors specifically developed to handle floating-point operations are now available, and they are quite swift.

Floating-Point Roundoff Errors

Take a number. Add 1 to it, and subtract the original number. What do you get? You get 1. But a floating-point calculation may give another answer:

```
/* floaterror */
main()
{
  float a,b;

  b = 2.0e20 + 1.0;
  a = b - 2.0e20;

  printf("%f \n", a);
}
```

The output:

```
0.000000
```

The reason for this odd result is that the computer doesn't keep track of enough decimal places to do the operation correctly. The number 2.0e20 is 2 followed by 20 zeros, and by adding 1, we are trying to change the 21st digit. To do this correctly, the program would need to be able to store a 21-digit number. But a **float** number is just 6 or 7 digits scaled to bigger or smaller numbers with an exponent. The attempt is doomed. On the other hand, if we used, say, 2.0e4 instead of 2.0e20, we would get the correct answer; for here we are trying to change the 5th digit, and **float** numbers are precise enough for that.

C Data Types

Now let's take a look at the specifics for the basic types used by C. For each type, we will show how to declare a variable, how to represent a constant, and what a typical use would be. Some C compilers do not support all these types, so check your manual to see which ones you have available.

The *int* Type

C offers a variety of integer types. They vary in the range of values offered and in whether or not negative numbers can be used. The **int** type is the basic choice, but should you need other choices to meet the requirements of a particular task or machine, they are available.

The **int** type is a *signed integer.* That means it must be a whole number and it can be positive, negative, or zero. The range in possible values depends on the computer system. Typically, an **int** uses one machine-word for storage. Thus, an IBM PC, which has a 2-byte word, uses 2 bytes (16 bits) to store an **int**. This allows a range in values from −32768 to +32767. Other machines may have different ranges. See Table 3.1 near the end of this chapter for examples.

Declaring an **int** *Variable*—As we saw in Chapter 2, the keyword **int** is used to declare variables of that type. First comes **int**, then the chosen name of the variable, then a semicolon. To declare more than one variable, you can declare each variable separately, or you can follow the **int** with a list of names in which each name is separated from the next by a comma. The following are valid declarations:

```
int erns;
int hogs, cows, goats;
```

We could have used a separate declaration for each variable, or we could have declared all four variables in the same statement. The effect is the same: arrange storage space for four **int**-sized variables and associate a name with each one. Declarations that create storage for the variable are termed *definitions* of the variable. So far, all the declarations we've used are definitions, but in Chapter 10 we'll see that this need not be the case. That is, not all declarations cause storage to be set aside for a variable. Some declarations merely announce that you plan to use a variable defined elsewhere. But until we get to Chapter 10, all our declarations will be definitions, so you can visualize them as requesting storage for variables.

These declarations create variables, then, but they don't provide values for them. How do variables get values? They can pick up values in the program. For example, there could be a line like this:

```
cows = 112;
```

Or a variable could pick up a value from a function, from **scanf( )**, for example. Finally, if we know in advance the starting value for a variable, we can "initialize" that variable.

Initializing a Variable—To *initialize* a variable means to assign it an initial value. In C, this can be done in the declaration. Just follow the variable name with an equals sign and the value you want the variable to have. Here are some examples:

```
int hogs = 21;
int cows = 32, goats = 14;
int dogs, cats = 94;
```

In the last line, only **cats** is initialized. A quick reading might lead one to think that **dogs** is also initialized to **94,** so it is best to avoid putting initialized and noninitialized variables in the same declaration statement.

In short, the declaration (when a definition) creates and labels the storage, and the initialization process places a value there. See Figure 3.4.

Figure 3.4
Defining and initializing a variable

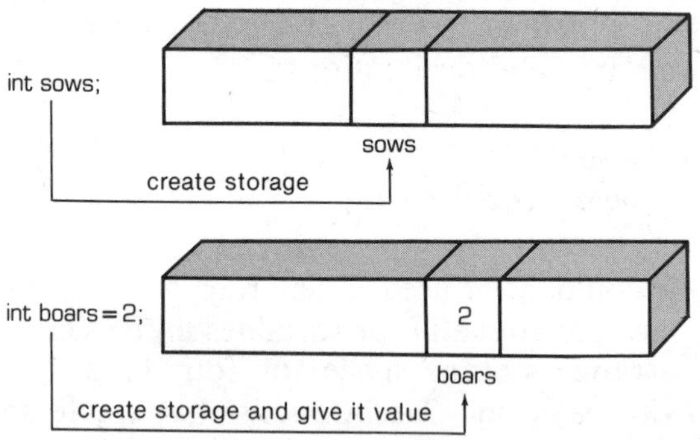

Type **int** *Constants*—The various integers (**21, 32, 14,** and **94**) in the last example are integer constants. When you write a number without a decimal point and without an exponent, C recognizes it as an integer. Thus, 22 and −44 are integer constants, while 22.0 and 2.2E1 are not. C treats most integer constants as type **int.** Very large integers may be treated differently; see the later discussion of the **long int** type.

Normally, C assumes you are writing integers as decimal integers, that is, in the base 10 number system. However, octal (base 8) and hexadecimal (base 16) numbers are popular with many programmers. Because 8 and 16 are powers of 2, and 10 is not, these number systems are more natural for computers. For example, the number 65536, which often pops up in 16-bit machines, is just 0x10000 in hexadecimal. Appendix G will tell you more about these other number systems. The important point for now is that C lets you write numbers in octal or hexadecimal (or "hex") notations. You just have to use the correct prefixes so that C will know which system you are using. A **0** (zero) prefix means you are writing in octal. For example, the decimal value 16 is written as 020 in C octal. Similarly, a prefix of **0x** or **0X** (zero-exe) means you are writing in hexadecimal, so 16 is written as 0x10 or 0X10 in hexadecimal.

One important point to realize, however, is that this option of using different number systems is provided as a service for your convenience. It doesn't affect how the number is stored. That is, you can write 16 or 020 or 0x10, and the number will be stored exactly the same way in each case—in the binary code used internally by computers.

Printing **int** *Values*—We can use the **printf( )** function to print **int**s. As we saw in Chapter 2, the **%d** notation is used to indicate just where in a line the integer is to be printed. Each **%d** must be matched by an **int** value, which can be an **int** variable, an **int** constant, or any other expression having an **int** value. Here, for example, is a simple program that initializes a variable and prints some values:

```
main()
{
     int ten = 10;
     printf("%d minus %d is %d\n", ten, 2, ten - 2);
}
```

Compiling and running the program produces this output:

```
10 minus 2 is 8
```

Thus, the first **%d** represents the **int** variable **ten**, the second **%d** represents the **int** constant **2**, and the third **%d** represents the **int** expression **ten − 2**.

Just as C lets you write a number in any one of three number systems, it also lets you print a number in any of these three systems. To print an integer in octal notation instead of decimal, use **%o** instead of **%d**. To print an integer in hexadecimal, use **%x**. Here is a short example:

```
main()
{
     int x = 100;
     printf("dec = %d; octal = %o; hex = %x\n", x, x, x);
}
```

Compiling and running this program produces this output:

```
dec = 100; octal = 144; hex = 64
```

We see the same value displayed in three different number systems; the **printf( )** function makes the conversions. Note that the special prefixes are not used in output.

Other Integer Types

When you are just learning the language, the **int** type is probably the only integer type you will need. But, to be complete, we'll look at the other forms now. If you like, you can skim over this section to the discussion of the **char** type and return here when you have a need.

C offers three "adjective" keywords to modify the basic type: **unsigned**, **long**, and **short**.

1. The type **short int**, or, more briefly, **short**, may use less storage than **int**, thus saving space when only small numbers are needed.

2. The type **long int**, or **long**, may use more storage than **int**, thus allowing larger integers to be used.

3. The type **unsigned int**, or **unsigned**, shifts the range of numbers that can be stored. For example, a 2-byte **unsigned int** allows a range from 0 to 65535 in value instead of from −32768 to +32767. Many C implementations also recognize **unsigned long int**, or **unsigned long**, and **unsigned short int**, or **unsigned short**, as valid types.

Why do we say **long** and **short** types "may" use more or less storage than **int**? Because all that C guarantees is that **short** is no longer than **int** and that **long** is no shorter than **int**. The idea is to fit the types to the machine. On an IBM PC, for example, an **int** and a **short** are both 16 bits, while a **long** is 32 bits. On a VAX, however, a **short** is 16 bits, while both **int** and **long** are 32 bits. The natural word size on a VAX is 32 bits. Since this allows integers in excess of 2 billion (see Table 3.1), the implementors of C on the VAX did not see a necessity for anything larger; thus, **long** is the same as **int**. But for many uses, integers of that size are not needed, so a space-saving **short** was created. The IBM PC, on the other hand, has only a 16-bit word, which means that a larger **long** was needed.

The most common practice today is to set up **long** as 32 bits, **short** as 16 bits, and **int** to either 16 bits or 32 bits, depending on the machine's natural word size.

When do you use the various **int** types? First, consider **unsigned** types. It is natural to use them for counting, since you don't need negative numbers and the unsigned types let you reach higher positive numbers than the signed types.

Use the **long** type if you need to use numbers that **long** can handle and that **int** cannot. However, on systems for which **long** is bigger than **int**, using **long** may slow down calculations, so don't use **long** if it is not essential. One further point: If you are writing code on a machine for which **int** and **long** are synonymous, and if you do need 32-bit integers, you can use **long** instead of **int** so that the program would function if transferred to a 16-bit machine.

Use **short** to save storage space or if, say, you need a 16-bit value on a system where **int** is 32-bit. Saving storage space usually is important only if your program uses large arrays of integers.

Integer Overflow

What happens if an integer tries to get too big for its type? Let's set an integer to its largest possible value, add to it, and see what happens.

```
/* toobig */
main()
{
  int i = 32767;

  printf("%d %d %d\n", i, i+1, i+2);
}
```

Here's the result for our system:

```
32767 -32768 -32767
```

The integer **i** is acting like a car's odometer. When it reaches its maximum value, it starts over at the beginning. The main difference is that an odometer begins at 0, while our **int** begins at −32768.

Notice that you are not informed that **i** has exceeded ("overflowed") its maximum value. You would have to include your own programming to keep tabs on that.

The behavior we have described here is not mandated by the rules of C, but it is the typical implementation.

Declaring Other Integer Types—Other integer types are declared in the same manner as the **int** type. The following list shows several examples; not all compilers will recognize the last two:

```
long int estine;
long johns;
short int erns;
short ribs;
unsigned int s_count;
unsigned players;
unsigned long headcount;
unsigned short yesvotes;
```

Type **long** *Constants*—Normally, when you use a number like 2345 in your program code, it is stored as an **int** type. But what if you use a number like 1000000 on a system in which **int** will not hold such a large number? Then the compiler treats it as a **long int**, assuming that type is large enough.

Sometimes you may need to store a small number as a **long** integer. Programming that involves explicit use of memory addresses on an IBM PC, for instance, can create such a need. Also, some standard C functions require type **long** values. To cause a constant to be stored as type **long**, you can add an **l** (lowercase "ell") or **L** as a suffix. We recommend the second form, since it looks less like the digit 1. Thus, on a system with a 16-bit **int** and a 32-bit **long**, the integer 7 is stored in 2 bytes, and the integer 7L is stored in 4 bytes. The **l** and **L** suffixes also can be used with octal and hex integers.

Printing **long** *and* **unsigned** *Types*—To print an **unsigned** number, use the %**u** notation; to print a **long** value, use %**ld**. (If **int** and **long** are the same on your system, just %**d** will suffice, but your program will not work properly when transferred to a system on which the two types are different.) Also, your system may support a %**lu** notation for printing **unsigned long** types. Here is a sample:

```
main()
{
    unsigned un = 40000;
    long ln = 2000000000;
    unsigned long uln = 2 * 2000000000;

    printf("un = %u and not %d\n", un, un);
    printf("n = %ld and not %d\n", ln, ln);
    printf("uln = %lu and not %u\n", uln, uln);
}
```

And here is the output:

```
un = 40000 and not -25536
ln = 2000000000 and not -27648
uln = 4000000000 and not 10240
```

This example points out that using the wrong specification can produce unexpected results. (We used **2 * 2000000000** instead of 4000000000 because our implementation does not recognize written decimal integers beyond the **long** limit. The * symbol is used in C to indicate multiplication.)

Using Characters: Type *char*

The **char** type, we've said, is used for storing characters such as letters and punctuation marks, but technically it is an integer type. Why? Because the **char** type actually stores integers, not characters. After all, a computer can only store a pattern of 1s and 0s. To handle characters, the computer uses a numerical code in which certain integers represent certain characters. The most commonly used code is the ASCII code given in Appendix I. It is the code we will assume for this book. In it, for example, the integer 65 represents an uppercase A. So to store the letter A, we actually need to store the integer 65. (Many IBM mainframes use a different code, called EBCDIC, but the principle is the same.)

The standard ASCII code runs numerically from 0 to 127. This is small enough that 7 bits can hold the largest code value. The **char** type typically is defined as a 1-byte (or 8-bit) unit of memory, so it is more than large enough to encompass the standard ASCII code. Many systems, such as the IBM PC and the Apple Macintosh, offer extended ASCII codes (not the same for both systems) that still stay within an 8-bit limit.

Declaring Type **char** *Variables*—As you might expect, **char** variables are declared in the same manner as other variables. Here are some examples:

```
char response;
char itable, latan;
```

This program would create three **char** variables: **response**, **itable**, and **latan**.

Signed or Unsigned?—Some C implementations make **char** a signed type; this means it can hold values in the range −128 through +127. Other implementations make **char** an unsigned type. This provides a range from 0 through 255. Your compiler manual should tell you which type **char** is.

Many newer implementations allow you to use the keywords **signed** and **unsigned** with **char**. Then, regardless of what **char** is, **signed char** would be signed, and **unsigned char** would be unsigned.

Character Constants and Initialization—Suppose you want to initialize a character constant to the letter A. You *can* use the numerical code:

```
char grade = 65;
```

In this example, **65** is type **int**, but, since the value is smaller than the maximum **char** size, it can be assigned to **grade** without any problems.

But computer languages are supposed to make things easy for us; we shouldn't have to memorize the ASCII code. And we don't. We can assign the character A to **grade** with the following initialization:

```
char grade = 'A';
```

A single letter contained between single quotes is a C character constant. When the compiler sees '**A**', it converts it to the proper code value. (On an EBCDIC system, for example, the compiler would use the EBCDIC code for the letter A.)

The single quotes are essential:

```
char broiled;        /* declare a char variable */
broiled = 'T';       /* OK */
broiled = T;         /* NO! Thinks T is a variable */
broiled = "T";       /* NO! Thinks "T" is a string */
```

If you leave off the quotes, the compiler will think **T** is the name of a variable. If you use double quotes, it will think you are using a "string." We'll discuss strings in the next chapter.

Nonprinting Characters—The single quote technique is fine for characters, digits, and punctuation marks, but if you look through Appendix I, you will see that some of the ASCII characters are "nonprinting." For example, some represent actions such as backspacing or going to the next line or making the terminal bell ring (or speaker beep). How can these be represented? C offers three ways.

The first way we have already mentioned: just use the ASCII code. For example, the ASCII code for the beep character is 7, so we can do this:

```
char beep = 7;
```

The second way is to use a special form of the ASCII code. Take the octal ASCII code, precede it with a backslash (\), and put the whole thing in single quotes. We did this in our program **goldenyou**:

```
beep = '\007';
```

You can omit the leading zeros, so '**\07**' or even '**\7**' will do. This notation causes numbers to be interpreted as octal even if there is no initial **0**.

How is using '**\007**' different from using **7**, as we did earlier? One difference is that '**\007**' can be incorporated into a string, which is a sequence of characters, while **7** cannot.

Many new implementations accept a hexadecimal form for character constants. In this case, the backslash is followed by an **x** or **X** and one to three hexadecimal digits. For example, the [control-p] character has an ASCII hex code of 10 (16, in decimal), so it can be expressed as '**\x10**' or '**\X010**'.

When you use ASCII code, note the difference between numbers and number characters. For example, the *character* "4" is represented by ASCII code value 52. This represents the symbol "4" and not the numerical value 4.

The third way to represent awkward characters in C is to use special symbol sequences. These are called *escape sequences* and are as follows:

```
\n        newline
\t        tab
\b        backspace
\r        carriage return
\f        form feed
\\        backslash(\)
\'        single quote(')
\"        double quote(")
```

These, too, would be enclosed in single quotes when assigned to a character variable. For example, we could make the statement:

```
nerf = '\n';
```

and then print the variable **nerf** to advance the printer or screen one line.

The first five escape sequences are common printer control characters. A newline starts a new line. A tab moves the cursor or printhead over a fixed amount, often 5 or 8 spaces. A backspace moves back one space. A carriage return moves to the beginning of a line. A form feed advances printer paper one page. The last three let you use \, ', and " as character constants. (Because these symbols are used to *define* character constants as part of a **printf( )** command, the situation could get confusing if you use them literally.) If you want to print out the line:

Figure 3.5
Writing constants within the *int* family

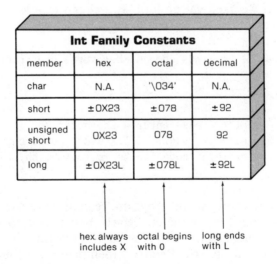

Int Family Constants			
member	hex	octal	decimal
char	N.A.	'\034'	N.A.
short	±0X23	±078	±92
unsigned short	0X23	078	92
long	±0X23L	±078L	±92L

hex always includes X   octal begins with 0   long ends with L

```
Gramps sez, "a \ is a backslash."
```

use:

```
printf("Gramps sez, \"a \\ is a backslash.\"\n");
```

At this point you may have two questions. One, why didn't we enclose the escape sequences in single quotes in the last example? Two, when should you use the ASCII code, and when should you use the escape sequences we just showed? (We hope that these are your two questions, for they are the ones we are about to answer.)

1. When a character, be it an escape sequence or not, is part of a string of characters enclosed in double quotes, don't enclose it in single quotes. Notice that none of the other characters in this example (G,r,a,m,p,s, etc.) are marked off by single quotes. A string of characters enclosed in double quotes is called a *character string*. We will explore this topic in the next chapter.

2. If you have a choice between using one of the special escape sequences, say '**\f**', or an equivalent ASCII code, say '**\016**', use the '**\f**'. First, the representation is more mnemonic. Second, it is more portable. If you have a system that doesn't use ASCII code, the '**\f**' will still work.

Printing Characters—The **printf( )** function uses **%c** to indicate that a character should be printed. Recall that a character is stored as an integer; so if we just print the value of a **char** variable, we should get an integer. The **%c** specifier tells **printf( )** to convert the integer to the corresponding character. If we like, we can look at a **char** variable both ways, as shown in this program:

```
main() /* finds code number for a character */
{
   char ch;

   printf("Please enter a character.\n");
   scanf("%c", &ch);      /* user inputs character */
   printf("The code for %c is %d.\n", ch, ch);
}
```

When you use the program, remember to use the [enter] or [return] key after typing the character. **Scanf( )** then fetches the character you typed, and the ampersand (**&**) sees to it that the character is assigned to the character variable **ch. Printf( )** then prints out the value of **ch** twice, first as a character (prompted by the **%c** code), then as a decimal integer (prompted by the **%d** code).

Types *float* and *double*

The various integer types serve well for most software development projects. However, mathematically oriented programs often make use of "floating-point" numbers. In C, such numbers are called type **float**; they correspond to the **real** types of FORTRAN and Pascal. This approach, as we have already mentioned, allows you to represent a much greater range of numbers, including decimal fractions. Floating-point numbers are analogous to scientific notation, a system used by scientists to express very large and small numbers. Let's take a look.

In scientific notation, numbers are represented as decimal numbers times powers of ten. Here are some examples.

Number	Scientific Notation	Exponential Notation
1,000,000,000	$= 1.0 \times 10^9$	$= 1.0e9$
123,000	$= 1.23 \times 10^5$	$= 1.23e5$
322.56	$= 3.2256 \times 10^2$	$= 3.2256e2$
0.000056	$= 5.6 \times 10^{-5}$	$= 5.6e-5$

The first column shows the usual notation, the second column scientific notation, and the third column exponential notation, which is the way scientific notation is usually written for and by computers, with the "e" followed by the power of ten.

Usually 32 bits are used to store a floating-point number. Eight bits are used to give the exponent its value and sign, and 24 bits are used to represent the nonexponent part. The important things for you to know are that this produces a digit precision of six or seven decimals and a range of $\pm(10^{-37}$ to $10^{+38})$. This can come in handy if you like to use numbers such as the mass of the sun (2.0e30 kilograms) or the charge of a proton (1.6e$-$19 coulombs). (We love using these numbers.)

Many systems also support type **double** (for double precision), which uses twice as many bits, typically 64. Some systems use all 32 additional bits for the nonexponent part. This increases the number of significant figures and reduces roundoff errors. Other systems use some of the bits to accommodate a larger exponent; this increases the range of numbers that can be accommodated.

Declaring Floating-Point Variables—Floating-point variables are declared and initialized in the same manner as their integer cousins. Here are some examples:

```
float noah, jonah;
double trouble;
float planck = 6.63e-34;
```

Figure 3.6
Some floating-point numbers

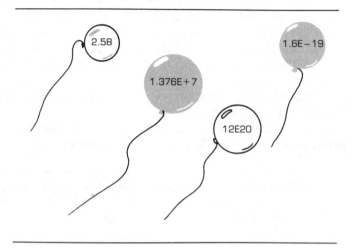

Floating-Point Constants—We have many choices open to us when we write a floating-point constant. The basic form of a floating-point constant is a signed series of digits including a decimal point, then an **e** or **E**, then a signed exponent indicating the power of 10 used. Here are two examples:

$$-1.56E+12 \qquad 2.87e-3$$

You can leave out positive signs. You can do without a decimal point or an exponential part, but not both simultaneously. You can omit a fractional part or an integer part, but not both (that wouldn't leave much!). Here are some more valid floating-point constants:

$$3.14159 \qquad .2 \qquad 4e16 \qquad .8E-5 \qquad 100.$$

Don't use spaces in a floating-point constant.

$$\text{WRONG} \qquad 1.56 \quad E+12$$

Floating-point constants are taken to be double precision. Suppose, for example, that **some** is a **float** variable, and that you have the statement

```
some = 4.0 * 2.0;
```

Then the 4.0 and 2.0 are stored as **double,** using (typically) 64 bits for each. The product (8, if you are wondering) is calculated using double precision arithmetic, and only then is the answer trimmed down to regular **float** size. This ensures maximum precision for your calculations.

Printing Floating-Point Values—The **printf( )** function uses %f to print type **float** and **double** numbers using decimal notation, and it uses %e to print them in exponential notation:

```
main()
{
        float value = 32000.0;

        printf("%f can be written %e\n", value, value);
}
```

This is the output:

```
32000.000000 can be written 3.200000e+004
```

This illustrates the default output. The next chapter discusses how to control the appearance of this output by setting field widths and the number of places to the right of the decimal.

Other Types

That finishes our list of fundamental data types. For some of you, that may seem like a lot. Others of you might be thinking that these are not enough. What about a Boolean type or a string type? C doesn't have them, but it still can deal quite well with logical manipulations and with strings. We will take a first look at strings in the next chapter.

C does have other types derived from the basic types. These types include arrays, pointers, structures, and unions. Although these are subject matter for later chapters, we already have smuggled some pointers into this chapter's examples. (Pointers are used by **scanf( )** and are indicated in that case by the & prefix.)

Floating-Point Overflow and Underflow

What happens if you try to make a **float** variable exceed its limits? For example, suppose you multiply 10e38 by 100 (overflow) or divide 10e−37 by 1000 (underflow)? The result depends on the system. On our system, any number that overflows will abort the program and will print an "overflow" message, and any number that underflows will be replaced by 0. Other systems may not issue warnings or may offer you a choice of responses. If this matter concerns you, you'll have to check out the rules on your system. If you can't find the information, don't be afraid to try a little trial and error.

Summary: The Basic Data Types

Keywords:
The basic data types are set up using the following seven keywords: **int, long, short, unsigned, char, float, double.**

Signed Integers:
These can have positive or negative values.

int: the basic integer type for a given system.
long or **long int**: can hold an integer at least as large as the largest **int** and possibly larger.
short or **short int**: the largest **short** integer is no larger than the largest **int** and may be smaller. Typically, **long** will be bigger than **short**, and **int** will be the same as one of the two. For example, IBM PC Microsoft C has both 16-bit **short** and **int** and 32-bit **long**. It all depends on the system.

Unsigned Integers:
These have zero or positive values only. This extends the range of the largest possible positive number. Use the keyword **unsigned** before the desired type: **unsigned int, unsigned long, unsigned short.** A lone **unsigned** is the same as **unsigned int.**

Characters:
These are typographic symbols such as A, &, and +. Typically, just 1 byte of memory is used.

char: the keyword for this type

Some implementations use a signed **char**, while others use an unsigned **char**. Many implementations allow you to use the keywords **signed** and **unsigned** to specify which form you want.

Floating Point:
These can have positive or negative values.

float: the basic floating-point type for the system.
double or **long float**: a (possibly) larger unit for holding floating-point numbers. It may allow more significant figures and perhaps larger exponents.

Summary: How to Declare a Simple Variable

1. Choose the type you need.
2. Choose a name for the variable.
3. Use this format for a declaration statement:
   type-specifier variable-name;. The *type-specifier* is formed from one or more of the type keywords. Here are some examples:
   int erest;
   unsigned short cash;
4. You may declare more than one variable of the same type by separating the variable names with commas:
   char ch, init, ans;
5. You can initialize a variable in a declaration statement:
   float mass = 6.0E24;

Type Sizes

Table 3.1 shows type sizes for some common C environments.

Table 3.1.
Type Facts for Representative Systems

. Word Size	DEC PDP-11 16 Bits	DEC VAX 32 Bits	Intel 80386 Processor 32 Bits	IBM PC (Microsoft) 16 Bits
char	8	8	8	8
int	16	32	32	16
short	16	16	16	16
long	32	32	32	32
float	32	32	32	32
double	64	64	64	64
exponent range (double)	±38	±38	−307 to 308	−307 to 308

Figure 3.7
C data types for a typical system

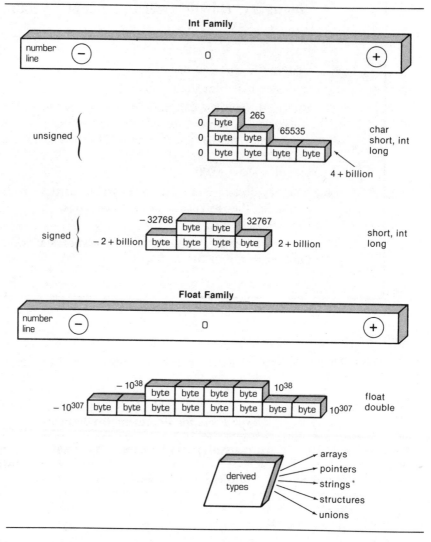

What is your system like? Try running this program to find out.

```
main()
{
  printf("Type int has a size of %d bytes.\n", sizeof(int));
  printf("Type char has a size of %d bytes.\n", sizeof(char));
  printf("Type long has a size of %d bytes.\n", sizeof(long));
  printf("Type double has a size of %d bytes.\n",
                   sizeof(double));
}
```

C has a built-in operator called **sizeof** that gives the size of things in bytes. Our output from this program was:

```
Type int has a size of 2 bytes.
Type char has a size of 1 bytes.
Type long has a size of 4 bytes.
Type double has a size of 8 bytes.
```

We found the size of just four types, but you can easily modify this program to find the size of any other type that interests you.

Incidentally, notice in the last line how we spread the **printf( )** statement over two lines. It is okay to do this as long as the break does not occur in the section in quotes or in the middle of a word.

Using Data Types

When you develop a program, take note of the variables you need and of what type they should be. Most likely you can use **int** or possibly **float** for the numbers and **char** for the characters. Declare them at the beginning of the function that uses them. Choose a name for the variable that suggests its meaning. When you initialize a variable, match the constant type to the variable type.

```
int apples = 3;           /* RIGHT */
int oranges = 3.0;        /* WRONG */
```

C is more forgiving about such mismatches than, say, Pascal, but it is best not to develop sloppy habits.

What You Should Have Learned

This chapter covered a lot of material, and we'll now summarize the most important topics. As in the previous chapter, we will include short examples as room permits. Here, then, are some things you should know.

What the basic C data types are: **int, short, long, unsigned, char, float, double**

How to declare a variable of any type: **int beancount; float rootbeer;** etc.

How to write an **int** constant: **256, 023, 0XF5,** etc.

How to write a **char** constant: **'r', 'U', '\007', '?',** etc.

How to write a **float** constant: **14.92, 1.67e−27,** etc.

How to use some of the **printf( )** specifiers: %d, %x, %o, %l, %c, %f, %e

What words, bytes, and bits are
When to use different data types

Review Questions

Working through these questions will help you digest the material in this chapter.

1. Which data type would you use for each of the following kinds of data?
   a. The population of Rio Frito.
   b. The average weight of a Rembrandt painting.
   c. The most common letter in this chapter.
   d. The number of times that letter occurs.

2. Identify the type and meaning, if any, of each of the following constants:
   a. '\b'
   b. 1066
   c. 99.44
   d. 0XAA
   e. 2.0e30

3. Virgila Ann Xenopod has concocted an error-laden program. Help her find the mistakes.

```
#include <stdio.h>
main
(
   float g; h;
   float tax, rate;

   g = e21;
   tax = rate*g;
)
```

4. Identify the data type (as used in declaration statements) and the **printf** format specifier for each of the following constants:

	Constant	Type	Specifier
a.	12		
b.	0X3		
c.	'C'		
d.	2.34E07		
e.	'\040'		
f.	7.0		
g.	6L		

5. Suppose that **ch** is a type **char** variable. Show how to assign the carriage-return character to **ch** by using an escape sequence, a decimal value, an octal character constant, and a hex character constant.

6. Correct this silly program. (The / in C means division.)

```
main() / this program is perfect /
{
   cows, legs integer;

   printf("How many cow legs did you count?\n);
   scanf("%c", legs);
   cows = legs / 4;
   printf("That implies there are %f cows.\n", cows)
}
```

Answers

1. **a. int,** possibly **short or unsigned** or **unsigned short;** population is a whole number
   b. float; it's unlikely the average will be an exact integer
   c. char
   d. int, possibly **unsigned**

2. **a. char,** the backspace character
   b. int, a historic date
   c. float, a measure of soap purity
   d. hexadecimal **int;** the decimal value is 170
   e. float, the mass of the sun in kg

3. Line 1: Fine.
   Line 2: Should have a parentheses pair follow **main;** i.e., **main( ).**
   Line 3: Use {, not (.
   Line 4: Should be a comma, not a semicolon, between **g** and **h.**
   Line 5: Fine.
   Line 6: (blank) Fine.
   Line 7: There should be at least one digit before the **e.** Either **1e21** or **1.0e21** is okay.
   Line 8: Fine.
   Line 9: Use }, not).
   Missing Lines: First, **rate** is never assigned a value. Second, the variable **h** is never used. Also, the program never informs us of the results of its calculation. Neither of these errors will stop the program from running (although you may be given a warning about the unused variable), but they do detract from its already limited usefulness.

4. **a. int,** %**d**
   b. int, %**x**
   c. char, %**c**
   d. float, %**e**
   e. char, %**c**
   f. float, %**f**
   g. long, %**l**

5. Your program should look like this:

```
ch = '\r';
ch = 13;
ch = '\15';
ch = '\XD';
```

6. Line 1: Use /* and */
   Line 3: **int cows, legs;**
   Line 5: **count?\n");**
   Line 6: **%d**, not **%c**
   Line 6: **&legs**
   Line 8: **%d**, not **%f**

Exercise

Exercises are problems for which we don't provide answers. One way to tell if you are right is to see if your answer works when you run it as a program.

1. Find out what your system does with integer overflow, floating-point overflow, and floating-point underflow by using the experimental approach; i.e., write programs having these problems.

4

Character Strings, #define, printf( ), and scanf( )

Concepts

- Character strings
- The C preprocessor
- Formatted output

In this chapter we go beyond basic data types and look at the character string. First we'll take a look at an important C facility, the C preprocessor, and learn how to define and use symbolic constants. Then we will look again at ways to communicate data to and from a program, this time exploring the features of **printf( )** and **scanf( )** more fully. By now you probably expect a sample program at the beginning of the chapter, and we won't disappoint you.

```
/* talkback */
#define DENSITY 62.4 /* human density in lbs per cu ft */
main() /* nosy, informative program */
{
   float weight, volume;
   int size, letters;
   char name[40];

   printf("Hi! What's your first name?\n");
   scanf("%s", name);
   printf("%s, what's your weight in pounds?\n", name);
   scanf("%f", &weight);
   size = sizeof name;
   letters = strlen(name);
   volume = weight/DENSITY;
   printf("Well, %s, your volume is %2.2f cubic feet.\n",
        name, volume);
   printf("Also, your first name has %d letters,\n",
        letters);
```

```
    printf("and we have %d bytes to store it in.\n", size);
}
```

Running **talkback** produces results such as the following:

```
Hi! What's your first name?
Angelica
Angelica, what's your weight in pounds?
102.5
Well, Angelica, your volume is 1.64 cubic feet.
Also, your first name has 8 letters,
and we have 40 bytes to store it in.
```

Here are the main new features of this program.

1. We have used an "array" to hold a "character string," in this case, someone's name.
2. We used the %s "conversion specification" to handle the input and output of the string. Note that **name**, unlike **weight**, does not use the **&** prefix when used with **scanf( )**. (As we will see later, **&weight** and **name** are both addresses.)
3. We used the C preprocessor to define the symbolic constant **DENSITY.**
4. We used the C function **strlen( )** to find the length of a string.

The C approach may seem a little complex compared to the input/output modes of, say, BASIC. However, this complexity buys a finer control of I/O and a greater program efficiency. And it is not all that difficult once you get into it.

Let's flesh out these new ideas.

Character Strings—An Introduction

A *character string* is a series of one or more characters. An example of a string is:

```
"Zing went the strings of my heart!"
```

The double quotes are not part of the string. They are there to mark off the string, just as single quotes are used to mark off a character.

C has no special variable type for strings. Instead, strings are stored in an "array" of **char** type. This means you can think of the characters in a string as being stored in adjacent memory cells, one character per cell. See Figure 4.1.

Note in the figure that we show the character **\0** in the last array

Figure 4.1
A string in an array

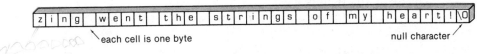

position. This is the *null character,* and C uses it to mark the end of a string. The null character is not the digit zero; it is the nonprinting character whose ASCII code number is 0. The presence of the null character means that the array must have at least one more cell than the number of characters to be stored.

Now just what is an array? We can think of an array as several memory cells in a row. Or, if you prefer more formal and exact language, an *array* is an ordered sequence of data elements of one type. In our example, we created an array of 40 memory cells, each of which can store one **char**-type value. We accomplished this with the declaration:

```
char name [40];
```

The brackets identify **name** as an array, the 40 indicates the number of elements, and the **char** identifies the type of each element.

Figure 4.2
Declaring an array name of type *char*

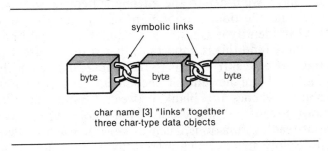

One compiler we used required this declaration instead:

```
static char name[40];
```

Here **static** is a "storage class" specifier (an item that we will discuss in Chapter 10). This difference was due to a bug in the **scanf( )** function for that implementation. The bug has been fixed, but we mention this difference to point out that there may be discrepancies between C as we describe it and C as it exists on your system.

Using a character string is beginning to sound complicated: you have to create an array, pack in the characters of a string one by one, and remember to add a \0 at the end! Fortunately for us, the computer can take care of most of the details itself.

Try this program to see how easily it works in practice.

```
/* praise1 */
#define PRAISE "My sakes, that's a grand name!"
main()
{
    char name[50];

    printf("What's your name?\n");
    scanf("%s", name);
    printf("Hello, %s. %s\n", name, PRAISE);
}
```

The %s tells **printf( )** to print a string. Running **praise1** should produce an output similar to this:

```
What's your name?
Elmo Blunk
Hello, Elmo. My sakes, that's a grand name!
```

We did not have to put in the null character ourselves. That task was done for us when **scanf( )** read the input. **PRAISE** is a "character string constant." We'll get to the **#define** statement soon; for now, you should know that the double quotation marks that enclose the phrase following **PRAISE** identify it as a string and take care of putting in the null character.

Note (and this is important) that **scanf( )** just reads Elmo Blunk's first name. After **scanf( )** starts to read input, it stops at the first "white space" (blank, tab, or newline) it encounters. Thus, it stops scanning for **name** when it reaches the blank between "Elmo" and "Blunk." In general, **scanf( )** reads just single words, not whole phrases as a string. C has other input-reading functions, such as **gets( )**, for handling general strings. We will explore strings much more fully in later chapters.

The string "**x**" is not the same as the character '**x**'. One difference is that '**x**' is a basic type (**char**), while "**x**" is a derived type, an array of **char**. A second difference is that "**x**" really consists of two characters, '**x**' and the null character.

String Length—*strlen( )*

In the last chapter we unleashed the **sizeof** operator, which gave us the size of things in bytes. The **strlen( )** function gives us the length of a string in characters. Since it takes one byte to hold one character, you might suppose

Figure 4.3
The character 'x' and the string "x"

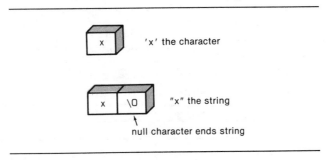

'x' the character

"x" the string

null character ends string

both would give the same result when applied to a string, but they don't. Let's add a few lines to our example and see why.

```
/* praise2 */
#define PRAISE "My sakes, that's a grand name!"
main()
{
  char name[50];

  printf("What's your name?\n");
  scanf("%s", name);
  printf("Hello, %s. %s\n", name, PRAISE);
  printf("Your name of %d letters occupies %d memory cells.\n",
        strlen(name), sizeof name);
  printf("The phrase of praise has %d letters ", strlen(PRAISE));
  printf("and occupies %d memory cells.\n", sizeof PRAISE);
}
```

Notice, incidentally, that we have used two methods to handle long **printf( )** statements. We spread one print statement over two lines. We can break a line between arguments but not in the middle of a string. Then we used two **printf( )** statements to print just one line. We did this by using the newline character (**\n**) only in the second statement. Running the program could produce this interchange:

```
What's your name?
Perky
Hello, Perky. My sakes, that's a grand name!
Your name of 5 letters occupies 50 memory cells.
The phrase of praise has 30 letters and occupies 31 memory cells.
```

See what happens. The array **name** has 50 memory cells, and that is what **sizeof** reports to us. But only the first five cells are needed to hold **Perky,** and that is what **strlen( )** reports to us. The sixth cell in the array

name contains the null character, and its presence tells **strlen( )** when to stop counting.

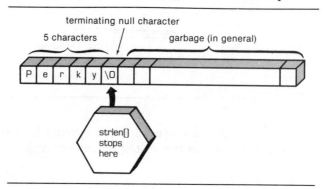

Figure 4.4
The *strlen( )* function knows when to stop

When we get to **PRAISE,** we find that **strlen( )** again gives us the exact number of characters (including spaces and punctuation) in the string. The **sizeof** operator gives us a number one larger, for it also counts the invisible null character used to end the string. We didn't tell the computer how much memory to set aside to store the phrase. It had to count the number of characters between the double quotes itself.

One other point: in the preceding chapter we used **sizeof** with parentheses, and in this chapter we didn't. Whether or not you use parentheses depends on whether you want the size of a type class or the size of a particular quantity. That is, you would use **sizeof(char)** or **sizeof(float),** but **sizeof name** or **sizeof 6.28.**

In the last example, our use of **strlen( )** and **sizeof** was not a very important one. We merely wanted to satisfy our curiosity. Actually, however, **strlen( )** and **sizeof** are important programming tools. **Strlen( ),** for example, is useful in all sorts of character-string programs, as we'll see in Chapter 13.

Let's move on to the **#define** statement.

Constants and the C Preprocessor

Sometimes we need to use a constant in a program. For example, we could give the circumference of a circle as:

```
circ = 3.14 * diameter;
```

Here we used the constant 3.14 to represent the famous constant pi. To use a constant, we can just type in the actual value, as we did here. There are good reasons to use a "symbolic constant" instead, however. That is, we could use a statement like:

```
circ = pi * diameter;
```

and have the computer substitute in the actual value later.

Why is this a better way? First, a name tells us more than a number does. Compare these two statements:

```
owed = 0.015 * housevl;
owed = taxrate * housevl;
```

If we are reading through a long program, the meaning of the second version is plainer.

Second, suppose we have used a constant in several places, and it becomes necessary to change its value. After all, tax rates do change, and a state legislature once passed a law stating that the value of pi would henceforth be a simple 3 1/7. (Presumably many a circle became a fugitive from justice.) Then we need merely alter the definition of the symbolic constant, rather than find and change every occurrence of the constant in the program.

Okay, how do we set up a symbolic constant? One way is to declare a variable and set it equal to the desired constant. We could do this:

```
float taxrate;
taxrate = 0.015;
```

This is all right for a small program, but it is a little wasteful because the computer has to go peek into the **taxrate** memory location every time it is used. This is an example of *execution time* substitution, for the substitutions take place while the program is running. Fortunately, C has a better idea.

The better idea is the C preprocessor. We've already seen in Chapter 2 how the preprocessor uses **#include** to include information from another file. The preprocessor also lets us define constants. Just add a line like this at the top of the file containing your program:

```
#define TAXRATE 0.015
```

When your program is compiled, the value 0.015 will be substituted everywhere you have used **TAXRATE**. This is called a *compile time* substitution. By the time you run the program, all the substitutions already have been made.

Note the format. First comes **#define.** It should start at the far left. Then comes the symbolic name for the constant, then the value for the constant. No semicolon is used, since this is not a C statement. Why is **TAXRATE** capitalized? It is a sensible C tradition to type constants in uppercase. Then, when you come across one in the depths of a program, you will know at once that it is a constant and not a variable. It is just another example of trying to make programs readable. Your programs will still work if you don't capitalize the constants, but you should feel a little guilty about it.

Here is a simple example:

```
/* pizza */
#define PI 3.14159
main()        /* learning about your pizza */
{
   float area, circum, radius;

   printf("What is the radius of your pizza?\n");
   scanf("%f", &radius);
   area = PI * radius * radius;
   circum = 2.0 * PI *radius;
   printf("Your basic pizza parameters are as follows:\n");
   printf("circumference = %1.2f, area = %1.2f\n", circum, area);
}
```

The %**1.2f** in the **printf( )** statement causes the printout to be rounded to two decimal places. Of course, this program may not reflect your major pizza concerns, but it does serve to fill a small niche in the world of pizza programs. Here is a sample run:

```
What is the radius of your pizza?
6.0
Your basic pizza parameters are as follows:
circumference = 37.70, area = 113.10
```

The **#define** statement can be used for character and string constants, too. Just use single quotes for the former and double quotes for the latter. Thus, the following examples are valid:

```
#define BEEP '\007'
#define ESS 'S'
#define NULL '\0'
#define OOPS "Now you have done it!"
```

Now we have a special treat for the lazy. Suppose you develop a whole packet of programs that use the same set of constants. You can do the following:

1. Collect all your **#define** statements in one file; call it, say, **const.h.**

Figure 4.5
What you type versus what is compiled

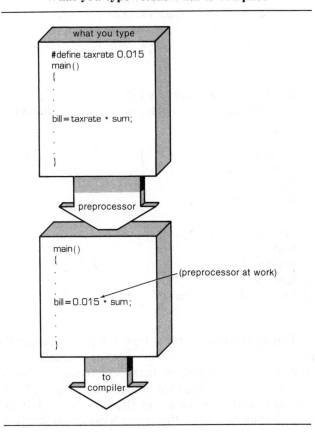

2. At the head of each file of programs, insert the statement
#include "const.h".

Then, when you run the program, the preprocessor will read the file
const.h and use all the **#define** statements there for your program. Incidentally, the **.h** at the end of the file name is a reminder to you that the file is a
header, i.e., full of information to go at the head of your program. The
preprocessor itself doesn't care if you use a **.h** in the name or not.

C—A Master of Disguise: Creating Aliases

The capabilities of **#define** go beyond the symbolic representation of constants. Consider, for instance, the following program:

```
#include "alias.h"
program
  begin
```

```
            whole yours, mine then
            spitout("Give me an integer, please.\n ") then
            takein("%d", &yours) then
            mine = yours times TWO then
            spitout("%d is twice your number!\n ", mine) then
        end
```

Hmm, this looks vaguely familiar, a little like Pascal, but it doesn't seem to be C. The secret, of course, is in the file **alias.h.** What's in it? Read on.

```
alias.h
#define program main()
#define begin    {
#define end      }
#define then     ;
#define takein   scanf
#define spitout  printf
#define TWO      2
#define times    *
#define whole    int
```

This example illustrates how the preprocessor works. Your program is searched for items defined by **#define** statements, and finds are then replaced. In our example, all **thens** are rendered into semicolons at compilation. The resulting program is identical to what we would have received by typing in the usual C terms in the first place. (By the way, this example is meant to illustrate how the preprocessor works; it is not intended to be a model to emulate.)

This powerful ability can be used to define a "macro," which is sort of a poor man's function. We will return to this topic in Chapter 11.

There are some limitations. For example, parts of a program within double quotes are immune to substitution. For instance, this combination wouldn't work:

```
#define MN "minimifidianism"
printf("He was a strong believer in MN.\n");
```

The printout would just read:

```
He was a strong believer in MN.
```

However, the statement

```
printf("He was a strong believer in %s.\n", MN);
```

would produce:

```
He was a strong believer in minimifidianism.
```

In this case, the **MN** was outside the double quotes, so it was replaced by its definition.

The C preprocessor is a useful, helpful tool, so take advantage of it when you can. We'll show you more applications as we move along.

Exploring and Exploiting *printf( )* and *scanf( )*

The functions **printf( )** and **scanf( )** let us communicate with a program. We call them input/output functions, or I/O functions for short. These are not the only I/O functions we can use with C, but they are the most versatile. These functions are *not* part of the definition of C. Indeed, C leaves the implementation of I/O up to the compiler writers; this makes it possible to better match I/O to specific machines. However, in the interests of compatibility, various systems all come with versions of **scanf( )** and **printf( ).** What we say here should be true for most systems, but don't be astonished if you find your version to be different in some small fashion. The ANSI C Standard, discussed in Chapter 16, describes standard versions of these functions, so discrepancies should disappear as the standard is implemented.

Generally, **printf( )** and **scanf( )** work much the same, each using a "control string" and a list of "arguments." We will show how these work first with **printf( ),** then with **scanf( ).**

The instructions we give **printf( )** when we ask it to print a variable depend on what type the variable is. For instance, we have used the %**d** notation when printing an integer and the %**c** notation when printing a character. Let's list the common identifiers that the **printf( )** function uses, and then we'll show how to use them. First, here are the identifiers and the type of output they cause to be printed. The first five serve most needs, but the other four are available if you desire them.

Identifier	Output
%d	decimal integer
%c	a single character
%s	character string
%e	floating-point number, e-notation
%f	floating-point number, decimal notation
%g	use %f or %e, whichever is shorter
%u	unsigned decimal integer
%o	unsigned octal integer
%x	unsigned hexadecimal integer

New implementations may offer further choices; check your manual to see what your version offers. Meanwhile, let's see how these representative identifiers are used.

Using *printf( )*

Here is a program that uses some of the examples we will discuss:

```
/* printstuff */
#define PI 3.141593
main()
{
    int number = 5;
    float ouzo = 13.5;
    int cost = 31000;

    printf("The %d women drank %f glasses of ouzo.\n",number,ouzo);
    printf("The value of pi is %f.\n", PI);
    printf("Farewell! thou art too dear for my possessing,\n");
    printf("%c%d\n", '$', cost);
}
```

The output, of course, is:

```
The 5 women drank 13.500000 glasses of ouzo.
The value of pi is 3.141593.
Farewell! thou art too dear for my possessing,
$31000
```

The format for using **printf( )** is this:

```
printf(Control, item1, item2,...);
```

Item1, item2, and so on, are the items to be printed. They can be variables or constants, or even expressions that are evaluated first before the value is printed. **Control** is a character string describing how the items are to be printed. For example, in the statement

```
printf("The %d women drank %f glasses of ouzo.\n", number, ouzo);
```

control would be the phrase in double quotes (after all, it is a character string), and **number** and **ouzo** would be the items or, in this case, the values of two variables.

Figure 4.6
Arguments for *printf( )*

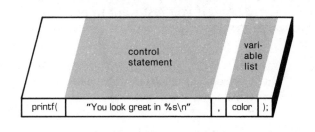

Here is a second example:

```
printf("The value of pi is %f.\n", PI);
```

This time, the list of items has just one member—the symbolic constant PI.
We see that **control** contains two distinct forms of information:

1. Characters that are actually printed.
2. Data identifiers, also called *conversion specifications.*

Figure 4.7
Anatomy of a control string

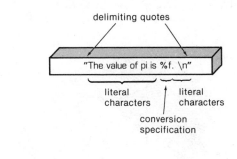

There should be one conversion specification for each item in the list
following **control.** Woe (or is it whoa?) unto you should you forget this
basic requirement! Don't do this:

```
printf("The score was Squids %d, Slugs %d.\n", score1);
```

Here, there is no value for the second **%d.** The result of this faux pas will depend on your system, but at best you will get nonsense.

If you just want to print a phrase, you don't need any conversion specifications. And if you just want to print data, you can dispense with the running commentary. Thus, each of the following statements is quite acceptable.

```
printf("Farewell! thou art too dear for my possessing,\n");
printf("%c%d\n", '$', cost);
```

In the second statement, note that the first item on the print list was a character constant rather than a variable.

Since the **printf( )** function uses the % symbol to identify the conversion specifications, there is a slight problem if you wish to print the % sign itself. If you just use a lone % sign, the compiler will think you have bungled a conversion specification. The way out is simple. Just use two % symbols:

```
pc = 2*6;
printf("Only %d%% of Sally's gribbles were edible.\n", pc);
```

The following output would result:

```
Only 12% of Sally's gribbles were edible.
```

Conversion Specification Modifiers for *printf( )*

We can modify a basic conversion specification by inserting modifiers between the % and the defining conversion character. Here is a list of the symbols you can place there legally. If you use more than one modifier, they should be in the same order as they appear in this table. Not all combinations are possible.

Modifier	Meaning
—	The item will be printed beginning at the left of its field width (as defined below). Normally the item is printed so that it ends at the right of its field. Example: %**—10d**
digit string	The minimum field width. A wider field will be used if the printed number or string won't fit in the field. Example: %**4d**
.digit string	Precision. For floating types, the number of digits to be printed to the right of the decimal. For character strings, the maximum number of characters to be printed. Example: %**4.2f** (2 decimal places in a field 4 characters wide)
l	The corresponding data item is **long** rather than **int.** Example: %**ld**

Examples—Let's put these modifiers to work. We'll begin by looking at the effect of the field width modifier on printing an integer. Consider the following program:

```
main()
{
  printf("/%d/\n", 336);
  printf("/%2d/\n", 336);
  printf("/%10d/\n", 336);
  printf("/%-10d/\n", 336);
}
```

This program prints the same quantity four times, but using four different conversion specifications. We used a slash (/) to let you see where each field begins and ends. The output looks like this:

```
/336/
/336/
/        336/
/336        /
```

The first conversion specification is **%d** with no modifiers. We see that it uses a field with the same width as the integer. This is the so-called *default* option; i.e., what gets done if you don't give further instructions. The second conversion specification is **%2d**. This should produce a field with a width of 2, but since the integer is three digits long, the field is expanded automatically to fit the number. The next conversion specification is **%10d**. This produces a field ten spaces wide, and, indeed, there are seven blanks and three digits between the /'s, with the number tucked into the right end of the field. The final specification is **%−10d**. It also produces a field ten spaces wide, and the − puts the number at the left end, just as advertised. Once you get used to it, this system is easy to use and gives you nice control over the appearance of your output.

Okay, let's look at some floating-point formats. Let the program look like this:

```c
main()
{
    printf("/%f/\n", 1234.56);
    printf("/%e/\n", 1234.56);
    printf("/%4.2f/\n", 1234.56);
    printf("/%3.1f/\n", 1234.56);
    printf("/%10.3f/\n", 1234.56);
    printf("/%10.3e/\n", 1234.56);
}
```

This time we get this output:

```
/1234.560000/
/1.234560e+003/
/1234.56/
/1234.6/
/  1234.560/
/1.235e+003/
```

Again we begin with the default version, **%f**. In this case there are two defaults: the field width and the digits to the right of the decimal. The second default is six digits, and the field width is whatever it takes to hold the number.

Next is the default for %**e.** We can see that it prints one digit to the left of the decimal point and six places to the right. We seem to be getting a lot of digits! The cure is to specify the number of decimal places to the right of the decimal, and the last four examples in this segment do that. Notice how the fourth and the sixth examples cause the output to be rounded off.

Now let's examine some of the string options. Consider this example:

```
#define BLURB "Outstanding acting!"
main()
{
    printf("/%2s/\n", BLURB);
    printf("/%22s/\n", BLURB);
    printf("/%22.5s/\n", BLURB);
    printf("/%-22.5s/\n", BLURB);
}
```

Here's the output:

```
/Outstanding acting!/
/   Outstanding acting!/
/                 Outst/
/Outst                 /
```

Notice how the field is expanded to contain all the specified characters. Also notice how the precision specification limits the number of characters printed. The .5 in the format specifier tells **printf( )** to print just five characters.

Okay, you've seen some examples. Now how would you set up a statement to print something having the following form?

```
The NAME family just may be $XXX.XX dollars richer!
```

Here NAME and XXX.XX represent values that will be supplied by variables in the program, say, **name[40]** and **cash.**

Here is one solution:

```
printf("The %s family just may be $%.2f richer!\n",name,cash);
```

So far we have played it safe and matched the conversion specification to the variable type, %**f** for type **float,** and so on. But, as we saw in our program to find the ASCII code for a character, we can also use **printf( )** to make type conversions! But we have to keep reasonable and stay within the family of integer types.

Using *printf( )* to Make Conversions

Once again, we will print an integer. Since we now know about fields, we won't bother using slashes to mark them.

```
main()
{
    printf("%d\n", 336);
    printf("%o\n", 336);
    printf("%x\n", 336);
    printf("%d\n", -336);
    printf("%u\n", -336);
}
```

Our system produces the following results:

```
336
520
150
-336
65200
```

First, as you would expect, the **%d** specification gives us the number 336, just as it did a few lines ago. But look what happens when you ask the program to print this decimal integer as an octal integer. It prints 520, which is the octal equivalent of 336 ($5 \times 64 + 2 \times 8 + 0 \times 1 = 336$). Similarly, 150 is the hex equivalent to 336.

Thus, we can use the **printf( )** conversion specifications to convert decimal to octal or hexadecimal, and vice versa. Just ask for the number to be printed in the form you want; use **%d** to get decimal, **%o** to get octal, or **%x** to get hex. It doesn't matter in what form the number originally appeared in the program.

But there is more to the output. Printing −336 using **%d** produces no surprise. But the **%u** (unsigned) version came out as 65200, not as the 336 you might have expected. This results from the way negative numbers are represented on our reference system. It uses a method called the "two's complement." In this method, the numbers 0 to 32767 represent themselves, and the numbers 32768 to 65535 represent negative numbers, with 65535 being −1, 65534 being −2, etc. Thus **−366** is represented by **65536 − 336** or 65200. Not all systems use this method to represent negative integers. Nonetheless, there is a moral: don't expect a **%u** conversion simply to strip the sign from a number.

Now we come to an interesting example that we have used already—using **printf( )** to find the ASCII code of a character. For instance,

```
printf ("%c %d\n", 'A', 'A');
```

produces

```
A 65
```

for output. **A** is the letter, of course, and **65** is the decimal ASCII code for the character **A.** We could use %**o** if we want the octal ASCII code.

This gives us an easy way to find the ASCII code for various characters and vice versa. Of course, you may prefer to look them up in Appendix G.

What happens if you try to convert a number bigger than 255 to a character? The following program line and its output give the answer.

```
printf("%d %c\n", 336, 336);
336 P
```

The ASCII decimal code for **P** is 80, and **336** is just 256 + 80. Apparently the number is interpreted modulo 256. (That's math talk meaning the remainder when the number is divided by 256.) In other words, whenever the computer reaches a multiple of 256, it starts counting over again, and 256 is considered to be 0, 257 is 1, 511 is 255, 512 is 0, 513 is 1, etc.

Finally, we try printing an integer (65616) that's larger than the maximum **int** (32767) allowed on our system:

```
printf("%ld %d \n", 65616, 65616);
```

The result is:

```
65616 80
```

Again, the computer does its modulo thing. This time the counting is done in groups of 65536. A number between 32767 and 65536 would be printed as a negative number because of the way negative numbers are stored. Systems with different integer sizes would have the same general behavior, but with different numerical values.

We haven't exhausted all possible combinations of data and conversion specifications, so feel free to try some yourself. Better yet, see if you can predict in advance what the result will be when a certain item is printed using the conversion specification of your choice.

Using *scanf( )*

We will not be making extensive use of **scanf( )** until later, so we will only highlight its use here.

Like **printf( )**, **scanf( )** uses a control string followed by a list of arguments. The chief difference is in the argument list. **Printf( )** uses variable names, constants, and expressions. **Scanf( )** uses pointers to variables. Fortunately, we don't have to know anything about pointers to use the function. Just remember these two rules:

1. If you wish to read in a value for one of the basic variable types, precede the variable name with an &.
2. If you wish to read in a value for a string variable, don't use an &.

This is a valid program:

```
main()
{
    int age;
    float assets;
    char pet[30];

    printf("Enter your age, assets, and favorite pet.\n");
    scanf("%d %f", &age, &assets);
    scanf("%s", pet); /* no & for char array */
    printf("%d $%.0f %s\n ", age, assets, pet);
}
```

And here is a sample exchange:

```
Enter your age, assets, and favorite pet.
82
8345245.19 rhino
82 $8345245 rhino
```

Scanf( ) uses white space (blanks, tabs, and spaces) to decide how to divide the input into separate fields. It matches up consecutive conversion specifications to consecutive fields, skipping over the white space in-between. Note how we spread our input over two lines. We could just as well have used one or five lines, as long as we had at least one newline, space, or tab between each entry. The only exception to this is the %c specification, which reads the very next character, even if it is white space.

The **scanf( )** function uses pretty much the same set of conversion-specification characters as **printf( )** does. The main differences for **scanf( )** are these:

1. There is no %g option.
2. The %f and the %e options are equivalent. Both accept an optional sign, a string of digits with or without a decimal point, and an optional exponent field.
3. There is a %h option for reading **short** integers.

Scanf( ) is not the most commonly used input function in C. We have featured it here because of its versatility (it can read all the different data types), but C has several other input functions, such as **getchar( )** and

gets( ) that are better suited for specific tasks, such as reading single characters or reading strings containing spaces. We will cover some of these functions in Chapters 6, 13, and 15.

The * Modifier with *printf( )* and *scanf( )*

Both **printf( )** and **scanf( )** can use * to modify the meaning of a specifier, but they do so in dissimilar fashions. First, let's see what the * can do for **printf( )**.

Suppose that you don't want to commit yourself to a field width in advance but that you want the program to specify it. You can do this by using * instead of a number for the field width. But you also have to use an argument to tell what the field width should be. Here is a short example showing how this works:

```
/* varwid.c -- uses variable-width output field */
main()
{
  unsigned width;
  int number = 256;

  printf("What field width?\n");
  scanf("%d", &width);
  printf("The number is :%*d:\n", width, number);
}
```

The variable **width** provides the **field width,** and **number** is the number to be printed. Because the * precedes the **d** in the specifier, **width** comes before **number** in the argument list. Here is a sample run:

```
What field width?
6
The number is :   256:
```

We replied to the question with **6,** so that was the field width used.

The technique also can be used with floating-point values:

```
printf("Weight = %*.*f\n", width, precision, weight);
```

Here, **width** and **precision** would be variables previously set to the desired values. A program, for example, could decide on values for these variables after looking at the value of **weight.**

The * serves quite a different purpose for **scanf( ).** When placed between the % and the specifier letter, it causes that function to skip over corresponding input. Here is an example:

```
/* skip2.c -- skips over first two integers of input */
```

```
main()
{
    int n;

    printf("Please enter three integers:\n");
    scanf("%*d %*d %d", &n);
    printf("The last integer was %d\n", n);
}
```

This **scanf( )** instruction says, "Skip two integers and copy the third into **n**." Here is a sample run:

```
Please enter three integers:
445 345 1212
The last integer was 1212
```

This skipping facility is useful, for example, if a program needs to read just certain items from a file that has data arranged in a standard format.

Usage Tips

Specifying fixed field widths is useful when you want to print columns of data. Since the default field width is just the width of the number, the repeated use of, say,

```
printf("%d %d %d\n", val1, val2, val3);
```

would produce ragged columns if the numbers in a column had different sizes. For example, the output could look like this:

```
12 234 1222
4 5 23
22334 2322 10001
```

(This assumes that the value of the variables has been changed between print statements.)

The output can be cleaned up using a sufficiently large fixed field width. For example, using

```
printf("%9d %9d %9d\n", val1, val2, val3);
```

would yield:

```
        12        234       1222
         4          5         23
     22334       2322      10001
```

Leaving a blank between one conversion specification and the next ensures that one number will never run into the next, even if it overflows its own field. This is so because the regular characters in the control string, including spaces, are printed out.

On the other hand, if a number is to be embedded in a phrase, it often is convenient to specify a field as small or smaller than the expected number width. This makes the number fit in without unnecessary blanks. For example,

```
printf("Count Beppo ran %.2f miles in 3 hours.\n", distance);
```

might produce:

```
Count Beppo ran 10.22 miles in 3 hours.
```

On the other hand, changing the conversion specification to %10.2f would give:

```
Count Beppo ran       10.22 miles in 3 hours.
```

What You Should Have Learned

What a character string is: some characters in a row
How to write a character string: **"some characters in a row"**
How a string is stored: **"some characters in a row \0"**
Where to store a string: **char phrase[25]** or **static char phrase[25]**
How to find the length of a string: **strlen(phrase)**
How to print out a string: **printf("%s", phrase)**
How to read in a one-word string: **scanf("%s," name)**
How to define a numerical constant: **#define TWO 2**
How to define a character constant: **#define WOW '!'**
How to define a string constant: **#define WARN "Don't do that!"**
I/O conversion specifications: %d %f %e %g %c %s %u %o %x
How to fine-tune output format: %−10d %3.2f
How to make conversions: **printf("%d %o %c\n", WOW, WOW, WOW);**
How to use variable field widths: **printf("%*d\n", width, q);**
How to skip over input: **scanf("%*s");**

Review Questions

1. Run the opening program again, but this time give your first and last name when it asks you for your first name. What happens? Why?

2. Assuming that each of the following examples is part of a complete program, what will each one print?

   a. `printf("He sold the painting for $%2.2f.\n", 2.345e2);`
   b. `printf("%c%c%c\n", 'H', 105, '\41');`
   c. `#define Q "His Hamlet was funny without being vulgar."`
      `printf("%s\nhas %d characters.\n", Q, strlen(Q));`
   d. `printf("Is %2.2e the same as %2.2f?\n", 1201.0, 1201.0);`

3. In Question 2c, what changes could we make so that string Q is printed out enclosed in quotes?

4. It's find the error time!

```
define B booboo
define X 10
main()
{
    int age;
    char name;

    printf("Please enter your first name.");
    scanf("%s", name);
    printf("All right, %c, what's your age?\n", name);
    scanf("%f", age);
    xp = age + X;
    printf("That's a %s! You must be at least %d.\n", B, xp);
}
```

5. Suppose a program starts like this:

```
#define BOOK "War and Peace"
main()
{
float cost =12.99;
float percent = 80.0;
```

Construct a **printf( )** statement that uses **BOOK** and **cost** to print the following:

```
This copy of "War and Peace" sells for $12.99.
That is 80% of list.
```

Answers

1. The program bombs. The first **scanf( )** statement reads just your first name, leaving your last name untouched but still stored in the input "buffer." (This

buffer is just a temporary storage area used to store the input.) When the next **scanf( )** statement comes along looking for your weight, it picks up where the last reading attempt ended, and reads your last name as your weight. This produces garbage. On the other hand, if you respond to the name request with something like "Lasha 144," it will use 144 as your weight even though you typed it before your weight was requested.

2. **a.** `He sold the painting for $234.50.`
   b. `Hi!` (Note: The first character is a character constant, the second is a decimal integer converted to a character, and the third is ASCII representation of a character constant.)
   c. `His Hamlet was funny without being vulgar.`
   `has 41 characters.`
   d. `Is 1.20e+003 the same as 1201.00?`

3. Remember the escape sequences of Chapter 3 and try:

   `printf("\"%s\"\nhas %d characters.\n", Q, strlen(Q));`

4. Line 1: The **#** was omitted before **define. booboo** should be "**booboo**".
   Line 2: The **#** was omitted before **define.**
   Line 6: **name** should be an array; **char name[25]** would serve.
   Line 8: There should be **\n** in the control string.
   Line 10: The **%c** should be **%s.**
   Line 11: Since **age** is an integer, use **%d**, not **%f**. Also, use **&age**, not **age.**
   Line 12: **xp** never was declared
   Line 13: Okay, but it will be messed up by improperly defined B. Also, the program is guilty of poor manners.

5. Recall the **%%** construction for printing **%**.

   `printf("This copy of \"%s\" sells for $%0.2f.\n", BOOK, cost);`
   `printf("That is %d%% of list.\n", percent);`

Exercises

1. Write a program that asks for your first name, then your last name, and then prints the names in the format last, first.

2. Write a program that requests your first name and does the following with it:
   a. Prints it enclosed in double quotation marks.
   b. Prints it in a field 20 characters wide, with the whole field in quotes.
   c. Prints it at the left end of a field 20 characters wide, with the whole field enclosed in quotes.
   d. Prints it in a field 3 characters wider than the name.

5

Operators, Expressions, and Statements

Concepts
- Operators and operands
- Doing arithmetic
- Using *while*
- Expressions
- Simple and compound statements
- Type conversions

Keywords
- *while*

Operators
- `+ - * / % ++ -- (type)`

I n Chapters 3 and 4 we talked about the kinds of data that C recognizes. Now we will look at ways to do things to the data. C offers many possibilities. We will start with basic arithmetic: addition, subtraction, multiplication, and division. To make our programs more interesting and useful, we will take a first look at loops in this chapter.

Introducing Loops

Here is a sample program that does a little arithmetic and introduces the **while** loop.

```
/* shoesize1 */
#define OFFSET 7.64
#define SCALE 0.325
main()
{
 /* this program converts shoe size to foot size in inches */
  float shoe, foot;

  shoe = 9.0;
  foot = SCALE*shoe + OFFSET;
  printf("Shoe size (men's)    foot length\n");
  printf("%10.1f %13.2f inches\n", shoe, foot);
}
```

Wow! Here is a program with multiplication *and* addition. It takes your shoe size (if you wear a size 9) and tells you how long your foot is in inches. But you say you could solve this problem by hand more quickly than you could type the program? That's a good point. It is a waste of time and effort to produce a one-shot program that does just one shoe size. We could make it more useful by writing it as an interactive program, but that still barely taps the potential of a computer.

What we need is some way to have a computer do repetitive calculations. After all, that is one of the main reasons for using a computer to do arithmetic. C offers several methods to accomplish repetitive calculations, and we will outline one here. This approach, called a **"while** loop," will enable us to make a more interesting exploration of operators. Here, then, is our improved shoe sizing program.

```
/* shoesize2 */
#define OFFSET 7.64
#define SCALE 0.325
main()
{
/* this program converts shoe size to foot size in inches */
 float shoe, foot;

 printf("Shoe size (men's)    foot length\n");
 shoe = 3.0;
 while (shoe < 18.5) {
    foot = SCALE*shoe + OFFSET;
    printf("%10.1f %15.2f inches\n", shoe, foot);
    shoe = shoe + 1.0;
    }
 printf("If the shoe fits, wear it.\n");
}
```

Here is a condensed version of **shoesize2**'s output:

```
Shoe size (men's)     foot length
        3.0           8.61 inches
        4.0           8.94 inches
        ...            ...
        ...            ...
       17.0          13.16 inches
       18.0          13.49 inches
If the shoe fits, wear it.
```

(Incidentally, the constants for this conversion were obtained during an incognito visit to a shoe store. The only shoe-sizer left lying around was for men's sizes. Those of you interested in women's sizes will have to make your own visit to a shoe store.)

This is how the **while** loop works. When the program first reaches the **while** statement, it checks to see if the condition in parentheses is true or not. In this case the expression is:

```
shoe < 18.5
```

where the < symbol means "less than." Well, **shoe** was initialized to **3.0**, which certainly is less than **18.5**. Thus the condition is true. In this case the program proceeds to the next statement, which converts the size to inches. Then it prints out the results. The next statement,

```
shoe = shoe + 1.0;
```

increases **shoe** by 1.0, making it 4.0. At this point the program returns to the **while** portion to check the condition. Why at this point? Because the next line is a closing brace (}), and we have used a set of braces ({ }) to mark the extent of the **while** loop. The statements between the two braces are the ones that may be repeated. Now back to our program. Is **4** less than **18.5?** Yup. So the whole cycle of embraced commands following the **while** is repeated. (In computerese, the program is said to "loop" through these statements.) This continues until **shoe** reaches a value of **19.0**. At this point the condition

```
shoe < 18.5
```

becomes false, since **19.0** is not less than **18.5.** When this happens, control passes to the next statement following the **while** loop. In our case, that is the final **printf( )** statement.

You easily can modify this program to do other conversions. For example, change **SCALE** to **1.8** and **OFFSET** to **32.0,** and you have a program that converts Centigrade to Fahrenheit. Or change **SCALE** to **0.6214** and **OFFSET** to **0,** and you convert kilometers to miles. If you make these changes, you probably should change the printed messages, too, to prevent confusion.

The **while** loop gives us a convenient, flexible means of controlling a program. Now let us turn to the fundamental operators that we can use in our programs.

Fundamental Operators

C uses *operators* to represent arithmetic operations. For example, the + operator causes the two values flanking it to be added together. If the term "operator" seems odd to you, please reflect that they had to call those things something. "Operator" does seem to be a better choice than, say, "those things" or "arithmetical transactors." We'll look now at =, +, −, *, and /. (C does not have an exponentiating operator. In a later chapter we will present a function to accomplish this task.)

Assignment Operator: =

In C, the equals sign does not mean "equals." Instead, it is a value-assigning operator. The statement

```
bmw = 2002;
```

assigns the value 2002 to the variable named **bmw.** That is, the item to the left of the = sign is the *name* of a variable, and the item on the right is the *value* of the variable. We call the = symbol an "assignment operator." Again, don't think of the line as saying, "**bmw** equals 2002." Instead, read it as "assign the value 2002 to the variable **bmw.**" The action goes from right to left for this operator.

Perhaps this distinction between the name of a variable and the value of a variable seems like hair-splitting, but consider the following very common type of computer statement:

```
i = i + 1;
```

As mathematics, it makes no sense. If you add one to a finite number, the result isn't equal to the number you started with. But as a computer assignment statement, it is perfectly reasonable. It means, in long-winded English, "find the value of the variable whose name is **i.** To that value, add 1, then assign this new value to the variable whose name is **i.**"

Figure 5.1
The statement $i = i + 1;$

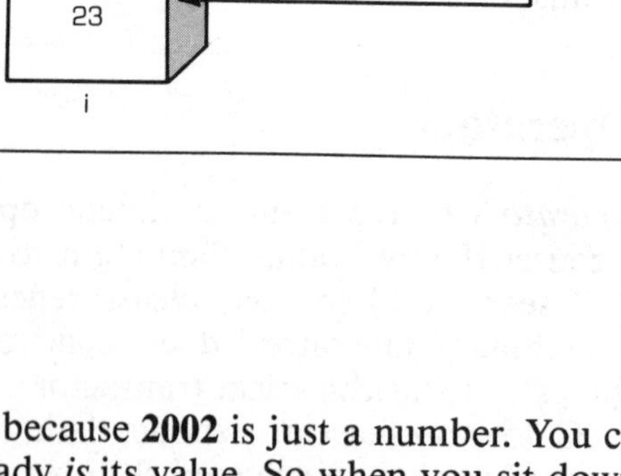

```
i = i + 1;
i = 22 + 1;
i = 23;
```

A statement such as

```
2002 = bmw;
```

makes no sense in C because **2002** is just a number. You can't assign a value to a constant; it already *is* its value. So when you sit down at the keyboard, remember that the item to the left of $=$ sign must be the name of a variable. (Actually, the left-hand side must refer to a storage location. The simplest way is to use the name of a variable, but, as you will see later, a "pointer" can be used to point to a location.)

For those of you who like to get the names of things right, the proper term for what we have called "items" is *operands*. Operands are what operators operate on. For example, you can describe eating a hamburger as applying the "eat" operator to the "hamburger" operand.

The basic C assignment operator is a little flashier than most. Try this short program:

```
/* golf tournament score card */
main()
{
  int jane, tarzan, cheeta;

  cheeta = tarzan = jane = 68;
  printf("                    cheeta    tarzan    jane\n");
  printf("First round score %4d %8d %8d\n",cheeta,tarzan,jane);
}
```

Many languages would boggle at the triple assignment made in this program, but C accepts it routinely. The assignments are made right to left; first **jane** gets the value 68, then **tarzan** does, and finally **cheeta** does. Thus, the output is:

```
                    cheeta    tarzan    jane
First round score     68        68      68
```

C has several other assignment operators that work differently from the one described here, and we promise to tell you about them in a later chapter.

Addition Operator: $+$

The addition operator causes the two values on either side of it to be added together. For example, the statement

```
printf("%d", 4 + 20);
```

causes the number **24** to be printed and not the expression

```
4 + 20.
```

The operands can be variables as well as constants. Thus, the statement

```
income = salary + bribes;
```

will cause the computer to look up the values of the two variables on the right, add them up, and assign this total to the variable **income**.

The + operator is termed a "binary" or "dyadic" operator, meaning that it takes *two* operands.

Subtraction Operator: —

The subtraction operator causes the number after the — sign to be subtracted from the number before the sign. The statement

```
takehome = 224.00 - 24.00;
```

assigns the value 200.0 to **takehome.**

Sign Operator: —

The minus sign also is used to indicate or to change the algebraic sign of a value. For instance, the sequence

```
rocky = -12;
smokey = -rocky;
```

gives **smokey** the value **12.**

When the minus sign is used this way, it is called a "unary" operator, meaning that it takes just one operand.

Multiplication Operator: *

Multiplication is indicated by the * symbol. The statement

```
cm = 2.54 * in;
```

multiplies the variable **in** by **2.54** and assigns the answer to **cm.**

By any chance do you want a table of squares? C doesn't have a squaring function, but we can use multiplication.

```
/* squares */
main () /* produces table of squares */
{
    int num = 1;

    while ( num < 21) {
        printf("%10d %10d\n", num, num*num);
        num = num + 1;
        }
}
```

Figure 5.2
Unary and binary operators

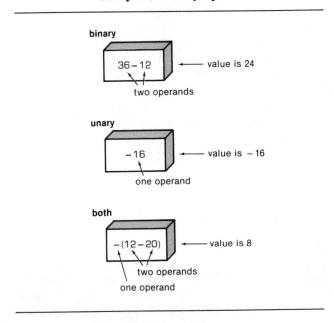

This program prints out the first 20 integers and their squares, as you can verify for yourself.

Let's look at a more interesting example.

You probably have heard the story of the powerful ruler who seeks to reward a scholar who has done him a great service. When the scholar is asked what he would like, he points to a chessboard and says, just one grain of wheat on the first square, two on the second, four on the third, eight on the next, and so on. The ruler, lacking mathematical erudition, is astounded at the modesty of this request, for he had been prepared to offer great riches. The joke, of course, is on the ruler, as this next program shows. It calculates how many grains go on each square and keeps a running total. Since you may not be up-to-date on wheat crops, we also compare the running total to a rough estimate of the annual wheat crop in the United States.

```
/* wheat */
#define SQUARES 64 /* squares on a checkerboard */
#define CROP 7E14 /* US wheat crop in grains */
main()
{
    double current, total;
    int count = 1;

    printf("square   grains added   total grains   ");
    printf("fraction of \n");
```

```
        printf("                                         ");
        printf("    US total");
        total = current = 1.0; /*start with one grain */
        printf("%4d %15.2e %13.2e %12.2e\n", count, current,
          total, total/CROP);
        while ( count < SQUARES )
           {
          count = count + 1;
          current = 2.0 * current; /*double grains on next square*/
          total = total + current; /* update total */
          printf("%4d %15.2e %13.2e %12.2e\n", count, current,
              total, total/CROP);
           }
     }
```

The output begins innocuously enough:

square	grains added	total grains	fraction of US total
1	1.00E+00	1.00E+00	1.43E-15
2	2.00E+00	3.00E+00	4.29E-15
3	4.00E+00	7.00E+00	1.00E-14
4	8.00E+00	1.50E+01	2.14E-14
5	1.60E+01	3.10E+01	4.43E-14
6	3.20E+01	6.30E+01	9.00E-14
7	6.40E+01	1.27E+02	1.81E-13
8	1.28E+02	2.55E+02	3.64E-13
9	2.56E+02	5.11E+02	7.30E-13
10	5.12E+02	1.02E+03	1.46E-12

After ten squares, the scholar has acquired just a little over a thousand grains of wheat. But look what has happened by square 50!

50	5.63E+14	1.13E+15	1.61E+00

The haul has exceeded the total U.S. annual output! If you want to see what happens by the 64th square, you will have to run the program yourself.

This example illustrates the phenomenon of exponential growth. The world population growth and our use of energy resources have followed the same pattern.

Division Operator: /

C uses the / symbol to represent division. The value to the left of the / is divided by the value to the right. For example,

```
four = 12.0/3.0;
```

gives **four** the value of 4.0. Division works differently for integer types than it does for floating types. Floating-type division gives a floating-point answer, but integer division yields an integer answer. An integer has to be a whole number, which makes dividing 5 by 3 awkward since the answer isn't a whole number. In C, any fraction resulting from integer division is discarded. This process is called *truncation*.

Try this program to see how truncation works and how integer division differs from floating-point division.

```
/* divisions we have known */
main()
{

    printf ("integer division: 5/4   is %d \n", 5/4);
    printf ("integer division: 6/3   is %d \n", 6/3);
    printf ("integer division: 7/4   is %d \n", 7/4);
    printf ("floating division: 7./4. is %1.2f \n", 7./4.);
    printf ("mixed division:    7./4  is %1.2f \n", 7./4);
}
```

We also included a case of "mixed types" by having a real number divided by an integer. C is a more forgiving language than some and will let you get away with this, but normally you should avoid mixing types. Now for the results:

```
integer division: 5/4  is 1
integer division: 6/3  is 2
integer division: 7/4  is 1
floating division: 7./4. is 1.75
mixed division:    7./4  is 1.75
```

Notice how integer division does not round to the nearest integer, but always rounds down. And when we mixed integers with floating point, the answer came out the same as floating point. When a calculation like this has both types, the integer is converted to floating point before division.

The properties of integer division turn out to be quite handy for some problems. We will give an example fairly soon. First, there is another important matter to raise. Namely, what happens when you combine more than one operation into one statement? That is our next topic.

Operator Precedence

Consider the line:

```
butter = 25.0 + 60.0*n/SCALE;
```

This statement has an addition, a multiplication, and a division. Which operation takes place first? Is 25.0 added to 60.0, the result of 85.0 then multiplied by n, and that result then divided by **SCALE?** Or is 60.0 multiplied by n, the result added to 25.0, and that answer then divided by **SCALE?** Or is it some other order? Let's take **n** to be 6.0 and **SCALE** to be 2.0. If you work through using these values, you will find that the first approach yields a value of 255. The second approach gives 192.5. A C program must have some other order in mind, for it would give a value of 205.0 for **butter.**

Clearly the order of executing the various operations can make a difference, so C needs unambiguous rules for choosing what to do first. C does this by setting up an operator pecking order. Each operator is assigned a precedence level. Multiplication and division have a higher precedence than addition and subtraction, so they are performed first. What if two operators have the same precedence? Then they are executed according to the order in which they occur in the statement. For most operators the order is from left to right. (The = operator was an exception to this.) Therefore, in the statement

```
butter = 25.0 + 60.0*n/SCALE;
```

the order of operations is:

60.0*n	the first * or / in the statement then (assuming n = 6 so that 60.0*n = 360.0)
360.0/SCALE	the second * or / in the statement and finally (since SCALE = 2.0)
25.0 + 180	the first + or − in the statement to yield 205.0.

Many people like to represent the order of evaluation with a type of diagram called an "expression tree." Figure 5.3 is an example of such a diagram. The diagram shows how the original expression is reduced by steps to a single value.

But what if you want, say, an addition to take place before a division. Then you can do as we do in this line:

```
flour = (25.0 + 60.0*n)/SCALE;
```

Whatever is enclosed in parentheses is executed first. Within the parentheses, the usual rules hold. For this example, first the multiplication takes

Figure 5.3
Expression trees showing operators, operands, and order of evaluation

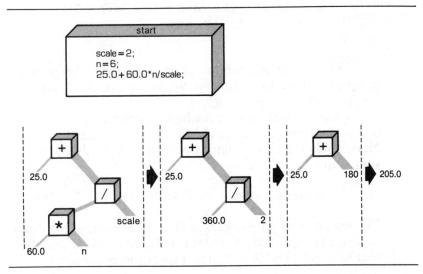

place, then the addition. That takes care of what was in the parentheses. Only then is the result divided by **SCALE.**

Table 5.1 summarizes our rules for the operators we've used so far. (Appendix C contains a table covering all operators.)

Table 5.1
Operators in Order of Decreasing Precedence

Operators	Associativity
( )	¦left to right
− (unary)	¦left to right
* /	¦left to right
+ − (subtraction)	¦left to right
=	¦right to left

Notice that the two uses of the minus sign have different priorities. The associativity column tells us how an operator associates with its operands. For example, the unary minus sign associates with the quantity to its right, and in division the left operand is divided by the right.

Let's try out these rules on a more complex example.

```
/* precedence test */
main()
```

```
{
    int top, score;
    top = score = -(2 + 5)*6 + (4 + 3*(2 + 3));
    printf("top = %d \n", top);
}
```

What value will this program print out? Figure it out, then run the program or read the following description to check your answer. (We think you probably will get it right.)

Okay, parentheses are the highest priority. Going from left to right, the first pair of parentheses is **(2+5),** so we evaluate the contents, obtaining 7. Next, apply the unary minus operator to 7 to obtain −7. Now, the expression is this:

```
    top = score = -7*6 + (4 + 3*(2 + 3))
```

The next pair of parentheses is **(4 + 3*(2 + 3)),** so we evaluate its contents, that is, the expression **4 + 3*(2 + 3).** Aha! More parentheses! So the first step here is to find 2 + 3. The expression becomes:

```
    top = score = -7*6 + (4 + 3*5)
```

We still have to finish up what is in the parentheses. Since * has priority over +, the expression becomes:

```
    top = score = -7*6 + (4 + 15)
```

and then

```
    top = score = -7*6 + 19
```

What's next? Multiply −7 by **6** and get this expression:

```
    top = score = -42 + 19
```

Then addition makes it:

```
    top = score = -23
```

Then **score** is assigned the value **−23,** and, finally, **top** gets the value **−23.** Remember that the = operator associates from right to left.

Some Additional Operators

C has about 40 operators, but some are used much more than others. The ones we just covered are the most common, and we would like to add three more useful operators to the list.

Modulus Operator: %

The modulus operator is used in integer arithmetic. It gives the remainder that results when the integer to its left is divided by the integer to its right. For example, **13 % 5** (read as "13 modulo 5") has the value 3, since 5 goes into 13 twice, with a remainder of 3.

Don't bother trying to use this operator with floating-point numbers; it just won't work.

At first glance, this operator may strike you as an esoteric tool for mathematicians, but actually it is rather practical and helpful. One common use is to help you control the flow of a program. Suppose, for example, you are working on a bill-preparing program that is designed to add in an extra charge every third month. Just have the program evaluate the month number modulo 3 (i.e., **month % 3**) and check to see if the result is 0. If so, add in the extra charge. Once we get to "if statements," you'll see better how this works.

Here's an example using %:

```
/* sectomin */
/* converting seconds to minutes and seconds */
#define SM 60 /* seconds in a minute */
main()
{
    int sec, min, left;

    printf("Convert seconds to minutes and seconds!\n");
    printf("Enter the number of seconds you wish to convert.\n");
    scanf("%d", &sec);  /* number of seconds is read in */
    min = sec/SM;    /* truncated number of minutes  */
    left = sec % SM; /* number of seconds left over  */
    printf("%d seconds is %d minutes, %d seconds.\n", sec, min, left);
}
```

Here is a sample output:

```
Convert seconds to minutes and seconds!
Enter the number of seconds you wish to convert.
234
234 seconds is 3 minutes, 54 seconds.
```

One problem with this interactive program is that it processes just one input value. Can you figure out a way to have the program prompt you repeatedly for new input values? We will return to that problem in this chapter's question section, but if you work out your own solution first, we will be pleased.

Increment and Decrement Operators: ++ and −−

The increment operator performs a simple task; it increments (increases) the value of its operand by one. The operator comes in two varieties. The first variety has the ++ come before the affected variable; this is the *prefix* mode. The second variety has the ++ come after the affected variable; this is the *postfix* mode. The two modes differ with regard to the precise time the incrementing takes place. We'll look at the similarities first and then return to that difference. This short example shows how the increment operators work.

```
/* addone */
main() /*incrementing: prefix and postfix */
{   int ultra = 0, super = 0;

    while (super < 5) {
        super++;
        ++ultra;
        printf("super = %d, ultra = %d \n", super, ultra);
    }
}
```

Running **addone** produces:

```
super = 1, ultra = 1
super = 2, ultra = 2
super = 3, ultra = 3
super = 4, ultra = 4
super = 5, ultra = 5
```

Gosh, we've counted to 5! Twice! Simultaneously! (If you have a need to count further, just change the limit in the **while** statement.)

We confess we could have achieved exactly the same results by replacing the two increment statements with:

```
super = super + 1;
ultra = ultra + 1;
```

These are simple enough statements. Why bother creating one, let alone two, abbreviations?

One reason is that the compact form makes your programs neater and easier to follow. These operators give your programs an elegant gloss that cannot fail to please the eye. For instance, we can rewrite part of **shoesize2** this way:

```
shoe = 3.0;
while (shoe < 18.5) {
```

```
foot = SCALE*size + OFFSET;
printf("%10.1f %20.2f inches\n", shoe, foot);
++shoe;
}
```

But we still haven't taken full advantage of the increment operator. We can shorten the fragment this way:

```
shoe = 2.0;
while (++shoe < 18.5) {
    foot = SCALE*shoe + OFFSET;
    printf("%10.1f %20.2f inches\n", shoe, foot);
    }
```

Here we have combined the incrementing process and the **while** comparison into one expression. This type of construction is so common in C that it merits a closer look. First, how does it work? Simply. The value of **shoe** is increased by one, then compared to **18.5.** If it is less, the statements between the braces are executed once. Then **shoe** is increased by one again, and the cycle is repeated until the **shoe** gets too big. We changed the initial value of **shoe** from **3.0** to **2.0** to compensate for **shoe** being incremented before the first evaluation of **foot.**

Second, what's so good about this approach? It is more compact. More important, it gathers in one place the two processes that control the loop. The first process is the test: do we continue or not? In this case, the test is checking to see if the shoe size is less than 18.5. The second process changes an element of the test; in this case, the shoe size is increased.

Figure 5.4
Through the loop once

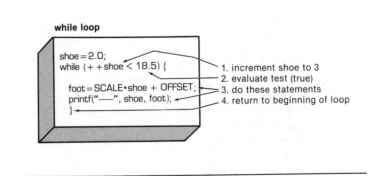

Suppose we forgot to change the shoe size. Then **shoe** would *always* be less than **18.5,** and the loop would never end. The computer would churn out line after identical line, caught in a dreaded "infinite loop." Eventually, you would lose interest in the output and have to kill the program somehow. Having the loop test and the loop change at one place instead of at separate locations makes it easier to remember to include a loop change.

Another advantage of the increment operator is that it usually produces slightly more efficient machine language code, since it is similar to actual machine language instructions.

Finally, these operators have an additional feature that can be of use in certain delicate situations. To learn what this feature is, try running the next program.

```
main()
{
    int a = 1, b = 1;
    int aplus, plusb;

    aplus = a++;       /* postfix */
    plusb = ++b;       /* prefix  */
    printf("a aplus b plusb \n");
    printf("%3d %5d %5d %5d\n", a, aplus, b, plusb);
}
```

If you do this correctly and if we remember correctly, you should get this as the result:

a	aplus	b	plusb
2	1	2	2

Both **a** and **b** were increased by 1, as promised. However, **aplus** has the value of **a** before **a** changed, while **plusb** has the value of **b** after **b** changed. This is the difference between the prefix form and the postfix form.

aplus = a++   postfix: **a** changed *after* its value was used
plusb = ++b   prefix: **b** changed *before* its value was used

Figure 5.5
Prefix and postfix

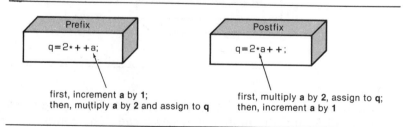

Prefix	Postfix
q=2*++a;	q=2*a++;
first, increment **a** by 1; then, multiply **a** by 2 and assign to **q**	first, multiply **a** by 2, assign to **q**; then, increment **a** by 1

When one of these increment operators is used by itself, as in a solitary **ego++;** statement, it doesn't matter which form you use. The choice does matter, however, when the operator and its operand are part of a larger expression, as in the assignment statements we just saw. In this kind of situation you must give some thought to the result you want. For instance, recall our use of

```
while (++shoe < 18.5)
```

This gave us a table up to size 18. But if we had used **shoe++** instead, the table would have gone to size 19, since **shoe** would be increased after the comparison instead of before.

Of course, you could fall back on the less subtle

```
shoe = shoe + 1;
```

form, but then no one will believe you are a true C programmer.

We suggest that you pay special attention to the examples of increment operators as you read through this book. Ask yourself if we could have used either one or if circumstances dictated a particular choice. Speaking of examples, here comes another one.

Do computers ever sleep? Of course they do, but they usually don't tell us. This program reveals what really goes on.

```
/* sheep */
#define MAX 40
main()
{
    int count = 0;

    printf("I count sheep to go to sleep.\n");
    while (++count < MAX )
      printf("%d million sheep and still not asleep...\n", count);
    printf("%d million sheep and zzzzzz....\n",count);
}
```

Try it and see if it does what you think it will. (Incidentally, what would be the effect of replacing the prefix form of the increment operator with the postfix form?)

Decrementing: ——

For each increment operator, there is a corresponding decrement operator. Instead of ++, we use ——.

```
-- count;   /* prefix form of decrement operator */
count --;   /* postfix form of decrement operator */
```

Here is an example illustrating that computers can be accomplished lyricists:

```
/* bottles */
#define MAX 100
main()
{
  int count = MAX + 1;

  while( --count > 0) {
  printf("%d bottles of beer on the wall, %d bottles of beer!\n",
          count, count);
  printf("Take one down and pass it around,\n");
  printf("%d bottles of beer!\n\n", count-1);
  }
}
```

The output starts like this:

```
100 bottles of beer on the wall, 100 bottles of beer!
Take one down and pass it around,
99 bottles of beer!

99 bottles of beer on the wall, 99 bottles of beer!
Take one down and pass it around,
98 bottles of beer!
```

It goes on a bit and ends this way:

```
1 bottles of beer on the wall, 1 bottles of beer!
Take one down and pass it around,
0 bottles of beer!
```

Apparently our accomplished lyricist has a problem with plurals, but that could be fixed by using the conditional operators of Chapter 7.

Incidentally, the > operator stands for "greater than." Like <, it is a "relational operator." We will take a longer look at relational operators in Chapter 7.

Precedence

The increment and decrement operators have a very high precedence of association; only parentheses are higher. Thus, **x*y++** means **(x)*(y++)**

and not **(x∗y)++**, which is fortunate, since the latter is meaningless. (The increment and decrement operators affect a *variable,* and the combination **x∗y** is not itself a variable, although its parts are.)

Don't confuse precedence of these two operators with the order of evaluation. Suppose we have:

```
y = 2;
n = 3;
nextnum = (y + n++)*6;
```

What values does **nextnum** get? Well, by substituting in values,

```
nextnum = (2 + 3)*6 = 5*6 = 30
```

Only after **n** is used is it increased to **4.** Precedence tells us that the **++** is attached only to the **n.** It also tells us when the value of **n** is used for evaluating the expression, but the nature of the increment operator determines when the value of **n** is changed.

When **n++** is part of an expression, you can think of it as meaning "use **n**; then increment it." On the other hand, **++n** means "increment **n**; then use it."

Don't Be Too Clever

You can get fooled if you try to do too much at once with the increment operators. For example, you might think that you could improve on our program to print integers and their squares by replacing the **while** loop with this one:

```
while ( num < 21) {
    printf("%10d %10d\n", num, num*num++);
    }
```

This looks reasonable. We print the number **num,** we multiply it by itself to get the square, and then we increase **num** by one. In fact, this program may even work on some systems. But not all. The problem is that when **printf( )** goes to get the values for printing, it may evaluate the last argument first and increment **num** before getting to the other argument. Thus, instead of printing, say,

5	25

it will print

6	25

C gives the compiler the freedom to choose which arguments in a function to evaluate first; this freedom increases compiler efficiency but can cause trouble if you use an increment operator on an argument.

Another possible source of trouble is a statement like:

```
ans = num/2 + 5*(1 + num++);
```

Again, the problem is that the compiler may not do things in the same order you have in mind. You would think that it would find **num/2** first, then move on. But it might do the last term first, increase **num,** and use the new value in **num/2.** There is just no guarantee.

It is easy enough to avoid these problems.

1. Don't use increment or decrement operators on a variable that is part of more than one argument of a function.
2. Don't use increment or decrement operators on a variable that appears more than once in an expression.

Expressions and Statements

We have been using the terms "expression" and "statement" throughout these first few chapters, and now the time has come to study their meanings more closely. Statements form the basic program steps of C, and most statements are constructed from expressions. This suggests we look at expressions first, and we will.

Expressions

An *expression* consists of a combination of operators and operands. (An operand, recall, is what an operator operates on.) The simplest expression is a lone operand, and you can build in complexity from there. Here are some expressions:

```
4
-6
4+21
a*(b + c/d)/20
q = 5*2
x = ++q % 3
q > 3
```

As you can see, the operands can be constants, variables, or combinations of the two. Some expressions are combinations of smaller expressions, which we can call *subexpressions*. For instance, **c/d** is a subexpression of our fourth example.

An important property of C is that every C expression has a value. To find the value, we perform the operations in the order dictated by operator precedence. The value of the first few expressions is clear, but what about the ones with = signs? Those expressions simply have the same value that the variable to the left of the = sign receives. Thus, the expression **q=5*2** as a whole has the value **10**. And the expression **q > 3**? Such relational expressions have the value **1** if true and **0** if false. Here are some expressions and their values:

Expression	Value
-4+6	2
c = 3 + 8	11
5 > 3	1
6 +(c = 3 + 8)	17

That last one looks strange! But it is perfectly legal in C, for it is just the sum of two subexpressions, each of which has a value.

Order of Subexpressions— C leaves some latitude to implementors in deciding the order in which subexpressions are evaluated. Consider an expression like this:

```
a*b/c + d*c
```

C guarantees that the subexpressions **a*b/c** and **d*c** will be evaluated before the addition. Furthermore, the left-to-right rule for multiplication and division guarantees that **a** is multiplied by **b** and then the product is divided by **c**. But there is no rule governing whether **a*b/c** is evaluated before or after **d*c**. That's left open for the designers of the compiler to decide. You might think the left-to-right rule says to do the left-most subexpression first, but that rule just applies to a sequence of operations of the same level. That is, it applies to multiplication and division in **a*b/c**, but it ends there since the next operator (+) has a different precedence level.

Because of this indeterminacy, you should not use expressions like this:

```
a * b + c * b++
```

One compiler might evaluate the right term last, causing both terms to use the same value for **b**, but a second compiler might evaluate the right term first and increment **b** before it is used in the left term.

Statements

Statements are the primary building blocks of a program. A *program* is just a series of statements with a little punctuation thrown in. A statement is a complete instruction to the computer. In C, statements are indicated by a semicolon at the end. Thus:

```
legs = 4
```

is just an expression (which could be part of a larger expression), but

```
legs = 4;
```

is a statement.

What makes an instruction complete? It has to complete an action. The expression

```
2 + 2
```

is not a complete instruction. It tells the computer to add 2 and 2, but it fails to tell the computer what to do with the answer. If we say

```
kids = 2 + 2;
```

however, we tell the computer to store the answer (4) in the memory location labeled **kids.** With the number 4 thus disposed of, the computer can move on to the next task.

Although a statement is a complete instruction, not all complete instructions are statements. Consider the following statement:

```
x = 6 + (y = 5);
```

In it, the subexpression **y = 5** is a complete instruction, but it is only part of the statement. Because a complete instruction is not necessarily a statement, a semicolon is needed to identify instructions that truly are statements.

So far we have encountered four kinds of statements. Here is a short sample that uses all four:

```
/* addemup */
main()                          /*finds sum of first 20 integers */
{
   int count, sum;              /* declaration statement */

   count = 0;                   /* assignment statement   */
   sum = 0;                     /*         ditto          */
   while ( count++ < 20 )       /*         while          */
       sum = sum + count;       /*       statement        */
   printf("sum = %d\n", sum);   /* function statement     */
}
```

Let's discuss the example. By now you must be pretty familiar with the declaration statement. Nonetheless, we will remind you that it establishes the names and type of variables and causes memory locations to be set aside for them.

The assignment statement is the workhorse of most programs; it assigns a value to a variable. It consists of a variable name followed by the assignment operator ($=$) followed by an expression followed by a semicolon. Note that the **while** statement includes an assignment statement within it.

A function statement causes the function to do whatever it does. In our example, the **printf( )** function is invoked to print out some results.

Figure 5.6
Structure of a simple *while* loop

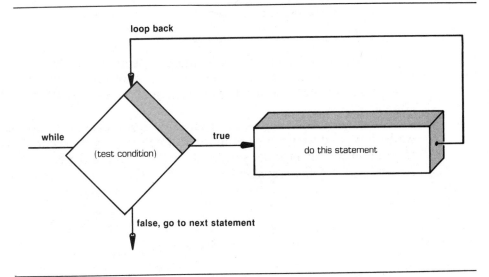

A **while** statement has three distinct parts. First is the keyword **while.** Then, in parentheses, comes a test condition. Finally comes the statement that is performed if the test is met. Only one statement is included in the loop. It can be a simple statement, as in this example, in which case no braces are needed to mark it off. Or the statement can be a compound statement, like some of our earlier examples, in which case braces are required. Read about compound statements just ahead.

The **while** statement belongs to a class of statements sometimes called *structured statements* because they possess a structure more complex than that of a simple assignment statement. In later chapters we will encounter many other kinds of structured statements.

Compound Statements (Blocks)

A *compound statement* is two or more statements grouped together by enclosing them in braces; it also is called a *block*. We used one in our **shoesize2** program in order to let the **while** statement encompass several statements. Compare the following program fragments:

```
/* fragment 1 */
index = 0;
```

```
while (index++ < 10 )
    sam = 10*index + 2;
printf ("sam = %d\n", sam);


 /* fragment 2 */
index = 0;
while (index++ < 10 ) {
    sam = 10*index + 2;
    printf ("sam = %d\n", sam);
    }
```

In fragment 1, only the assignment statement is included in the **while** loop. (In the absence of braces, a **while** statement runs from the **while** to the next semicolon.) The printout will occur just once, after the loop has been completed.

In fragment 2, the braces ensure that both statements are part of the **while** loop, and we get a printout each time the loop is executed. The entire compound statement is considered to be the single statement in terms of the structure of a **while** statement.

Style Tips

Look again at the two **while** fragments and notice how we have used indentation to mark off the body of the **while** loops. The indentation makes no difference whatsoever to the compiler; it uses the braces and its knowledge of the structure of **while** loops to decide how to interpret our instructions. The indentation is there for us, so that we can see at a glance how the program is organized.

We have shown one popular style for positioning the braces for a block, or compound statement. Another very common style is this:

```
while (index++ < 10)
    {
    sam = 10*index + 2;
    printf("sam = %d \n", sam);
    }
```

This style emphasizes that the statements form a block, while the other style highlights the attachment of the block to the **while**. Again, as far as the compiler is concerned, both forms are identical.

To sum up, use indentation as a tool to point out the structure of a program.

Figure 5.7
While **loop with a compound statement**

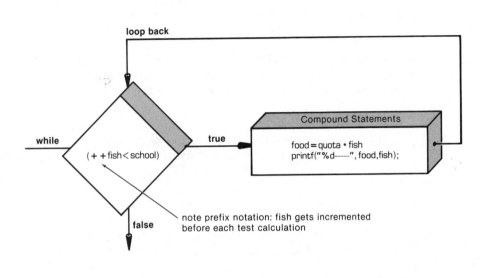

Type Conversions

Statements and expressions normally should use variables and constants of just one type. If, however, you mix types, C doesn't stop dead in its tracks the way, say, Pascal does. Instead, it uses a set of rules to make type conversions automatically. This can be a convenience, but it also can be a danger, especially if you are mixing types inadvertently. (The **lint** program, found on many UNIX systems, checks for type "clashes.") It is a good idea to have at least some knowledge of the type conversion rules.

The basic rules are these:

1. In any operation involving two types, both values are converted to the "higher" ranking of the two types. This process is called *promotion*.
2. The ranking of types, from highest to lowest, is **double, float, long, int, short,** and **char.** Also, **unsigned** outranks the corresponding signed type.
3. In an assignment statement, the final result of the calculations is converted to the type of the variable that is being assigned a value. This process can result in promotion, as described in Rule 1, or *demotion,* in which a value is converted to a lower-ranking type.

117

Summary: Expressions and Statements

Expressions:

An expression is a combination of operators and operands. The simplest expression is just a constant or a variable with no operator, such as **22** or **beebop**. More complex examples are **55 + 22** and **vap = 2*(vip + (vup = 4))**.

Statements:

A statement is a command to the computer. There are simple statements and compound statements. *Simple statements* terminate in a semicolon. Examples are:

```
1. Declaration statements    int toes;
2. Assignment statements     toes = 12;
3. Function call statements  printf("%d\n", toes);
4. Control statements        while ( toes < 20 )
                                    toes = toes + 2;
5. Null statement            ; /*does nothing*/
```

Compound statements, or *blocks,* consist of one or more statements (which themselves can be compound) enclosed in braces. The following **while** statement contains an example:

```
while ( years < 100 )
    {
    wisdom = wisdom + 1;
    printf("%d %d\n", years, wisdom);
    years = years + 1;
    }
```

Promotion usually is a smooth, uneventful process, but demotion can lead to real trouble. The reason is simple: the lower-ranking type may not be big enough to hold the complete number. A **char** variable can hold the integer **101** but not the integer **22334**.

This sample illustrates the working of these rules.

```
/* conversions */
main()
{
    char ch;
    int i;
```

```
    float fl;

    fl = i = ch = 'A';      /* line 8 */
    printf("ch = %c, i = %d, fl = %2.2f\n", ch, i, fl);
    ch = ch + 1;            /* line 10 */
    i = fl + 2*ch;          /* line 11 */
    fl = 2.0*ch + i;        /* line 12 */
    printf("ch = %c, i = %d, fl = %2.2f\n", ch, i, fl);
    ch = 2.0e30;            /* line 14 */
    printf("Now ch = %c\n", ch);
}
```

This is what running **conversions** produces:

```
ch = A, i = 65, fl = 65.00
ch = B, i = 197, fl = 329.00
Now ch =
```

This is what happened.

Lines 8 and 9: The character 'A' is stored as a character by **ch**. The integer variable **i** receives the integer conversion of 'A' (65). Finally, **fl** receives the floating conversion of **65**, which is **65.00**.

Lines 10 and 13: The character variable 'A' is converted to the integer **65**, which then is added to the **1**. The resulting integer **66** then is converted to the character **B** and stored in **ch**.

Lines 11 and 13: The value of **ch** is converted to an integer (**66**) for the multiplication by **2**. The resulting integer (**132**) is converted to floating point in order to be added to **fl**. The result (**197.00**) is converted to **int** and stored in **i**.

Lines 12 and 13: The value of **ch** ('**B**') is converted to floating point for multiplication by **2.0**. The value of **i** (**197**) is converted to floating point for the addition, and the result (**329.00**) is stored in **fl**.

Lines 14 and 15: Here we try a case of demotion, setting **ch** equal to a rather large number. The results are poor. Whatever cramming and truncating took place resulted in producing code for some nonprinting character on our system.

Actually, there is one other kind of conversion that took place. In order to preserve numerical accuracy, *all* **float** values are converted to **double** when arithmetic calculations are done. This greatly reduces roundoff error. The final answer, of course, is converted back to **float** if that is the declared type. This conversion you needn't worry about, but it is nice to know that the compiler is looking after your best interests.

Cast Operator

Usually it is best to steer clear of type conversions, especially of demotions. But sometimes it is convenient to make conversions, providing you exercise care in what you do. The type conversions we've discussed so far are done automatically. It also is possible for you to demand the precise type conversion you want. The method is called a *cast* and consists of preceding the quantity with the name of the desired type in parentheses. The parentheses and type name together constitute a *cast operator*. The general form of a cast operator is

```
(type)
```

where the actual type desired is substituted for the word "type."

Consider these two lines, in which **mice** is an **int** variable. The second line contains two casts to type **int**.

```
mice = 1.6 + 1.7;
mice = (int) 1.6 + (int) 1.7;
```

The first example uses automatic conversion. First **1.6** and **1.7** are added to yield **3.3**. This number is then converted through truncation to the integer **3** in order to match the **int** variable. In the second example, **1.6** is converted to an integer (**1**) before addition, as is **1.7**, so that **mice** is assigned the value **1+1**, or **2**.

Normally, you shouldn't mix types; that's why some languages don't allow it. But there are occasions when it is useful. The C philosophy is to avoid putting barriers in your way and to give you the responsibility of not abusing that freedom.

Summary: Operating in C

Here's what the operators we have discussed so far do.

Assignment Operator:

=   Assigns value at its right to the variable at its left.

Arithmetic Operators:

+   Adds value at its right to the value at its left.

−   Subtracts value at its right from the value at its left.

−   As a unary operator, changes the sign of the value at its right.

*   Multiplies value at its right by the value at its left.

/   Divides value at its left by the value at its right. Answer is truncated if both operands are integers.

%   Yields the remainder when the value at its left is divided by the value to its right (integers only).

++   Adds 1 to the value of the variable to its right (prefix mode) or of the variable to its left (postfix mode).

−−   Like ++, but subtracts 1.

Miscellaneous Operators:

sizeof   Yields the size, in bytes, of the operand to its right. The operand can be a type-specifier in parentheses, as in **sizeof (float)**, or it can be the name of a particular variable or array, etc., as in **sizeof foo.**

(type)   Cast operator: converts following value to the type specified by the enclosed keyword(s). For example, **(float)** 9 converts the integer **9** to the floating-point number **9.0.**

An Example Program

In Figure 5.8 we've put together a useful program (if you're a runner or know one) that just happens to illustrate several of the ideas in this chapter. It looks long, but all the calculations are done in six lines near the end. The bulk of the program relays information between the computer and the user. We've tried using enough comments to make it nearly self-explanatory, so read it through, and when you are done, we'll clear up a few other points.

Figure 5.8
A useful program for runners

```
/* running */
#define SM      60 /* seconds in a minute  */
#define SH    3600 /* seconds in an hour    */
#define MK 0.62137 /* miles in a kilometer */
main()
{
    float distk, distm; /* distance run in km and in miles  */
    float rate;         /* average speed in mph             */
    int min, sec;       /* minutes and seconds of running time*/
    int time;           /* running time in seconds only     */
    float mtime;        /* time in seconds for one mile      */
    int mmin, msec;     /* minutes and seconds for one mile*/

    printf("This program converts your time for a metric race\n");
    printf("to a time for running a mile and to your average\n");
    printf("speed in miles per hour.\n");
    printf("Please enter, in kilometers, the distance run.\n");
    scanf("%f", &distk);
    printf("Next enter the time in minutes and seconds.\n");
    printf("Begin by entering the minutes.\n");
    scanf("%d", &min);
    printf("Now enter the seconds.\n");
    scanf("%d", &sec);
    time = SM*min + sec;        /* converts time to pure seconds */
    distm = MK*distk;           /* converts kilometers to miles */
    rate = distm/time*SH;   /* miles per sec × sec per hour = mph */
    mtime =(float) time/distm;  /* time/distance = time per mile */
    mmin = (int) mtime / SM;             /* find whole minutes */
    msec = (int) mtime % SM;            /* find remaining seconds */
    printf("You ran %1.2f km (%1.2f miles) in %d min, %d sec.\n",
            distk, distm, min, sec)
    printf("That pace corresponds to running a mile in %d min,",
            mmin);
    printf("%d sec.\nYour average speed was %1.2f mph.\n",msec,
            rate);
}
```

We utilized the same approach we used in **sectomin** to convert the final time to minutes and seconds, but we also had to make type conversions. Why? Because we need integer arguments for the seconds-to-minutes part of the program, but the metric-to-mile conversion involves floating-point numbers. We have used the cast operator to make these conversions explicit.

To tell the truth, it should be possible to write the program using just automatic conversions. In fact, we did so, using **mtime** of type **int** to force the time calculation to be converted to integer form. However, that version failed to run on one of the three systems that we tried. Using casts makes your intent clearer not only to the reader, but perhaps to the compiler as well.

Here's a sample output:

```
This program converts your time for a metric race
to a time for running a mile and to your average
speed in miles per hour.
Please enter, in kilometers, the distance run.
10.0
Next enter the time in minutes and seconds.
Begin by entering the minutes.
36
Now enter the seconds.
23
You ran 10.00 km (6.21 miles) in 36 min, 23 sec.
That pace corresponds to running a mile in 5 min, 51 sec.
Your average speed was 10.25 mph.
```

What You Should Have Learned

How to use several operators: +, −, *, /, %, ++, −−, **(type)**
What an operand is: that which an operator acts on
What an expression is: a combination of operators and operands
How to evaluate an expression: follow the order of precedence
How to recognize a statement: by its semicolon
Several kinds of statements: declaration, assignment, **while,** compound
How to form a compound statement: enclose a series of statements within
    braces { }
How to form a **while** statement: **while (test)** statement
What happens in expressions of mixed types: automatic conversion

Review Questions

1. Assume all variables are of type **int.** Find the value of each of the following variables:

   a. x = (2 + 3) * 6;

b. x = (12 + 6)/2*3;

c. y = x = (2 + 3)/4;

d. y = 3 + 2*(x = 7/2);

e. x = (int) 3.8 + 3.3;

f. x = (2 + 3) * 10.5;

g. x = 3 / 5 * 22.0;

h. x = 22.0 * 3 / 5;

2. We suspect that there are some errors in the next program. Can you help us find them?

```
main()
{
  int i = 1,
  float n;
  printf("Watch out! Here come a bunch of fractions!\n");
  while (i < 30)
    n = 1/i;
    printf(" %f", n);
  printf("That's all, folks!\n");
}
```

3. Here's a first attempt at making **sectomin** interactive. The program is not satisfactory; why not? How can it be improved?

```
#define SM 60
main()
{
  int sec, min, left;

  printf("This program converts seconds to minutes and");
  printf("seconds.\n");
  printf("Just enter the number of seconds.\n");
  printf("Enter 0 to end the program.\n");
  while ( sec > 0 ) {
    scanf("%d", &sec);
    min = sec/SM;
    left = sec % SM;
    printf("%d sec is %d min, %d sec. \n", sec, min, left);
    printf("Next input?\n");
    }
  printf("Bye!\n");
}
```

4. What will this program print?

```
#include <stdio.h>
#define FORMAT "%s is a string\n"
main()
{
```

```
        int num = 0;

        printf(FORMAT,FORMAT);
        printf("%d\n", ++num);
        printf("%d\n", num++);
        printf("%d\n", num--);
        printf("%d\n", num);
}
```

5. What will this program print?

```
main()
{
        char c1, c2;
        int diff;
        float num;

        c1 = 'D';
        c2 = 'A';
        diff = c1 - c2;
        num = diff;
        printf("%c%c%c:%d %3.2f\n", c1, c2, c1, diff, num);
}
```

6. What will this program print?

```
#include <stdio.h>
#define TEN 10
main()
{
        int n = 0;

        while (n++ < TEN)
             printf("%5d", n);
        printf("\n");
}
```

7. Modify the last program so that it prints the letters **a** through **g** instead.

8. If the following fragments were part of a complete program, what would they print?
   a. int x = 0;

```
      while ( ++x < 3 )
         printf("%4d", x);
```
   b. int x = 100;

```
      while ( x++ < 103 )
         printf("%4d\n",x);
      printf("%4d\n",x);
```

```
c. char ch = 's';

   while (ch < 'w')
      {
      printf("%c", ch);
      ch++;
      }
   printf("%c\n",ch);
```

9. What will the following program print?

```
#define MESG "COMPUTER BYTES DOG"
#include <stdio.h>
main()
{
   int n = 0;

   while ( n < 5 )
      printf("%s\n", MESG);
      n++;
   printf("That's all.\n");
}
```

Answers

1. **a.** 30
   b. 27 (not 3). (12 + 6)/(2*3) would give 3
   c. x = 1, y = 1   (integer division)
   d. x = 3 (integer division) and y = 9
   e. x = 6, for (**int**) 3.8 = 3; 3 + 3.3 = 6.3, which becomes 6, since x is **int**
   f. x = 52, for 5*10.5 is 52.5, which truncates to 52
   g. x = 0, for 3 / 5 is 0 (integer division). Left-to-right precedence means this is the first calculation made
   h. x = 13. This time the first operation is 22.0 * 3, which yields 66.0 (floating). Division by 5 yields 13.2, truncated to 13

2. Line 3: Should end in a semicolon, not a comma.
   Line 7: The **while** statement sets up an infinite loop, for the value of **i** remains 1 and is always less than 30. Presumably we meant to write **while(i++ < 30).**
   Lines 7–9: The indentation implies we wanted lines 8 and 9 to form a block, but the lack of braces means the **while** loop includes only line 8. Braces should be added.
   Line 8: Since **1** and **i** are both integers, the result of the division will be **1** when **i** is **1**, and 0 for all larger values. Using **n = 1.0/i;** would cause **i** to be converted to floating-point before division and yield nonzero answers.
   Line 9: We omitted a newline character (**\n**) in the control statement; this will cause the numbers to be printed on one line, if possible.

3. The main problem lies in the relationship between the test statement (is **sec** greater than 0?) and the **scanf( )** statement that fetches the value of **sec**. In particular, the first time the test is made, the program hasn't had a chance to even get a value for **sec**, and the comparison will be made to some garbage value that happens to be at that memory location. One solution, albeit an inelegant one, is to initialize **sec** to, say, **1** so that the test is passed the first time through. This uncovers a second problem. When we finally type **0** to halt the program, **sec** doesn't get checked until after the loop is finished, and we get the results for **0** seconds printed out. What we really want is to have a **scanf( )** statement just before the **while** test is made. We can accomplish that by altering the central part of the program to read this way:

```
scanf("%d", &sec);
while ( sec > 0 ) {
  min = sec/SM;
  left = sec % SM;
  printf("%d sec is %d min, %d sec. \n", sec, min, left);
  printf("Next input?\n");
  scanf("%d", &sec);
  }
```

The first time through, the **scanf( )** outside the loop is used. Thereafter, the **scanf( )** at the end of the loop (and hence just before the loop begins again) is used. This is a common method for handling problems of this sort.

4. Here is the output:

```
%s is a string
 is a string
1
1
2
1
```

Let us explain. The first **printf()** statement is the same as:

```
printf("%s is a string\n","%s is a string\n");
```

The second print statement first increments **num** to **1**, then prints the value. The third print statement prints **num**, which is **1**, then increments it to **2**. The fourth print statement prints the current value of **n**, which still is 2, then decrements **n** to **1**. The final print statement prints the current value of **n**, **1**.

5. Here is the output:

```
DAD:3 3.00
```

Since '**D**' and '**A**' really represent the ASCII codes 68 and 65, the difference is 3. You don't need to know the codes, however. You just have to know that the letters are coded with consecutive numbers, making '**D**' 3 greater than '**A**'.

6. It prints the digits 1 through 10 in 5-column-wide fields on one line and then starts a new line:

```
    1    2    3    4    5    6    7    8    9   10
```

7. Here are two approaches. An okay approach is:

```
#define END 7
main()
{
    int n = 0;

    while (n++ < END)
        printf("%5c", 'a' - 1 + n);
    printf("\n");
}
```

The better one is:

```
#include <stdio.h>
#define END 'h'
main()
{
char ch = 'a';

while (ch < END)
    printf("%5c", ch++);
printf("\n");
}
```

In Chapter 7 we will introduce the "less than or equal to" operator. Using that, we could make the test **ch** <= **'g'**.

8. Here is the output for each example:

a. 1   2

Note that **x** is incremented, then compared. The cursor is left on the same line.

b. 101
102
103
104

Note that this time **x** is compared, then incremented. In both this case and in example a, **x** is incremented before printing takes place. Note, too, that indenting the second **printf( )** statement does not make it part of the **while** loop. Thus, it is called only once, after the **while** loop ends.

c. stuvw

Here there is no incrementing until after the first **printf( )**.

9. It prints COMPUTER BYTES DOG indefinitely, since the incrementing statement is not part of the **while** loop; braces are needed to fix the program.

Exercises

1. Use a **while** loop to convert time in minutes to time in hours and minutes. Use a **#define** and a sensible method of ending the loop.

2. Write a program that asks for an integer and then prints out all the integers from (and including) that value up to (and including) a value larger by 10. (That is, if the input is 5, the output runs from 5 to 15.)

3. Change our program **addemup** that found the sum of the first 20 integers. (If you prefer, you can think of it as a program that calculates how much money you get in 20 days if you receive $1 the first day, $2 the second day, $3 the third day, and so on.) Modify the program so that you can tell it interactively how far the calculation should go; that is, replace the **20** with a variable that is read in.

4. Now modify the program so that it computes the sum of the squares of the integers. (Or, if you prefer, how much money you get if you get $1 the first day, $4 the second day, $9 the third day, and so on. This looks like a much better deal!) C doesn't have a squaring function, but you can use the fact that the square of n is just n*n.

5. Now modify the program so that when it finishes a calculation, it asks you for a new limit so that it can repeat the process. Have the program terminate when you enter a **0**. (Hint: use a loop within a loop. Also, see Question 3 and its answer.)

6

Input/Output Functions and Redirection

Concepts

- Input and output (I/O)
- *getchar( )* and *putchar( )*
- End-of-File (EOF)
- Redirection: < and >
- System-dependent I/O
- Time-delay loops

The words "input" and "output" have more than one use in computing. We can talk about input and output *devices,* such as keyboards, disk drives, and dot matrix printers. Or we can talk about the *data* that are used for input and output. And we can talk about the *functions* that perform input and output. Our main intent in this chapter is to discuss functions used for input and output (I/O for short), but we will also touch on the other meanings of I/O.

By I/O functions we mean functions that transport data to and from your program. We've used two such functions already: **printf( )** and **scanf( )**. Now we will look at some of the other options that C gives.

Input/output functions are not part of the definition of C; their development is left to the implementors of C. If you are putting together a C compiler, you can create whatever input/output functions you like. If the system for which you are designing has some special feature, such as the 8086 microprocessor port I/O approach, you can build in special I/O functions using that feature. We will look at an example of this at the end of this chapter. On the other hand, everyone benefits if there are standard I/O functions available on all systems. This allows you to write "portable" programs that can be moved easily from one system to another. One of the goals of the ANSI C standard (Chapter 16) is to create a standard library common to all implementations. The **printf( )** and **scanf( )** functions fall into that class, as will the next two I/O functions we examine, **getchar( )** and **putchar( )**.

These two functions perform input and output one character at a time. That may strike you at first as a rather silly way of doing things. After all, you and I easily read groupings larger than a single character. But this method does suit the ability of a computer. Furthermore, this approach is the heart of most programs that deal with text, that is, with ordinary words.

We'll see how to parlay these two simple functions into programs that count characters, read files, and copy files. En route, we will learn about buffers, echoes, and redirection.

Figure 6.1
Word-processing workhorses: *getchar( )* **and** *putchar( )*

Single-Character I/O: *getchar( )* and *putchar( )*

The **getchar( )** function gets one character (hence the name) from your keyboard and delivers it to an executing program. The **putchar( )** function gets one character from an executing program and puts it on your screen. Here is a very simple example. All it does is fetch one character from the keyboard and print it on the screen. We will modify this program step by step until it acquires a variety of useful abilities. You'll have to read on to find out what they are, but first look at our humble beginning version.

```
/* getput1 */
#include <stdio.h>
main()
{
```

```
    char ch;

    ch = getchar();    /* line 1 */
    putchar(ch);       /* line 2 */
}
```

On most systems the definitions of **getchar** and **putchar** are found in the system file **stdio.h,** and that is why we have included that file in the program. Using this program produces exchanges like this:

```
g [enter]
g
```

or possibly like this:

```
gg
```

The **[enter]** is our way of indicating that you press the [enter] key. In each case you type the first **g** and the computer produces the second **g.**

The result depends on whether or not your system has "buffered" input. If you had to press the [enter] key before getting a response, then your system is buffered. Let's finish looking at **getchar( )** and **putchar( )** before we dive into buffers.

The **getchar( )** function has no argument (i.e., nothing within the parentheses). It simply fetches the next character and makes it available to the program. We say that the function "returns" a value. A statement such as **ch = getchar( );** assigns the return value to **ch.** Thus, if you type the letter **g,** the **getchar( )** function reads the character and makes it into a return value. And the assignment statement then assigns the return value to **ch.**

The **putchar( )** function, on the other hand, takes an argument. You must place between the parentheses whatever single character you wish printed. The argument can be a single character (including the escape sequences of Chapter 3) or a variable or function whose value is a single character. These all are valid uses of **putchar( ):**

```
putchar('S');      /* note that single quotes are */
putchar('\n');     /* used for character constants */
putchar('\007');
putchar(ch);       /* where ch is type char variable */
putchar(getchar());
```

We can use the last form to rewrite our program as:

```
#include <stdio.h>
main()
{
 putchar(getchar());
}
```

This is compact and uses no variables. Instead, the return value of **getchar( )** becomes the argument to **putchar( )**, which then prints it. This form is more efficient than the first one, but perhaps less clear.

Now that we see how these two functions work, we can turn to the subject of buffers.

Buffers

When you run this program (either version) on some systems, the letter you input is repeated ("echoed") immediately. On other systems, nothing happens until you press the [enter] key. The first case is an instance of *unbuffered* (or *direct*) input, meaning that the character you type is immediately made available to the waiting program. The second case is one of *buffered* input, in which the characters you type are collected and stored in an area of temporary storage called a *buffer*. Pressing the [enter] key then causes the block of characters (or single character, if that is all you typed) to be made available to your program. For our program, only the first character would be used, since there is just one use of **getchar( )**. For example, a buffered system would cause our program to work like this:

```
Here is a long line of input. [enter]
H
```

The unbuffered system, on the other hand, would return the **H** as soon as you typed it. The input-output might look like this:

```
HHere is a long line of input.
```

The second **H** came from the program butting in immediately. In either case only one character is processed by the program, since **getchar( )** is invoked but once.

Why have buffers? First, it is much less time-consuming to transmit several characters as a block than one by one. Second, if you mistype, you can use your keyboard correction facilities to fix your mistake. When you finally press [enter], the corrected version can be transmitted.

Unbuffered input, on the other hand, may be desired for some interactive programs. In a word processor, for instance, you would like each command to take place as soon as you press a key. So both buffered and unbuffered output have their uses.

Which do you have? You can find out by running our program and seeing which behavior results. Some C compilers give you your choice. On our microcomputer system, for example, **getchar( )** provides buffered input while **getche( )** gives direct input. Also, some operating systems provide a choice. On UNIX, for example, the **stty** command and the **ioctl( )** function let you specify the type of input that you want. In this book, we will assume that you are using buffered input.

Figure 6.2
Buffered versus unbuffered input

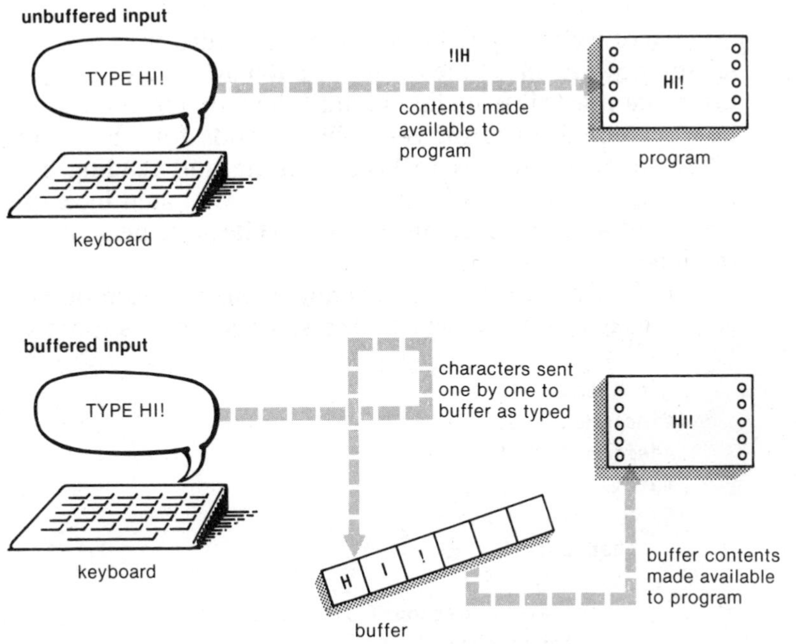

Onward

Let's tackle something a little more ambitious than reading and printing just one character. Let's take on lots of characters. We would like the program to stop eventually, so let's design it to stop when some particular character, say an asterisk (*), is typed. We can do this with a **while** loop.

```
/* getput2 */
/*this program fetches and prints characters until stopped*/
#include <stdio.h>
#define STOP '*' /* give the * character the symbolic name STOP */
main()
{
   char ch;

   ch = getchar();              /* line 9  */
   while ( ch != STOP) {        /* line 10 */
      putchar(ch);              /* line 11 */
```

```
        ch = getchar();            /* line 12 */
        }
    }
```

Here we've used the program structure we discussed in Question 3, Chapter 5. The first time through, **putchar( )** gets its argument from line 9; after that it gets it from line 12 until the loop terminates. We've introduced a new relational operator, **!=**, which stands for "not equal to." Thus, the **while** statement means to keep printing and reading characters until the program runs across a **STOP** character. We could have omitted the **#define** statement and just used an * in the **while** statement, but our choice makes the intent more obvious.

Before you rush to get this marvelous program on your machine, look at our next version. It will do the same job but is more C-like in its style.

```
/* getput3 */
#include <stdio.h>
#define STOP '*'
main()
{
    char ch;

    while ((ch = getchar()) != STOP) /* line 8 */
        putchar(ch);
}
```

Line 8 of this marvel replaces lines 9, 10, and 12 of **getput2.** How does it work? Start with the contents of the inner parentheses:

```
ch = getchar()
```

This is an expression. Its effect is to activate **getchar( )** and to assign its return value to **ch.** That takes care of what **getput2** did in lines 9 and 12. Next, recall that an expression has a value and that an assignment expression has the same value as a whole that the variable to the left of the = sign has. Thus, the value of **(ch = getchar( ))** is just the value of **ch,** so

```
(ch = getchar()) != STOP
```

has the same effect as

```
ch != STOP
```

This takes care of what **getput2** did in line 10. This sort of construction (combining an assignment with a comparison) is very common in C.

Like our earlier example using **while (++shoe < 18.5),** this form has the advantage of putting in one place the loop test and the action that

Figure 6.3
Evaluating the *while* loop condition

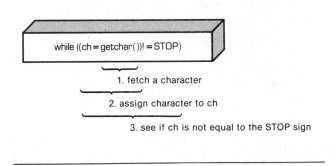

1. fetch a character

2. assign character to ch

3. see if ch is not equal to the STOP sign

changes the test. The structure closely resembles the way we might think of the process: "I want to read a character, look at it, and decide what to do next."

Now let's return to our program and try it out. If you are using an unbuffered system, the result might look like this:

```
II  wwoonnddeerr  iiff  tthhiiss  wwoorrkkss..*I guess it did.
```

All the characters up to the stop signal (the asterisk) are echoed back as you type. Even the spaces are doubled. Once you type in the stop signal, however, the program stops and what you type appears on the screen without an echo.

Now let's switch to a buffered system. This time nothing happens until we press the [enter] key. Here is a possible exchange:

```
I wonder if this works.*Hmm, I can't tell. [enter]
I wonder if this works.
```

The whole first line was sent to the program. The program read it one character at a time and printed out one character at a time until it found the asterisk *.

Now let's make the program a little more useful. We'll have it count the characters it reads. We need to make only a few changes.

```
/* charcount1 */
#define STOP '*'
main()
{
```

```
      char ch;
      int count = 0;      /* initialize character counter to 0 */

      while ((ch = getchar()) ! = STOP) {
            putchar(ch);
            count++;                        /* add one to the count */
            }
      printf("\nA grand total of %d characters were read.\n",
            count);
}
```

We can omit the **putchar( )** line if we want just to count without echoing the characters. This little program counts characters, and it is only a few small steps away from a program that can count lines and words. The next chapter will provide the tools we need to do that.

Reading a Single Line

Meanwhile, let's see what other improvements we can make with just the tools at hand. One thing we can change easily is the stop signal. Can we come up with a better choice than the asterisk *? One possibility is to use the newline (\n) character. All we need to do is redefine **STOP**.

```
      #define STOP '\n'
```

What effect will this have? Well, a newline character is transmitted when you press the [enter] key, so this will cause our program to operate on one line of input. For example, suppose we make this change in **charcount1** and then type the following input:

```
      Oh to be in Fresno now that summer's here, [enter]
```

The response would be:

```
      Oh to be in Fresno now that summer's here,
      A grand total of 42 characters were read.
```

(If we had left out the initial \n in the final **printf( )** statement, the counting message would have been tacked on right after the comma following **here.** We elected to avoid such tacky tacking on.)

The count of 42 does not include the [enter] key, for the counting is done inside the loop.

We now have a program that reads in one line. Depending on what statements we leave inside the **while** loop, the program can echo the line, count the characters in the line, or both. This looks potentially useful, perhaps as part of some larger program. But it would be nice to be able to read larger chunks of data, perhaps even a file of data. It can be done with the proper choice for **STOP**.

Reading a File

What would the ideal **STOP** character be? It should be one that normally does not show up in text. That way it won't pop up accidentally in the middle of some input, stopping the program before we want it to stop.

This kind of problem is not new, and, fortunately for us, it already has been solved by the people who design computer systems. Actually, their problem was slightly different, but we still can use their answer. Their problem concerned "files." A *file* is just a block of memory in which information is stored. Normally a file would be kept in some sort of permanent memory, such as on a floppy disk, a hard disk, or tape. A computer operating system needs some way to tell where each file begins and ends. One method to detect the end of a file is to place a special character there. This is the method used, for example, for CP/M, IBM-DOS, and MS-DOS "text" files. These operating systems use the [control-z] character to mark the ends of files. Figure 6.4 illustrates this approach.

Figure 6.4
A file with an end-of-file marker

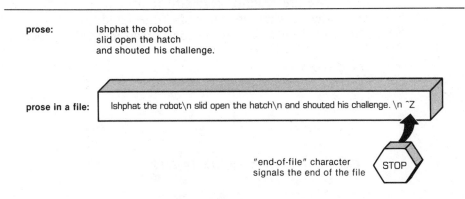

prose:
Ishphat the robot
slid open the hatch
and shouted his challenge.

prose in a file: Ishphat the robot\n slid open the hatch\n and shouted his challenge. \n ˆZ

"end-of-file" character
signals the end of the file   STOP

A second approach is for the operating system to store information on the size of the file. If a file has 3000 bytes and a program has read 3000 bytes, then it has reached the end. MS-DOS and its relatives use this approach for "binary" files, since it allows the files to hold all characters, including [control-z]'s. UNIX uses that approach for all files.

The way C handles this variety of choices is to have the **getchar( )** function return a special signal when the end of a file is detected, regardless of the method actually used to find the end of file. The name given to this signal is **EOF** (end of file). Thus, the return value for **getchar( )** when it detects an end of file is **EOF**.

Typically, EOF is defined in the **stdio.h** file as follows:

```
#define EOF (-1)
```

Why −1? Normally, **getchar( )** returns a value in the range 0 through 127, since those are values corresponding to the standard character set. Or it might return values from 0 through 255 if the system recognizes an extended character set. In either case, the value −1 does not correspond to any character, so it can be used as a signal.

Some systems may define the **EOF** constant to have a different numerical value, but always in such a way that it is different from a return value produced by a legitimate character. But if you include the **stdio.h** file and use the **EOF** symbol, you don't have to worry about the numerical definition. The important point to keep in mind is that **EOF** represents a signal from **getchar( )** that it found the end of a file; it is not a symbol actually found in the file.

Okay, how can we use **EOF** in a program? We compare the return value of **getchar( )** with **EOF**. If they are different, we have not yet reached the end of a file. In other words, we can use an expression like this:

```
while ( (ch = getchar() ) != EOF)
```

But what if we are reading keyboard input and not a file? Most systems provide a way to simulate an end-of-file condition from the keyboard. Knowing that, we can rewrite our basic read and echo program this way:

```
/* getput4 */
#include <stdio.h>
main()
{
   int ch;

   while ((ch = getchar()) != EOF)
      putchar(ch);
}
```

Note these points:

1. We don't have to define EOF, for **stdio.h** takes care of that.

2. We don't have to worry about the actual value of EOF, for the **#define** statement in **stdio.h** lets us use the symbolic representation EOF.

3. We've changed **ch** from type **char** to type **int.** We did this

because **char** variables may be represented by unsigned integers in the range 0 to 255, but EOF may have the numerical value −1. That is an impossible value for an unsigned **char** variable, but not for **int**. Fortunately, **getchar( )** is actually of type **int** itself, so it can read the EOF character. Implementations that use a signed **char** type can get by with declaring **ch** as type **char**, but it is better to use the more general form.

4. The fact that **ch** is an integer doesn't faze **putchar( )**. It still prints out the character equivalent.

5. To use this program on keyboard input, we need a way to type the EOF character. No, you can't just type the letters E-O-F, and you can't just type −1. (Typing −1 would transmit two characters: a hyphen and the digit 1.) Instead, you have to find out what the system requires. On most UNIX systems, for example, typing [control-d] at the beginning of a line causes the end-of-file signal to be transmitted. Many microcomputing systems recognize a [control-z] typed anywhere on a line as an end-of-file signal.

Here is a buffered example of running **getput4**:

```
She walks in beauty, like the night
She walks in beauty, like the night
  Of cloudless climes and starry skies...
  Of cloudless climes and starry skies...
              Lord Byron
              Lord Byron
[control-z]
```

Each time we press [enter], the characters stored in the buffer are processed, and a copy of the line is printed out. This continues until we simulate the end of file.

Let's stop for a moment and think about the possibilities for **getput4**. It copies onto the screen whatever input we feed it. Suppose we could somehow feed a file to it. Then it would print the contents of the file onto the screen, stopping when it reached the end of the file, for it would find an EOF signal then. Or suppose instead that we could find a way to direct the program's output to a file. Then we could type data on the keyboard and use **getput4** to store what we type. Or suppose we could do both simultaneously; suppose we could direct input from one file into **getput4** and send the output to another file. Then we could use **getput4** to copy files. Thus, our little program has the potential to look at the contents of files, to create new files, and to make copies of files—pretty good for such a short program! The key is to control the flow of input and output, and that is our next topic.

Redirection and Files

Input and output involve functions, data, and devices. Consider, for instance, our **getput4** program. It uses the input function **getchar( )**. The input device (we have assumed) is a keyboard, and the input data are individual characters. We would like to keep the same input function and the same kind of data, but to change where the program looks for data. A good question to ask (and to answer) is "How does a program know where to look for its input?"

By default, a C program looks to the "standard input" as a source for input. This *standard input* is whatever has been set up as the usual way for reading data into the computer. It could be magnetic tape, punched cards, a teletype, or (as we will continue to assume) a video terminal. A modern computer is a suggestible tool, however, and we can influence it to look elsewhere for input. In particular, we can tell a program to seek its input from a file instead of from a keyboard.

There are a couple ways to get a program to work with files. One way is to explicitly use special functions that open files, close files, read files, write in files, and so forth. We don't want to get that involved yet. The second way is to use a program designed to work with keyboard and screen, but to "redirect" input and output along different channels, to and from files, for example. This approach is more limited in some respects than the first, but it is much simpler to use. It is the one that we will use.

UNIX

Redirection is a feature of the UNIX operating system, not of C itself. But it is such a useful aid that when people transported C to other systems, they often brought along a form of redirection with it. Furthermore, many of the newer operating systems, including MS-DOS 2 and 3, have included redirection. So even if you are not on a UNIX system, there is a good chance that you have some form of redirection available. We will discuss UNIX redirection first, then non-UNIX redirection.

Redirecting Input—Suppose you have compiled our **getput4** program and placed the executable version in a file called **getput4.** Then to run the program, you just type the file name

```
getput4
```

and the program runs as we described earlier, taking its input from what you type at the keyboard. Now suppose that you wish to use the program on the "text file" called **words.** (A *text file* is one containing text, that is, data stored as characters. It could be an essay or a program in C, for example. A file containing machine language instructions, such as the file holding the executable version of a program is *not* a text file. Since our program works with characters, it should be used with text files.) All you need do is enter this command instead of the previous one:

```
getput4 <words
```

The < symbol is a UNIX redirection operator. It causes the contents of the **words** file to be channelled into **getput4.** The **getput4** program itself doesn't know (or care) that the input is coming from a file instead of the keyboard. All it knows is that a stream of characters is being fed to it, so it reads them and prints them one character at a time until the end of file shows up. UNIX puts files and I/O devices on the same footing, so the file is now the I/O "device." Try it!

```
getput4 <words
```

Here is the output:

```
To see a World in a grain of sand,
And a Heaven in a wild flower,
Hold Infinity in the palm of your hand,
And Eternity in an hour.
```

Of course we cannot guarantee that William Blake will turn up in the file you choose.

Redirecting Output—Now suppose (assuming your supposer is still working) that you wish to have the words you type sent to a file called **mywords.** Then you can enter

```
getput4 >mywords
```

and begin typing. The > is a second UNIX redirection operator. It causes a new file called **mywords** to be created for your use, and then it redirects the output of **getput4** (that output is a copy of the characters you type) to that file. If you already have a file with the name **mywords,** normally it would be erased and then replaced by the new one. (Some UNIX systems give you the option of protecting existing files, however.) All that appears on the screen are the letters you type, and the copies go to the file instead. To end the program, type a [control-d] at the beginning of a line. Try it. If you can't think of anything to type, just imitate this example. Here we show the UNIX prompt, which we take to be a %. Remember to end each line with a [return] so as to send the buffer contents to the program.

```
% getput4 >mywords
   You should have no problem recalling which redirection
operator does what. Just remember that each operator points
in the direction the information flows. Think of it as a
funnel.
[control-d]
%
```

Once the [control-d] is processed, the program terminates and returns control to the UNIX operating system, as is indicated by the return of the UNIX prompt. Did the program work? The UNIX **ls** command, which lists file names, should show you that the file **mywords** now exists. You can use the UNIX **cat** command to check the contents, or you can use **getput4** again, this time redirecting the file *to* the program.

```
% getput4 <mywords
   You should have no problem recalling which redirection
operator does what. Just remember that each operator points
in the direction the information flows. Think of it as a
funnel.
%
```

Combined Redirection—Now crank up your supposer one more time and suppose you want to make a copy of the file **mywords** and call it **savewords.** Just issue the command

```
getput4 <mywords >savewords
```

and the deed is done. The command

```
getput4 >savewords <mywords
```

would have served as well, since the order of redirection operations doesn't matter.

Don't use the same file for both input and output in one command.

```
getput 4 <mywords >mywords WRONG
```

The reason for not doing this is that the **>mywords** causes the original **mywords** to be erased before it is ever used as input.

Figure 6.5
Combined redirection

Perhaps we now should summarize the rules governing the use of the two redirection operators < and >.

1. A redirection operator connects an *executable* program (including standard UNIX commands) with a file. It cannot be used to connect one file to another or one program to another.

2. Input cannot be taken from more than one file, nor can output be directed to more than one file using these operators.

3. Normally the spaces between the names and operators are optional, except occasionally when some characters with special meaning to the UNIX shell are used. We could, for example, have used **getput4<words** or the much more attractive **getput4 < words.**

We already have given several proper examples. Here are some wrong examples, with **addup** and **count** as executable programs and **fish** and **stars** as text files.

fish > stars	Violates Rule 1
addup < count	Violates Rule 1
addup < fish < stars	Violates Rule 2
count > stars fish	Violates Rule 2

UNIX also features a > > operator, which lets you add data to the end of an existing file, and the pipe operator (|) which lets you connect the output of one program to the input of a second program. See a UNIX book (the forthcoming second edition of *UNIX™ Primer Plus,* Waite, Prata, and Martin, Indianapolis: Howard W. Sams, 1987, comes to mind) for more information on all these operators.

Let's try one more example and construct a very simple cypher program. We'll alter **getput** slightly and obtain:

```
/* simplecode */
/* this program replaces each text character by the next */
/* in the ASCII sequence */
#include <stdio.h>
main()
{
  int ch;

  while ((ch = getchar()) != EOF)
    putchar(ch + 1);
}
```

The **putchar( )** function converts the integer "**ch + 1**" to the appropriate character.

Now compile the program and store the executable version in a file called, say, **simplecode.** Next, put the following into a file called **original.** (You can use your system editor, or you can use **getput4** as we showed earlier.)

```
Good spelling is an aid
to clear writing.
```

Now give the command:

```
simplecode <original
```

The result should be something like this:

```
Hppe!tqfmmjoh!jt!bo!bje^Kup!dmfbs!xsjujoh^K
```

The **G** is changed to an **H,** the **o** to a **p,** and so on. You may have a couple of surprises. Notice that the spaces become exclamation marks. This reminds us that a space is a character on the same footing as other characters. Second, two lines were compressed into one. Why? Because **original** contains a newline character at the end of the first line; that's how the computer knows to start the next word on a new line. But that character also was changed. On our system it was changed to ^**K,** which is another way to write [control-k], and so no new line was started. If we want an encyphering program that preserves the original line structure, we need a way to change all the characters *except* the newline character. The next chapter will give us the tools to do that.

Non-UNIX

We'll deal mainly with the differences from redirection in UNIX, so if you skipped over UNIX redirection, go back and read it (it's pretty easy going). There are two varieties in this category:

1. Other operating systems with redirection.
2. C compilers with redirection.

We can't cover all possible operating systems, so we will give just one example, but of one that is in widespread use. That system is MS-DOS 2. MS-DOS began as an offshoot of CP/M, but it is now evolving towards XENIX, a UNIX-like system. Version 2 of MS-DOS instituted redirection operators < and >, which work just as we described in the previous section.

We also can't cover all possible C compilers. However, five out of the six microcomputer versions of C compilers that we've looked at use the < and > symbols for redirection. Compiler-generated redirection differs in two respects from UNIX redirection:

1. It works only with C programs, while UNIX redirection works for any executable program.
2. There must be a space between the program name and the operator, and there must be no space between the operator and the file name. Here is an example of the proper form:

```
getput4 <words
```

Comment—Redirection is a simple yet potent tool. With it we can make our tiny **getput4** program into a file producer, a file reader, and a file copier. The approach exemplifies the C (and UNIX) philosophy of creating simple tools that can be combined in a variety of ways to perform a variety of tasks.

Summary: How to Redirect Input and Output

With most C systems you can use redirection, either for all programs through the operating system or else just for C programs, courtesy of the C compiler. In the following, let **prog** be the name of the executable program and let **file1** and **file2** be names of files.

Redirecting Output to a File: >

```
prog >file1
```

Redirecting Input from a File: <

```
prog <file2
```

Combined Redirection:

```
prog <file2 >file1    or
prog >file1 <file2
```

Both forms use **file2** for input and **file1** for output.

Spacing:
Some systems (C compilers, especially) require a space to the left of the redirection operator and no space to the right. Other systems (UNIX, for example) will accept either spaces or no spaces on either side.

A Graphic Example

We can use **getchar( )** and **putchar( )** to produce geometric patterns using characters. Here is a program to do that. It reads a character and then prints it a number of times, the number depending on the ASCII value. It also prints a sufficient number of spaces to center each line.

```
/* patterns */
/* produces a symmetric pattern of characters */
#include <stdio.h>
main()
{
  int ch;  /* read character */
  int index;
  int chnum;

  while ((ch = getchar()) != '\n') {
     chnum = ch % 26; /* produces a number from 0 to 25 */
     index = 0;
     while (index++ < (30 - chnum))
         putchar(' '); /* spaces to center pattern */
     index = 0;
     while (index++ < (2*chnum + 1))
         putchar(ch); /* print ch several times */
     putchar('\n');
     }
}
```

The only new technical point is that we have used subexpressions, such as **(30 − chnum)** in the **while** loop conditions. One **while** loop controls the printing of the initial spaces, and the second controls the printing of the characters.

What you get depends on the data you input. If, for example, you type

What's up?

then the response is:

```
            WWWWWWWWWWWWWWWWWWW
                     h
     aaaaaaaaaaaaaaaaaaaaaaaaaaaaaaaaaaaaaaaaa
          ttttttttttttttttttttttttttt
          ''''''''''''''''''''''''''''
             sssssssssssssssssssssss
```

```
uuuuuuuuuuuuuuuuuuuuuuuuuuuu
ppppppppppppppppppp
?????????????????????????
```

What can you do with this program? You can ignore it. You can tinker with it to change the kinds of patterns it makes. You can try to find combinations of input characters that produce a pretty pattern. For example, the input

    hijklmnopqrstuiii

produces:

```
                 h
                iii
               jjjjj
              kkkkkkk
             lllllllll
            mmmmmmmmmmm
           nnnnnnnnnnnnn
          ooooooooooooooo
         ppppppppppppppppp
        qqqqqqqqqqqqqqqqqqq
       rrrrrrrrrrrrrrrrrrrrr
      sssssssssssssssssssssss
     ttttttttttttttttttttttttt
    uuuuuuuuuuuuuuuuuuuuuuuuuuu
                iii
                iii
                iii
```

System-Dependent I/O: 8086/8088 I/O Ports

Let's look at a different sort of I/O device as we turn now to an example of fitting C to the requirements of a specific system. Many of the new generation of microcomputers are based on the Intel's 8086 and 8088 microprocessor chips. The best-known example is the IBM PC, which uses the 8088. We will discuss a particular example for the IBM PC, but the principles involved apply to other users for the 8086/8088 family.

A computer like the IBM has more to it than just the 8088 chip. It has a keyboard, a speaker, perhaps a cassette drive or a disk drive, a monitor, built-in memory, timers, and other microprocessors to control the flow of data. The central processing unit (incorporated into the 8088 chip) needs a way to communicate with the other parts of the computer. Some of this is done by using memory addresses, and some is done by using input/output "ports." The 8088 chip has 65536 ports that it can use for communication. Each device is assigned its own particular port or ports to use for communicating with the 8088. (Not all 65536 are used!) For example, ports 992, 993, and 1000 to 1004 are used to communicate with the color/graphics adapter. The speaker is controlled using port 97. The speaker sounds a bit simpler than the color/graphics adapter, so we will use the speaker to illustrate the use of I/O ports.

Port 97 doesn't control the speaker directly. The device that does is something called an 8255 Programmable Parallel Interface Controller. This microprocessor has three *registers* (small, easily accessed memory units), each of which holds a number. The numbers in the registers control what the device does. Each register is connected with the 8088 through a port, and port 97 is connected to the register that controls the speaker. We program the control by using the port to change the number in the register. The right number will cause the speaker to sound a tone. The wrong number can cause problems. Thus, we need to know what number to send and how to send it. In particular, we need to know how to use C to send the number.

Figure 6.6
The 8088-8255 connection

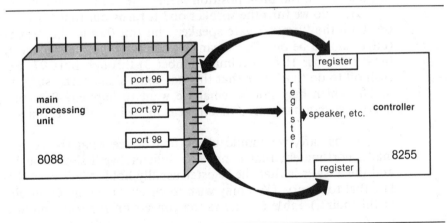

First, let's look into what numbers to send. The first thing to know is that an 8255 register accepts an 8-bit number, which is stored as a binary number, such as 01011011. Each of the 8 storage bits is regarded as an on-off switch for some device or action. The presence of a 0 or 1 in a particular bit position determines whether or not the device is on. For example, bit 3 (the bits are numbered from 0 to 7 going from right to left) determines whether the cassette motor is on; bit 7 enables and disables the keyboard. Notice the need for caution. If we turn the speaker on and neglect the other bits, we might accidentally turn the keyboard off! So let's take a look at what each bit does by examining Figure 6.7. (The information is from IBM's Technical Reference Manual, and we don't have to know what most of it means.)

Figure 6.7
Port 97: what each bit controls

```
bit 0 + timer 2 gate speaker
bit 1 + speaker data
bit 2 + (read read/write memory size) or (read spare key)
bit 3 + cassette motor off
bit 4 - enable read/write memory
bit 5 - enable i/o ch ck
bit 6 - hold kbd clk low
bit 7 - (enable kbd) or + (clr kbd & enable sense sw's)
```

Note the little plus and minus signs in the figure. A plus sign indicates that a 1 means the condition holds, and a minus indicates that a 0 means the condition holds. Thus, a 1 in the bit-3 position means the cassette motor is off, and a 0 in the bit-4 position means the read/write memory is enabled.

How do we turn the speaker on? It turns out that for the speaker to be on, both the "timer 2 gate speaker" bit (bit 0) and the "speaker data" bit (bit 1) should be on. This means we can turn the speaker on by sending the binary number 11 (or decimal number 3) through port 97. But before you rush off to do that, note that this has some side effects, such as setting bit 4 to off, which may not be what we want to happen. Preventing you from making such a hasty error is one reason we haven't yet told you how to use the ports!

To be safe, we should check first to see what the register reads normally. Fortunately, that is not too difficult (we'll show you in a moment), and the answer is that the register usually holds "76" or "77." Let's translate that to binary. (You may wish to check Appendix G on binary numbers at this point.) Table 6.1 shows the conversion for some numbers.

Table 6.1
Binary Conversions of Some Decimal Numbers

Decimal	Bit Number	7	6	5	4	3	2	1	0
76		0	1	0	0	1	1	0	0
77		0	1	0	0	1	1	0	1
78		0	1	0	0	1	1	1	0
79		0	1	0	0	1	1	1	1

Without going into what "hold keyboard clock low" might mean, it is clear that the safest course of action is to leave all the bit positions other than 0 and 1 unchanged. This corresponds to sending binary number 01001111, or decimal 79, to the register. As an added precaution, we should read the original value in the register and then restore the register to that value when we are done sounding the speaker. (The bitwise operators discussed in Appendix F offer another approach for setting the register.)

Okay, we are ready to sound the speaker. What do we do next?

Using a Port

There are two things you can do with a port. You can send information from the 8088 to the attached device, or you can read information from the attached device to the 8088. In assembly language these tasks are accomplished using the OUT and the IN instructions. In C the method depends on the compiler. Some compilers offer an analogous C function. Lattice C and Microsoft C, for example, use **outp( )** and **inp( )**. Other compilers may use slightly different names. If you are using a compiler that doesn't offer this function, most likely you can use assembly language to define such a function. Check your compiler documentation. Meanwhile, we will assume that you have access to the **outp( )** and **inp( )** functions.

Here, then, is a first pass at beeping your beeper.

```
/* beep1 */
/* a program to make the speaker beep */
main()
{
  int store;

  store = inp(97); /* store the initial port 97 reading */
  printf("port 97 = %d\n", store); /* check results */
  outp(97,79);    /* send 79 to port 97; turns speaker on */
  outp(97,store);         /* restore to initial condition */
}
```

You probably can tell what the **inp( )** and **outp( )** functions do, but here is a formal description.

inp(portnumber)	This function returns an 8-bit integer value (which is converted to a 16-bit **int** by adding zeros to the left) from input port **portnumber.** It does not alter whatever the port is connected to.
outp(portnumber, value)	This function sends the 8-bit integer value to output port **portnumber.**

Note that a port can be both an input and an output port, depending on how it is used.

Now run the program. You may not be very satisfied, for it doesn't take very long for the computer to turn the speaker off after turning it on. It would be much more satisfactory if we could get the computer to wait a bit before turning the speaker off. Can that be done? Yes, we just have to give the computer something to do in the meantime. That can be arranged, as the next program shows.

```
/* beep2 */
/* a longer beep */
#define LIMIT 10000
main()
{
    int store;
    int count = 0; /* something for the computer to count with */

    store = inp(97);
    outp(97,79);
    while(count++ < LIMIT)
        ; /* whiling away time doing nothing */
    outp(97,store);
}
```

Notice that all the **while** statement does is increase **count** until it reaches **LIMIT**. The semicolon following the **while** statement is the "null" statement, one that does nothing. Thus, **beep2** turns the speaker on, counts to 10000, then turns the speaker off. You can adjust the size of **LIMIT** to control how long the sound continues. Or you can replace **LIMIT** with a variable and use **scanf( )** to read in a value controlling the duration.

It would be nice if we could control the pitch, too. Well, we can. After we study functions more fully, you can check Appendix H for a program that makes the terminal keyboard into a musical keyboard.

Summary

Once again we have dealt with I/O devices, I/O data, and I/O functions. The devices were the 8255 controller and the speaker, the data were the numbers communicated to and from one of the 8255 registers, and the functions were **inp( )** and **outp( )**. Using these functions or their assembly code equivalents is necessary if we want to use the 8086/8088 I/O ports, and C compilers give you one or both options.

Tapping the Hidden Horsepower of Your Computer

Want to unlock the awesome number-crunching potential of the beast? We have created an amazing program (revealed in Figure 6.8) that does just that. It is a program that you must run to appreciate fully. Warning: for proper effect, you should choose a LIMIT value appropriate for your system. More on that in a moment, but, first, here is the program.

Figure 6.8
A number-crunching program

```
/* hans */
#include <stdio.h>
#define LIMIT 8000L
main()
{
  int num1, num2;
  long delay = 0;
  int count = 0;

  printf("Hans the computer horse will add two very ");
  printf("small integers for your pleasure.\n");
  printf("Please enter the first small integer.\n");
  scanf("%d", &num1);
  printf("Thank you. Now enter the second integer.\n");
  scanf("%d", &num2);
  printf("Okay, Hans, how much is that?\n");
  while( delay++ < LIMIT);
  while( count++ < (num1 + num2 -1))
    {
    putchar('\007');
    delay = 0;
    while( delay++ < LIMIT);
    putchar('\n');
    }
  printf("Yes?\n");
  delay = 0;
  while( delay++ < 3*LIMIT);
  putchar('\007');
  printf("Very good, Hans!\n");
}
```

Technical notes: The **while** statements containing **delay** do nothing but mark time. The semicolon at the end of the line indicates that the **while** loop ends there and does not include any of the following lines. The use of a **while** loop within another **while** loop is called *nesting*. We find that 8000 is a good value for **LIMIT** on the IBM PC. For a VAX 11/750 we prefer a value around 50000, but the time-sharing load on the system can affect that choice. We set **LIMIT** equal to a **long** constant (that's what the terminal **L** does) to avoid problems with the maximum **int** size. (This wasn't really necessary for the value of **8000,** but even changing the value to 12000 on an IBM would have made it necessary, for then the expression **3∗LIMIT** would be 36000, which is larger than the maximum **int** on that system.)

If your system doesn't have a speaker or a bell, perhaps you could replace **putchar('\007')** with **printf("CLOP").**

This program will impress your friends and probably soothe those who fear computers. We think that it can form the core of a "C Calculator," but we leave the development of the concept to our readers.

What You Should Have Learned

What **getchar( )** does: fetches a character from the keyboard
What **putchar(ch)** does: sends the character **ch** to the screen
What != means: not equal to
What **EOF** is: a special character indicating the end of a file
How to redirect input from a file: **program < file**
How to redirect output to a file: **program > file**
What ports are: I/O accesses to attached devices
How to use ports: **inp( )** and **outp( )**

Review Questions

1. **putchar(getchar( ))** is a valid expression. Is **getchar(putchar( ))** also valid?

2. What would each of the following statements accomplish?
   a. putchar('H');
   b. putchar('\007');
   c. putchar('\n');
   d. putchar('\b');

3. Suppose you have a program **count** that counts the characters in its input. Devise a command that counts the number of characters in the file **essay** and stores the result in a file named **essayct.**

4. Given the program and files of Question 3, which of the following are valid commands?
   a. essayct <essay
   b. count essay
   c. essay >count

5. What does the statement **outp(212,23)** do?

6. What is the output of each of the following fragments for the indicated input (assume that **ch** is **type int** and that the input is buffered):

   a. The input is as follows:
```
If you quit, I will. [return]
```
   The fragment is as follows:
```
while (( ch = getchar() ) != 'i' )
    putchar(ch);
```
  b. The input is as follows:
```
Harhar [return]
```
   The fragment is as follows:
```
while ( ( ch = getchar() ) != '\n' )
    {
    putchar(ch++);
    putchar(++ch);
    }
```

Answers

1. No, **getchar( )** doesn't use an argument and **putchar( )** needs one.

2. **a.** print the letter H
   b. output the character '\007', which produces a beep
   c. start a new line
   d. backspace one space

3. **count** <**essay** >**essayct** or else **count** >**essayct** <**essay**

4. **a.** invalid; **essayct** is not an executable program
   b. invalid; the redirection operator was omitted (however, you later will
     learn to write programs that don't need the redirection operator)
   c. invalid; this setup implies that **essay** is a program and that **count** is a file

5. It sends the number 23 out through port number 212.

6. **a.** The output is as follows:
```
If you qu
```
   Note that the character **I** is distinct from the character **i**. Also note that
   the **i** is not printed, for the loop quits upon detecting it.
  b. The output is as follows:
```
HJacrthjacrt
```
   The first time through, **ch** has the value **H**. The **ch++** causes the value to
   be used (printed), then incremented (to **I**). Then the **++ch** causes the
   value to be incremented (to **J**), then be used (printed). After that, the
   next character (**a**) is read, and the process is repeated. An important
   point here is that the incrementations affect the value of **ch** after it has
   been assigned a value; they don't somehow cause the program to move
   through the input queue.

Exercises

1. Produce the program described in Question 3. That is, devise a program that counts the number of characters in its input.

2. Modify **count** so that it beeps each time it counts a character. Insert a short counting loop to separate one beep from the next.

3. Modify **beep2** so that you can input the counting loop limit when the program runs.

4. Write a program that reads input until encountering **EOF**. Have the program print out each input character and its ASCII decimal code.

7

Choosing Alternatives

Concepts
- Making decisions
- True and false in C
- Making comparisons
- Logic in C

Keywords
- *if, else, switch, break, case, default*

Operators
- `> >= <= < == != && || / ?:`

D o you want to create powerful, intelligent, versatile, and useful programs? Then you need a language that provides the three basic forms of program "flow" control. According to computer science (which is the science of computers and not science by computers—yet), a good language should provide these three forms of program flow:

1. Executing a series of statements.
2. Repeating a sequence of statements until some condition is met.
3. Using a test to decide between alternative actions.

The first form we know well; all our programs have consisted of a sequence of statements. The **while** loop is one example of the second form, and we will pick up other methods in Chapter 8. The final form, choosing between different possible courses of action, makes a program much more "intelligent" and increases enormously the usefulness of a computer. We will explore that topic in this chapter.

The *if* Statement

Let's start with a very simple example of an "if" statement." We already have a program that counts the number of characters in a file. Suppose we want to count lines, instead. We can do that by counting the number of newline characters in a file. Here's how:

```
/* linecounter */
```

```
#include <stdio.h>
main()
{
  int ch;
  int linecount = 0;

  while ( (ch = getchar()) != EOF)
       if (ch == '\n')
           linecount++;
  printf("I counted %d lines.\n", linecount);
}
```

The core of this program is the statement

```
if (ch == '\n')
    linecount++;
```

This **if** statement instructs the computer to increase **linecount** by 1 *if* the character just read (**ch**) is the newline character. The == is not a misprint; it means "is equal to." Don't confuse this operator with the assignment operator (=).

What happens if **ch** is not equal to a newline character? Nothing happens, and the **while** loop moves on to read the next character.

The **if** statement we just used counts as a single statement, running from the initial **if** to the closing semicolon. That is why we didn't have to use braces to mark the limits of the **while** loop.

It is a simple matter to make the program count both characters and lines, so let's do it.

```
/*line and character counter */
#include <stdio.h>
main()
{
  int ch;
  int linecount = 0;
  int charcount = 0;

  while ( (ch = getchar()) != EOF)
       {
       charcount++;
       if (ch == '\n')
           linecount++;
       }
  printf("I counted %d characters and %d lines.\n",
       charcount, linecount);
}
```

Now the **while** loop encompasses two statements, so we use braces to mark off the body of the loop.

We will call the compiled program **lcc** and use redirection to count the characters and lines in a file called **chow**.

```
lcc <chow
I counted 8539 characters and 233 lines.
```

The next step in developing this program will be to have it count words. That's only a little harder than what we've done so far, but we need to learn a little more about using **if** statements first.

Adding *else* to the *if* Statement

The simplest form of an **if** statement is the one we just used:

```
if(expression)
    statement
```

Normally the expression is a relational expression; that is, it compares the magnitude of two quantities ($x > y$ or $c == 6$, for example). If the expression is true (x is greater than y, or c does equal 6), then the statement is executed. Otherwise, it is ignored. More generally, any expression can be used, and an expression with a 0 value is taken to be false—more on that a little later.

The statement portion can be a simple statement, as in our example, or it can be a compound statement or block, marked off by braces:

```
if ( score > big)
    printf("Jackpot!\n"); /* simple statement */

if ( joe > ron)
    {
    joecash++;
    printf("You lose, Ron.\n");
    }                       /* compound statement */
```

The simple form of an **if** statement gives you the choice of executing a statement (possibly compound) or skipping it. C also lets us choose between two statements by using the **if-else** structure.

Choice: *if-else*

In the last chapter we presented a very simple cypher program that converted each character to the next one in the ASCII sequence. Unfortunately, it even converted the newline character, causing several lines to combine. We can eliminate that problem by creating a program that makes a simple choice: if the character is a newline, leave it alone; otherwise, convert it. Here is how this can be done in C:

```
/* code1 */
#include <stdio.h>
main()
{
  char ch;

  while ((ch = getchar()) != EOF) {
      if (ch == '\n')          /*  leave the newline      */
          putchar(ch);         /*  character unchanged    */
      else
          putchar(ch + 1);     /* change other characters */
      }
}
```

Last time we used a file containing the following text.

```
Good spelling is an aid
to good writing.
```

Using the same text with our new program gives this result:

```
Hppe!tqfmmjoh!jt!bo!bje
up!hppe!xsjujoh/
```

Gosh! It works. Incidentally, we can easily make a decoding program. Just duplicate **code1**, but replace **(ch + 1)** with **(ch − 1)**.

Did you note the general form of the **if-else** statement? It's

```
if(expression)
    statement
else
    statement
```

If the expression is true, the first statement is executed. If the expression is false, the statement following the **else** is executed. The statements can be simple or compound. The indentation is not required by C, but it is the standard style. It shows at a glance those statements whose execution depends on a test.

The **if** lets us choose whether or not to do one action. The **if-else** lets us choose between two actions. What if we need more choices than that?

Figure 7.1
If versus *if-else*

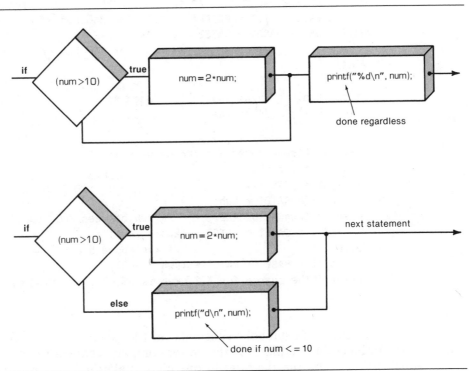

Multiple Choice: *else-if*

Often life offers us more than two choices. We can extend the **if-else** structure with **else-if** to accommodate this fact. Let's look at a particular example. Utility companies often have charges that depend on the amount of energy you use. Here are the rates we are charged for electricity, based on kilowatt-hours (kWh).

first 240 kWh:	$0.05418 per kWh
next 300 kWh:	$0.07047 per kWh
over 540 kWh:	$0.09164 per kWh

If you worry about your energy management, you might wish to prepare a program to calculate your energy costs. Here is a first step in that direction.

```
/* electbill */
```

```
/* calculates electric bill   */
#define RATE1 0.05418      /* rate for first 240 kwh */
#define RATE2 0.07047      /* rate for next 300 kwh  */
#define RATE3 0.09164      /* rate for over 540 kwh  */
#define BREAK1 240.0       /* first breakpoint for rates  */
#define BREAK2 540.0       /* second breakpoint for rates */
#define BASE1 RATE1 * BREAK1 /* cost for 240 kwh */
#define BASE2 BASE1 + RATE2 * (BREAK2 - BREAK1)
                           /* cost for 540 kwh */
main()
{
   float kwh;    /* kilowatt-hours used */
   float bill;   /* charges */

   printf("Please enter the kwh used.\n");
   scanf("%f", &kwh);
   if (kwh <= BREAK1)
       bill = RATE1 * kwh;
   else if (kwh <= BREAK2)      /* kwh between 240 and 540 */
       bill = BASE1 + RATE2 * (kwh - 240);
   else                         /* kwh above 540 */
       bill = BASE2 + RATE3 * (kwh - 540);
   printf("The charge for %.1f kwh is $%1.2f.\n", kwh, bill);
}
```

We have used symbolic constants for the rates. This way our constants are gathered in one place. If the power company changes its rates (and this can happen), having the rates in one place makes it less likely that we will fail to update a rate. We also expressed the rate breakpoints symbolically. They, too, are subject to change. **BASE1** and **BASE2** are expressed in terms of the rates and breakpoints. Then, if the rates or breakpoints change, the bases are updated automatically. You may recall that the preprocessor does not do calculations. Where **BASE1** appears in the program, it will be replaced by **0.05418 * 240.0**. The compiler, however, does evaluate this expression to its numerical value (13.00) so that the program code uses this final value.

The flow of the program is straightforward, with the program selecting one of three formulas, depending on the value of **kwh**. Figure 7.2 illustrates the flow. We should point out that the only way the program can reach the first **else** is if **kwh** is equal to or greater than **240**. Thus, the **else if (kwh <=BREAK2)** line really is equivalent to demanding that **kwh** is between **240** and **540**, as we noted in the program comment. Similarly, the final **else** can be reached only if **kwh** equals or exceeds **540**. Finally, note that **BASE1** and **BASE2** represent the total charges for the first 240 and 540 kilowatt-hours, respectively. Thus, we need only add on the additional charges for electricity in excess of those amounts.

Figure 7.2
Program flow for "electbill"

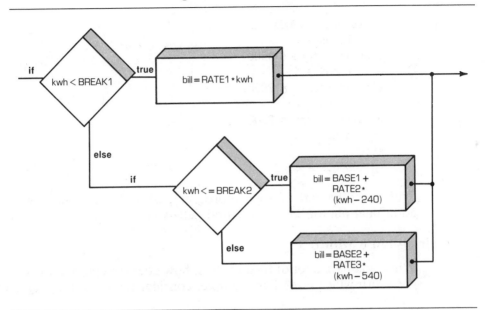

Actually, the **else-if** is just a variation on what we already knew. For example, the core of our program is just another way of writing

```
if ( kwh <=BREAK1 )
     bill = RATE1 * kwh;
else
    if ( kwh <=BREAK2 )
         bill = BASE1 + RATE2 * (kwh - 240);
    else
         bill = BASE2 + RATE3 * (kwh - 540);
```

That is, the program consists of an **if-else** statement for which the statement part of the **else** is another **if-else** statement. The second **if-else** statement is said to be "nested" in the first. (Incidentally, the entire **if-else** structure counts as a single statement, which is why we didn't have to enclose the nested **if-else** in braces.)

These two forms are perfectly equivalent. The only differences are in where we put spaces and newlines, and these are ignored by the compiler. Nonetheless, the first form is preferred, for it shows more clearly that we are making a three-way choice. This form makes it easier to scan the program and see what the choices are. Save the nested forms for when they are needed, for instance, when you must test two separate quantities. An example would be if there were a 10% surcharge for kilowatt-hours in excess of 540 during the summer only.

You may string together as many **else-ifs** as you need (within compiler limits, of course), as illustrated by this fragment:

```
if (score < 1000)
     bonus = 0;
else if (score < 1500)
     bonus = 1;
else if (score < 2000)
     bonus = 2;
else if (score < 2500)
     bonus = 4;
else
     bonus = 6;
```

(This could be part of a game program, where **bonus** represents how many additional photon bombs or food pellets you get for the next round.)

Pairing *else's* with *if's*

When you have a lot of **ifs** and **elses**, how does the computer decide which **if** goes with which **else?** For example, consider the program fragment

```
if ( number > 6 )
    if ( number < 12 )
        printf("You're close!\n");
else
    printf("Sorry, you lose a turn!\n");
```

When does "Sorry, you lose a turn!" get printed: when **number** is less than or equal to **6,** or when **number** is greater than **12?** In other words, does the **else** go with the first **if** or the second?

The answer is, it goes with the second **if.** That is, you would get these responses:

Number	Response
5	none
10	You're close!
15	Sorry, you lose a turn!

The rule is that an **else** goes with the most recent **if** unless braces indicate otherwise. We indented our example to make it look as if the **else** goes with the first **if,** but remember that the compiler ignores indentation. If we really want the **else** to go with the first **if,** we can write the fragment this way:

```
if ( number > 6 )
    {
    if (number < 12 )
```

```
        printf("You're close!\n");
    }
else
    printf("Sorry, you lose a turn!\n");
```

Now we would get these responses:

Number	Response
5	`Sorry, you lose a turn!`
10	`You're close!`
15	none

Figure 7.3
The rule for *if-else* pairings

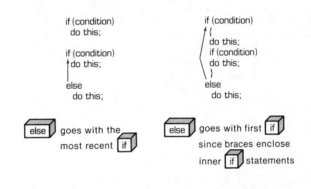

Summary: Using *if* Statements for Making Choices

Keywords: *if, else*

General Comments:
In each of the following forms, the *statement* can be either a simple statement or a compound statement. A "true" expression, more generally, means one with a nonzero value.

Form 1:

```
if ( expression )
    statement
```

The *statement* is executed if the *expression* is true.

Form 2:

```
if ( expression )
    statement1
  else
    statement2
```

If the *expression* is true, *statement1* is executed. Otherwise *statement2* is executed.

Form 3:

```
if ( expression1 )
    statement1
  else if ( expression2 )
    statement2
  else
    statement3
```

If *expression1* is true, then *statement1* is executed. If *expression1* is false but *expression2* is true, *statement2* is executed. Otherwise, if both expressions are false, *statement3* is executed.

Example:

```
if (legs == 4)
    printf("It might be a horse.\n");
else if (legs > 4)
    printf("It is not a horse.\n");
else    /* case of legs < 4 */
    {
    legs++;
    printf("Now it has one more leg.\n")
    }
```

Which is Bigger: Using Relational Operators and Expressions

Relational operators are used to make comparisons. We have used several already, and now we will show you the complete list of C relational operators.

Operator	Meaning
<	is less than
<=	is less than or equal to
==	is equal to
>=	is greater than or equal to
>	is greater than
!=	is not equal to

That pretty much covers all the possibilities for numerical relationships. (Numbers, even complex ones, are less complex than humans.) The main caution we offer is don't use = for ==. Some computer languages (BASIC, for example) do use the same symbol for the assignment operator as for the relational equality operator, but the two operations are quite different. The assignment operator *assigns* a value to the left-hand variable. The relational equality operator, however, checks to see if the left-hand and right-hand sides are already equal. It doesn't change the value of the left-hand variable, if one is present.

    canoes = 3   assigns the value 3 to canoes.
    canoes == 5   checks to see if canoes has the value 5.

Some care is needed, for a compiler will let you use the wrong form in some cases, yielding results other than what you expect. We will show an example shortly.

Table 7.1
Assignment and Relational Equality Operators in Some Common Languages

Language	Assignment	Relational Equality
BASIC	=	=
FORTRAN	=	.EQ.
C	=	==
Pascal	:=	=
PL/I	=	=
Logo	make	=

The relational operators are used to form the relational expressions used in **if** and **while** statements. These statements check to see if the expression is true or false. Here are four unrelated statements containing examples of relational expressions; the meaning, we hope, is clear.

```
if ( number < 6)
    printf("Your number is too small.\n");

while ( ch != '$')
    count++;

if ( total == 100)
    printf("You have hit the jackpot!\n");
if ( ch > 'M' )
    printf ("Send this person to another line.\n");
```

Figure 7.4
The relational operator == and the assignment operator =

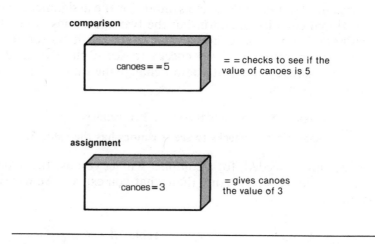

Note that the relational expressions can be used with characters, too. The machine code (which we have been assuming is ASCII) is used for the comparison. However, you can't use the relational operators to compare strings; in Chapter 13 we will show you what to use for strings.

The relational operators can be used with floating-point numbers, too. However, you should limit yourself to using only < and > in floating-point comparisons. The reason is that roundoff errors can prevent two numbers from being equal even though logically they should be. Consider, for example, this decimal system analogue. Certainly the product of 3 and 1/3 is 1.0, but if we express 1/3 as a six-place decimal fraction, the product is .999999, which is not quite equal to 1.

Each relational expression is judged to be "true" or "false." This raises an interesting question.

What Is Truth?

We can answer this age-old question, at least as far as C is concerned. First, recall that an expression in C always has a value. This is so even for relational expressions, as this next example shows. In it we find the values of two relational expressions, one true and one false.

```
/* trueandfalse */
main()
{
  int true, false;

  true = ( 10 > 2);    /* value of a true relationship  */
  false = ( 10 == 2); /* value of a false relationship */
  printf("true = %d; false = %d \n", true, false);
}
```

Here we have assigned the values of two relational expressions to two variables. Being straightforward, we assigned **true** the value of a true expression, and **false** the value of a false expression. Running the program produces the following simple output:

```
true = 1; false = 0
```

Aha! For C, truth is **1** and falsity is **0**. We can check that easily enough by running the next program.

```
/* truthcheck */
main()
{
  if (1)
       printf("1 means true.\n");
  else
       printf("1 doesn't mean true.\n");
  if (0)
       printf("0 doesn't mean false.\n");
  else
       printf("0 means false.\n");
}
```

We say that the **1** should evaluate as a true statement, and the **0** should evaluate as a false statement. If what we say is accurate, then the first **if** statement should take its first branch (the **if** branch), and the second **if** statement should take its second branch (the **else** branch). Try it out and see if we are right.

FOUR OF THE GREATEST INVENTIONS IN HUMAN HISTORY . . . .

THE WHEEL

THE LIGHT BULB

THE MICROCOMPUTER

MICROCOMPUTER MANUAL AND RESOURCE BOOK AUTHORS

So What Else Is True?

If we can use a **1** or a **0** as an **if** statement test expression, can we use other numbers? If so, what happens? Let's experiment.

```
/* iftest */
main()
{
    if(200)
      printf("200 is true.\n");
    if (-33)
      printf("-33 is true.\n");
}
```

The results:

```
200 is true.
-33 is true.
```

Apparently C regards **200** and **−33** as "true," also. Indeed, all nonzero values are regarded as "true," and only **0** is recognized as "false." C has a very tolerant notion of truth!

Many programmers make use of this definition of truth. For example, the phrase

```
if(goats != 0)
```

can be replaced by

```
if(goats)
```

since the expression **(goats != 0)** and the expression **(goats)** both become **0** or false only when **goats** has the value **0.** We think the second form is not as clear in meaning as the first. It can be more efficient, however, for it requires fewer processing operations for the computer when the program runs. But some compilers are clever enough to use the same efficient code for either form.

Troubles with Truth

C's tolerant notion of truth can lead to trouble. Consider the following program:

```
/* employment */
main()
{
  int age = 20;

  while (age++ <= 65)
    {
       if (( age % 20) == 0) /* is age divisible by 20? */
         printf("You are %d. Here is a raise.\n", age);
       if (age = 65)
         printf("You are %d. Here is your gold watch.\n", age);
    }
}
```

At first glance you might think the output of this program would be:

```
You are 40. Here is a raise.
You are 60. Here is a raise.
You are 65. Here is your gold watch.
```

The actual output, however, is:

```
You are 65. Here is your gold watch.
You are 65. Here is your gold watch.
You are 65. Here is your gold watch.
You are 65. Here is your gold watch.
You are 65. Here is your gold watch.
        ...
```

and so on indefinitely.

What has happened! Not only did we design the program poorly, but we ignored our own cautionary remarks and used

```
if (age = 65)
```

instead of

```
if (age == 65)
```

The effect is disastrous. When the program reaches that line, it looks at the expression **(age = 65)**. As you will remember, an assignment expression (which this is) takes the value of the variable, **65** in this case. Since **65** is nonzero, the expression is evaluated as "true" and the following print instruction is executed. Then, when the program returns to the **while** test, **age** is **65**, which is less than or equal to 65. The test is met, **age** is then increased to **66** (because of the postfix increment operator **++),** and the loop is traversed again. Will it stop next time? It should, because **age** is now greater than **65**. But when the program reaches our faulty **if** statement again, **age** gets set back to **65** again! So the message is printed out once more, and the loop is repeated again, ad infinitum. (Unless, of course, you eventually decide to abort the program.)

To sum up, the relational operators are used to form relational expressions. Relational expressions have the value "1" if true and "0" if false. Statements (such as **while** and **if**) that normally use relational expressions as tests can use any expression as a test, with nonzero values recognized as "true" and zero values as "false."

Priority of Relational Operators

The priority of the relational operators is less than that of + and − and greater than that of assignment. This means, for example, that

```
x > y + 2
```

means the same as

```
x > (y + 2)
```

It also means that

    ch = getchar() != EOF

is the same as

    ch = (getchar() != EOF)

since the higher priority of **!=** means that operation is done before assignment. Thus, **ch** would receive either **1** or **0** for a value, for **(getchar( ) != EOF)** is a relational expression whose value is assigned to **ch.** Since our program examples up to now have given **ch** the value of **getchar( ),** we have used parentheses to get the correct grouping:

    (ch = getchar()) != EOF

The relational operators are themselves organized into two different priorities.

>   Higher priority group: < <= >= >
>   Lower priority group: == !=

Like most other operators, the relational operators associate from left to right. Thus,

    ex != wye == zee

is the same as

    (ex != wye) == zee

First C checks to see if **ex** and **wye** are equal. Then the resulting value of **1** or **0** (true or false) is compared to the value of **zee.** We don't anticipate using this sort of construction, but we feel that it is our duty to point out such sidelights.

We remind the reader who wishes to keep his or her priorities straight that Appendix C has a complete priority ranking of all operators.

Let's Get Logical

Sometimes it is useful to combine two or more relational expressions. For instance, suppose we want a program that counts only nonwhite-space characters. That is, we wish to keep track of characters that are not spaces, not newline characters, and not tab characters. We can use "logical" operators to meet this need. Here is a short program illustrating the method.

```
/* chcount */
/* counts nonwhite-space characters */
main()
{
   int ch;
   int charcount = 0;
   while ((ch = getchar()) != EOF)
      if( ch != ' ' && ch != '\n' && ch != '\t')
             charcount++;
   printf("There are %d nonwhite-space characters.\n", charcount);
}
```

The action begins as it often has in past programs: the program reads a character and checks to see if it is the end-of-file character. Next comes something new, a statement using the logical "and" operator **&&.** We can translate the **if** statement thus: If the character is not a blank **AND** if it is not a newline character **AND** if it is not a tab character, then increase **charcount** by one.

Summary: Relational Operators and Expressions

Relational Operators:
Each of these operators compares the value at its left to the value at its right.

<	less than
<=	less than or equal to
==	equal to
>=	greater than or equal to
>	greater than
!=	unequal to

Relational Expressions:
A simple relational expression consists of a relational operator with an operand on each side. If the relation is true, the relational expression has the value 1. If the relation is false, the relational expression has the value 0.

Examples:
5 > 2 is true and has the value 1.
(2+a) == a is false and has the value 0.

All three conditions must be true if the whole expression is to be true. The logical operators have a lower priority than the relational operators, so it was not necessary to use additional parentheses to group the subexpressions.

There are three logical operators in C:

Operator	Meaning
&&	and
¦¦	or
!	not

Suppose **exp1** and **exp2** are two simple relational expressions like **cat > rat** or **debt == 1000.** Then we can state the following:

1. **exp1 && exp2** is true only if both **exp1** and **exp2** are true.
2. **exp1 ¦¦ exp2** is true if either or both of **exp1** and **exp2** are true.
3. **!exp1** is true if **exp1** is false and vice versa.

Here are some concrete examples:

```
5 > 2 && 4 > 7     is false because only one subexpression is true.
5 > 2 ¦¦ 4 > 7     is true because at least one of the subexpressions is true.
!(4 > 7)           is true because 4 is not greater than 7.
```

The last expression, incidentally, is equivalent to

```
4 <= 7.
```

If you are unfamiliar or uncomfortable with logical operators, remember that

```
(practice && time) == perfect
```

Priorities

The **!** operator has a very high priority, higher than multiplication, the same as the increment operators, and just below that of parentheses. The **&&** operator has higher priority than ¦¦, and both rank below the relational operators and above assignment in priority. Thus, the expression

```
a > b && b > c ¦¦ b > d
```

would be interpreted as

```
((a > b) && (b > c)) || (b > d)
```

That is, **b** is between **a** and **c,** or **b** is greater than **d.**

Order of Evaluation

Ordinarily C does not guarantee which parts of a complex expression will be evaluated first. For example, in the statement

```
apples = (5 + 3) * (9 + 6);
```

the expression **5 + 3** might be evaluated before **9 + 6** or it might be evaluated afterwards. (However, operator priorities do guarantee that both will be evaluated before the multiplication takes place.) This ambiguity was left in the language to enable compiler designers to make the most efficient choice for a particular system. The exception to this rule (or lack of rule) is the treatment of logical operators. C guarantees that logical expressions are evaluated from left to right. Furthermore, it guarantees that as soon as an element is found which invalidates the expression as a whole, the evaluation stops. These guarantees make it possible to use constructions such as:

```
while((c = getchar()) != EOF && c != '\n')
```

The first subexpression gives a value to **c** which then can be used in the second subexpression. Without the order guarantee, the computer might try to test the second expression before finding out what value **c** had.

Another example is:

```
if ( number != 0 && 12/number == 2)
    printf("The number is 5 or 6.\n");
```

If **number** has the value **0,** the expression is false, and the relational expression is not evaluated any further. This spares the computer the trauma of trying to divide by zero. Many languages do not have this feature. After seeing that **number** is 0, they still plunge ahead to check the next condition.

Now let's apply our understanding in two examples. Our first example is a handy one.

A Word-Count Program

Now we have the tools to make a word-counting program. (We may as well count characters and lines while we are at it.) The key point is to devise a way for the program to recognize a word. We will take a relatively simple approach and define a word as a sequence of characters that contains no white space. Thus, "glymxck" and "r2d2" are words. We will use a variable called **word** to keep track of whether or not we are in a word. When we

---

Summary: Logical Operators and Expressions

Logical Operators:
Logical operators normally take relational expressions as operands. The !
operator takes one operand. The rest take two, one to the left, one to the
right.

```
&&        and
¦¦        or
!         not
```

Logical Expressions:

expression1 && expression2   is true if and only if both expressions are
true.

expression1 ¦¦ expression2   is true if either one or both expressions are
true.

!expression   is true if the expression is false, and vice
versa.

Order of Evaluation:
Logical expressions are evaluated from left to right; evaluation stops as soon
as something is discovered that renders the expression false.

Examples:
```
6 > 2 && 3 == 3      is true.
! ( 6 > 2 && 3 ==3 ) is false.
x != 0 && 20/x < 5   the second expression is evaluated only if x is
                     nonzero.
```

encounter white space (a blank, tab, or newline), we will know we've
reached the end of a word. Then the next nonwhite-space character will
mark the start of a new word, and we can increment our word count by 1.
Here's the program:

```
#include <stdio.h>
#define YES 1
#define NO 0
main()
{
    int ch;         /* read-in character      */
    long nc = 0L;   /* number of characters   */
```

```
        int nl = 0;      /* number of lines        */
        int nw = 0;      /* number of words        */
        int word = NO;   /* ==YES if ch is in a word */

        while(( ch = getchar()) != EOF)
          {
          nc++;    /* count characters */
          if (ch == '\n')
          nl++;    /* count lines      */
          if( ch != ' ' && ch != '\n' && ch != '\t' && word == NO)
             {
             word = YES;  /* starting a new word */
             nw++;        /* count word          */
             }
          if(( ch == ' ' || ch == '\n' || ch == '\t') &&
             word == YES)
             word = NO;   /* reached end of word */
        }
          printf("characters = %ld, words = %d, lines = %d\n",
          nc,nw,nl);
     }
```

Since there are three different white-space characters, we had to use the logical operators to check for all three possibilities. Consider, for example, the line

```
    if( ch != ' ' && ch != '\n' && ch != '\t' && word == NO)
```

It says, "if **ch** is *not* a space and *not* a newline and *not* a tab, and if we are not in a word." (The first three conditions together ask if **ch** is not white space.) If all four conditions are met, then we must be starting a new word, and **nw** is incremented. If we are in the middle of a word, then the first three conditions hold, but **word** will be **YES**, and **nw** is not incremented. When we reach the next white-space character, we set **word** equal to **NO** again.

Check the coding to see whether or not the program gets confused if there are several spaces between one word and the next.

To run this program on a file, use redirection.

Character Sketches

Now let's look at something less utilitarian and more decorative. Our plan is to create a program with which you can draw rough, filled-in figures using characters. Each line of output consists of an unbroken row of characters. We choose the character and the length and position of the row. The program keeps reading our choices until it finds EOF. Figure 7.5 presents the program.

Suppose we call the executable program **sketcher.** To run the program, we type its name. Then we enter a character and two numbers. The program responds, we enter another set of data, and the program responds again until we provide an EOF signal. On a UNIX system an exchange could look like this:

```
% sketcher
B 10 20
            BBBBBBBBBBB
Y 12 18
              YYYYYYY
[control-d]
%
```

Figure 7.5
Character sketch program

```c
 /* sketcher */
/* this program makes solid figures */
#include <stdio.h>
#define MAXLENGTH 80
main()
{
   int ch;             /* character to be printed */
   int start, stop;    /* starting and stopping points */
   int count ;         /* position counter */

   while((ch = getchar()) != EOF) /* read in character */
     {
     if ( ch != '\n' && ch != ' ') /* skip newlines, spaces */
       {
       scanf("%d %d", &start, &stop); /* read limits */
       if( start  > stop||start < 1||stop > MAXLENGTH)
         printf("Inappropriate limits were entered.\n");
       else
         {
         count = 0;
         while (++count < start)
            putchar(' '); /* print blanks to starting point */
         while ( count++ <= stop)
            putchar(ch);  /* print char to stopping point */
         putchar('\n');   /* end line and start a new one  */
         }   /* end of else */
       }     /* end of ch if */
```

```
      }        /* end of while loop */
   }           /* end of main */
```

The program printed out the character **B** in columns 10 to 20, and it printed **Y** in columns 12 to 18. Unfortunately, when we use the program interactively, our commands are interspersed with the output. A much more satisfactory way to use the program is to create a file containing suitable data and then to use redirection to feed the file to the program. Suppose, for example, the file **fig** contains the following data:

```
_ 30 50
| 30 50
| 30 50
| 30 50
| 30 50
| 30 50
= 20 60
: 31 49
: 30 49
: 29 49
: 27 49
: 25 49
: 30 49
: 30 49
/ 30 49
: 35 48
: 35 48
```

Then the command **sketcher** < **fig** produces the output shown in Figure 7.6.

(Note: Printers and screens have different values for the vertical-to-horizontal ratio for characters, and this causes figures of this sort to look more compressed vertically when printed than when displayed on a screen.)

Analyzing the Program

This program is short, but it is more involved than the examples we have given before. Let's look at some of its elements.

Line Length—We limited the program to print no farther than the 80th column, since 80 characters is the standard width of many video monitors and of normal-width paper. However, you can redefine the value of **MAXLENGTH** if you wish to use the program with a device having a different output width.

Figure 7.6
Output of character sketch program

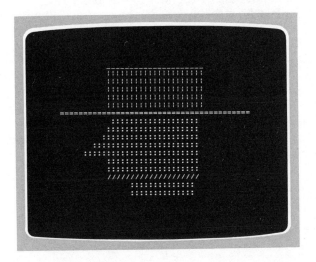

Program Structure—Our program has three **while** loops, one **if** statement, and one **if-else** statement. Let's see what each does.

```
while((ch = getchar()) != EOF)
```

The purpose of the first **while** loop is to allow us to read in several data sets. (Each data set consists of a character and of the two integers that indicate where the character is to be printed.) By reading the character first, we were able to combine reading the character with testing for EOF. If the EOF signal is found, then the program stops without trying to read values for **start** and **stop.** Otherwise, values for **start** and **stop** are read using **scanf( )**, and then the program processes them. That completes the loop. Then a new character is read, and the procedure is repeated.

Note that we used two statements, not one, to read in the data. Why didn't we just use a single statement?

```
scanf("%c %d %d", &ch, &start, &stop);
```

Suppose we had. Consider what happens when the program finishes reading the last line of data from a file. When the loop begins again, nothing remains to be read in the file. When **scanf( )** goes to read a value for **ch,** it encounters the end of file and assigns **EOF** to **ch.** Then it tries to read a value for **start,** but there is nothing left in the file to read! The computer belches forth a complaint, and your program dies ignominiously. By separating the character read from the rest, we gave the computer a chance to test for EOF *before* attempting to read further.

```
if (ch != '\n' && ch != ' ' )
```

The purpose of the first **if** statement is to make it easier to enter data. We explain how this works in the section following this one.

```
if ( start > stop || start < 1 || stop > MAXLENGTH)
    printf("Inappropriate limits were entered.\n");
else
```

The purpose of the **if-else** statement is to let the program skirt around values of **start** and **stop** that would lead to trouble. This, too, we will discuss later. Note, however, how we have used logical and relational operators to check for any one of three dangers.

CHIP `N´ DIP

The main body of the program consists of the compound statement that follows the **else.**

```
count = 0;
```

First, a counter called **count** is set to zero.

```
while (++count < start)
    putchar(' ');
```

Then a **while** loop starts printing blanks until the **start** position is reached. If **start** is, say, 10, then 9 spaces are printed. Thus, the character printing will start in the 10th column. Note how using the prefix form of the increment operator with the $<$ operator acts to yield this result. If we had used **count++** $<$ **start,** the comparison would have taken place before **count** was incremented, and one more space would have been permitted.

```
while ( count++ <= stop)
    putchar(ch);
```

The second **while** loop in this block performs the task of printing the character from the **start** column to the **stop** column. This time we used the postfix form and the $<=$ operator. This combination produces the desired result of printing the character up to and including the stop position. You can use logic or trial-and-error to verify this.

```
putchar('\n');
```

Finally, we use **putchar('\n')** to finish the line and start a new one.

Data Form—When we write a program, we need to understand how it is going to interact with the input data, so we will look into that now. We'll assume that buffered input is used.

The data used for input should be in a form compatible with the input functions used by the program. Here the burden is on the user to get the data in the right form. A more sophisticated program would shift more of that burden to the program itself. The clearest form for entering data is:

```
H 10 40
I 9 41
```

with the character followed by its starting column position and its stopping column position. But our program also accepts this form:

```
H
10
40
I
9
41
```

or this form:

```
H 10 40 I 9 41
```

and this, too:

```
H10 40I 9 41
```

Suppose, then, we type this sequence:

```
H10 40 [return]
I9  41 [return]
```

The **getchar( )** function reads the **H**. Then **scanf( )** reads the **10** and the **40**. That provides the data for one output line. But to enter the data, we must press the [return] key, and that generates a newline character. So the next time through the loop, **getchar( )** finds a newline character sitting there, and it assigns it to **ch**. Then **scanf( )** goes to read an integer, but the next item in the queue is the letter **I**. That stymies **scanf( )**. To avoid that problem, we added the **if** statement comparing **ch** to '\n'. If **ch** is the newline character, then the loop skips over to the next **getchar( )** so that **ch** becomes **I**, as intended. Similarly, the loop skips to the next **getchar( )** if **ch** is a space; that lets us input data in this format:

```
H 10 40 I 9 41 [return]
```

This way, after the program reads the **40**, **getchar( )** assigns a space to **ch**, the program skips over the rest of the loop, and **getchar( )** then assigns **I** to **ch**. Then **scanf( )** is allowed to read the next set of numbers.

Thus, that one **if** statement greatly adds to the program's flexibility in reading data.

If, however, we omit the line

```
if ( ch != '\n' && ch!= ' ')
```

from the program, only the last form of data entry would work. To say why this is so, we have to look into how **getchar( )** and **scanf( )** work.

The **getchar( )** function reads the first character it finds, whether it is an alphabetic character, a space, a newline, or whatever. The **scanf( )** function does the same if it is reading in the %c (character) format. But when **scanf( )** reads in the %d (integer) format, it skips over spaces and newlines. Thus, any spaces or newlines between the character read by **getchar( )** and the next integer read by **scanf( )** are ignored. Then **scanf( )** reads in digits until it runs into a nondigit, such as a space, newline, or alphabetic character. Hence we need a space or newline between the first and second integer so that **scanf( )** can tell when one ends and the next begins.

Error-Checking—The problem of getting the user to input data that the computer can use properly is a pervasive one. One technique is to use *error-checking*. This means having the computer check the data to see if it is okay before using it. We have included a beginning effort at error-checking in this program with the lines

```
if ( start > stop || start < 1 || stop > MAXLENGTH)
printf("Inappropriate limits were entered.\n");
```

This was part of an **if-else** structure which indicated that the main part of the program took place only if none of the **if** tests were true.

What were we protecting against? First, it makes no sense for the starting position to come after the final position; terminals normally print from left to right, not vice versa. So the expression **start > stop** checks for that possible error. Second, the first column on a screen is column 1; we can't write to the left of the left margin. The **start < 1** expression guards against making an error there. Finally, the expression **stop > MAXLENGTH** checks to see that we don't try to print past the right margin.

Are there any other erroneous values we could give to **start** and **stop**? Well, we could try to make **start** greater than **MAXLENGTH.** Would that pass our test? No. It is true that we don't check for this error directly. However, suppose **start** is greater than **MAXLENGTH.** Then, either **stop** is also greater then **MAXLENGTH**—in which case that error is caught—or else **stop** isn't greater than **MAXLENGTH.** But if **stop** is less than **MAXLENGTH,** it must also be less than **start,** so this case gets caught by the first test. Another possible error is that **stop** is less than 1. We leave it to you to make sure that this error doesn't sneak through, either.

We kept the test pretty simple. If you design a program for serious use, you should put more effort than we did into this part of the program. For instance, you should put in error messages to identify which values are wrong and why. And you could inject more personality into the messages. Here are some possibilities:

```
Your value of 897654 for stop exceeds the screen width.
Oh my! Your START is bigger than your STOP. Please try again.
THE START VALUE SHOULD BE BIGGER THAN 0, TURKEY.
```

The personality you inject, of course, is up to you.

Another potential input problem is having letters when **scanf( )** expects numbers. We'll look at some ways to handle that problem in Chapter 10.

The Conditional Operator: ?:

C offers a shorthand way to express one form of the **if-else** statement. It is called a *conditional expression* and uses the **?:** conditional operator. This is a two-part operator that has three operands. Here is an example that yields the absolute value of a number:

```
x = ( y < 0 ) ? -y : y;
```

Everything between the = and the semicolon is the conditional expression. The meaning of the statement is this: If **y** is less than zero, then **x =** −**y**; otherwise, **x = y.** In **if-else** terms:

```
if (y < 0)
    x = -y;
```

```
else
    x = y;
```

The general form of the conditional expression is

expression1 ? *expression 2* : *expression 3*

If expression1 is true (nonzero), then the whole conditional expression has the same value as expression2. If expression1 is false (0), the whole conditional expression has the same value as expression3.

You can use the conditional expression when you have a variable to which could be assigned two possible values. A typical example is setting a variable equal to the maximum of two values:

```
max = (a > b) ? a : b;
```

Conditional expressions are not necessary, since **if-else** statements can accomplish the same end. They are, however, more compact, and they usually lead to more compact machine language code.

Summary: The Conditional Operator

The Conditional Operator: ?:
This operator takes three operands, each of which is an expression. They are arranged this way: *expression1* ? *expression2* : *expression3*. The value of the whole expression equals the value of *expression2* if *expression1* is true, and equals the value of *expression3* otherwise.

Examples:

```
( 5 > 3 ) ? 1 : 2    has the value 1.
( 3 > 5 ) ? 1 : 2    has the value 2.
( a > b) ? a : b     has the value of the larger of a or b.
```

Multiple Choice: *switch* and *break*

The conditional operator and the **if-else** construction make it easy to write programs that choose between *two* alternatives. Sometimes, however, a program needs to choose one of *several* alternatives. We can do this by using **if-else if- . . . -else,** but in many cases it is more convenient to use the C **switch** statement. Here is an example showing how it works. This program reads in a letter, then responds by printing an animal name that begins with that letter.

Figure 7.7
Animal names program

```c
/* animals */
main()
{
  char ch;

  printf("Give me a letter of the alphabet, and I will give ");
  printf("an animal name\nbeginning with that letter.\n");
  printf("Please type in a letter; type a # to end my act.\n");
  while((ch = getchar()) != '#')
    {
    if (ch != '\n') /* skip over newline */
      {
      if ( ch >= 'a' && ch <= 'z') /* Lowercase only */
        switch (ch)
        {
        case 'a' :
              printf("argali, a wild sheep of Asia\n");
              break;
        case 'b' :
              printf("babirusa, a wild pig of Malay\n");
              break;
        case 'c' :
              printf("coati, racoonlike mammal\n");
              break;
        case 'd' :
              printf("desman, aquatic, molelike critter\n");
              break;
        case 'e' :
              printf("echidna, the spiny anteater\n");
              break;
        default :
              printf("That's a stumper!\n");
        }
      else
          printf("I only recognize lowercase letters.\n");
      printf("Please enter another letter or a #.\n");
      } /* end of skip newline if */
    } /* while loop end */
  }
```

We got a little lazy and stopped at "e." Let's look at a sample run before explaining the program further.

```
Give me a letter of the alphabet, and I will give an animal name
beginning with that letter.
Please type in a letter; type a # to end my act.
a [return]
argali, a wild sheep of Asia
Please enter another letter or a #.
d [return]
desman, aquatic, molelike critter
Please enter another letter or a #.
r [return]
That's a stumper!
Please enter another letter or a #.
Q [return]
I only recognize lowercase letters.
Please enter another letter or a #.
# [return]
```

This is how the **switch** statement works. The expression in the parentheses following the word **switch** is evaluated. In this case it has whatever value we last entered for **ch.** Then the program scans the list of "labels" (**case 'a' :, case 'b' :,** etc., in this instance) until it finds one that matches that value. The program then jumps to that line. What if there is no match? If there is a line labeled **default :,** the program jumps there. Otherwise, the program proceeds to the statement following the **switch.**

What about the **break** statement? It causes the program to break out of the **switch** and skip to the next statement after the switch. (See Figure 7.8.) Without the **break** statement, every statement from the matched label to the end of the **switch** would be processed. For example, if we removed all the **break** statements from our program, then ran the program using the letter **d,** we would get this exchange.

```
Give me a letter of the alphabet, and I will give an animal name
beginning with that letter.
Please type in a letter; type a # to end my act.
d [return]
desman, aquatic, molelike critter
echidna, the spiny anteater
That's a stumper!
Please enter another letter or a #.
# [return]
```

All the statements from **case 'd' :** to the end of the **switch** were executed.

Figure 7.8
Program flow in switches with and without breaks

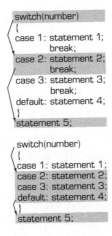

in each case, number has the value 2

If you are familiar with Pascal, you will recognize the **switch** statement as being similar to the Pascal **case** statement. The most important difference is that the **switch** statement requires the use of a **break** if you want only the labeled statement to be processed.

The **switch** labels must be integer-type (including **char**) constants or constant expressions (expressions containing only constants). You can't use a variable for a label. The expression in the parentheses should be one with an integer value (again, including type **char**). This, then, is the structure of a **switch:**

```
switch(integer expression)
    {
    case constant1 :
            statements; (optional)
    case constant2 :
            statements; (optional)
        ...
    default : (optional)
            statements; (optional)
    }
```

Summary: Multiple Choice with *switch*

Keyword: *switch*

General Comments:
Program control jumps to the statement bearing the value of *expression* as a label. Program flow then proceeds through the remaining statements unless redirected again. Both *expression* and labels must have integer values (type **char** is included), and the labels must be constants or expressions formed solely from constants. If no label matches the expression value, control goes to the statement labeled **default,** if present. Otherwise, control passes to the next statement following the **switch** statement.

Form:

```
switch ( expression )
    {
    case label1 : statement1
    case label2 : statement2
    default     : statement3
    }
```

There can be more than two labeled statements, and the **default** case is optional.

Example:

```
switch ( letter )
    {
    case 'a' :
    case 'e' : printf("%d is a vowel\n", letter);
    case 'c' :
    case 'n' : printf("%d is in \"cane\"\n", letter);
    default  : printf("Have a nice day.\n");
    }
```

If **letter** has the value 'a' or 'e', all three messages are printed; 'c' and 'n' cause the last two to be printed. Other values print just the last message.

We can use labels without statements when we want several labels to have the same result. For instance, the fragment

```
case 'F' :
case 'f' :
    printf(ferret, a weasellike mammal.\n);
    break;
```

would cause either **F** or **f** to trigger the printing of the ferret message. If **F** is entered, for example, the program jumps to that line. There are no statements there, so the program moves on until it reaches the **break.**

Our program has two other small features we wish to mention. First, since it is intended to be used interactively, we decided to use **#** instead of EOF as a stop signal. A computer innocent might feel baffled if asked to enter an EOF character or even a control character, but a **#** is pretty straightforward. Since this makes it unnecessary for the program to read an EOF, we don't have to declare **ch** to be type **int.** Second, we installed an **if** statement that causes the program to ignore newline characters when reading in characters. This, too, is a concession to the interactiveness of the program. Without this **if** statement, each time we press the [return] key, it would be processed as a character.

When should you use a **switch** and when should you use the **else-if** construction? Often you don't have a choice. You can't use a **switch** if your choice is based on evaluating a **float** variable or expression. Nor can you conveniently use a **switch** if a variable must fall into a certain range. It is simple to write

```
if (integer < 1000 && integer > 2 )
```

but covering this possibility with a **switch** would involve setting up case labels for each integer from 3 to 999. However, if you can use a **switch,** your program will run more efficiently.

The material here will let you tackle programs much more powerful and ambitious than those you worked with before. Just compare some of the examples in this chapter to those of the earlier chapters, and you will see the truth of that claim. But there is even more to learn, and that's why there are still a few more chapters for you to wander through.

What You Should Have Learned

How to choose between executing a statement or not: **if**
How to choose between two alternatives: **if-else**
How to choose among multiple alternatives: **else-if, switch**
The relational operators: >   >=   ==   <=   <   !=
The logical operators: **&& || !**
The conditional operator: **?:**

Review Questions

1. Determine which expressions are true and which are false.
   a. 100 > 3
   b. 'a' > 'c'
   c. 100 > 3 && 'a' > 'c'
   d. 100 > 3 || 'a' > 'c'
   e. !(100 > 3)

2. Construct an expression to express the following conditions.
   a. **number** is equal to or greater than 1 but smaller than 9.
   b. **ch** is not a **q** or a **k.**
   c. **number** is between 1 and 9 but is not a 5.
   d. **number** is not between 1 and 9.

3. The following program has unnecessarily complex relational expressions as well as some outright errors. Simplify and correct it.

```
main()                                             /* 1 */
{                                                  /* 2 */
  int weight, height; /*weight in lbs, height in inches */
                                                   /* 4 */
  scanf("%d, weight, height);                      /* 5 */
  if ( weight < 100)                               /* 6 */
    if ( height >= 72 )                            /* 7 */
      printf("You are very tall for your weight.\n");
    else if ( height < 72 && > 64)                 /* 9 */
      printf( "You are tall for your weight.\n");
  else if ( weight > 300 && !(weight <= 300) )     /* 11 */
    if ( !(height >= 48)                           /* 12 */
        printf( " You are quite short for your weight.\n");
  else                                             /* 14 */
    printf("Your weight is ideal.\n");             /* 15 */
                                                   /* 16 */
}
```

4. Write a program that prints this message:

   GUESS MY SECRET INTEGER!

   Have the program read the user's answer. As long as the user fails to guess the number 2001, have the program respond by displaying

   WRONG! GUESS AGAIN

   and then reading the next guess. When the user guesses correctly, have the program congratulate the user, say goodbye, and end.

5. What is the numerical value of each of the following expressions?
   a. 5 > 2
   b. 3+4 > 2 && 3 < 2
   c. x >= y || y > x

d. d = 5 + (6 > 2)

e. 'X' > 'T' ? 10 : 5

f. x > y ? y > x : x > y

6. What would the following program print?

```
main()
{
    int i = 0;
    while ( i < 3) {
        switch(i++) {
            case 0 : printf("Merry);
            case 1 : printf("Merr");
            case 2 : printf("Mer");
            default: printf("Oh no!");
            }
        putchar('\n');
        }
}
```

7. Using **if-else** statements, write a program that reads input up to **EOF**, replaces each period with an exclamation mark, replaces each exclamation mark initially present with two exclamation marks, and reports at the end the number of substitutions it has made.

8. Redo Question 7, but use a **switch**.

Answers

1. True: a, d

2. **a. number >= 1 && number < 9**

   b. ch != 'q' && ch != 'k'
   Note: **ch != 'q' ¦¦ ch != 'k'** would always be true, for if **ch** was a **q** then it couldn't be **k.** So the second alternative would be true, making the whole "or" combination true.

   c. number > 1 && number < 9 && number != 5

   d. !(number > 1 && number < 9)
   or
   number <= 1 ¦¦ number >= 9
   Note: saying that a number *isn't* between 1 and 9 is the same as saying that it *is* equal to or less than 1 or equal to or greater than 9. The second form is more awkward as words but slightly simpler as an expression.

3. Line 5: Should be **scanf("%d %d", &weight, &height);**. Don't forget those **&**s for **scanf( )**. Also this line should be preceded by a line prompting input.
   Line 9: What is meant is **(height < 72 && height > 64)**. However, the first part of the expression is unnecessary, since **height** must be less than **72**

for the **else-if** to be reached in the first place. Thus, a simple **(height > 64)** will serve.

Line 11: the condition is redundant; the second subexpression (**weight** not less than or equal to 300) means the same as the first. A simple (**weight > 300)** is all that is needed. But there is more trouble. Line 11 gets attached to the wrong **if!** Clearly this **else** is meant to go along with line 6. By the most recent **if not** rule, however, it will be associated with the **if** of line 9. Thus, line 11 is reached when **weight** is less than 100 and **height** is 64 or under. This makes it impossible for **weight** to exceed 300 when this statement is reached.

Lines 7 through 9: Should be enclosed in braces. Then line 11 will become an alternative to line 6, not to line 9.

Line 12: Simplify the expression to (**height < 48**).

Line 14: This **else** associates with the last **if,** the one on line 12. Enclose lines 12 and 13 in braces to force this **else** to associate with the **if** of line 11. Note that the final message is printed only for those weighing between 100 and 300 pounds.

4. Here is one possibility.

```
#define SECNUM 2001
main()
{
    int num;

    printf("GUESS MY SECRET INTEGER!\n");
    scanf("%d",&num);
    while ( num != SECNUM) {
        printf("WRONG! GUESS AGAIN\n");
        scanf("%d",&num);
        }
    printf("That's it! Congratulations and goodbye!\n");
}
```

5. a. 1. The assertion is true, which numerically is a **1.**

b. 0. 3 is not less than 2.

c. 1. If the first expression is false, the second is true, and vice versa; just one true expression is needed.

d. 6. The relational expression is true, or 1.

e. 10. 'X' is greater than 'T', so the first alternative is chosen.

f. 0. If **x > y** is true, then the first alternative, **y > x**, is chosen. But in that case, **y > x** is false, or **0.** Now suppose **x > y** is false. Then the second alternative, **x > y**, is chosen. In this case that alternative is false, or **0.**

6. Here's what is printed:

```
MerryMerrMerOh no!
MerrMerOh no!
MerOh no!
```

Note that the **switch** contained no **break** statements, so when **i** is **0**, all the choices are printed. Also note that **i** is incremented *after* it is used to select a case.

7. Here is one possibility:

```c
/* adman1.c -- hyperbole program */
#include <stdio.h>
main()
{
   int ch;
   int subs =0;
   while ( (ch = getchar() ) != EOF)
       if ( ch == '.')
           {
           putchar('!');
           subs++;
           }
       else if (ch == '!')
           {
           putchar('!');
           putchar('!');
           subs++;
           }
       else
           putchar(ch);
   printf("There were %d substitutions.\n", subs);
}
```

8. Here is one possibility. Note that we made use of how a **switch** can "fall through" to the next **case** in the absence of a **break**.

```c
#include <stdio.h>
main()
{
   int ch;
   int subs = 0;
   while ( (ch = getchar() ) != EOF)
      switch(ch)
         {
         case '!' : putchar('!');
         case '.' : putchar('!');
                    subs++;
                    break;
         default  : putchar(ch);
         }
   printf("There were %d substitutions.\n", subs);
}
```

Exercises

1. Write a program that reads input until encountering **EOF** and that reports back:
   a. The number of spaces read
   b. The number of newline characters read
   c. The total number of all other characters read

2. Write a program that reads input until encountering **EOF**. Have the program print out each input character and its ASCII decimal code. Print eight character-code pairs per line. Suggestion: use a character count and the **modulus operator (%)** to print a newline character every eight cycles of the loop.

3. Write a program that reads input up to **EOF** and reports back the number of times that the sequence **ei** occurs. Note: the program will have to "remember" the preceding character as well as the current character. Test it with input like "Receive your eieio award."

4. Write a program that requests the hours worked in a week and then prints the gross pay, the taxes, and the net pay. Assume the following:
   a. Basic pay rate = $10.00/hr
   b. Overtime (in excess of 40 hours) = time and a half
   c. Tax rate = 15% of the first $300
          20% of the next $150
          25% of the rest

   Use #defined constants, and don't worry if the example does not conform to current tax law.

5. Modify assumption **a** in Exercise 4 so that the program presents a menu of pay rates to choose from. Use a switch to select the pay rate. The beginning of a run should look something like this:

```
********************************************************************
Enter the number corresponding to the desired pay rate or action:
1) $8.75/hr                          2) $9.33/hr
3) $10.00/hr                         4) $11.20/hr
5) quit
********************************************************************
```

   If choices **1-4** are selected, then the program should request the hours worked. The program should recycle until **5** is entered. If something other than choices **1-5** is entered, the program should remind the user what the proper choices are, and then recycle. Use #defined constants.

8

Loops and Other
Control Aids

Concepts
- Looping
- Nested loops
- Making program jumps
- Using loops with arrays

Keywords
- *while, do, for, break, continue, goto*

Operators
- += −= *= /= %= ,

As you tackle more complex tasks, the flow of your programs becomes more involved. You need structures and statements to control and organize the workings of these programs. C provides you with valuable tools to meet this need. Already we have seen how useful the **while** loop is when we need to repeat an action several times. C provides two more loop structures: the **for** loop and the **do . . . while** loop. In this chapter we will explore the workings of these control structures and explain how to make the best use of each. We will discuss **break, continue, goto,** and the comma operator, all of which can be used to control the flow of a program. Also, we will talk a bit more about arrays, which are often used with loops.

The *while* Loop

We have used the **while** loop extensively, but let us review it with a simple, perhaps simple-minded, program to guess a number.

```
    /* numguess1 */
/* an inefficient number-guesser */
#include <stdio.h>
main()
{
   int guess = 1;
   char response;

   printf("Pick an integer from 1 to 100. I will try to guess ");
   printf("it.\nRespond with a y if my guess is right and");
```

```
        printf("\nwith an n if it is wrong.\n");
        printf("Uh...is your number %d?\n", guess);
        while((response = getchar()) != 'y')          /* get response */
           if( response != '\n')               /* ignore newline character */
              printf("Well, then, is it %d?\n", ++guess);
        printf("I knew I could do it!\n");
}
```

Note the logic. If you respond with a **y,** the program quits the loop and goes to the final print statement. The program asks you to respond with an **n** if the guess is wrong, but in fact any response other than **y** sends the program through the loop. However, if the character is a newline character, the effect of the loop is to do nothing. Any other character causes the next larger integer to be guessed. (What would happen if we had used **guess++** instead of **++guess?**)

The **if(response != '\n')** portion tells the program to ignore the extraneous newline character that is transmitted when you use the [enter] key.

This **while** loop did not require braces because the two-line **if** statement counts as a single statement.

You probably noticed that this is a rather dumb program. It is written in proper C and gets the job done, but its approach is very inefficient. This example illustrates that correctness is not the only criterion by which to judge a program. Efficiency, too, is important. We'll come back to this program later and try to spiff it up a bit.

The general form of the **while** loop is

```
while( expression )
     statement
```

Our examples have used relational expressions for the expression part, but

Figure 8.1
Structure of the *while* loop

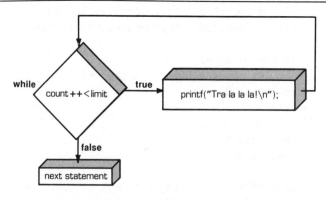

the expression can be of any sort. The statement part can be a simple statement with a terminating semicolon or it can be a compound statement enclosed in braces. If the expression is true (or, more generally, nonzero), the statement is executed once, and then the expression is tested again. This cycle of test and execution is repeated until the expression becomes false (or, more generally, zero). Each cycle is called an *iteration*. The structure is very similar to that of an **if** statement. The chief difference is that in an **if** statement, the test and (possibly) the execution are done just once; but in the **while** loop, the test and execution may be repeated several times.

Terminating a *while* Loop

Here is a CRUCIAL point about **while** loops. When you construct a **while** loop, it must include something that changes the value of the test expression so that the expression eventually becomes false. Otherwise, the loop will never terminate. Consider this example:

```
index = 1;
 while ( index < 5 )
    printf("Good morning!\n");
```

This fragment prints its cheerful message indefinitely, for nothing in the loop changes the value of **index** from its initial value of 1.

```
index = 1;
 while ( --index < 5 )
    printf("How are the old atoms vibrating!\n");
```

This fragment isn't much better. It changes the value of **index,** but in the wrong direction! At least this version will terminate eventually when **index** drops below the most negative number the system can handle.

The **while** loop is a *conditional* loop using an *entry condition*. It is called conditional because the execution of the statement portion depends on the condition we describe through the expression portion. Is **index** less than 5? Is the last character read the EOF signal? The expression forms an entry condition because the condition must be met *before* the body of the loop is entered. In a situation like the following, the body of the loop is never entered because the condition is false to begin with.

```
index = 10;
   while ( index++ < 5)
      printf("Have a fair day or better.\n");
```

Change the first line to

```
index = 3;
```

and you have a working program.

Algorithms and Pseudocode

Okay, let's return to our dim-witted number-guessing program. The fault with this program is not in the programming per se, but in the *algorithm*—that is, the method used to guess the number. We can represent the method this way:

> ask user to choose a number
>
> computer guesses 1
>
> while guess is wrong, increase guess by 1

This, incidentally, is an example of *pseudocode,* which is the art of expressing a program in simple English that parallels the forms of a computer language. Pseudocode is useful for working out the logic of a program. Once the logic seems right, you then can attend to the details of translating the pseudocode to the actual programming code. The advantage of pseudocode is that it lets you concentrate on the logic and organization of a program while sparing you the effort of simultaneously worrying how to express the ideas in a computer language.

If we want to improve the program, we need to improve the algorithm. One method is to choose a number halfway between 1 and 100 (50 is close enough) and to have the user reply whether the guess is high, low, or correct. If the user replies that the guess is too high, that immediately eliminates all the numbers from 50 to 100. The program's next guess would be a number halfway between 1 and 49. Again, a high or low answer would eliminate half the remaining choices, and by continuing the process, the program rapidly narrows the choices until the correct number is guessed. Let's put that into pseudocode. We'll let **highest** stand for the highest possible value the number could have and **lowest** stand for the lowest possible value. Initially these will be 100 and 1, respectively, so we can start there.

> set **highest** to **100**
>
> set **lowest** to **1**
>
> ask user to choose a number
>
> guess (**highest** + **lowest**)/2
>
> while guess is wrong, do the following:
>
>   { if guess is high, set **highest** to old guess minus 1
>
>   if guess is low, set **lowest** to old guess plus 1
>
>   new guess is (**highest** + **lowest**)/2 }

Note the logic: If the first guess of 50 is high, then the highest possible value the number could have is 49. If 50 is too low, then the lowest possible value is 51.

Now we will convert this approach to C. Figure 8.2 presents the program.

Figure 8.2
Number-guessing program

```
   /* numguess2 */
/* a better number-guesser */
#include <stdio.h>
#define HIGH 100
#define LOW  1
main()
{
   int guess = (HIGH + LOW)/2;
   int highest = HIGH;
   int lowest = LOW;
   char response;

   printf("Pick an integer from %d to %d.  I will try ",LOW,HIGH);
   printf("to guess it.\nRespond with a y if my guess is right,");
   printf("with an h if it\nis high, and with an l if my");
   printf("guess is low.\n");
   printf("Uh...is your number %d?\n", guess);
   while((response = getchar()) != 'y')
      {
      if ( response != '\n')
          {
          if (response == 'h')
           {  /* reduce upper limit if guess is too high */
          highest = guess - 1;
          guess = (highest + lowest)/2;
          printf("Too high, huh. Is your number %d?\n", guess);
          }
      else if (response == 'l')
          { /* increase lower limit if guess is too low */
          lowest = guess + 1;
          guess = (highest + lowest)/2;
          printf("Too low, huh. Is your number %d?\n", guess);
          }
      else
          {  /* guide user to correct response   */
          printf("I don't understand; please type a y, h,");
          printf("or l.\n");
          }
      }
```

```
    }
  printf("I knew I could do it!\n");
}
```

The final **else** gives the user another chance to reply whenever he or she makes a nonstandard response. Also, notice that we used symbolic constants to make it simple to change the range.

Does the program work? Here is a sample run. Our number is 71.

```
Pick an integer from 1 to 100.  I will try to guess it.
Respond with a y if my guess is right, with an h if it
is high, and with an l if my guess is low.
Uh...is your number 50?
 n
I don't understand; please type a y, h, or l.
 l
Too low, huh. Is your number 75?
 h
Too high, huh. Is your number 62?
 l
Too low, huh. Is your number 68?
 l
Too low, huh. Is your number 71?
 y
I knew I could do it!
```

Can anything go wrong with this program? We've protected it against people typing unwanted characters, so that shouldn't be a problem. The one thing that can mess it up is someone typing an **h** when he means **l,** or vice versa. Unfortunately there is no way to make the user truthful and error-free. However, there are some steps you can take if you are sufficiently interested. (You may, for example, desire to distract your six-year-old niece.) First, notice that our approach needs at most seven guesses to get any number. (Each guess cuts the possibilities in half. Seven guesses cover 2^7-1, or 127, possibilities, enough to handle the hundred numbers.) You can alter the program so that it counts the number of guesses. If the count exceeds 7, you can print out a complaining message, then reset **highest, lowest,** and the count to their original values. Other changes you could make are to modify the **if** statements so they accept both upper- and lowercase letters.

Our last example of a **while** loop uses an indefinite condition; we don't know in advance how many times the loop will be executed before the expression becomes false. Many of our examples, however, have used **while** loops to count out a definite number of repetitions. Here is a short example of a **while** counting loop:

Summary: The *while* Statement

Keyword: *while*

General Comments:
The **while** statement creates a loop that repeats until the test *expression* becomes false, or zero. The **while** statement is an *entry-condition* loop; the decision to go through one more pass of the loop is made *before* the loop is traversed. Thus, it is possible that the loop is never traversed. The *statement* part of the form can be a simple statement or a compound statement.

Form:

```
while ( expression )
        statement
```

The *statement* portion is repeated until the *expression* becomes false or zero.

Examples:

```
while ( n++ < 100 )
        printf(" %d %d\n",n, 2*n+1 );

while ( fargo < 1000 )
        {
        fargo = fargo + step;
        step = 2 * step;
        }
```

```
count = 1;                              /* initialization */
   while ( count <= NUMBER )            /* test           */
     {
     printf("Be my Valentine!\n");      /* action         */
     count++;                           /* increment count */
     }
```

Although this form works fine, it is not the best form for this type of situation, since the actions defining the loop are not all gathered together. Let's elaborate on that point.

Three actions are involved in setting up a loop that is to be repeated a fixed number of times. A counter must be initialized, compared with some limiting number, and incremented each time the loop is traversed. The **while** loop condition takes care of the comparison. The increment operator takes care of the incrementation. As we have done elsewhere, we can combine these two actions into one expression by using **count++ <= NUMBER**. But the initialization of the counter is done outside the loop, as in our statement **count = 1;**. This makes it possible to forget to initialize a counter, and what *might* happen *will* happen eventually. Let's look at a control statement that avoids these problems.

The *for* Loop

The **for** loop gathers all three actions into one place. By using a **for** loop, we can replace the preceding fragment with one statement:

```
for( count = 1; count <= NUMBER; count++)
    printf("Be my Valentine!\n");
```

The parentheses contain three expressions separated by semicolons. The first expression is an initialization. It is done just once, when the **for** loop first starts. The second expression is a test condition; it is evaluated before each potential execution of a loop. When the expression is false (when count is greater than number), the loop is terminated. The third expression is evaluated at the end of each loop. We have used it to increment the value of **count,** but it needn't be restricted to that use. The **for** statement is completed by following it with a simple or compound statement. Figure 8.3 summarizes the structure of a **for** loop.

Figure 8.3
Structure of a *for* loop

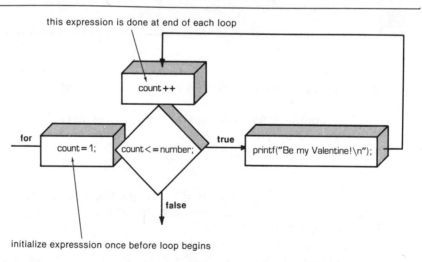

Here we use a **for** loop in a program that prints a table of cubes:

```
/* forcubed */
main()
{
  int num;
  printf(" n    n cubed\n");
  for ( num = 1; num <= 6; num++)
     printf("%5d %5d\n", num, num*num*num);
}
```

This prints the integers 1 through 6 and their cubes:

```
n  n cubed
1    1
2    8
3    27
4    64
5   125
6   216
```

Looking at the first line of the **for** loop tells us immediately all the information about the loop parameters: the starting value of **num,** the final value of **num,** and the amount that **num** increases each looping.

One common use of a **for** loop is to have the computer mark time, slowing its responses down to human levels.

```
for( n = 1; n <= 10000; n++)
    ;
```

This loop has the computer count to 10000. The lone semicolon on the second line tells us that nothing else is done in the loop. We can think of a solitary semicolon as a *null* statement, a statement that does nothing.

Using *for* for Flexibility!

Although the **for** loop looks similar to the FORTRAN DO loop, the Pascal FOR loop, and the BASIC FOR . . . NEXT loop, it is much more flexible than any of these. This flexibility stems from how the three expressions in a **for** specification can be used. So far we have used the first expression to initialize a counter, the second expression to express the limit for the counter, and the third expression to increase the counter by 1. When used this way, the C **for** statement is very much like the others we have mentioned. But there are many other possibilities, and here we will show you nine variations.

1. You can use the decrement operator to count down instead of to count up.

```
for ( n = 10; n > 0; n--)
      printf("%d seconds!\n", n);
printf("We have ignition!\n");
```

2. You can count by twos, tens, etc., if you want.

```
for ( n = 2;  n < 60; n = n + 13)
      printf( "%d \n", n);
```

This would increase **n** by 13 each cycle, printing the digits 2, 15, 28, 41, and 54.

Incidentally, C offers a shorthand notation for incrementing a variable by a fixed amount. Instead of

```
n = n + 13
```

we can use

```
n += 13
```

The += is the *additive assignment operator,* and it adds whatever expression is at its right to the variable name at its left. See the box on page 220 for more details.

3. You can count by characters instead of by numbers.

```
for ( ch = 'a'; ch <= 'z'; ch++)
      printf("The ASCII value for %c is %d.\n", ch, ch);
```

This program will print out the letters **a** through **z** along with their ASCII values. It works because characters are stored as integers, so this fragment really counts by integers anyway.

4. You can test some condition other than the number of iterations. In our **forcubed** program we can replace

```
for ( num = 1; num <= 6; num++)
```

by

```
for (num = 1; num*num*num <= 216; num++)
```

We would do this if we were more concerned with limiting the size of the cube than in limiting the number of iterations.

5.   You can let a quantity increase geometrically instead of arithmetically; that is, instead of adding a fixed amount each time, you can multiply by a fixed amount.

```
for ( debt = 100.0; debt < 150.0; debt = debt*1.1 )
    printf("Your debt is now $%.2f.\n", debt);
```

This program fragment multiplies **debt** by 1.1 each cycle, increasing it by 10%. The output looks like this:

```
Your debt is now $100.00.
Your debt is now $110.00.
Your debt is now $121.00.
Your debt is now $133.10.
Your debt is now $146.41.
```

As you may have guessed, there is a shorthand notation for multiplying **debt** by 1.1. We could have used the expression

```
debt *= 1.1
```

to accomplish that multiplication. The *=* operator is the *multiplicative assignment operator,* and it multiplies the variable to its left by whatever is to its right. (See the box on page 220.)

6.   You can use any legal expression you want for the third expression. Whatever you put in will be updated each iteration.

```
y = 55;
for ( x = 1; y <= 75; y = ++x*5 + 50)
    printf("%10d %10d\n", x, y);
```

This fragment prints out the values of **x** and of the algebraic expression **5*x + 50**. The output would look like this:

```
1          55
2          60
3          65
4          70
5          75
```

Notice that the test involved **y** and not **x.** Each of the three expressions in the **for** loop control can use different variables.

Although this example is valid, it does not show good style. The program would be clearer if we didn't mix the updating process with an algebraic calculation.

7. You can even leave one or more expressions blank (but don't omit the semicolons). Just be sure to include within the loop itself some statement that will eventually cause the loop to terminate.

```
ans = 2;
for (n = 3; ans <= 25; )
    ans = ans*n;
```

This loop will keep the value of **n** at 3. The variable **ans** will start with the value 2, then increase to 6, 18, and obtain a final value of 54. (The value 18 is less than 25, so the **for** loop goes through one more iteration, multiplying 18 by 3 to get 54.)

The loop

```
for( ; ; )
    printf("I want some action\n");
```

goes on forever, since an empty test is considered to be true.

8. The first expression need not initialize a variable. It could, instead, be a **printf( )** statement of some sort. Just remember that the first expression is evaluated or executed just once, before any other parts of the loop are executed.

```
for ( printf("Keep entering numbers!\n"); num != 6;  )
        scanf("%d", num);
printf("That's the one I want!\n");
```

This fragment prints the first message once, then keeps accepting numbers until you enter a 6.

9. The parameters of the loop expressions can be altered by actions within the loop. For example, suppose you have the loop set up like this:

```
for(n = 1; n < 10000; n += delta)
```

If after a few iterations your program decided **delta** was too small or too large, an **if** statement inside the loop could change the size of **delta.** In an interactive program, **delta** could be changed by the user as the loop was working.

In short, the freedom you have in selecting the expressions that control a **for** loop makes this loop able to do much more than just perform a fixed number of iterations. The power of the **for** loop is enhanced further by the operators we will discuss shortly.

Summary: The *for* Statement

Keyword: *for*

General Comments:
The **for** statement uses three control expressions, separated by semicolons, to control a looping process. The *initialize* expression is executed once, before any of the loop statements are executed. If the **test** expression is true (or nonzero), the loop is cycled through once. Then the **update** expression is evaluated, and it is time to check the **test** expression again. The **for** statement is an *entry-condition* loop; the decision to go through one more pass of the loop is made *before* the loop is traversed. Thus, it is possible that the loop is never traversed. The *statement* part of the form can be a simple statement or a compound statement.

Form:
```
for ( initialize ; test ; update )
        statement
```
The loop is repeated until *test* becomes false or zero.

Example:
```
for ( n = 0;  n < 10 ; n++ )
        printf(" %d %d\n", n, 2*n+1 );
```

The Comma Operator

The comma operator extends the flexibility of the **for** loop by allowing you to include more than one initialization or update in a **for** loop specification. For example, here is a program that prints out first class postage rates. (At the time of this writing, the rate is 22 cents for the first ounce and 17 cents for each additional ounce.)

More Assignment Operators: $+=$, $-=$, $*=$, $/=$, $\%=$

Some time ago we mentioned that C had several assignment operators. The most basic one, of course, is $=$, which simply assigns the value of the expression at its right to the variable at its left. The other assignment operators update variables. Each is used with a variable name at its left and an expression at its right. The variable is assigned a new value equal to its old value adjusted by the value of the expression at the right. The exact adjustment depends on the operator. For example:

```
scores += 20    is the same as   scores = scores + 20
dimes -= 2      is the same as   dimes = dimes - 2
bunnies *= 2    is the same as   bunnies = bunnies * 2
time /= 2.73    is the same as   time = time / 2.73
reduce %= 3     is the same as   reduce = reduce % 3
```

We used simple numbers on the right, but we could have used more elaborate expressions:

```
x *= 3*y + 12    is the same as   x = x * (3*y + 12)
```

These assignment operators have the same low priority that $=$ does, i.e., less than that of $+$ or $*$. This is reflected in the last example.

You are not required to use these forms. They are, however, more compact, and they usually produce more efficient machine code than the longer form. They are particularly useful if you are trying to squeeze something into a **for** loop specification.

```
/* postalrates */
#define FIRST 22
#define NEXT  17
main()
{
    int ounces, cost;


    printf(" ounces  cost\n");
    for(ounces=1, cost=FIRST; ounces<= 16; ounces++, cost += NEXT)
        printf("%5d %7d\n", ounces, cost);
}
```

The first four lines of output look like this:

```
ounces  cost
   1     22
   2     39
   3     56
```

We used the comma operator in the first and the third expressions. Its presence in the first expression causes **ounces** *and* **cost** to be initialized. Its second occurrence causes **ounces** to be increased by 1 and **cost** to be increased by 17 (the value of **NEXT**) each iteration. All the calculations are done in the **for** loop specifications.

Figure 8.4
The comma operator and the *for* loop

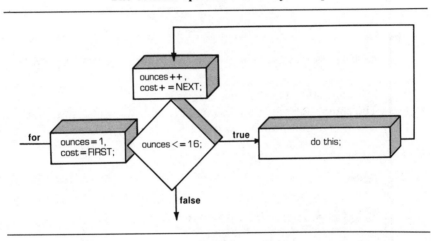

The comma operator is not restricted to **for** loops, but that is where it is most often used. The operator has one further property: it guarantees that the expressions it separates will be evaluated in a left-to-right order. Thus, **ounces** is initialized before **cost**. That is not important for this example, but it would be important if the expression for **cost** contained **ounces**.

The comma also is used as a separator. Thus, the commas in

```
char ch, date;
```

and

```
printf("%d %d\n", chimps, chumps);
```

are separators, not comma operators.

Summary: Our New Operators

Assignment Operators:
Each of these operators updates the variable at its left by the value at its right, using the indicated operation. We use r-h for right-hand, and l-h for left-hand.

```
+=   Adds the r-h quantity to the l-h variable.
-=   Subtracts the r-h quantity from the l-h variable.
*=   Multiplies the l-h variable by the r-h quantity.
/=   Divides the l-h variable by the r-h quantity.
%=   Gives the remainder from dividing the l-h variable by the r-h quantity.
```

Example:

```
rabbits *= 1.6;   is the same as   rabbits = rabbits * 1.6;
```

Miscellaneous: The Comma Operator
The comma operator links two expressions into one and guarantees that the left-most expression is evaluated first. It is typically used to include more information in a **for** loop control expression.

Example:

```
for ( step = 2, fargo = 0; fargo < 1000; step *= 2)
        fargo += step;
```

Zeno Meets the *for* Loop

Let's see how the comma operator can help solve an old paradox. The Greek philosopher Zeno once argued that an arrow will never reach its target. First, he said, the arrow covers half the distance to the target. Then it has to cover half of the remaining distance. Then it still has half of what's left to cover, ad infinitum. Since the journey has an infinite number of parts, Zeno argued, it would take the arrow an infinite amount of time to reach its journey's end. We doubt, however, that Zeno would have volunteered to be a target just on the strength of this argument.

Let's take a quantitative approach and suppose that it takes the arrow 1 second to travel the first half. Then it would take 1/2 second to travel half of what was left, 1/4 second to travel half of what was left next, etc.

We can represent the total time by the infinite series $1+1/2+1/4+1/8+1/16+\ldots$.

We can write a short program to find the sum of the first few terms.

```
/* zeno */
#define LIMIT 15
main()
{
 int count;
 float time, x;

 for(time=0.0, x=1.0, count=1; count <= LIMIT; count++, x *= 2.0)
    {
    time += 1.0/x;
    printf("time = %f when count = %d.\n", time, count);
    }
}
```

This gives the sum of the first 15 terms:

```
time = 1.000000 when count = 1.
time = 1.500000 when count = 2.
time = 1.750000 when count = 3.
time = 1.875000 when count = 4.
time = 1.937500 when count = 5.
time = 1.968750 when count = 6.
time = 1.984375 when count = 7.
time = 1.992188 when count = 8.
time = 1.996094 when count = 9.
time = 1.998047 when count = 10.
time = 1.999023 when count = 11.
time = 1.999512 when count = 12.
time = 1.999756 when count = 13.
time = 1.999878 when count = 14.
time = 1.999939 when count = 15.
```

We can see that although we keep adding more terms, the total seems to level out. Indeed, mathematicians have proven that the total approaches 2.0 as the number of terms approaches infinity, just as our program suggests. Thank heavens, for if Zeno were right, motion would be impossible. (But if motion were impossible, there would be no Zeno.)

What about the program itself? It shows that we can use more than one comma operator in an expression. We initialized **time, x,** and **count.** Once we set up the conditions for the loop, the program itself is extremely brief.

An Exit-Condition Loop: *do while*

The **while** loop and the **for** loop are both entry-condition loops. The test condition is checked before each iteration of the loop. C also has an *exit-condition* loop in which the condition is checked after each iteration of the loop. This variety is a **do while** loop and looks like this:

```
do
    {
    ch = getchar();
    putchar(ch);
    } while (ch != '\n');
```

How does this differ from, say,

```
while ((ch = getchar()) != '\n')
    putchar(ch);
```

The difference comes when the newline character is read. The **while** loop prints out all the characters *up to* the first newline character, and the **do while** loop prints out all the characters *up to and including* the newline character. Only after it has printed the newline character does the loop check to see if a newline character has shown up. In a **do while** loop that action comes before the test condition.

The general form of the **do while** loop is:

```
do
    statement
        while ( expression );
```

The statement can be simple or compound.

A **do while** loop always is executed at least once, since the test is made after the body of the loop is executed. A **for** loop or a **while** loop, on the other hand, may be executed zero times, since the test is made before execution. You should restrict the use of **do while** loops to cases that require at least one iteration. For instance, we could have used a **do while** loop for our number-guessing programs. In pseudocode we could structure the program this way:

```
do
    {
    make a guess
    get a response of y, h, or l
    } while ( response isn't y )
```

Figure 8.5
Structure of a *do while* loop

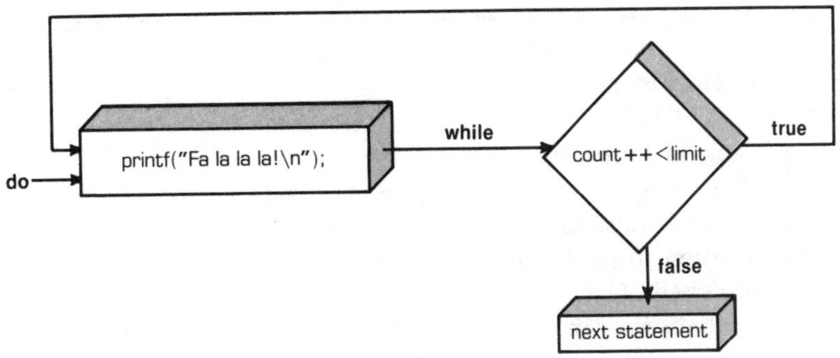

You should avoid a **do while** structure of the type shown in the following pseudocode:

    ask user if he or she wants to continue
    do
        some clever stuff
        while (answer is yes)

Here, after the user answers "no," some clever stuff gets done anyway because the test comes too late.

Which Loop?

Once you decide you need a loop, which one should you use? First, decide whether you need an entry-condition loop or an exit-condition loop. Your answer should usually be an entry-condition loop. Kernighan and Ritchie (*The C Programming Language,* Englewood Cliffs: Prentice-Hall, 1978) estimate that the exit-condition loop (**do while**) is needed for about 5% of loops. There are several reasons why computer scientists consider an entry-condition loop superior. One is the general principle that it is better to look before you leap (or loop) than after. A second is that a program is easier to read if the loop test is found at the beginning of the loop. Finally, in many uses, it is important that the loop be skipped entirely if the test is not initially met.

Assume you need an entry-condition loop. Should it be a **for** or a **while?** This is partly a matter of taste, since what you can do with one, you can do with the other. To make a **for** like a **while,** you can omit the first and third expressions:

Summary: The *do while* Statement

Keywords: *do, while*

General Comments:

The **do while** statement creates a loop that repeats until the test *expression* becomes false or zero. The **do while** statement is an *exit-condition* loop; the decision to go through one more pass of the loop is made *after* the loop is traversed. Thus, the loop must be executed at least once. The *statement* part of the form can be a simple statement or a compound statement.

Form:

```
do
    statement
        while ( expression );
```

The *statement* portion is repeated until the *expression* becomes false or zero.

Example:

```
do
    scanf("%d", &number)
        while( number != 20 );
```

```
for ( ;test; )
```

is the same as

```
while(test)
```

To make a **while** like a **for,** preface it with an initialization and include update statements:

```
initialize;
while (test)
  {
  body;
  update;
  }
```

is the same as

```
for (initialize; test; update)
    body;
```

In terms of style, it seems appropriate to use a **for** loop when the loop involves initializing and updating a variable and to use a **while** loop when the conditions are otherwise. Thus, **while** is natural for the

```
while((ch = getchar()) !=EOF)
```

idiom we have used. The **for** loop is a more natural choice for loops involving counting with an index:

```
for ( count = 1; count <= 100; count++)
```

Nested Loops

A *nested loop* is a loop that is inside another loop. Here is a problem that uses nested loops to find all the prime numbers up to a given limit. A prime number is one that can be divided evenly only by two distinct numbers, 1 and itself. The first primes are 2, 3, 5, 7, and 11.

A straightforward approach to find out if a number is prime is to divide it by all the numbers between 1 and itself. If it can be divided by any of them evenly, then the number is not prime. We can use the modulus operator (%) to see if the division is even. (You remember the modulus operator, don't you? It yields the remainder when the first operand is divided by the second. If a number can be divided evenly, then the modulus operator yields a 0.) Once we find a divisor, there is no point in checking further, so we will want to terminate the process as soon as a divisor is found.

We'll start by checking a single number. This will use just one loop.

```
/* prime1 */
main()
{
    int number, divisor;

    printf("Which number do you wish to test for primeness?\n");
    scanf("%d", &number);               /* get response */
    while (number < 2)                  /* no go */
        {
        printf("Sorry, we don't accept numbers less than 2.\n");
        printf("Please try again.\n");
        scanf("%d", &number);
```

```
        }
    for ( divisor = 2; number % divisor != 0; divisor++)
        ; /* prime test made inside loop specifications */
    if (divisor == number) /* executed after loop terminates*/
        printf("%d is prime.\n", number);
    else
        printf("%d is not prime.\n", number);
    }
```

We used a **while** structure to steer clear of input values that would crash the program.

Notice that all the calculation is done inside the **for** loop specification section. The quantity **number** is divided by progressively larger divisors until one goes in evenly (i.e., **number % divisor** becomes 0). If the first divisor to go in evenly is the number itself, then **number** is prime. Otherwise, it will have a smaller divisor and that will terminate the loop earlier.

To find all the primes up to a certain value, we need to enclose our **for** loop in another loop. In pseudocode,

for number = 1 to limit

    check if number is prime

The second line represents our preceding program. Translating to C, we get

```
/* prime2 */
main()
{
    int number, divisor, limit;
    int count = 0;

    printf("Please enter the upper limit for the prime search.\n");
    printf("The limit should be 2 or larger.\n");
    scanf("%d", &limit);
    while ( limit < 2)  /* second chance if entry error */
        {
        printf("You weren't paying attention! Try again.\n");
        scanf("%d", &limit);
        }
    printf("Here come the primes!\n");
    for ( number = 2; number <= limit; number++)  /* outer loop */
        {
        for (divisor =2; number % divisor != 0; divisor++)
            ;
        if(divisor == number)
            {
            printf("%5d ", number);
            if ( ++count % 10 == 0)
```

```
        printf("\n");    /* start new line every 10 primes */
      }
    }
  printf("\nThat's all!\n");
}
```

The outer loop selects each number in turn from 2 to **limit** for testing. The inner loop performs the testing. We used **count** to keep track of the number of primes. Every tenth prime we start a new line. Here is a sample output:

```
Please enter the upper limit for the prime search.
The limit should be 2 or larger.
250
Here come the primes!
    2     3     5     7    11    13    17    19    23    29
   31    37    41    43    47    53    59    61    67    71
   73    79    83    89    97   101   103   107   109   113
  127   131   137   139   149   151   157   163   167   173
  179   181   191   193   197   199   211   223   227   229
  233   239   241
That's all!
```

This approach is quite straightforward but is not the ultimate in efficiency. For example, if you are testing to see if 121 is prime, there is no need to check divisors past 11. If any divisor bigger than 11 went in evenly, the result of the division would be a number smaller than 11, and that divisor would have been found earlier. Thus, we only need to check divisors up to the square root of the number, but the programming for that is a bit trickier. We leave it as an exercise for the clever reader. (Hint: rather than compare the divisor to the square root of the number, compare the square of the divisor to the number itself.)

Other Control Statements: *break, continue, goto*

The looping statements we have just discussed and the conditional statements (**if, if-else,** and **switch**) are the most important control mechanisms in C. They should be used to provide the overall structure of a program. The three statements we discuss next should be used more sparingly. Using them excessively will make a program harder to follow, more error prone, and harder to modify.

The *break* Statement

The most important of these three control statements is **break,** which we encountered when studying **switch.** It can be used with **switch,** where often

227

it is necessary, and also with any of the three loop structures. When encountered, it causes the program to break free of the **switch, for, while,** or **do while** that encloses it and to proceed to the next stage of the program. If the **break** statement is inside nested structures, it affects only the innermost structure containing it.

Sometimes **break** is used to leave a loop when there are two separate reasons to leave. Here's an echo loop that stops when it reads either an EOF character or a newline character:

```
while ( ( ch = getchar()) != EOF )
   {
   if (ch == '\n')
        break;
   putchar(ch);
   }
```

We can make the logic clearer if we put both tests in one place:

```
while ( ( ch = getchar()  ) != EOF && ch != '\n' )
      putchar(ch);
```

If you find that you have used a **break** as a part of an **if** statement, see if you can re-express the condition (as we did in the preceding fragment) so that the need for the **break** is ended.

The *continue* Statement

This statement can be used in the three loop forms, but not in a **switch.** Like **break,** it interrupts the flow of a program. Instead of terminating the whole loop, however, **continue** causes the rest of an iteration to be skipped and the next iteration to be started. Let's replace the **break** in the last fragment with a **continue:**

```
while ( ( ch = getchar()  ) != EOF  )
    {
    if ( ch == '\n' )
        continue;
    putchar(ch);
    }
```

The **break** version quits the loop entirely when a newline character is encountered. The **continue** version merely skips over the newlines and quits only when an EOF character is encountered.

Of course, this fragment could have been expressed more economically as:

```
while ( ( ch = getchar() ) != EOF )
    if ( ch != '\n')
        putchar(ch);
```

Often, as in this case, reversing an **if** test will eliminate the need for a **continue.**

On the other hand, the **continue** statement can shorten some programs, particularly if they involve nested **if-else** statements.

The *goto* Statement

The **goto** statement, bulwark of BASIC and FORTRAN, is available in C. However, C, unlike those two languages, can get along quite well without it. Kernighan and Ritchie refer to the **goto** statement as "infinitely abusable" and suggest that it "be used sparingly, if at all."

First we will show you how to use it; then we will show why you don't need to.

The **goto** statement has two parts: the **goto** and a label name. The label is named following the same conventions used in naming a variable. An example is

```
goto part2;
```

For this statement to work, there must be another statement bearing the **part2** label. This is done by beginning a statement with the label name followed by a colon.

```
part2: printf("Refined analysis:\n");
```

Avoiding the goto—In principle, you never need to use the **goto** in a C program. But if you have a background in FORTRAN or BASIC, both of which require its use, you may have developed programming habits that depend on using the **goto**.

To help you get over that dependence, we will outline some familiar **goto** situations and then show you a more C-like approach.

1. Handling an **if** situation that requires more than one statement:

```
if ( size > 12)
    goto a;
goto b;
a: cost = cost * 1.05;
    flag = 2;
b: bill = cost * flag;
```

(In standard BASIC and FORTRAN only the single statement immediately following the **if** condition is attached to the **if.** We have translated that pattern into the equivalent C.)

The standard C approach of using a compound statement or block is much easier to follow:

```
if (size > 12)
    {
    cost = cost * 1.05;
    flag = 2;
    }
bill = cost * flag;
```

2. Choosing from two alternatives:

```
if ( ibex > 14)
    goto a;
sheds = 2;
goto b;
a: sheds = 3;
b: help = 2 * sheds;
```

Having the **if-else** structure available allows C to express this choice much more cleanly:

```
if ( ibex > 14)
    sheds = 3;
else
```

```
    sheds = 2;
help = 2 * sheds;
```

3. Setting up an indefinite loop:

```
readin: scanf("%d", &score);
if( score < 0)
    goto stage2;
lots of statements;
goto readin;
stage2: more stuff;
```

Use a **while** loop instead:

```
scanf("%d", &score);
while( score >= 0)
    {
    lots of statements;
    scanf("%d", &score);
    }
more stuff;
```

4. Skipping to the end of a loop: use **continue** instead.

5. Leaving a loop: use **break** instead. Actually, **break** and **continue** are specialized forms of a **goto.** The advantages of using them are that their names tell you what they are supposed to do and that since they don't use labels, there is no danger of putting a label in the wrong place.

6. Leaping madly about to different parts of a program: don't!

There is one use of **goto** that is tolerated by some C practitioners, and that is to get out of a nested set of loops if trouble shows up. (A single **break** just gets you out of the innermost loop.)

```
while ( funct > 0 )
    {
    for (i = 1, i <= 100; i++)
        {
        for ( j= 1; j <= 50; j++)
            {
            statements galore;
            if ( big trouble)
                goto help;
            statements;
            }
        more statements;
        }
```

```
        yet more statements;
        }
and more statements;
help : bail out;
```

As you can see from our examples, the alternative forms are clearer than the **goto** forms. This difference grows even greater when you mix several of these situations together. Which **gotos** are helping **ifs,** which are simulating **if-elses,** which are controlling loops, which are just there because you have programmed yourself into a corner? A gung-ho **goto** approach lets you create a labyrinth of program flow. If you aren't familiar with **gotos,** keep it that way. If you are used to using them, try to train yourself not to. Ironically, C, which doesn't need a **goto,** has a better **goto** than most languages because it lets you use descriptive words for labels instead of numbers.

Summary: Program Jumps

Keywords: *break, continue, goto*

General Comments:
These three instructions cause program flow to jump from one location of a program to another location.

The *break* **Command:**
The **break** command can be used with any of the three loop forms and with the **switch** statement. It causes program control to skip over the rest of the loop or **switch** containing it and to resume with the next command following the loop or **switch.**

Example:

```
switch (number )
    {
    case  4:  printf("That's a good choice.\n");
              break;
    case  5:  printf("That's a fair choice.\n");
              break;
    default:  printf("That's a poor choice.\n");
    }
```

The *continue* Command:

The **continue** command can be used with any of the three loop forms but not with a **switch.** It causes program control to skip the remaining statements in a loop. For a **while** or **for** loop, the next loop cycle is started. For a **do while** loop, the exit condition is tested and then, if necessary, the next loop cycle is started.

Example:

```
while ( (ch = getchar())  != EOF)
    {
    if ( ch == ' ' )
            continue;
    putchar(ch);
    chcount++;
    }
```

This fragment echoes and counts nonspace characters.

The *goto* Command:

A **goto** statement causes program control to jump to a statement bearing the indicated label. A colon is used to separate a labeled statement from its label. Label names follow the rules for variable names. The labeled statement can come either before or after the **goto.**

Form:

```
goto label;
    ...
label : statement
```

Example:

```
top : ch = getchar();
    ...
if ( ch != 'y' )
        goto top;
```

Arrays

Arrays are important features in many programs. They let you store lots of related information in a convenient fashion. We will devote a whole chapter to arrays later, but because arrays often hang around loops, we want to start using them now.

An *array* is a series of variables that share the same basic name and that are distinguished from one another by a numerical tag. For instance, the declaration

```
float debts[20];
```

announces that **debts** is an array with twenty members or "elements." The first element of the array is called **debts[0]**, the second element is called **debts[1]**, etc., up to **debts[19]**. Note that the numbering of array elements starts with 0 and not 1. Because we declared the array to be type **float**, each element can be assigned a **float** value. For example, we can have

```
debts[5] = 32.54;
debts[6] = 1.2e+21;
```

An array can be of any data type:

```
int nannies[22];      /* an array to hold 22 integers    */
char alpha[26];        /* an array to hold 26 characters  */
long big[500];      /* an array to hold 500 long integers */
```

Earlier, for example, we talked about strings, which are a special case of **char** arrays. (A **char** array in general is one whose elements are assigned **char** values. A string is a **char** array in which the null character, '\0', is used to mark the end of the string.)

Figure 8.6
Character arrays and strings

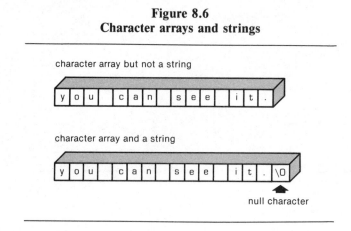

The numbers used to identify the array elements are called *subscripts* or *indices*. The subscripts must be integers, and, as we mentioned, the

subscripting begins with 0. The array elements are stored next to each other in memory, as shown in Figure 8.7.

Figure 8.7
The "char" and "int" arrays in memory

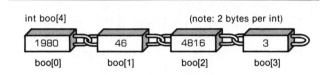

int boo[4]   (note: 2 bytes per int)

| 1980 | 46 | 4816 | 3 |
| boo[0] | boo[1] | boo[2] | boo[3] |

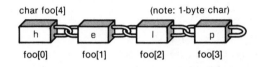

char foo[4]   (note: 1-byte char)

| h | e | l | p |
| foo[0] | foo[1] | foo[2] | foo[3] |

There are many, many uses for arrays. Here is a relatively simple one. Suppose you want a program that reads in ten scores, which will be processed later on. By using an array, you can avoid inventing ten different variable names, one for each score. Also, you can use a **for** loop to do the reading.

```
/* scoreread */
main()
{
  int i, score[10];

  for (i = 0; i <= 9; i++)
      scanf("%d", &score[i]);  /* read in the ten scores  */
  printf("The scores read in are as follows:\n");
  for (i=0; i < = 9; i++)
      printf("%5d", score[i]);  /* verify input */
  printf("\n");
}
```

It is good practice to have a program repeat or "echo" the values it has just read in. It helps ensure that the program is processing the data you think it is.

Our approach here is much more convenient than using ten separate **scanf( )** statements and ten separate **printf( )** statements to read in and verify the ten scores. The **for** loop provides a very simple and direct way to utilize the array subscripts.

What sort of operations might we perform on these scores? We could

235

find the average, we could find the standard deviation (yes, we know how), we could find the highest score, we could sort the scores. Let's tackle the two easiest parts: finding the average and finding the highest score.

To find the average, we can add this to the program:

```
int sum, average;

for (i = 0, sum = 0; i <=9; i++)  /* two initializations */
    sum += score[i];   /* add up the array elements */
average = sum/10;     /* time-honored method of averaging */
printf("The average of these scores is %d.\n", average);
```

To find the highest score, we can add this to the program:

```
int highest;
for (highest = score[0], i = 1; i <= 9; i++)
    if ( score[i] > highest)
        highest = score[i];
printf("The highest score is %d.\n", highest);
```

Here we begin by setting **highest** equal to **score[0].** Then we compare **highest** to each element of the array. Whenever we find a value higher than the current value of **highest,** we set **highest** equal to the new, higher value.

Now put the parts together. In pseudocode,

read in scores

echo scores back

find and print average

find and print highest score

While we are at it, we will generalize slightly.

```
/* scores */
#define NUM 10
main()
{
int i, sum, average, highest, score[NUM];

printf("Enter the %d scores now.\n,NUM);
for (i = 0; i < NUM; i++)
    scanf("%d", &score[i]); /* read in the ten scores  */
printf("The scores read in are as follows:\n");
for (i = 0; i < NUM; i++)
    printf("%5d", score[i]); /* verify input */
printf("\n");
for (i = 0, sum = 0; i < NUM; i++)
```

```
    sum += score[i];  /* add up the array elements */
average = sum/NUM;       /* time-honored method of averaging */
printf("The average of these scores is %d.\n", average);
for (highest = score[0], i = 1; i < NUM; i++)
    if ( score[i] > highest) /* see which is bigger */
        highest = score[i];
printf("The highest score is %d.\n", highest);
}
```

We replaced **10** with a symbolic constant, and we used the fact that **i** $<=$ **(NUM − 1)** is the same as **i** $<$ **NUM**.

Let's check to see if it works; then we can make a few comments.

```
Enter the 10 scores now.
76 85 62 48 98 71 66 89 70 77
The scores read in are as follows:
   76    85    62    48    98    71   66   89   70   77
The average of these scores is 74.
The highest score is 98.
```

One point to note is that we used four separate **for** loops. You may wonder if this was really necessary. Could we have combined some of the operations in one loop? The answer is that we could have done so. That would have made the program more compact. However, we were swayed (impressionable folks that we are) by the principle of modularity. The idea behind this phrase is that a program should be broken into separate units or "modules," with each module having one task to perform. (Our pseudocode reflects the four modules to this program.) This makes it easier to read a program. Perhaps even more importantly, it makes it much easier to update or modify a program if different parts of it are not intermingled. Just pop out the offending module, replace it with a new one, and leave the rest of the program unchanged.

The second point to note is that it is rather unsatisfying to have a program that processes exactly ten numbers. What if someone drops out and only nine scores are available? True, by using a symbolic constant for 10, we made it simple to change the program, but still you would have to recompile it. Are there other choices? We will look at that next.

A Question of Input

There are several approaches to reading in a series, say, of numbers. We will outline some here, going from least convenient to more convenient.

In general, the least convenient approach is the one we just used—writing a program to accept a fixed number of input items. (However, the approach is fine for situations in which the number of input items never changes.) If the number of input items changes, then the program must be recompiled.

The next step up is to ask the user how many items will be read in. Since the size of the array is fixed by the program, the program should check to see that the user's answer is no larger than the array size. Then the user can input the data. We can remake the beginning of our program into the following:

```
printf("How many data items will you be entering?\n");
scanf("%d", &nbr);
while ( nbr > NUM)
    {
    printf("I can handle only up to %d items; please enter a");
    printf("smaller value.\n", NUM);
    scanf("%d", &nbr);
    } /* ensures that nbr <= NUM, the maximum array size */
for ( i = 0; i < nbr ; i++)
        scanf("%d", &score[i]);
```

We would continue by replacing every **NUM** in the program (except in the **#define** statement and in the array declaration) by **nbr.** This makes the various operations affect only those elements of the array that are filled with data.

The problem with this approach is that it relies on the user to count correctly, and relying on the user to do things right leads to fragile programs.

This problem leads to the next approach, which is to let the computer count the number of numbers entered. After all, computers do have some aptitude in that direction. The main problem here is how to let the computer know when you are done entering numbers. One method is to have the user give a special signal to announce the end. This signal has to be of the *same data type* as the rest of the data in order to be read by the same program statement. But it must also be *distinct* from ordinary data. For instance, if we were reading in scores for a test on which a person could score from 0 to 100 points, we wouldn't choose 74 as a signal, because that could be a legitimate test score. A number like 999 or −3, on the other hand, would make a suitable stop signal, since it isn't a legitimate score. Here is an implementation of this approach:

```
/* scores1 */
#define STOP 999 /* signal to stop reading input */
#define NUM 50
main()
{
  int i, count, temp, score[NUM];

  printf("Begin entering score values.  Enter 999 to signify\n");
```

```
      printf("the end of data. The maximum number of scores you\n");
      printf("can enter is %d.\n", NUM);
      count = 0;
      scanf("%d", &temp); /* read in a value */
      while( temp != STOP && count <= NUM)   /* check for STOP sign */
            {                      /* and check to see if room is left */
            score[count++] = temp; /* store value and update count */
            if (count < NUM + 1)
                scanf("%d", &temp);   /* read in next value */
            else
                print("I ain't takin' no mo' data.\n");
            }
   printf("You entered %d scores, as follows:\n", count);
   for (i = 0; i < count; i++)
        printf("%5d\n", score[i]);
   }
```

We read input into a temporary variable **temp** and assign the value to the array only if the value is not the STOP signal. It's not really necessary to do it this way; we just thought it might make the testing process a bit clearer.

Notice that we check for two things: first, to see if the STOP signal has been read and second, to see if there is room in the array for another number. If we fill the array before getting a STOP signal, the program politely informs us so and quits reading in data.

Note, too, that we use the postfix form of the increment operator. Thus, when **count** is 0, **score[0]** is assigned the value of **temp,** and then **count** is increased to 1. After each iteration of the **while** loop, **count** is one larger than the last subscript used for the array. This is what we want, since **score[0]** is the first element, **score[20]** is the 21st element, and so on. When the program finally leaves the loop, **count** equals the total number of data numbers read. We then use **count** as the upper limit for the following **for** loops.

This scheme works well as long as we have a fund of numbers that would never be entered as data. But what if we want a program to accept *any* number of the proper data type as data? Then that would leave no number to use as a STOP signal.

We faced a problem like that before when we sought an end-of-file marker. The solution then was to have a character-fetching function (**getchar( )**) that was actually a type **int.** This enabled the function to report a "character" (EOF) that really wasn't an ordinary character. What would be useful for our current example is a function that fetches an integer but is also capable of reading a noninteger which can be used as a STOP symbol.

Fortunately, **scanf( )** has a property that can help out with this task. In addition to assigning values to variables, as in **scanf("%d", &temp)**, this function also has a return value. That is, we can have statements like this:

```
status = scanf("%d", &temp);
```

This not only places a value in **temp**, it also assigns a return value to the **int** variable **status**. An important point is that the return value is *not* the value that is being read and assigned to **temp**. Instead, the return value for **scanf( )** is a report on its success in attempting to read input. Here are the possible results:

1. Normally, **scanf( )** returns the number of items read. In the preceding example, this would be the integer 1.

2. If **scanf( )** is unable to read the first item on its list because of a format problem, it returns the value 0. For example, if you specify type "**%d**" but try to enter the character **j**, **scanf( )** stops and returns a value of 0. The **j** remains in the input queue; this means that the next attempt to read input will start at the **j**.

3. If **scanf( )** encounters the end of file before reading the first input, it returns the value **EOF**, as defined in the file **stdio.h**.

These facts let us set up a number-reading loop as illustrated in the next small program, which reads in integers and prints the total.

```c
/* sums -- sums integer input */
#include <stdio.h>
main()
{
    int n;
    long sum = 0L;

    printf("This program sums the integers you enter.");
    printf(" So enter some.\n");
    printf("To halt, enter a nondigit or EOF.\n");
    while ( scanf("%d", &n) == 1 )
        sum +=n;
    printf("The total is %d.\n", sum);
}
```

As long as **scanf( )** reads an integer, it returns a **1**, and the loop continues. But when a noninteger or an end of file shows up, the return value is **0** or **EOF**, and the loop halts. Here is a sample run:

```
This program sums the integers you enter. So enter some.
To halt, enter a nondigit or EOF.
10 20 30 [return]
40 50 q 1000 [return]
The total is 150.
```

Note that, with buffered input, the numbers are not transmitted to the program until [return] is pressed. But although **1000** is sent, the processing ends with the **50**, for the **q** terminates the loop. Note, too, that since **scanf( )** skips over spaces and newlines when reading integers, the input can have several numbers on the same line as well as numbers on different lines.

Summary

Our main topic was program control. C offers many aids for structuring your programs. The **while** and the **for** statements provide entry-condition loops. The latter are particularly suited for loops that involve initialization and updating. The comma operator lets you initialize and update more than one variable in a **for** loop. For the rare occasion when an exit-condition loop is needed, C provides the **do while** statement. The **break, continue,** and **goto** statements provide further means of controlling the flow of a program.

We also discussed arrays further. Arrays are declared in the same fashion as ordinary variables, but they have a number in brackets to indicate the number of elements. The first element of an array is numbered 0, the second is numbered 1, etc. The subscripts used to number arrays can be manipulated conveniently by using loops.

What You Should Have Learned

C's three loop forms: **while, for,** and **do while**
The difference between entry-condition and exit-condition loops

Why entry-condition loops are used much more often than exit-condition loops

The other assignment operators: += −= *= /= %=

How to use the comma operator

When to use **break** and **continue:** sparingly

When to use **goto:** when you want clumsy, hard-to-follow programs

How to use a **while** to protect a program from faulty input

What an array is and how to declare one: **long arms[8]**

How to use the return value for **scanf( )**

Review Questions

1. Find the value of quack after each line.

```
int quack = 2;
quack += 5;
quack *= 10;
quack -= 6;
quack /= 8;
quack %= 3;
```

2. What output would the following loop produce?

```
for ( value = 36; value > 0; value /= 2)
     printf("%3d", value);
```

3. How can you modify the **if** statements in **numguess2** to accept both upper- and lowercase letters?

4. We suspect the following program is not perfect. What errors can you find?

```
main()                             /* line 1 */
{                                  /* line 2 */
   int i, j, list(10);             /* line 3 */

   for (i = 1, i <= 10,  i++)      /* line 5 */
      {                            /* line 6 */
      list[i] = 2*i + 3;           /* line 7 */
      for (j = 1, j > = i, j++)    /* line 8 */
          printf("%d\n", list[j]); /* line 9 */
      }                            /* line 10 */
```

5. Use nested loops to write a program that produces this pattern:

```
$$$$$$$$
$$$$$$$$
$$$$$$$$
$$$$$$$$
```

6. Write a program that creates an array with 26 elements and stores the 26 lowercase letters in it.

7. What does each of the following programs print out?

   a.
```
main()
{
      int i = 0;

      while ( ++i < 4)
          printf("Hi! ");
      do
          printf("Bye! ");
          while ( i++ < 8);
}
```
   b.
```
#include <stdio.h>
main()
{
      int i;
      char ch;

      for (i = 0, ch = 'A'; i < 4; i++, ch += 2 * i)
             putchar(ch);
}
```

8. Given the input "Saddle up my horse!", what would each of the following programs produce for output? (The ! follows the space character in the ASCII sequence.)

   a.
```
#include <stdio.h>
main()
{
      int ch;

      while ( (ch = getchar()) != 'o' )
             putchar(ch);
}
```
   b.
```
#include <stdio.h>
main()
{
      int ch;
      while ( (ch = getchar()) != 'o' )
             putchar(++ch);
}
```
   c.
```
#include <stdio.h>
main()
{
      int ch;

      do {
```

243

```
            ch = getchar();
            putchar(ch);
              } while ( ch != 'o' );
    }
```

d. ```
   #include <stdio.h>
   main()
   {
       int ch;

       for (ch = '!'; ch != 'o'; ch = getchar())
           putchar();
   }
   ```

9. What will the following program print?

```
#include <stdio.h>
main()
{
    int n, m;

    for (n = 0; n < 8; n++)
        {
        printf("%d", n);
        switch (n % 3)
            {
            case 0 : putchar('H');
            case 1 : putchar('E');
                    break;
            case 2 : putchar('\n');
            }
        }

    printf("\n***\n");

    n = 10;
    while (++n <= 13)
        printf("%d",n);
    do
        printf("%d",n);
        while (++n <= 12);

    printf("\n***\n");

    for (n = 1; n*n < 60; n +=3)
        printf("%d\n", n);

    printf("\n***\n");
```
```

```
for ( n = 1, m = 5; n < m; n *= 2, m+= 2)
     printf("%d %d\n", n, m);

printf("\n***\n");

for ( n = 4; n > 0; n--)
     {
     for ( m = 0; m <= n; m++)
          putchar('+');
     putchar('\n');
          }
}
```

10. Write a program that reads input character-by-character up to end of file. Have it count separately the number of times each digit character appears in the input. Use an array to store the counts, with the 0-element holding the number of '0' characters, and so on. Note that if **ch** is a digit character, then **ch** − '0' is the corresponding array subscript.

Answers

1. 2, 7, 70, 64, 8, 2

2. **36 18 9 4 2 1** Recall how integer division works: 1 divided by 2 is 0, so the loop terminates after value equals 1.

3. `if ( response == 'h' || response == 'H')`

4. Line 3: Should be **list[10]**.
   Line 5: Commas should be semicolons.
   Line 5: Range for **i** should be from 0 to 9, not 1 to 10.
   Line 8: Commas should be semicolons.
   Line 8: >= should be <=. Otherwise, when **i** is **1**, the loop never ends.
   Line 10: There should be another closing brace between lines 9 and 10. One brace closes the compound statement, and one closes the program.

5.
```
main()
{
int i,j;

for(i = 1; i <= 4; i++)
    {
    for(j = 1; j <= 8; j++)
         printf("$");
    printf("\n");
    }
}
```

6.
```
main()
    {
```

```
        int i;
        char ch, alpha[26];

        for ( i = 0, ch = 'a'; i < 26; i++, ch++)
            alpha[i] = ch;
    }
```

7. **a.** Hi! Hi! Hi! Bye! Bye! Bye! Bye! Bye!
   b. ACGM

8. **a.** Saddle up my h
   b. The increment operator changes the value of **ch** after it is read.
      Tbeemf!vq!nz!i
   c. Notice the difference between a **while** and a **do while**.
      Saddle up my ho
   d. The first **getchar( )** call does not take place until the end of the first
      cycle.
      !Saddle up my h

9. Here is the output we get:

```
0HE1E2
3HE4E5
6HE7E
***
11121314
***
1
4
7
***
1 5
2 7
4 9
8 11
***
+++++
++++
+++
++
```

10. Here is one solution. Note that the increment operator may be applied to
    individual array elements.

```
#include <stdio.h>
main()
{
        int d_ct[10]; /* array for storing digit counts */
        int ch, i;
```

```
      for (i = 0; i < 10; i++ )
            d_ct[i] = 0;     /* initialize counts to 0 */

      while ( (ch = getchar() ) != EOF )
            if ( ch >= '0' && ch <= '9')
                  d_ct[ch - '0']++;
      for ( i = '0'; i <= '9'; i++ )
            printf("# of %c's = %d\n", i, d_ct[i - '0'] );
}
```

Exercises

1. Modify **numguess2** along the lines we suggested to improve the program.

2. Implement our suggestion to improve the efficiency of the prime number program.

3. Use nested loops to produce the following pattern:

   ```
   $
   $$
   $$$
   $$$$
   $$$$$
   ```

4. Write a program that prints a table with each line giving an integer, its square, and its cube. Ask the user to input the lower and upper limits for the table. Use a **for** loop.

5. Revise Exercise 4 so that after each table is printed, the user is asked if he or she wishes to do another. If the user does, then the program should repeat. A **do while** loop would be appropriate here if at least one table will always be printed.

6. Consider these two infinite series:

   $$1.0 + 1.0/2.0 + 1.0/3.0 + 1.0/4.0 + \ldots$$
   $$1.0 - 1.0/2.0 + 1.0/3.0 - 1.0/4.0 + \ldots$$

   Write a program that evaluates running totals of these two series up to some limit of number of terms. Have the user enter the limit interactively. Look at the running totals after 20 terms, 100 terms, 500 terms. Does either series appear to be converging to some value? (Incidentally, you can use the modulus operator to set the sign for the second series, which requires a minus sign for even divisors. If **x % 2** is **0**, then **x** is even.)

7. Rewrite the **scores1** program so that it stops reading input when the last array element is filled or when a noninteger is encountered or when end of file is encountered. Incorporate the use of **scanf( )**'s return value, as was done in **sums**.

9

How to Function Properly

Concepts

- Functions
- Program building blocks
- Communicating between functions: arguments, pointers, return
- Function types

Keywords

- *return*

The design philosophy of C is based on using functions. Already we have used several functions to help our programming: **printf( )**, **scanf( )**, **getchar( )**, **putchar( )**, and **strlen( )**. These functions come with the system, but we also created several functions of our own, all called **main( )**. Programs always start by executing the instructions in **main( )**; after that, **main( )** can call other functions, like **getchar( )**, into action. Now we will learn how to create our own functions and make them available to **main( )** and to each other.

First, what is a function? A *function* is a self-contained unit of program code designed to accomplish a particular task. A function in C plays the same role that functions, subroutines, and procedures play in other languages, although the details may be different. Some functions cause action to take place. For example, **printf( )** causes data to be printed on your screen. Some functions find a value for the program to use. For instance, **strlen( )** tells a program how long a certain string is. In general, a function can both produce actions and provide values.

Why do we use functions? For one thing, they save us from repetitious programming. If we have to do a certain task several times in a program, we write an appropriate function once, then have the program use that function wherever needed. Or we can use the same function in different programs, just as we use **putchar( )** in many programs. Even if we do a task just once in just one program, it is worthwhile to use a function because functions make a program more modular, hence easier to read and easier to change or fix. Suppose, for example, we want to write a program that does the following:

read in a list of numbers

sort the numbers

find their average
print out a bar graph

We could use this program:

```
main()
{
  float list[50];

  readlist(list);
  sort(list);
  average(list);
  bargraph(list);
}
```

Of course, we would also have to write the four functions **readlist( )**, **sort( )**, **average( )**, and **bargraph( )** . . . mere details. By using descriptive function names, we have made it quite clear what the program does and how it is organized. We then can fiddle with each function separately until it does its job right. An added benefit is that if we make the functions general enough, they can prove useful in other programs.

Many programmers like to think of a function as a "black box" defined in terms of the information that goes in (its input) and of what it produces (its output). What goes on inside the black box is not our concern, unless we are the ones who have to write the function. For example, when we use **printf( )**, we know we have to give it a control string and, perhaps, some arguments. We also know what output **printf( )** should produce. We never had to think about the programming that went into creating **printf( )**. Thinking of functions in this manner helps us concentrate on the overall design of the program rather than on the details.

What do we need to learn about functions? We need to know how to define them properly, how to call them up for use, and how to set up communications between a function and the program that invokes it. To learn these things, we will begin with a very simple example and then bring in more features until we have the full story.

Creating and Using a Simple Function

Our modest first goal is to create a function that types 65 asterisks in a row. To give our function a context, we will include it in a program that prints a simple letterhead. Here is the complete program. It consists of the functions **main( )** and **starbar( )**.

```
/* letterhead1 */
#define NAME "MEGATHINK, INC."
```

```
        #define ADDRESS "10 Megabuck Plaza"
        #define PLACE "Megapolis, CA 94904"
        main()
        {
          starbar();
          printf("%s\n", NAME);
          printf("%s\n", ADDRESS);
          printf("%s\n", PLACE);
          starbar();
        }
        /* now comes the starbar() function */
        #include <stdio.h>
        #define LIMIT 65
        starbar()
        {
          int count;

          for ( count = 1; count <= LIMIT; count++)
              putchar('*');
          putchar('\n');
        }
```

Here is the output:

```
*****************************************************************
MEGATHINK, INC.
10 Megabuck Plaza
Megapolis, CA 94904
*****************************************************************
```

And here are the major points to note about this program:

1. We called (invoked, summoned) the function **starbar( )** from **main( )** by using just its name. It is a bit like summoning a demon, but, instead of inscribing a pentagon, we just follow the name with a semicolon, creating a statement:

```
starbar();
```

This is one form for calling up a function, but it isn't the only one. Whenever the computer reaches a **starbar( )** statement, it looks for the **starbar( )** function and follows the instructions there. When finished, it returns to the next line of the "calling program," **main( )**, in this case.

Figure 9.1
Control flow for letterhead 1

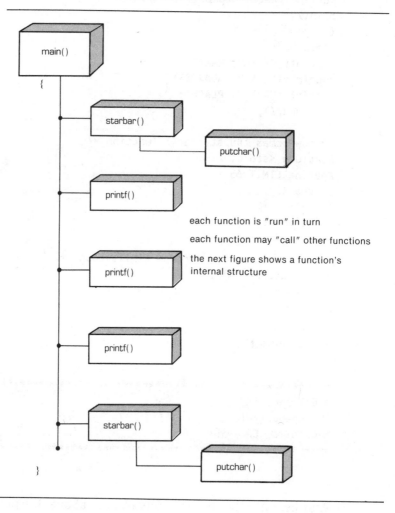

each function is "run" in turn

each function may "call" other functions

the next figure shows a function's
internal structure

2.   We followed the same form in writing **starbar( )** as we did in
main( ). First came the name, then the opening brace, then a declaration
of variables used, then the defining statements of the function, then the
closing brace. We even preceded the function with **#define** and **#include**
statements needed by it and not by **main( )**.

3.   We included **starbar( )** and **main( )** in the same file. We could
have used two separate files. The single-file form is slightly easier to
compile. Two separate files make it simpler to use the same function in
different programs. We will discuss using two or more files later. For now,
we will keep all our functions in one basket. The closing brace of **main( )**
tells the compiler where that function ends. The parentheses in **starbar( )**
tell the compiler that **starbar( )** is a function. Note that this instance of

starbar( ) is not followed by a semicolon; this lack of a semicolon tells the compiler that we are *defining* **starbar( )** rather than using it.

If we think of **starbar( )** as a black box, its output is the line of stars that is printed. It doesn't have any input because it doesn't need to use any information from the calling program. This function doesn't require any communication with the calling program.

Let's create a case where communication *is* needed.

Figure 9.2
Structure of a simple function

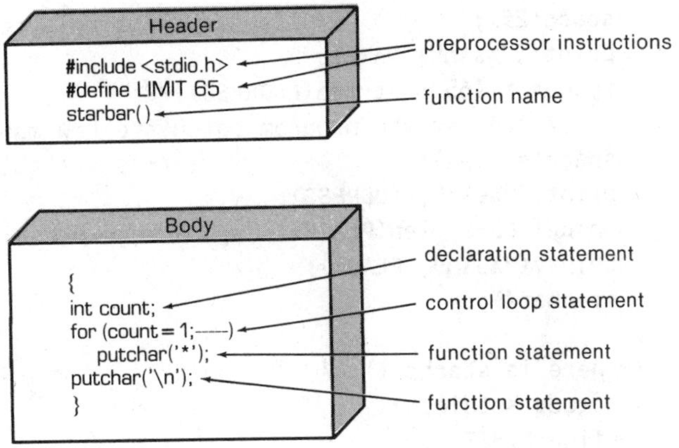

Function Arguments

The letterhead would look a little nicer if the text were centered. We can center the text by printing the right number of spaces before the rest of the line is printed. Let's use a function to print spaces. Our **space( )** function (let's call it that) will be a lot like our **starbar( )** function, except this time there has to be communication from **main( )** to the function telling it how many spaces to print.

Let's get more specific. Our bar of stars is 65 spaces wide, and MEGATHINK, INC. is 15 spaces wide. Thus, in our first version, there were 50 spaces following the heading. To center it, we should lead off with 25 spaces, which will result in 25 spaces on either side of the phrase. Therefore we want to be able to communicate the value "25" to the spacing function. We will use the same method we use to communicate the value '*' to **putchar( )**: use an argument. Then **space(25)** will mean to skip 25 spaces. The **25** is the argument. We will call **space( )** three times, once for each line of the address. Here is how it looks:

Figure 9.3
Letterhead program

```
  /* letterhead2 */
#define NAME "MEGATHINK, INC."
#define ADDRESS "10 Megabuck Plaza"
#define PLACE "Megapolis, CA 94904"
main()
{
  int spaces;

  starbar();
  space(25);           /*   space () using a constant as argument */
  printf("%s\n", NAME);
  spaces = (65 - strlen(ADDRESS))/2;
     /* we let the program calculate how many spaces to skip */
  space(spaces);                   /* a variable as argument */
  printf("%s\n", ADDRESS);
  space((65-strlen(PLACE))/2); /* an expression as argument */
  printf("%s\n", PLACE);
  starbar();
}
/* here is starbar() */
#include <stdio.h>
#define LIMIT 65
starbar()
{
  int count;

  for ( count = 1; count <= LIMIT: count++)
      putchar('*');
  putchar('\n');
}
/* and here is the space() function */
space(number)
int number;    /* declare argument before brace */
{
  int count;   /* declare other variable after brace */

  for ( count = 1; count <= number; count++)
      putchar(' ');
}
```

Notice that we experimented by expressing the argument in three different ways. Did they all work? Yes, and here is the proof.

```
****************************************************************
                        MEGATHINK, INC.
                        10 Megabuck Plaza
                        Megapolis, CA 94904
****************************************************************
```

First, let's look at how to set up a function with an argument. After that, we'll look at how it is used.

Defining a Function with an Argument: Formal Arguments

Our function definition begins with two lines:

```
space(number)
int number;
```

The first line informs the compiler that **space( )** uses an argument and that the argument will be called **number.** The second line is a declaration informing the compiler that **number** is of type **int.** Note that the argument is declared *before* the brace that marks the start of the body of the function. Incidentally, your compiler may allow you to condense these two lines to one:

```
space (int number)
```

With either form, the variable **number** is called a "formal" argument. It is, in fact, a new variable, and the computer must set aside a memory location for it.

Now let's see how we use this function.

Calling a Function with an Argument: Actual Arguments

The trick is to assign a value to the formal argument, **number,** in this case. Once that variable has a value, then the program does its task. We give **number** a value by using an "actual argument" in the function call. Consider our first use of **space( )**

```
space(25);
```

The actual argument is 25, and this *value* is assigned to the formal argument, the variable **number.** That is, the function call has this effect:

```
number = 25;
```

In short, the formal argument is a variable in the called program, and the actual argument is the particular value assigned to that variable by the calling program. As we showed in our example, the actual argument can be a constant, a variable, or an even more elaborate expression. Regardless of which it is, the actual argument is evaluated, and it is the value (in this case, an integer) that is sent to the function. For instance, consider our final use of **space( ):**

```
space((65-strlen(PLACE))/2);
```

First, that long expression forming the actual argument was evaluated to 23. Then the value 23 is assigned to the variable **number.** The function neither knows nor cares whether that number came from a constant, a variable, or a more general expression. Again, the actual argument is a specific value which is assigned to the variable known as the formal argument.

Figure 9.4
Formal arguments and actual arguments

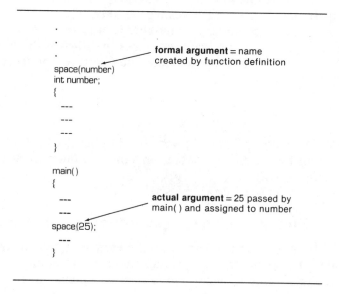

The Black Box Viewpoint

In the black box view of **space( ),** the input is the number of spaces to be skipped, and the output is the skipping of the spaces. The input is communicated to the function via an argument. It is the argument that provides a communication link between **main( )** and **space( ).** The variable **count,** on the other hand, is declared inside the body of the function, and other functions know nothing about **count.** It is part of the mechanism hidden within the black box. It is not the same variable as the **count** in **starbar( ).**

Multiple Arguments

If more than one argument is needed, you can provide an argument list, with the arguments separated by commas, as shown here.

```
printnum( i,j)
int i, j;
{
    printf("New points = %d.  Total points = %d.\n", i, j);
}
```

We have seen how to communicate information from the calling program to the called function. How can we send information the other way? That is our next topic.

Returning a Value from a Function: *return*

Let's construct an absolute value function. The absolute value of a number is its value when the sign is ignored. Hence the absolute value of 5 is 5, and the absolute value of −3 is 3. We'll call the function **abs( )**. The input to **abs( )** will be whatever number for which we want the absolute value. The output of the function will be the number shorn of any negative signs. We can handle the input with an argument. The output, as you shall see, is handled using the C keyword **return**. Since **abs( )** has to be called by another function, we will create a simple **main( )** whose sole purpose is to check to see if **abs( )** works. A program designed to test functions this way is called a *driver*. The driver takes a function for a spin. If the function pans out, then it can be installed in a more noteworthy program. (The term *driver* also is used for programs that run devices.) Here is our driver and our absolute value function:

```
/* abs.driver */
main()
{
    int a = 10, b = 0, c = -22;
    int d, e, f;

    d = abs(a);
    e = abs(b);
    f = abs(c);
    printf ("%d %d %d\n", d, e, f);
}
    /* absolute value function */
abs(x)
int x;
{
```

```
        int y;

        y = (x < 0) ? -x: x; /* remember the ?: operator */
        return y;    /* returns the value of y to calling program */
}
```

Here is the output:

```
    10 0 22
```

First, let's refresh our memory about **?:**, the conditional operator. The conditional operator in **abs( )** works this way: if **x** is less than **0**, **y** is set to **−x**; otherwise **y** is set to **x**. This is what we want, for if **x** is **−5**, then **y** is **−(−5)** or just **5**.

The keyword **return** causes the value of whatever expression follows it to be the return value of the function containing the **return.** Thus, when **abs( )** is first called by our driver, **abs(a)** returns the value 10, which then can be assigned to the variable **d.**

The variable **y** is private to **abs( ),** but the value of **y** is communicated back to the calling program with **return.** The effect of

```
    d = abs(a);
```

is as if we could say

```
    abs(a);
    d = y;
```

Can we actually say the latter? No, for the calling program doesn't even know that **y** exists.

The returned value can be assigned to a variable, as in our example, or it can be used as part of an expression. You can do this, for example:

```
    answer = 2*abs(z) + 25;
    printf("%d\n", abs(-32 + answer));
```

The return value can be supplied by any expression, not just a variable. For example, we can shorten our program to the following:

```
    /* absolute value function, second version */
    abs(x)
    int x;
    {
        return (x < 0) ? -x : x;
    }
```

The conditional expression is evaluated to either −**x** or **x**, and that value is returned to the calling program.

If you prefer to enclose the return value in parentheses for clarity or style, that is fine. But parentheses are not required.

Using **return** has one other effect. It terminates the function and returns control to the next statement in the calling function. This occurs even if the **return** statement is not the last in the function. Thus, we could have written **abs( )** this way:

```
/* absolute value function, third version */
abs(x)
int x;
{
   if ( x < 0)
       return (-x);
   else
        return(x);
}
```

This version is clearer. To the user, however, all three versions are the same, since all take the same input and produce the same output. Just the innards are different. Even this version works the same:

```
/* absolute value function, fourth version */
abs(x)
int x;
{
   if ( x < 0)
       return(-x);
   else
       return(x);
    printf("Professor Fleppard is a fopdoodle.\n")
}
```

The **return** statements prevent the **printf( )** statement from ever being reached. Professor Fleppard can use the compiled version of this function in his own programs and never learn the true feelings of his student programmer.

You can use a statement like this, too:

```
return;
```

It causes the containing function to terminate and return control to the calling function. Because no expression is included in parentheses, no value is given to the function.

Local Variables

Several times we have remarked that the variables in a function are private to it and not known to the calling function. Similarly, the variables of the calling function are not known to the called function. That is why we use arguments and **return** to communicate values back and forth. Variables known only to the one function that contains them are called *local* variables. So far these are the only kind of variables we have used, but C does provide for variables that are known to several functions. These nonlocal variables are termed *global* variables, and we will return to them later. Meanwhile, we want to emphasize that local variables are truly local. Even if we use the same name for variables in two different functions, the computer distinguishes between them. We can show this by using the **&** operator (not to be confused with the **&&** operator).

Finding Addresses: The & Operator

The **&** operator gives us the address at which a variable is stored. If **pooh** is the name of a variable, then **&pooh** is the address of the variable. We can think of the address as a location in memory, but we also can think of it as the label the computer uses to identify a variable. Suppose we have the statement

```
pooh = 24;
```

And suppose that the address where **pooh** is stored is 12126. Then the statement

```
printf("%d %u\n", pooh, &pooh);
```

would produce

```
24 12126
```

Furthermore, the machine code for the first statement would be something along the lines of "Store 24 in location 12126,"

Let's use this operator to see where variables of the same name, but in different functions, are kept.

```
/* locationcheck */
main()
{
  int pooh = 2, bah = 5;

  printf("In main(), pooh = %d and &pooh = %u\n", pooh, &pooh);
```

```
    printf("In main(), bah = %d and &bah = %u\n", bah, &bah);
    mikado(pooh);
}
mikado(bah)
int bah;
{
    int pooh = 10;

    printf("In mikado(), pooh = %d and &pooh = %u\n", pooh, &pooh);
    printf("In mikado(), bah = %d and &bah = %u\n", bah, &bah);
}
```

We used the %u (unsigned integer) format for printing the addresses in case they turn out to be larger than the maximum **int** size. On our system, the output of this little exercise is:

```
In main(), pooh = 2 and &pooh = 3644
In main(), bah = 5 and &bah = 3646
In mikado(), pooh = 10 and &pooh = 3636
In mikado(), bah = 2 and &bah = 3642
```

What does this show? First, the two **pooh**s have different addresses. The same is true of the two **bah**s. Thus, as promised, the computer considers these to be four separate variables. Second, the call **mikado(pooh)** did convey the value (2) of the actual argument (**pooh** of **main( )**) to the formal argument (**bah** of **mikado( )**). Note that just the value was transferred. The two variables involved (**pooh** of **main( )** and **bah** of **mikado( )**) retain their distinct identities.

We raise the second point because it is not true for all languages. In a FORTRAN subroutine, for example, the subroutine uses the variables in the calling program. The subroutine may call the variables by different names, but the addresses are the same. C doesn't do this. Each function uses its own variables. This is preferable, for it means that the original variables won't get altered mysteriously by some side effect of the called function. But it can make for some difficulties, too, as our next section shows.

Altering Variables in the Calling Program

Sometimes we want one function to make changes in the variables of a different function. For example, a common task in sorting problems is interchanging the values of two variables. Suppose we have two variables called **x** and **y** and that we wish to swap values. The simple sequence

```
x = y;
y = x;
```

does not work, for by the time the second line is reached, the original value of **x** has been lost. We have to put in an additional line to save the original value of **x**:

```
temp = x;
x = y;
y = temp;
```

Now that we have a working method, let's put it into a function and construct a driver to test it. To make clear which variables belong to **main( )** and which belong to the **interchange( )** function, we will use **x** and **y** for the first, and **u** and **v** for the second.

```
/* switch1 */
main()
{
   int x = 5, y = 10;

   printf("Originally x = %d and y = %d.\n", x , y);
   interchange(x,y);
   printf("Now x = %d and y = %d.\n", x, y);
}
interchange(u,v)
int u,v;
{
   int temp;

   temp = u;
   u = v;
   v = temp;
}
```

Next, we run the program.

```
Originally x = 5 and y = 10.
Now x = 5 and y = 10.
```

Oops! They didn't get switched! Let's put some printing statements in **interchange( )** to see what has gone wrong.

```
/* switch2 */
main()
{
   int x = 5, y = 10;
```

```
        printf("Originally x = %d and y = %d.\n", x , y);
        interchange(x,y);
        printf("Now x = %d and y = %d.\n", x, y);
}
interchange(u,v)
int u,v;
{
    int temp;

    printf("Originally u = %d and v = %d.\n", u , v);
    temp = u;
    u = v;
    v = temp;
    printf("Now u = %d and v = %d.\n", u, v);
}
```

Here is the new output:

```
Originally x = 5 and y = 10.
Originally u = 5 and v = 10.
Now u = 10 and v = 5.
Now x = 5 and y = 10.
```

Well, nothing is wrong with **interchange( )**; it does swap the values of **u** and **v**. The problem is communicating the results back to **main( )**. As we pointed out, **interchange( )** uses different variables from **main( )**, so interchanging the values of **u** and **v** have no effect on **x** and **y**! Can we use **return** somehow? Well, we could finish **interchange( )** with the line

```
return(u);
```

and change the call in **main( )** to

```
x = interchange(x,y);
```

This will give **x** its new value, but it leaves **y** in the cold.

*With **return** you can send just one value back to the calling program.* But we need to communicate *two* values. It can be done! All we have to do is use "pointers."

Pointers: A First Look

Pointers? What are they? Basically, a *pointer* is a symbolic representation of an address. For example, earlier we used the address operator to find the address of the variable **pooh.** Then **&pooh** is a "pointer to **pooh.**" The actual address is a number (56002, in our case), and the symbolic representation **&pooh** is a pointer *constant*. After all, the variable **pooh** is not going to change addresses while the program is running.

C also has pointer *variables*. Just as a **char** variable has a character as a value and an **int** variable has an integer as a value, the pointer variable has an address as a value. If we give a particular pointer the name **ptr,** then we can have statements like

```
ptr = &pooh;  /* assigns pooh's address to ptr */
```

We say that **ptr** "points to" **pooh.** The difference between **ptr** and **&pooh** is that **ptr** is a variable while **&pooh** is a constant. If we want, we can make **ptr** point elsewhere:

```
ptr = &bah;  /* make ptr point to bah instead of to pooh */
```

Now **ptr's** value is the address of **bah.**

The Indirection Operator: *

Suppose we know that **ptr** points to **bah.** Then we can use the indirection operator * to find the value stored in **bah.** (Don't confuse this *unary* indirection operator with the *binary* * operator of multiplication.)

```
val = *ptr;  /* finding the value prt points to  */
```

The last two C statements, taken together, amount to

```
val = bah;
```

Using the address and indirection operators is a rather indirect way of accomplishing this result, hence the name "indirection operator."

Summary: Pointer-related Operators

The Address Operator: &
When followed by a variable name, **&** gives the address of that variable.

Example:
&nurse   is the address of the variable **nurse.**

The Indirection Operator: *
When followed by a pointer, ***** gives the value stored at the pointed-to address.

Example:

```
nurse = 22;
ptr = &nurse;  /* pointer to nurse */
val = *ptr;
```

The net effect is to assign the value **22** to **val.**

Declaring Pointers

We know how to declare **int** variables and the like. How do we declare a pointer variable? You might guess like this:

```
pointer ptr;    /* not the way to declare a pointer  */
```

Why not? Because it is not enough to say that a variable is a pointer. We also have to say what kind of variable the pointer points to! The reason for this is that different variable types take up different amounts of storage, and some pointer operations require knowledge of the storage size. Also, the program has to know what kind of data is stored at the address. A **long** and a **float** may use the same amount of storage, but they store numbers quite differently. Here's how pointers are declared:

```
int *pi;        /* pointer to an integer variable */
char *pc;       /* pointer to a character variable */
float *pf,*pg;  /* pointers to float variables */
```

The type specification identifies the type of variable pointed to, and the asterisk (*) identifies the variable itself as a pointer. The declaration **int *pi;** says that **pi** is a pointer and that ***pi** is type **int**.

Similarly, the value (***pc**) of what **pc** points to is of type **char**. What of **pc** itself? We describe it as being of type "pointer to **char**." Its value, being an address, is an unsigned integer, so we would use the %**u** format to print **pc**'s value.

Figure 9.5
Declaring and using pointers

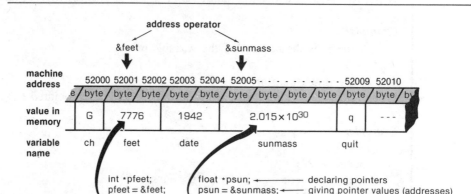

Using Pointers to Communicate between Functions

We have touched only the surface of the rich and fascinating world of pointers, but our concern here is using pointers to solve our communication problem. Here's a program that uses pointers to make the interchange function work. Let's look at it, run it, and then try to understand its workings.

```
/* switch3 */
main()
{
    int x = 5, y = 10;

    printf("Originally x = %d and y = %d.\n", x, y);
```

```
        interchange(&x,&y);  /* send addresses to function */
        printf("Now x = %d and y = %d.\n", x, y);
}
interchange(u,v)
int *u, *v;  /* u and v are pointers  */
{
    int temp;

    temp = *u;  /* temp gets value that u points to */
    *u = *v;
    *v = temp;
}
```

After all this trouble, does it really work?

```
Originally x = 5 and y = 10.
Now x = 10 and y = 5.
```

Yes, it works.

Now, let's see how it works. First, our function call looks like this:

```
interchange(&x,&y);
```

Instead of transmitting the *values* of **x** and **y**, we are transmitting their *addresses*. This means that the formal arguments **u** and **v** appearing in

```
interchange(u,v)
```

will have addresses as values; hence they should be declared as pointers. Since **x** and **y** are integers, **u** and **v** are pointers to integers; so we declare

```
int *u, *v;
```

Next, in the body of the function, we declare

```
int temp;
```

to provide the temporary storage we need. We want to store the value of **x** in **temp,** so we say

```
temp = *u;
```

Remember, **u** has the value **&x,** so **u** points to **x.** This means that *u gives us the value of **x,** which is what we want. We *don't* want to write

```
temp = u;    /* NO */
```

for that would store the *address* of **x** rather than its *value;* and we are trying to interchange values, not addresses.

Similarly, to assign **y**'s *value* to **x**, we use

```
*u = *v;
```

which translates to

```
x = y;
```

Let's summarize what we did. We wanted a function that would alter the values **x** and **y**. By telling the function the addresses of **x** and **y**, we gave it access to those variables. Using pointers and the * operator, the function could examine the values stored at those locations and change them.

More generally, we can communicate two kinds of information about a variable to a function. If we use a call of the form

```
function1(x);
```

we transmit the *value* of **x**. If we use a call of the form

```
function2(&x);
```

we transmit the *address* of **x**. The first form requires that the function definition include a formal argument of the same type as **x**:

```
function1(num)
int num;
```

The second form requires that the function definition include a formal argument that is a pointer to the right type:

```
function2(ptr)
int *ptr;
```

Use the first form if the function needs a value for some calculation or action. Use the second form if the function needs to alter variables in the calling program. We have been doing this all along with the **scanf( )** function. When we want to read in a value for a variable **num,** we use **scanf("%d", &num).** That function reads a value, then uses the address we give it when it stores the value.

Pointers let us get around the fact that the variables of **interchange( )** were local. They let our function reach out into **main( )** and alter what was stored there.

Pascal users may recognize the first form as being similar to Pascal's value parameter and the second form as being similar to Pascal's variable parameter. BASIC users may find the whole setup a bit unsettling. If this section does seem strange to you, be assured that a little practice will make it seem simple, normal, and convenient.

Variables: Names, Addresses, and Values

Our discussion of pointers hinges on the relationships between the names, addresses, and values of variables, so let's discuss these matters further.

When we write a program we think of a variable as having two attributes: a name and a value. (There are other attributes, including type, but that's another matter.) After the program has been compiled and loaded, the computer also thinks of the same variable as having two attributes: an address and a value. An address is the computer's version of a name.

In many languages, the address is the computer's business, concealed from the programmer. In C, however, we can learn and use the address through the **&** operator:

&barn is the address of the variable **barn.**

We can get the value from the name just by using the name:

printf(''%d\n'', barn) prints the value of **barn.**

We can get the value from the address by using the * operator:

Given pbarn = &barn;, then *pbarn is the value stored at address &barn.

Although we can print out an address to satisfy our curiosity, that is not the main use for the **&** operator. More importantly, using **&**, *, and pointers lets us manipulate addresses and their contents symbolically, as we did in **switch3.**

Putting Our Knowledge of Functions to Work

Now that we know a bit about functions, let's put together some useful examples. Let's see, what should we do?

How about a power function, one that lets you raise 2 to the 5th power or 3 to the 3rd, etc.? First, we must decide on what input the program

Figure 9.6
Names, addresses, and values in a "byte-addressable" system,
such as the IBM PC

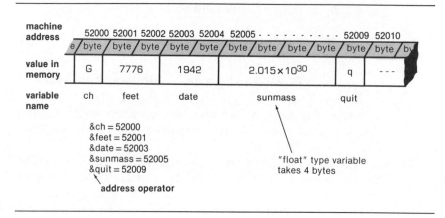

needs. That's clear; it needs to know the number and the exponent. We can handle that with two arguments:

```
power(base, exp)
int base, exp;
```

(At this point we have limited ourselves to integers and relatively small answers.)

Next, we need to decide on the output. That, too, is obvious. There should be one number for output, the answer. That we can do with

```
return(answer);
```

Now we decide on an algorithm for calculating the answer:

set answer equal to 1

multiply answer by the base as many times as exp says

Perhaps it's not clear how to perform the second step, so let's break it down further:

multiply answer by base and decrease exp by 1

stop when exp reaches 0

If exp is, say, 3, then this results in three multiplications, so this approach seems sound.

Okay, now put it in code.

```
/* finds base to the exp power */
```

```
power(base, exp)
int base, exp;
{
    int answer;

    for (answer = 1; exp > 0; exp--)
            answer = answer * base;
    return(answer);
}
```

Now test it with a driver.

```
/* powertest */
main()
{
    int x;

    x = power(2,3);
    printf("%d\n", x);
    x = power(-3,3);
    printf("%d\n", x);
    x = power (4,-2);
    printf("%d\n", x);
    x = power (5,10);
    printf("%d\n", x);
}
```

Put the two functions together, compile and run them. We get this output:

```
8
-27
1
761
```

Well, 2 to the 3rd power is 8, and −3 to 3rd power is −27. So far, so good. But 4 to the −2 power is 1/16, not 1. And 5 to the 10th power is 9,765,625—if memory serves us well.

What went wrong? First, the program is not designed to handle negative powers, so it bombs out on that problem. Second, type **int** on our system can't handle numbers beyond 65,535.

We can fix the program by including processing for negative powers and by using floating-point numbers for the base and answer. We need to keep the exponent an integer because that is the number of times we multiply; we can't perform 2.31 multiplications.

```
/* finds base to the exp power */
double power(base, exp)
double base;
int exp;
{
    double answer;

    if ( exp > 0)
        {
        for (answer = 1.0; exp > 0; exp--)
            answer *= base;
        return(answer);
        }
    else if (base != 0)
        {
        for (answer = 1.0; exp < 0; exp++)
            answer /= base;
        return(answer);
        }
    else  /* base = 0 and exp <= 0  */
        {
        printf("0 to the %d power is not allowed!\n", exp);
        return(0);
        }
}
```

There are some points to note here. Foremost is that we have to declare the function type! Since **answer** is type **double, power( )** itself must be **double,** because **power** is assigned the value returned by **return.** Why, you ask, did we not declare functions before? The answer is that C functions are assumed to be type **int** (and most are) unless otherwise declared.

Also, we wanted to show you that we haven't forgotten those new assignment operators we introduced in Chapter 8.

Third, we converted negative powers into division, as permitted by the laws of algebra. This brought up a disturbing possibility, division by zero, so we headed that off with an error message. We returned the value of 0 so that the program needn't stop.

We can use the same driver, providing we also declare **power( )**'s type there, too.

```
/* powertest */
main()
{
    double x;
    double power();  /* this is how to declare a function */

    x = power(2.0,3);
```

```
     printf("%.0f\n", x);
     x = power(-3.0,3);
     printf("%.0f\n", x);
     x = power (4.0,-2);
     printf("%.4f\n", x);
     x = power (5.0,10);
     printf("%.0f\n", x);
}
```

This time the output is satisfactory.

```
8
-27
0.0625
9765625
```

This example suggests we include the next short section.

Specifying Function Types

The type of a function is determined by the type of value it returns, not by the type of its arguments. Functions are assumed to be type **int** unless otherwise declared. If a function is not type **int,** you need to announce its type in two places:

1. Declare the function type in its definition:

```
char pun( ch, n)   /* a function that returns a character */
int n;
char ch;

float raft(num)   /* a function that returns type float */
int num;
```

2. Declare the function prior to its first appearance as a function call. This is termed a *forward declaration,* for it declares the function before it is defined. A forward declaration can be placed in the declaration segment of the calling function, or it can be declared above the calling function. In either case, just include the parentheses (no arguments) to identify it as a function. Either of the following is fine for a **main( )** function that calls on a **pun( )** function and a **raft( )** function defined later:

```
main()
```

```
{
char rch, pun();
float raft();
```

or

```
char pun();        /* function declared before main() */
float raft();
main()
{
char rch;
```

Don't forget now. If a function returns a non-**int** value, declare the function type where it is defined and where it is used.

The *void* Type

One function type merits discussion because we haven't mentioned it yet. What type should a function have if it has no return value? In the early days of C, such functions usually were declared without a type, making them type **int** by default. The recommended practice now, however, is to declare them to be type **void**. (This is "void" in the sense of empty, not in the sense of invalid.) Just as with other non-**int** types, **void** functions should be declared when used in another function.

What about functions like **printf( )**? We haven't called it **void**? Well, **printf( )** actually is type **int**. Like **scanf( )** it returns a status value, but usually the return value is ignored.

Summary: Functions

Form:
A typical function definition has this form:

> *name(argument list)*
> *argument declarations*
> *function body*

The presence of the argument list and declarations is optional. Variables other than the arguments are declared within the body, which is bounded by braces.

Example:

```
diff(x,y)      /* function name and argument list */
int x,y;       /* declare arguments */
```

```
{                  /* begin function body */
  int z;           /* declare local variable */

  z = x - y;
  return z;
}                  /* end function body */
```

Communicating Values:

Arguments are used to convey values from the calling program to the function. If variables **a** and **b** have the values 5 and 2, then the call

```
c = diff(a,b);
```

transmits 5 and 2 to the variables **x** and **y**. The values 5 and 2 are called *actual arguments,* and the **diff( )** variables **x** and **y** are called *formal arguments. The keyword* **return** communicates one value from the function to the calling program. In our example, **c** receives the value of **z**, which is 3. A function ordinarily has no effect on the variables in a calling program. Use pointers as arguments to directly affect variables in the calling program. This may be necessary if you wish to communicate more than one value back to the calling program.

Function Type:

Functions must have the same type as the value they return. Functions are assumed to be of type **int.** If a function is of another type, it must be declared so in the calling program and in the function definition.

Example:

```
main()
{
  float q, x, duff();  /* declare in calling program */
  int n;
  . . .
  q = duff(x,n);
  . . .
}
float duff( u, k )   /* declare in function definition */
float u;
int k;
{
  float tor;
  . . .
  return tor;   /* returns a float value */
}
```

All C Functions Are Created Equal

Each C function in a program is on equal footing with the others. Each can call any other function or be called by any other function. This makes the C function somewhat different from Pascal procedures, for Pascal procedures can be nested within other procedures. Procedures in one nest will be ignorant of procedures in another nest.

Isn't the function **main( )** special? Yes, it is a little special in that when a program of several functions is put together, execution starts with the first statement in **main( )**. But that is the limit of its preference. Even **main( )** can be called by other functions, as this example shows.

```
/* use.main */
#include <stdio.h>
main()
{
  char ch;
  void more();

  printf("Enter any character you want. A Q will end things.\n");
  ch = getchar();
  printf("Aha! That was a %c!\n", ch);
  if (ch != 'Q')
    more();
}
void more()
{
  main();
}
```

The function **main( )** calls **more( )**, and **more( )** calls **main( )**! When **main( )** is called, it starts at the beginning, so we have made a sneaky loop. Note that **more( )** is an example of a type **void** function.

Indeed, a function can even call itself. We can simplify the last example to this:

```
/* main.main */
#include <stdio.h>
main()
{
  char ch;

  printf("Enter any character you want. A Q will end things.\n");
  ch = getchar();
  printf("Aha! That was a %c!\n", ch);
  if (ch != 'Q')
```

Compiling Programs with Two or More Functions

The simplest approach to using several functions is to place them in the same file. Then just compile that file as you would a single-function file. Other approaches are more system dependent. Here are some:

UNIX

Suppose **file1.c** and **file2.c** are two files containing C functions. Then the command

```
cc file1.c file2.c
```

will compile both files and produce an executable file called **a.out.** In addition, two "object" files called **file1.o** and **file2.o** are produced. If you later change **file1.c** and not **file2.c,** you can compile the first and combine it with the object code version of the second file using the command

```
cc file1.c file2.o
```

Microsoft C

Compile **file1.c** and **file2.c** separately, producing the two object code files **file1.obj** and **file2.obj.** Use the linker to combine them with each other:

```
link file1 file2
```

Assembly-Code–Based Systems

Some systems allow you to compile several files at once à la UNIX:

```
cc file1.c file2.c
```

or equivalent. Or in some cases you can produce separate assembly-code modules and then combine those in the assembly process.

```
        main();
}
```

Here's some sample output to show that it works. Note how it even processes the newline character that gets transmitted when we used the [return] key.

```
Enter any character you want. A Q will end things.
I [return]
```

```
Aha! That was a I!
Enter any character you want. A Q will end things.
Aha! That was a
!
Enter any character you want. A Q will end things.
Q [return]
Aha! That was a Q!
```

The act of a function calling itself is termed *recursion*. The loop we set up using recursion doesn't work the same as a **while** or **do while** loop. When **main( )** calls itself, it doesn't simply repeat itself. It does go through the same set of instructions in memory, but it creates a new set of variables. If you print out the address of a variable in an ordinary loop, the address doesn't change from iteration to iteration. With the loop we have here, the address does change, for a new **ch** is created with each loop. If the program loops 20 times, 20 different variables will be created, each called **ch,** but each with its own address.

Summary

You should use functions as building blocks for larger programs. Each function should have a single, well-defined purpose. Use arguments to communicate values to a function, and use the keyword **return** to communicate a value back to the calling program. If the function returns a value not of type **int,** then you must specify the function type in the function definition and in the declaration section of the calling program. If you want the function to affect variables in the calling program, you should use addresses and pointers.

What You Should Have Learned

How to define a function

How to communicate information to a function: use arguments

The difference between a formal argument and an actual argument: one is a variable used by the function; the other is a value from the calling function

Where to declare arguments: after the function name and before the first brace

Where to declare other local variables: after the first brace

When and how to use **return**

When and how to use addresses and pointers for communication

When to declare function types: when they don't return an **int**

Where to declare function types: in the function definition and in or above the calling program

When to use the **void** type: for functions with no return value

Review Questions

1. Devise a function that returns the sum of two integers.

2. What changes, if any, would you need to make in order to have the function of Question 1 add two **float** numbers instead?

3. Devise a function **alter( )** that takes two **int** variables **x** and **y** and changes their values to their sum and their difference, respectively.

4. Anything wrong with this function definition?

```
void salami(num)
{
    int num, count;

    for(count = 1; count <= num; num++)
        printf(" O salami mio!\n");
}
```

5. Write a function that returns the largest of three integer arguments.

6. **a.** Write a function that displays a menu of four numbered choices and asks you to choose one. That is, the output should look like this:

```
Please choose one of the following:
1) copy files          2) move files
3) remove files        4) quit
Enter the number of your choice:
```

   b. Write a function that has two **int** arguments, a lower limit and an upper limit. The function should read an integer from input. If the integer is outside the limits, the function should print a menu (using the function from part **a.** and get a new value. When an integer in the proper limits is entered, the function should return that value to the calling program.
   c. Write a minimal program using the functions from parts **a.** and **b.** of this question. By minimal, we mean it need not actually perform the promised actions from the menu; it should just show the choices and get a valid response.

Answers

1. ```
   sum(j,k)
   int j, k;
   {
   return (j + k);
   }
   ```

2. ```
   float sum(j,k)
   float j, k;
   ```
   Also, declare **float sum( )** in the calling program.

3. Since we want to alter two variables in the calling program, we can use addresses and pointers. The call would be **alter(&x,&y)** A possible solution is:

```
void alter(px,py)
int *px, *py;   /* pointers to x and y */
{
    int sum, diff;

    sum = *px + *py;  /* add contents of two addresses */
    diff = *px - *py;
    *px = sum;
    *py = diff;
}
```

4. Yes; **num** should be declared before the first brace, not after. Also, it should be **count++**, not **num++**.

5. Here is one approach. It uses nested **if** statements. Technically, the second **else** can be omitted, since the previous **return** statements prevent the program from reaching **if (b > c)** unless **a <= b**. But its inclusion makes the logic more obvious.

```
int max3 (a, b, c)
int a, b, c;
{
    if ( a > b )
        if ( a > c )
            return a;
        else return c;
    else if ( b > c )
            return b;
    else return c;
}
```

Here's another. It uses nested conditional statements to produce an opaque coding style much beloved by some programmers.

```
int max3 (a, b, c)
int a, b, c;
{
    return  (a>b) ? ((a>c) ? a:c) : ((b>c) ? b:c);
}
```

6. Here is the minimal program; the **showmenu( )** and **getchoice( )** functions are possible solutions to parts **a.** and **b.**:

```
void showmenu();  /* declare functions used */
int getchoice();
main()
{
```

```
    int res;

    showmenu();
    res = getchoice(1,4);
    printf ("I don't know how to do choice %d: bye!\n", res);
}

void showmenu()
{
     printf("Please choose one of the following:\n");
     printf("1) copy files        2) move files\n");
     printf("3) remove files      4) quit\n");
     printf("Enter the number of your choice:\n");
}

int getchoice(low, high)
int low, high;
{
     int ans;

     scanf("%d", &ans);
     while ( ans < low ¦¦ ans  > high )
         {
         printf("%d is not a valid choice; try again\n", ans);
         showmenu();
         scanf("%d", &ans);
         }
     return ans;
}
```

Exercises

1. Devise a function **max(x,y)** that returns the larger of two values.

2. In the **letterhead2** program near the beginning of this chapter, we used two separate functions: **starbar( )** and **space( )**. The two functions are quite similar; each prints a certain character a certain number of times. Write a more general function that can be used for both tasks. It should take two arguments: a character to be printed, and the number of times it is to be printed.

3. Devise a function **chline(ch,i,j)** that prints the requested character in column **i** to column **j**. See **sketcher** in Chapter 7.

4. Write a function that takes three arguments: a character and two integers. The character is to be printed. The first integer specifies the number of times that the character is to be printed on a line, and the second integer specifies

the number of lines that are to be printed. Write a program that makes use of this function.

5. The harmonic mean of two numbers is obtained by taking the inverses of the two numbers, averaging them, and taking the inverse of the result. Write a function that takes two **double** arguments and returns the harmonic mean of the two numbers.

6. Write a function that takes an integer argument and returns two to that power. For example, if the function is called **twopow( )**, then **twopow(3)** would return a value of 2 cubed, or **8**.

7. The notation **n!** means the product of all the integers from **1** through **n**; it is read "n factorial." Write a function that takes an integer argument and returns the corresponding factorial. For example, if the function is called **fact( )**, then **fact(5)** would return **120**, which is **1*2*3*4*5**.

8. Modularize Exercise 5 of Chapter 7 by writing functions for the various tasks.

10

Storage Classes and Program Development

Concepts
- Local and global variables
- Storage classes
- Random number function
- Error-checking
- Modular programming
- Sorting

Keywords
- *auto, extern, static, register*

One of C's strengths is that it lets you control the fine points of a program. C's storage classes are an example of that control because they allow you to determine which functions know which variables and how long a variable persists in a program. Storage classes form the first topic of this chapter.

A second topic will be the idea that there is more to programming than just knowing the rules of the language, just as there is more to writing a novel (or even a letter) than knowing the rules of English. We will try to give you some general principles and concepts useful in designing programs. We will also develop several useful functions. As we do so, we will try to demonstrate some of the considerations that go into the designing of a function. In particular, we will emphasize the value of a modular approach, the breaking down of jobs into manageable tasks.

But first, we will discuss storage classes.

Storage Classes and Scope

We mentioned earlier that local variables are known only to the functions containing them. C also offers the possibility of global variables known to several functions. Suppose, for example, we want both **main( )** and **critic( )** to have access to the variable **units.** We can do this by assigning **units** to the "external" storage class, as shown here:

```
/* global.units */
int units;    /* an external variable */
main()
```

```
{
    extern int units;

    printf("How many pounds to a firkin of butter?\n");
    scanf("%d", &units);
    while ( units != 56)
        critic();
    printf("You must have looked it up!\n");
}
critic()
{
    extern int units;

    printf("No luck, chummy.  Try again.\n");
    scanf("%d", &units);
}
```

Here is a sample output:

```
How many pounds to a firkin of butter?
14
No luck, chummy.  Try again.
56
You must have looked it up!
```

(We did.)

Note how the second value for **units** was read by the **critic( )** function, yet **main( )** also knew the new value when it quit the **while** loop.

We made **units** an external variable by defining it outside of (external to) any function definition. Then, inside the functions that use the variable, we declare the variable by preceding the variable type with the keyword **extern.** The **extern** informs the computer to look for the definition of this variable outside the function. If we had omitted the keyword **extern** in, say, **critic( )**, the computer would have set up a separate variable private to **critic( )**, but also named **units.** Then the other **units** (the one in **main( )**) would never have its value reset.

Each variable, we know, has a type. In addition, each variable has a storage class. There are four keywords used to describe storage classes: **extern** (for external), **auto** (for automatic), **static,** and **register.** You haven't noticed storage classes before because variables declared within a function are considered to be class **auto** unless declared otherwise. (They are automatically automatic.)

The storage class of a variable is determined by where it is defined and by what keyword, if any, is used.

The storage class determines two things. First, it controls which functions have access to a variable. The extent to which a variable is available is called its *scope*. Second, the storage class determines how long the variable persists in memory. Let's go over the properties of each type.

Automatic Variables

By default, variables declared in a function are automatic. You can, however, make your intentions perfectly clear by explicitly using the keyword **auto:**

```
main()
{
   auto int plox;
```

You might do this, for example, to show that you intentionally are overriding an external function definition.

An automatic variable has local scope. Only the function in which the variable is defined knows the variable. (Of course, arguments can be used to communicate the value and the address of the variable to another function, but that is partial and indirect knowledge.) Other functions can use variables with the same name, but they will be independent variables stored in different memory locations.

An automatic variable comes into existence when the function that contains it is called. When the function finishes its task and returns control to its caller, the automatic variable disappears. The memory location can now be used for something else.

One more point about the scope of an automatic variable: the scope is confined to the block (paired braces) in which the variable is declared. We have always declared our variables at the beginning of the function block, so the scope is the whole function. But in principle one could declare a variable within a subblock. Then that variable would be known only to that subsection of the function. Normally, you wouldn't use this feature when designing a program. However, harried programmers sometimes use this option when trying to make a quick fix.

External Variables

A variable defined outside a function is external. An external variable also should be declared in a function that uses it by using the **extern** keyword. Declarations look like this:

```
int errupt;   /* 3 externally defined variables */
char coal;
double up;
main()
{
   extern int errupt;   /* declaring that 3 variables are */
   extern char coal;    /*      defined externally       */
   extern double up;
```

The group of **extern** declarations may be omitted entirely if the original definitions occur in the same file and before the function that uses them. Including the **extern** keyword allows a function to use an external variable even if it is defined later in a file or in a different file. (Both files, of course, have to be compiled, linked, or assembled at the same time.)

If just the **extern** is omitted from the declaration in a function, then a separate, automatic variable is set up by that name. You may want to label this second variable "auto" to show that this is a matter of intention and not of oversight.

These three examples show the four possible combinations:

```
/* Example 1 */
int hocus;
main()
{
    extern int hocus;  /* hocus declared external */
    ...
}
magic()
{
    extern int hocus;
    ...
}
```

Here there is one external variable **hocus,** and it is known to both **main( )** and **magic( ).**

```
/*Example 2 */
int hocus;
main()
{
    extern int hocus;  /* hocus declared external */
    ...
}
magic()
{
    /* hocus not declared at all */
    ...
}
```

Again, there is one external variable **hocus** known to both functions. This time, **magic( )** knows it by default.

```
/* Example 3 */
int hocus;
main()
{
    int hocus; /* hocus declared, is auto by default */
    ...
}
```

```
magic()
{
    auto int hocus; /* hocus declared automatic */
    ...
}
```

In this case, three separate variables are created. The **hocus** in **main( )** is automatic by default and is local to **main.** The **hocus** in **magic( )** is automatic explicitly and is known only to **magic( ).** The external **hocus** is not known to **main( )** or **magic( )** but would be known to any other function in the file that did not have its own local **hocus.**

These examples illustrate the scope of external variables. They persist as long as the program runs, and, since they aren't confined to any one function, they don't fade away when a particular function ends its task.

Note that if you use just the keyword **extern** without a type, the compiler interprets that as being **extern int.**

Definitions and Declarations

Consider this example:

```
int tern;
main()
{
        external int tern;
    ...
```

Here **tern** is declared twice. The first declaration causes storage to be set aside for the variable; hence it constitutes a "definition" of the variable. The second declaration merely tells the compiler to use the **tern** variable that previously has been created; thus, it is not a definition. The keyword **extern** always indicates that a declaration is not a definition, since it instructs the compiler to look elsewhere. Suppose, for instance, you do this:

```
extern int tern;
main()
{
    ...
```

Then the compiler would assume that the actual definition of **tern** is somewhere else in your program, perhaps in another file. This declaration will not cause space to be allocated. So don't use the keyword **extern** for an external definition; use it only to *refer* to an existing external definition.

Static Variables

The name *static variable* sounds like a contradiction, like a variable that can't vary. Actually, the "static" means the variable stays put. These variables have the same scope as automatic variables, but they don't vanish when the containing function ends its job. The computer remembers their values from one function call to the next. The next example illustrates this point and shows how to declare a static variable.

```
/* static variable */
main()
{
    int count;

    for (count = 1; count <= 3; count++)
        {
        printf("Here comes iteration %d:\n", count);
        trystat();
        }
}
trystat()
{
    int fade = 1;
    static int stay = 1;

    printf("fade = %d and stay = %d\n", fade++, stay++);
}
```

Note that **trystat( )** increments each variable after printing its value. Running the program gives this output:

```
Here comes iteration 1:
fade = 1 and stay = 1
Here comes iteration 2:
fade = 1 and stay = 2
Here comes iteration 3:
fade = 1 and stay = 3
```

The static variable **stay** remembers that its value was increased by 1, while the **fade** variable starts anew each time. This points out a difference in initialization: **fade** is initialized each time **trystat( )** is called, while **stay** is initialized just once, when **trystat( )** is compiled.

External Static Variables

You can also declare a **static** variable outside any function. This act creates an "external static" function. The difference between an ordinary external variable and an external static variable lies in the scope. The ordinary external variable can be used by functions in any file, while the external static variable can be used only by functions in the same file and below the variable definition. You set up an external static variable by placing the definition outside any function:

```
static randx = 1;
rand()
{
```

In just a bit we will show you an example for which you need this sort of variable.

Figure 10.1
External versus external static

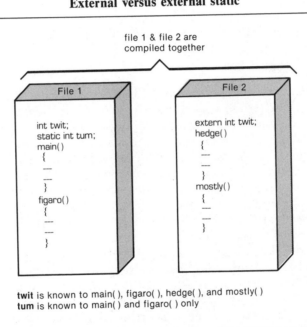

file 1 & file 2 are
compiled together

```
File 1

int twit;
static int tum;
main()
    {
    ---
    ---
    }
figaro()
    {
    ---
    ---
    }
```

```
File 2

extern int twit;
hedge()
    {
    ---
    ---
    }
mostly()
    {
    ---
    ---
    }
```

twit is known to main( ), figaro( ), hedge( ), and mostly( )
tum is known to main( ) and figaro( ) only

Register Variables

Variables normally are stored in computer memory. With luck, register variables are stored in the CPU registers, where they can be accessed and manipulated more rapidly than in memory. In other respects, register variables are the same as automatic variables. They are set up this way:

```
main()
{
    register int quick;
```

We say "with luck," for declaring a variable as register class is more a request than a direct order. The compiler has to weigh your demands against the number of registers that are available, so you may not get your wish. In that case, the variable becomes an ordinary automatic variable.

Scope Summary

At this point, let's summarize the scope of the various storage classes. The scope of an automatic variable (and that includes function formal arguments) is confined to the defining function. When a variable is declared external to a file, that external variable will be known to all functions following it in that file, whether or not those functions explicitly declare the variable as **extern**. If you want a function in a second file to access an external variable in the first file, then you must declare the variable in the second file using the keyword **extern.**

A static variable defined inside a function is local to the function, and a static variable defined outside a function is local to that file.

Which Storage Class?

The answer to the question "Which storage class?" almost always is "automatic." After all, why else was it selected as the default? Yes, we know that at first glance external storage is quite alluring. Just make all your variables external, and you'll never have to worry about using arguments and pointers to communicate back and forth between functions. Unfortunately, you will have to worry about function A sneakily altering variables in function C, although that was not your intention at all. The unquestionable evidence of untold years of collective computer experience is that the latter danger far outweighs the superficial charms of using external storage extensively.

One of the golden rules of protective programming is to observe the "need to know" principle. Keep the workings of each function as private as possible, sharing values only as they are needed.

Since there are times when the other classes are useful, they are available. But ask yourself if it is necessary to use one before doing so.

Now let's look at a function that makes use of an external static variable.

A Random Number Function

You should not be without a random number function. When someone demands a number of you, you can turn to this powerful resource instead of stammering a plea for more time. Less practically, you can use it in many computer games.

Actually, we will show you a "pseudorandom number generator." This means that the actual sequence of numbers is predictable (computers are not known for their spontaneity) but that they are spread pretty uniformly over the possible range of values.

The scheme starts with a number called the "seed." It uses the seed to

---

Summary: Storage Classes

Keywords: *auto, extern, static, register*

General Comments:
The storage class of a variable determines its scope and how long the variable persists. Storage class is determined by where the variable is defined and by the associated keyword. Variables defined outside a function are external and have global scope. Variables declared inside a function are automatic and local unless one of the other keywords is used. External variables defined above a function are known to it even if not declared internally.

Properties:

Storage Class	Keyword	Duration	Scope
automatic	`auto`	temporary	local
register	`register`	temporary	local
static	`static`	persistent	local
external	`extern`*	persistent	global (all files)
external static	`static`	persistent	global (one file)

Those above the dotted line are declared inside a function.
Those below the line are defined outside a function.

*The keyword **extern** is used only to redeclare variables that have been defined externally elsewhere; the act of defining the variable outside of a function makes it external.

---

produce a new number, which becomes the new seed. Then the new seed can be used to produce a newer seed, and so on. For this scheme to work, the random number function must remember the seed it used the last time it was called. Aha! This calls for a static variable.

Here is version 1. (Yes, version 2 comes soon.)

```
/* rand1 */
rand()
{
  static int randx = 1;

  randx = (randx * 25173 + 13849) % 65536; /* magic formula */
```

```
      return( randx);
}
```

The static variable **randx** starts out with the value 1 and is altered by the magic formula each time the function is called. The result on our system is a number somewhere in the range of -32768 to 32767. Systems with a different **int** size will produce different results.

Let's try it with this simple driver:

```
/* randdrive1 */
main()
{
    int count;

    for(count = 1; count <= 5; count++)
        printf("%d\n", rand());
}
```

Here's the output:

```
-26514
-4449
20196
-20531
3882
```

Well, that looks random enough. Let's run it again. This time the result is

```
-26514
-4449
20196
-20531
3882
```

Hmmm, that looks familiar; this is the "pseudo" aspect. Each time the main program is run, we start off with the same seed of 1. We can get around this problem by introducing a second function **srand( )** that lets you reset the seed. The trick is to make **randx** an external static variable known only to **rand( )** and **srand( )**. Keep these two functions in their own file and compile that file separately. Here is the modification:

```
/* file for rand() and srand() */
static int randx = 1;
```

```
rand()
{
  randx = (randx *25173 + 13849) % 65536;
  return( randx);
}
srand(x)
unsigned x;
{
   randx = x;
}
```

Use this driver:

```
 /* randdrive2 */
main()
{
   int count;
   int seed;

   printf("Please enter your choice for seed.\n");
   scanf("%d", &seed);
   srand(seed);     /* reset seed */
   for(count = 1; count <= 5; count++)
        printf("%d\n", rand());
}
```

Run the program once:

```
Please enter your choice for seed.
1
-26514
-4449
20196
-20531
3882
```

Using a value of 1 for **seed** yields the same values as before. Now let's try a value of 3:

```
Please enter your choice for seed.
3
23832
20241
-1858
-30417
-16204
```

Very good! We get a different set of numbers. Now let's develop a use for this set of functions.

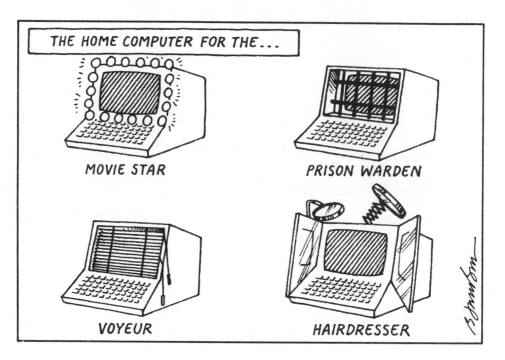

THE HOME COMPUTER FOR THE...

MOVIE STAR

PRISON WARDEN

VOYEUR

HAIRDRESSER

Roll 'Em

We are going to simulate that very popular random activity, dice-rolling. The most popular form of dice-rolling uses two 6-sided dice. But there are other possibilities. Many adventure-fantasy game players use all of the five geometrically possible dice: 4 sides, 6 sides, 8 sides, 12 sides, and 20 sides. (Those clever ancient Greeks proved that there are but five regular solids having all faces the same shape and size, and these solids are the bases for the dice varieties. One could make dice with other numbers of sides, but the faces would not all be the same, so they wouldn't all have equal odds of turning up.)

Computer calculations aren't limited by these geometric considerations, and we will devise an electronic die that can have any number of sides we want. Let's start with 6 sides, then generalize. We want a random number from 1 to 6, but **rand( )** produces the range -32768 to 32767, so we have some adjustments to make. Here's one approach.

1. Divide the random number by 32768. This results in a number x in the range $-1 <= x < 1$. (We'll have to convert to type **float** so that we can have decimal fractions.)

2. Add 1. Our new number satisfies the relationship $0 <= x < 2$.

3. Divide by 2. Now 0 <= x < 1.
4. Multiply by 6. Now 0 <= x < 6. (Close, but 0 is not a possible value.)
5. Add 1: 1<= x < 7. (Note: these are still decimal fractions.)
6. Truncate to an integer. Now we have an integer in the range of 1 to 6.
7. To generalize, just replace 6 in step 4 by the number of sides.

Here is a function that does these steps:

```
/* dice roller */
#define SCALE 32768.0
rollem(sides)
float sides;
{
    float roll;

    roll = ( (float) rand()/SCALE + 1.0) * sides / 2.0 + 1.0;
    return ( (int) roll);
}
```

We included two explicit type casts to emphasize where type conversions take place.

Now for a program that uses these tools:

```
/* multiple dice roll */
main()
{
    int dice, count, roll, seed;
    float sides;

    printf("Enter a seed value.\n");
    scanf("%d", &seed);
    srand(seed);
    printf("Enter the number of sides per die, 0 to stop.\n");
    scanf("%f", &sides);
    while (sides > 0)
        {
        printf("How many dice?\n");
        scanf("%d", &dice);
        for ( roll = 0, count = 1; count <= dice; count ++)
            roll += rollem(sides); /* running total of dice pips */
        printf("You have rolled a %d using %d %.of-sided dice.\n",
                    roll, dice, sides);
        printf("How many sides? Enter 0 to stop.\n");
        scanf("%f", &sides);
```

```
        }
    printf("GOOD FORTUNE TO YOU!\n");
}
```

Now let's use it:

```
Enter a seed value.
1
Enter the number of sides per die, 0 to stop.
6
How many dice?
2
You have rolled a 4 using 2 6-sided dice.
How many sides? Enter 0 to stop.
6
How many dice?
2
You have rolled a 7 using 2 6-sided dice.
How many sides? Enter 0 to stop.
0
GOOD FORTUNE TO YOU!
```

Thanks.

You can use **rollem( )** many ways. With **sides** equal to two, the function simulates a coin toss with "heads" = 2 and "tails" = 1 (or vice versa if you really prefer it). You can easily modify the program to show the individual results as well as the total. Or you can construct a craps simulator. If you require a large number of rolls (a dread Dungeon Master rolling character attributes), you can easily modify our program to produce output like this:

```
Enter a seed value.
10
Enter the number of sets; enter 0 to stop.
18
How many sides and how many dice?
6 3
Here are 18 sets of 3 6-sided throws.
   7    5    9    7   12   10    7   12   10   14
   9    8   13    9   10    7   16   10
How many sets? Enter 0 to stop.
0
```

Another use of **rand( )** (but not of **rollem( )**) would be to modify our number-guessing program so that the computer chooses and you guess, instead of vice versa.

If your C implementation gives you access to some changing quantity, such as the system clock, you can use that value (possibly truncated) to initialize the seed value.

Now let's develop some more functions. Our first project will be to design a function that reads integers.

An Integer-fetching Function: *getint( )*

Designing a function that reads integers may strike you as a rather simple project. After all, we can just use **scanf( )** with the **%d** format if we want to read in an integer. But this lazy approach has a drawback. If you mistakenly type, say, a **T** instead of a **6**, **scanf( )** will balk. What we would like to do is design a function that looks at input and warns you if it is not an integer. Actually, we can use the return value of **scanf( )** to solve the input problem (see Question 7), but we can learn more about programming and about C by developing our own function. We'll start by choosing a name: **getint( )**.

A Plan

Fortunately, we also have a strategy in mind. First, we note that any input can be read in as a string of characters. The integer 324, for example, can be read in as a string of three characters: the character '3', the character '2', and the character '4'. This suggests the following plan:

1. Read in the input as a character string.
2. See if the string consists just of digit characters, preceded, perhaps, by a plus or minus sign.
3. If so, convert it to the correct numerical value.
4. If not, issue a warning.

This plan is so clever, it should work. (The fact that it is a standard approach that has been around for years also gives us some confidence.) But before we plunge into writing the code, we should think more about what our function will do.

In particular, before we start fussing about the innards of **getint( )**, we should decide exactly how the function should interact with its environment: what the information flow will be. What information should it get from the calling program? What information should it give back? In what form should this information be? Once again we are looking at the function as a black box. Our first concern is what goes in and what goes out; after that we worry about what is inside. This approach helps produce a much smoother interaction between different parts of a program. Otherwise, you might find yourself in the position of trying to install a Volvo transmission in a Toyota. The general function is correct, but the interface is a problem.

Information Flow for *getint( )*

What output should our function have? It should surely give the value of the number it reads. Of course, **scanf( )** already does that. Second—and this is why we are taking the time to create this function—it should provide a status report. It should tell us whether or not it found an integer. To make the function really useful, it should also tell us if it finds an EOF. Then we could use **getint( )** in a **while** loop that keeps reading integers until it finds an EOF. In short, we want **getint( )** to return two values: the integer and the status.

Since we want two items of information, we can't use just a **return.** We could use two pointers. However, the common solution for this sort of problem is to use pointers to do the main work of the function and to use **return** to send back some sort of status code. Indeed, **scanf( )** does just this. It returns the numbers of items it has found, and it returns the EOF signal if that's what it found. We can use this feature with a call of this form:

```
status = scanf("%d", &number);
```

We will follow that model. Our function call would look like this:

```
status = getint(&number);
```

The right-hand side uses the address of **number** to get a value to **number,** and **return** is used to get a value to **status.**

Figure 10.2
Designing the *getint( )* function

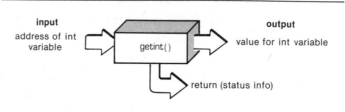

We have to decide on a code for the status report. Since undeclared functions are assumed to be type **int,** our code should consist of integers. Let's use this code for the status report:

−1 means EOF was found

1 means a string containing nondigits was found

0 means a digit string was found

In short, our **getint( )** function has one input, the address of the integer variable whose value is being read. It has two outputs. First, the value of the read integer is provided through a pointer. (Thus, the pointer argument is a two-way channel for information.) Second, a status code is provided by using **return**. This tells us that the skeleton of our function should look like this:

```
getint(ptint)
int *ptint;      /* pointer to integer */
{
    int status;
    ...
    return(status);
}
```

Great! Now we just have to fill in the interior of the function.

Inside *getint( )*

Our general plan, in rough pseudocode, for **getint( )** is this:

> read in the input as characters
> while no EOF is encountered, place the characters
>   into a character string
> if EOF is encountered, set status to STOP
> else
>   check string, convert to integer if possible, and
>   report status (YESNUM or NONUM)

Here we use STOP, YESNUM, and NONUM as symbolic constants representing the -1, 0, and 1 described previously.

We still have some design decisions to make. How does the function decide when it reaches the end of the input string? Should we put a limit on how long the string should be?

We enter a region where we have to decide between the convenience of the programmer and the convenience of the user. The simplest thing would be to have the user terminate a string by using the [enter] key. This would mean one entry per line. On the other hand, it would be nice for the user if several numbers could be placed on the same line:

    2   34   4542   2   98

We decided to give the user a break. The function will consider a string to begin with a nonblank, nonnewline character and to end when the next blank or newline is encountered. Thus, input can be on one line or several lines.

We'll limit the input string to 80 characters. Since strings are terminated with a null character, we will need an array of 81 characters to include the null. This is stupendously generous, since we need only 6 characters for a 16-bit integer and sign. You can enter longer numbers, but they will be cut down to size.

To make the program more modular, we'll delegate the actual conversion to another function, which we will call **stoi( )** for "string to integer." We also will have **stoi( )** return the proper status code to **getint( )**, and **getint( )** then can relay the status to its calling program. The function **stoi( )** will perform the last two lines of our pseudocode plan.

Figure 10.3 presents the code for **getint( )**; **stoi( )** will follow later:

Figure 10.3
Code for *getint ( )*

```
/*  getint()  */
#include <stdio.h>
#define LEN 81    /* maximum length of string */
#define STOP -1   /* status codes */
#define NONUM 1
#define YESNUM 0
getint(ptint)
int *ptint;       /* pointer to integer output */
{
    char intarr[LEN]; /* store input string */
    int  ch;
    int ind = 0; /* array index */

    while ((ch = getchar()) == '\n' ¦¦ ch == ' ' ¦¦ ch == '\t');
          /* skip over initial newlines, blanks, and tabs */
    while ( ch != EOF && ch != '\n' && ch != ' ' && ch != '\t' &&
          ind < LEN)
        {
        intarr[ind++] = ch;  /* put character into array */
        ch = getchar();      /* get next character */
        }
    intarr[ind] = '\0';  /* end array with null character */
    if (ch == EOF)
      return(STOP);
    else
       return ( stoi(intarr, ptint) );  /* does conversion */
}
```

We get a character **ch.** If it is a blank or newline or a tab, we get the next character until we get one that isn't. Then, if it isn't an EOF, we put it

in an array. We keep getting more cha'
find a forbidden character or until we
null character ('\0') in the next posit'
string. This puts the array into sta'
was the last character read, retu'
string. Here we invoke the new '
stoi( ) do? As input it takes a '
variable. It will use the pointer
use **return** to send a status re'
function that calls it.

A less compact way to repres

```
status = stoi(intarr, ptint);
return (status);
```

Here **status** would be an **int** variable. The first statemen.
to whatever **ptint** points to, and it also assigns a value to **status.** 1.
statement returns the value to the program that called **getint( ).** Our s.
program line has exactly the same effect, except that no intermediate variable **status** was needed.

Now we need to write **stoi( ),** and we will be done.

String-to-Integer Conversion: *stoi( )*

First, let's describe what input and output the **stoi( )** function should have.
The input will be a character string, so **stoi( )** will have a character string
argument. There will be two output values: the status and the integer conversion. We are using **return** for the status, so we will have to use a pointer
to return the other value. Thus there will be a second argument, a pointer-
to-integer. Our function skeleton will look like this:

```
stoi(string, intptr)
char string[]; /* input string */
int *intptr; /* pointer to variable getting integer value */
{
    int status;
    ...
    return(status);
}
```

The declaration for **string** may look odd, since the brackets are empty.
At this point, think of this declaration as setting up **string** as an alternative
name for the array used in the calling function (**intarr,** in this case). Chapters 12 and 13 will amplify on passing arrays to functions.

Okay, what about an algorithm for making the conversion? Let's ignore the sign for a moment and assume the string has only digits in it. Look
at the first character and convert it to its numerical equivalent. Suppose the

is '4'. This character has the ASCII numeric value 52, and that is
stored. If we subtract 48 from it, we get 4; that is,

$$ \text{'4'} - 48 = 4 $$

ut 48 is ASCII code for the character '0', so

$$ \text{'4'} - \text{'0'} = 4 $$

In fact, this last statement would be true for any code that uses consecutive numbers to represent consecutive digits. So if **num** is the numerical value and **chn** is a digit character, then

```
num = chn - '0';
```

Okay, we use this technique to convert the first digit to a number. Now we look at the next array member. If it is '\0', then there was only one digit, and we are done. Suppose, though, it is a '3'. We convert this to the numerical value 3. But if it is a 3, then the 4 must have been 40, and the total is 43:

```
num = 10 * num + chn - '0';
```

Now just continue this process, multiplying the old value of **num** by 10 every time we find one more digit. Our function will use this technique.

Here is the definition of **stoi( )**. We keep it in the same file as **getint( )** so that it can use the same **#define**'s.

```
/* converts string to integer and makes status report */
stoi(string, intptr)
char string[];      /* string to be converted to an integer */
int *intptr;        /* value of the integer */
{
    int sign = 1;            /* keep track of + or - */
    int index = 0;

    if ( string[index] == '-' || string[index] == '+' )
        sign = (string[index++] == '-') ? -1 : 1; /* set sign */
    *intptr = 0;  /* initialize value */
    while ( string[index] >= '0' && string[index] <= '9')
        *intptr = 10 * (*intptr) + string[index++] - '0';
    if ( string[index] == '\0')
        {
        *intptr = sign * ( *intptr );
        return(YESNUM);
        }
    else  /* found a nondigit other than sign or '\0' */
```

```
        return(NONUM);
}
```

The **while** statement jogs along, converting digits to numbers until it reaches a nondigit character. If that character is a '**\0**' character, all is fine because that marks the end of the string. Any other nondigit sends the program flow to the **else** to report failure.

The standard C library contains a function **atoi( )** (ASCII to integer) very much like **stoi( )**. The main differences are that **stoi( )** checks for nondigital strings, that **atoi( )** uses **return** instead of a pointer to give back the number, and that **atoi( )** does the blank skipping we did in **getint( )**. We could have done all the status checking in **getint( )** and used **atoi( )** instead of **stoi( )**, but we thought it would be more fun to develop our own approach.

Trying It Out

Is our logic as sound as we think? Let's try out our function in a sample program:

```
/* getint() tryout */
#define STOP -1
#define NONUM 1
#define YESNUM 0
main()
{
  int num, status;

  printf("This program stops reading numbers if EOF is read.\n");
  while ( (status = getint(&num)) != STOP )
      if (status == YESNUM)
         printf("The number %d has been accepted.\n", num);
      else
         printf("That was no integer! Try again.\n");
  printf("That's it.\n");
}
```

Here is a sample run.

```
This program stops reading numbers if EOF is read.
100     -23
The number 100 has been accepted.
The number -23 has been accepted.
+892
The number 892 has been accepted.
wonk
That was no integer! Try again.
```

```
23skidoo
That was no integer! Try again.
775
The number 775 has been accepted.
[control-z]        (sends the EOF signal on our system)
That's it.
```

As you can see, it works. Notice how we were able to set up a loop to read integers indefinitely until an EOF was typed. That is a handy feature.

Are there any bugs? There is at least one. If you follow a number directly with an EOF without an intervening blank or newline character, the input phase stops, ignoring that number:

```
706 EOF     /* 706 is accepted  */
706EOF      /* 706 not accepted */
```

We didn't want to make the example too complicated, so we let this bug pass. (It's not a bug for UNIX systems, since they require typing [control-d] at the *beginning* of a line to generate the EOF signal.) Also, this gives us a chance to say that further development is left as an exercise for the reader. (If you are interested in fixing that bug, you may be interested in the **ungetc( )** function, which places the last character read back in the input queue. It requires using a "stream" argument, as discussed in Chapter 15.)

Now that we have a handy function for fetching integers, let's turn to a new project that will use it.

Sorting Numbers

One of the most common tests for a computer is sorting. Here we'll develop a program to sort integers. Again, let's take a black box approach and think in terms of input and output. Our overall plan, shown in Figure 10.4, is pretty simple.

At this point, the program is still too vaguely defined to code. The next step is to identify the main tasks that the program must do to accomplish our goals. We can break down our example to three main tasks:

1. Read in the numbers.
2. Sort them.
3. Print out the sorted numbers.

Figure 10.5 shows this breakdown as we move from the top level of organization down to a more detailed level of organization.

Now we have three black boxes, each with its own input and output. We could assign each part to a different programming team, providing we

Figure 10.4
Sorting program: a black box view

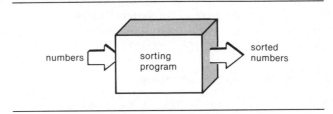

Figure 10.5
Sorting program: peeking inside

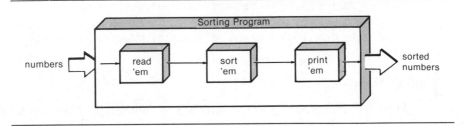

make sure that the numbers output by "read 'em" are in the same form that "sort 'em" uses for input.

As you can see, we are emphasizing modularity. We have broken the original problem into three smaller, more manageable problems.

What next? Now we apply our efforts to each of the three boxes separately, breaking them down to simpler units until we reach a point at which the code is obvious. As we do this, we pay attention to these important points: data-form choice, error-trapping, and information flow.

Figure 10.6
Sorting program: the first task

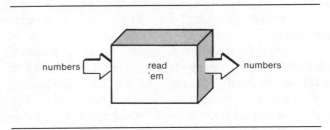

Let's continue with our example, tackling the reading section first.

Reading In Numeric Data

Many programs involve reading in numbers, so the ideas we develop here will be useful elsewhere. The general form for this part of the program is clear: use a loop to read in numbers until all the numbers are read. But there is more to it than you might think!

Choosing the Data Representation

How do we represent a bunch of numbers? We could use a bunch of variables, one for each number. That is just too much trouble to even think about. We could use an array, one element for each number. That sounds a lot better, so let's use an array.

But what kind of array? Type **int?** Type **double?** We need to know how the program is going to be used. Let's assume it is to be used with integers. (What if it is to be used with both? That's possible, but more work than we want right now.) We will use an array of integers to store the numbers we read.

Ending Input

How will the program know how many numbers to read? In Chapter 8 we discussed several solutions to this problem, most of which were unsatisfactory. Now that we have **getint( ),** however, there is no problem. Here is one approach:

> read a number
>
> while not EOF
>
>> assign it to an array and
>>
>> read the next number if the array isn't full

Note that there are two separate conditions that bring this section of the program to a close: an EOF signal or filling the array.

Further Considerations

Before we set this into C code, we still have decisions to make. What will we do about error-checking? Should we make this part of the program into a function?

By the first question we mean, what do we do about the possibility of the user entering faulty data, say a letter instead of an integer? Without **getint( ),** we would rely on the "perfect user theory," which states that the user makes no entry errors. However, we recognize that this theory may not apply to users other than ourselves. Fortunately, we can use **getint( )**'s status report feature to help out here.

The programming that is left can easily be fit into **main( ).** However, it is more modular to use a separate function for each of the three major parts of the program, so that is what we will do. The input to this function will be numbers from the keyboard or a file, and the function output will be an array containing the unsorted numbers. It would be nice if the function let the main program know how many numbers were read, so let's make that part of the output, too. Finally, we should try to make it a little user-friendly, so we will have it print a message indicating its limits, and we will have it echo its input.

The Functions *main( )* and *getarray( )*

Let's call our reading function **getarray( )**. We have defined the function in terms of input and output, and we have outlined the scheme in pseudocode. Let's write the function now and show how it fits into the main program.

First we give **main( )**:

```
/* sort1 */
#define MAXSIZE  100  /* limit to number of integers to sort */
main()
{
   int numbers[MAXSIZE]; /* array to hold input */
   int size;             /* number of input items */
   void sort(), print;

   size = getarray(numbers, MAXSIZE); /* put input into array */
   sort(numbers, size);     /* sort the array */
   print(numbers, size);    /* print the sorted array */
}
```

Here we have the overall view of the program. The function **getarray( )** places the input into the array **numbers** and reports back how many values were read in; that value is assigned to **size.** Then **sort( )** and **print( )**, which we have yet to write, sort the array and print the results. Giving them **size** makes their jobs easier and saves them from having to do their own counting. Also, we provide **getarray( )** with **MAXSIZE,** which tells it how big an array it has available for storage.

Now that we are adding **size** to the information flow, we should modify our black box sketch. See Figure 10.7.

Figure 10.7
Sorting program: adding details

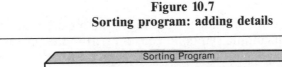
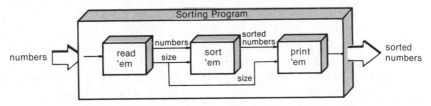

Now let's look at **getarray( )** in the following program:

```
/* getarray() using getint() */
#define STOP -1    /* EOF status */
#define NONUM 1    /* nondigit string status */
#define YESNUM 0   /* digit string status */
getarray( array, limit)
int array[], limit;
{
    int num, status;
    int index = 0;   /* array index */

    printf("This program stops reading numbers after %d values\n",
            limit);
    printf("or if an EOF character is entered.\n");
    while(  index < limit && (status = getint(&num)) != STOP )
        { /* stops reading at size limit or at EOF */
        if ( status == YESNUM)
            {
            array[index++] = num;
            printf("The number %d has been accepted.\n", num);
            }
        else if ( status == NONUM)
            printf("That was no integer! Try again.\n");
        else
            printf("This can't happen! Something's very wrong.\n");
        }
if ( index == limit )  /* report if array gets filled */
    printf("All %d elements of the array were filled.\n",
            limit);
    return(index);
}
```

This is a substantial chunk of program, and we have quite a few points to note.

Explanation

Since it is a little difficult to remember the meaning of, say, a -1 code, we have used mnemonic symbolic constants to represent the status codes.

Using these codes, we set up **getarray( )** to handle each of the possible status values. A **STOP** status causes the reading cycle to end when **getint( )** finds an EOF lurking in its path. A **YESNUM** status results in the number being stored in the awaiting array. Also, the number is "echoed" back to the user to let him or her know that it was accepted. A **NONUM** status sends the user back for another try. (That's being neighborly.)

But there is one more **else** statement. Logically, the only way that statement can be reached is if **getint( )** returns a value other than −1, 0, or 1. But those are the only values that can be returned, so this seems to be a useless statement. Why include it? We include it as an example of "defensive programming," the art of protecting a program from future fiddling. Someday, we, or someone else, may decide to go into **getint( )** and add a few more possible status values to its repertoire. Most likely we will have forgotten, and they may never have known, that **getarray( )** assumes that there are just three possible responses. So we include this final **else** to trap any new responses that show up, and future debugging will be that much simpler.

The size of the array is established in **main( )**. Therefore, we don't give the size of the array when we declare the array argument in **getarray( )**. We do, however, include the brackets in order to point out that the argument is an array.

```
int numbers[MAXSIZE];  /* give size in main */
int array[]; /* no size specification in called function */
```

In Chapter 12, we'll discuss the use of arrays in functions.

We decided to use the keyword **return** to communicate back the number of items read. Thus, our function call

```
size = getarray(numbers, MAXSIZE);
```

assigns a value to **size** and gives values to the **numbers** array.

You may be wondering why we didn't use pointers in the call

```
size = getarray (numbers, MAXSIZE);
```

After all, we are having the function change the value of something (the array) in the calling program. The answer is, we did use a pointer! In C, the name of an array is also a pointer to the first element of an array, that is:

```
numbers == &numbers[0]
```

When **getarray( )** sets up the array **array,** the address of **array[0]** is the same as the address of **numbers[0],** and so on for the other subscripts. Thus, all the manipulations that **getarray( )** does to **array[ ]** actually get done to **numbers[ ].** We will talk more about the relation between pointers and arrays in Chapter 12. The main point we need to know now is that if we use an array as a function argument, the function affects the array in the calling program.

In functions involving counters and limits, like this one, the most likely place to find errors is at the "boundary conditions," where counts reach their limits. Are we going to read a maximum of **MAXSIZE** numbers, or are we going to be off by one? We need to pay attention to details such as ++**index** versus **index**++ and < versus < =. We also have to keep in mind that arrays start their subscripting with **0,** not **1.** Check through our coding and see if it works as it should. The easiest way to do that is to imagine that **limit** is **1** and then walk through the procedure step by step.

Often the most difficult part of a program is getting it to interact in a convenient and dependable manner with the user. That is the case with this program. Now that we are through **getarray( )**, we will find **sort( )** to be easier and **print( )** easier yet. Let's move on to **sort( )** now.

Sorting the Data

Let's look at **main( )** again:

```
main()
{
  int numbers[MAXSIZE]; /* array to hold input */
  int size;             /* number of input items */
  void sort(), print();

  size = getarray(numbers, MAXSIZE); /* put input into array */
  sort(numbers, size);    /* sort the array */
  print(numbers, size);   /* print the sorted array */
}
```

We see that the input to **sort( )** is an array of integers to be sorted and a count of the number of elements to be sorted. The output is the array containing the sorted numbers. We still haven't decided how to do the sorting, so we have to refine this description further.

One obvious point to decide is the direction of the sort. Are we going to sort from large to small or vice versa? Again, we'll be arbitrary and say we will sort from large to small. (We could make a program to do either, but then we would have to develop a way to tell the program which choice we want.)

Figure 10.8
Sorting program: the second task

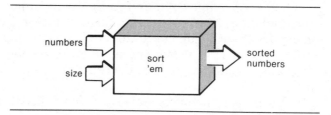

Now let's consider the method we will use to sort. Many sorting algorithms have been developed for computers; we'll use one of the simplest. Here is our plan in pseudocode:

for n = first to n = next-to-last element, find largest remaining
number and place it in the nth element

It works like this. First, n = 1. We look through the whole array, find
the largest number, and place it in the first element. Then n = 2, and we
look through all but the first element of the array, find the largest remaining
number, and place it in the second element. We continue this process until
we reach the next-to-last element. Now just two elements are left. We compare them and place the larger in the next-to-last position. This leaves the
smallest element of all in the final position.

This looks like a **for** loop task, but we still have to describe the "find
and place" process in more detail. How do we find the largest remaining
number each time? Here is one way. Compare the first and second elements
of the remaining array. If the second is larger, switch the two values. Now
compare the first element with the third. If the third is larger, switch those
two. Each time the larger element floats to the top. Continue this way until
you have compared the first with the last element. When you finish, the
largest number is now in the first element of the remaining array. In essence,
we have sorted the array for the first element, but the rest of the array is in a
jumble. In pseudocode:

for n = second element to last element, compare nth element with
first element; if nth is greater, swap values

This looks like another **for** loop. It will be nested in the first **for** loop.
The outer loop indicates which array element is to be filled, and the inner
loop finds the value to put there. Putting the two parts of the pseudocode
together and translating it into C, we get the following function:

```
/* sorts an integer array in decreasing order */
void sort(array, limit)
int array[], limit;
{
    int top, search;

    for ( top = 0 ; top < limit -1 ; top++)
        for ( search = top + 1; search < limit; search++)
            if ( array[search] > array[top])
                interchange( &array[search], &array[top] );
}
```

Here we were clever enough to remember that the first element has **0** for
a subscript. Also, we recalled that we developed a swapping function in
Chapter 9, so we have used it here. Since **interchange( )** works on two
elements of an array and not the whole array, we have used the addresses of
just the two concerned elements. (While the name **array** is a pointer to the

array as a whole, you need to use the **&** operator to point to individual members.)

We used **top** as the subscript for the array element that is to be filled, since it is at the top of the unsorted part of the array. The **search** index roams over the array below the current **top** element. Most texts use **i** and **j** for these indices, but that makes it harder to see what is happening.

Now we just have **print( )** to write.

Printing the Data

Figure 10.9
Sorting program: the third task

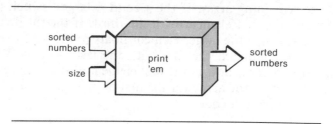

This one is pretty simple:

```
/* print an array */
void print(array, limit)
int array[], limit;
{
    int index;

    for ( index = 0; index < limit; index++)
        printf("%d\n", array[index]);
}
```

If we want something a little different, such as printing in rows instead of in one column, we can always come back and change this function, leaving the other functions untouched. Similarly, if we found a sorting algorithm we liked better, we could replace that module. That is one of the nice features about a modular program.

Results

Let's compile and test this package. To make checking the boundary conditions simpler, we'll temporarily change **MAXSIZE** to 5.

For our first test, we will feed numbers to the program until it refuses to take more.

```
This program stops reading numbers after 5 values
or if an EOF character is entered.
12 34 54 23 67
All 5 elements of the array were filled.
67
54
34
23
12
```

Good, it stopped when five numbers were read, and it sorted the results. Now we test to see if it stops when an EOF character is met.

```
This program stops reading numbers after 5 values
or if an EOF character is entered.
456 928
-23 +16
[control-z]          (transmits EOF on our system)
928
456
16
23
```

Faster than you can say "oikology is the science of housekeeping," the whole enormous array is sorted.

Success! It wasn't easy, but it wasn't impossible. By breaking the problem down into smaller parts and by thinking about what information should flow into and out of each part, we reduced the problem to manageable proportions. Furthermore, the individual modules we produced could be used as parts of similar programs.

That concludes our examples for this chapter. Now let's step back and look at the lessons of this chapter.

Overview

What have we accomplished? On the practical side we developed a random-number generator and an integer-sorting program. In the process we developed a **getint( )** function that we can use in other programs. On the educational side we illustrated some general principles and concepts useful in designing programs.

The most fundamental point to note is that programs should be *designed* rather than allowed to evolve through some random process of growth, trial, and error. You should think carefully about the form and content of input and output for a program. You should break the program down into well-defined tasks, then program these tasks separately, but with an eye to how they interface with one another. The idea is to achieve modularity. When necessary, break a module into smaller modules. Use functions to enhance the modularity and clarity of the program.

When designing a program, try to anticipate what might go wrong, and then program accordingly. Use error-trapping to steer around potential problems or, at least, to alert the user if a problem shows up. It's much better to give the user a second chance to enter data than to send the program crashing in ignominy.

When designing a function, first decide how it will interact with the calling function. Decide what information flows in and what information flows out. What will the arguments be? Will you use pointers, or **return,** or both? Once you have these design parameters in mind, you can turn your attention to the mechanics of the function.

Put these ideas to use, and your programs will be more reliable and less prone to crashing. You will acquire a body of functions that you can use in other programs. Your programming will take less time. All in all, it seems like a good recipe for healthy programming.

Don't forget about storage classes. Variables can be defined outside of functions, in which case they are called external (or global) variables and are available to more than one function. Variables defined within a function are local to that function and are not known to other functions. When possible, use the automatic variety of local variables. This keeps variables in one function from being contaminated by the actions of other functions.

What You Should Have Learned

How to think of a function: a black box with information flow
What "error-checking" is and why it is good
One algorithm for sorting
How to have a function change an array: **function(array)**
How to convert a digit string to a number
The storage classes: **auto, extern, static,** and **register**
The scope of each storage class.
Which storage class to use: **auto,** mostly

Review Questions

1. What might make our sorting algorithm inefficient?

2. How would you change the sorting routine to make it sort in increasing order instead of decreasing order?

3. Change **print( )** so that it prints five numbers per line.

4. How would you change **stoi( )** to handle strings that represent octal numbers?

5. Which functions know each variable in the following? Are there any errors?

```
   /* file 1 */
int daisy;
main()
{
int lily;
}
petal()
{
 extern int daisy, lily;
}
 /* file 2 */
static int lily;
int rose;
stem()
{
   int rose;
}
root()
{
   extern int daisy;
}
```

6. What will the following program print out?

```
#include <stdio.h>
char color= 'B';

main()
{
  extern char color;
  void first(), second();

  printf("color in main() is %c\n", color);
  first();
  printf("color in main() is %c\n", color);
  second();
  printf("color in main() is %c\n", color);
}

void first()
{
  char color;

  color = 'R';
  printf("color in first() is %c\n", color);
}

void second()
{
  color = 'G';
  printf("color in second() is %c\n", color);
}
```

7. Write a function that takes the address of an integer as an argument. Have it read an integer from input and place the value at the indicated address. If an input item is not an integer, have it skip to the next input item. Have it return 1 if it reads an integer and −1 if it detects EOF. To implement this function, use **scanf( )**. In particular, make use of **scanf( )**'s return value and of the fact that **scanf("%*s")** skips over the next input string, i.e., over the next contiguous set of visible characters.

Answers

1. Suppose we are sorting 20 numbers. Our sorting method makes 19 comparisons to find the one largest number. Then it makes 18 comparisons to find the next largest. All the information it obtained during the first search is forgotten, except for which is largest. The second largest number may have been in the number 1 spot for a while, then shuffled down to last. A lot of the comparisons made the first time through get repeated the second time through, and the third time, etc.

2. Replace **array[search]** $>$ **array[top]** with $<$ **array[top] array[search]**

3.
```
/* print an array */
print(array, limit)
int array[], limit;
{
    int index;

    for ( index = 0; index <= limit; index++)
        {
        printf("%10d ", array[index]);
        if (index % 5 == 4)
                printf("\n");
        }
    printf("\n");

}
```

4. First, limit the acceptable characters to the digits 0 through 7. Second, multiply by 8 instead of by 10 each time a new digit is detected.

5. **daisy** is known to **main( )** by default, and to **petal( )** and **root( )** because of the **extern** declaration. It is not known to **stem( )** because they are in different files. The first **lily** is local to **main:** the reference to **lily** in **petal( )** is an error because there is no external **lily** in either file. There is an external static **lily,** but it is known just to functions in the second file. The first external **rose** is known to **root( ),** but **stem( )** has overridden it with its own local **rose.**

6. We get this:

```
color in main() is B
color in first() is R
color in main() is B
color in second() is G
color in main() is G
```

The local declaration of **color** in **first( )** overrides the external definition, so the reassignment in **first( )** does not affect **color** in **main( ).** But **second( )** uses (by default) the external variable, which also is used by **main( ).** Hence, the changes made in **second( )** are reflected in **main( ).**

7. Here is one implementation:

```
int scanint ( pn )
int *pn;
{
    int status;

    while ( (status = scanf("%d", pn)) == 0 )
            scanf("%*s");
```

```
        return status;
    }
```

Here **scanf( )** attempts to read the next input item. If it is an integer, **status** is **1**, the value is stored at address **pn,** the loop is not entered, and the status of **1** is returned. If the next input item is a noninteger, the status is **0**, the item is skipped, and **scanf( )** is asked to read the next input item. If **EOF** is encountered, the loop is skipped, and -1 is returned. Note that since **pn** is a pointer, hence an address, it is a valid argument for **scanf( )**.

Exercises

1. Some users might be daunted by being asked to enter an EOF character.
    a. Modify **getarray( )** and its called functions so that a # character is used instead.
    b. Modify them so either an EOF or a # can be used.

2. Create a program that sorts **float** numbers.

3. Create a program that converts text of mixed lowercase and uppercase to uppercase only.

4. Create a program that double-spaces single-spaced text.

11

The C Preprocessor

Concepts
- Preprocessor directives
- Symbolic constants
- Macros and macro "functions"
- Macro side effects
- File inclusion
- Conditional compilation

Preprocessor Directives
- *#define, #include, #undef, #if, #ifdef,*
  #ifndef, #else, #endif

C was developed to meet the needs of working programmers, and working programmers like having a preprocessor. This useful aid looks at your program before it gets to the compiler (hence the term *pre*processor), and, following your direction, replaces the symbolic abbreviations in your program with the directions they represent. It looks for other files you request. It can also alter the conditions of compilation. This description does not do justice to the true utility and value of the preprocessor, so let's turn to examples. Of course, with **#define** and **#include,** we have provided examples all along, but now we can gather what we have learned in one place and add to it.

Symbolic Constants: *#define*

The **#define** preprocessor directive, like all preprocessor directives, begins with a **#** symbol in the far left column. (Note that the ANSI Standard permits the **#** symbol to be proceded by a space or a tab.) It can appear anywhere in the source file, and the definition holds from its place of appearance to the end of the file. We have used it heavily to define symbolic constants in our programs, but it has more range than that, as we will show. Here is an example that illustrates some of the possibilities and properties of the **#define** directive.

```
/*  simple preprocessor examples */
#define TWO 2     /* you can use comments if you like */
#define MSG "The old grey cat sang a merry \
song."
```

```
/* a backslash continues a definition to the next line */
#define FOUR  TWO*TWO
#define PX printf("X is %d.\n", x)
#define FMT  "X is %d.\n"
main()
{
   int x = TWO;

   PX;
   x = FOUR;
   printf( FMT, x);
   printf("%s\n", MSG);
   printf("TWO: MSG\n");
}
```

Each line has three parts. The first part is the **#define** directive. The second part is our chosen abbreviation, known as a *macro* in the computer world. The macro must have no spaces in it. Its name must conform to the same rules that C variables follow: only letters, digits, and the _ character can be used, and the first character cannot be a digit. The third part of the line is the string (called the *replacement string*) that the macro represents. When the preprocessor finds an example of one of your macros within your program, it almost always replaces it with the replacement string. (There is one exception as we will show you in just a moment.) This process of going from a macro to a final replacement string is called *macro expansion*. Note that we can insert comments in standard C fashion; they will be ignored by the preprocessor. Also, most systems allow you to use the backslash ("\") to extend a definition over more than one line.

Figure 11.1
Parts of a macro definition

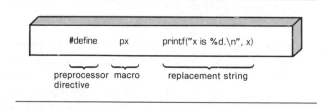

Let's run our example and see how it works.

```
X is 2.
X is 4.
The old grey cat sang a merry song.
TWO: MSG
```

Here's what happened. The statement

```
int x = TWO;   becomes   int x = 2;
```

as **2** is substituted for **TWO.** Then the statement

```
PX;   becomes   printf("X is %d.\n", x);
```

as that wholesale substitution is made. This is a new wrinkle, since up to now we've used macros only to represent constants. Here we see that a macro can express any string, even a whole C expression. Note, though, that this is a constant string; **PX** will print only a variable named **x.**

The next line also represents something new. You might think that **FOUR** is replaced by **4,** but the actual process is this:

```
x = FOUR'   becomes   x = TWO*TWO;   becomes   x = 2*2;
```

and ends there. The actual multiplication takes place, not while the preprocessor works, but during compilation, for the C compiler evaluates all constant expressions (expressions with just constants). The preprocessor does no calculation; it just makes the suggested substitutions very literally.

Note that a macro definition can include other macros. (Some compilers do not support this "nesting" feature.)

In the next line

```
printf (FMT, x);   becomes   printf("X is %d.\n",x);
```

as **FMT** is replaced by the corresponding string. This approach could be handy if you had a lengthy control string that you had to use several times.

In the next line **MSG** is replaced by the corresponding string. The quotes make the replacement string a character string constant; that is, once the program gets hold of it, it will be stored in an array terminated with a null character. Thus,

```
#define HAL 'Z'   defines a character constant, but
#define HAP "Z"   defines a character string:   Z\0
```

In general, wherever the preprocessor finds one of your macros in your program, it literally replaces it with the equivalent replacement string. If that string also contains macros, they, too, are replaced. The one exception to replacement is a macro found within double quotes. Thus,

```
printf("TWO: MSG");
```

prints **TWO: MSG** literally instead of printing

```
2: The old grey cat sang a merry song.
```

If you wanted this last line printed, you would use

```
printf("%d: %s\n", TWO, MSG);
```

for here the macros are outside the quotes.

When should you use symbolic constants? Probably you should use them for most numbers. If the number is some constant used in a calculation, a symbolic name makes its meaning clearer. If the number is an array size, a symbolic number makes it simpler to alter your program to handle a larger array. If the number is a system code for, say, EOF, a symbolic representation makes your program much more portable; just change one EOF definition. Mnemonic value, easy alterability, portability: these all make symbolic constants worthwhile.

Easy stuff, eh? Let's get more adventurous and look at the poor man's function, the macro with arguments.

MULTIFUNCTIONAL PREPROCESSOR

Using Arguments with *#define*

A macro with arguments looks very much like a function, since the arguments are enclosed within parentheses. Here are some examples that illustrate how such a "macro function" is defined and used. Some of the examples also point out possible pitfalls, so read them carefully.

```
/* macros with arguments   */
```

```
#define SQUARE(x) x*x
#define PR(x)    printf("x is %d.\n", x)
main()
{
     int x = 4
     int z;

     z = SQUARE(x);
     PR(z);
     z = SQUARE(2);
     PR(z);
     PR(SQUARE(x));
     PR(SQUARE(x+2));
     PR(100/SQUARE(2));
     PR(SQUARE(++x));
}
```

Wherever **SQUARE(x)** appears in our program, it is replaced by **x*x.** What is different from our earlier examples is that we are free to use symbols other than **x** when we use this macro. The **x** in the macro definition is replaced by the symbol used in the macro call in the program. Thus, **SQUARE(2)** is replaced by **2*2.** So the **x** really does act as an argument.

However, as we shall soon see, a macro argument does not work exactly like a function argument. Here are the results of running the program. Note that some of the answers are different from what you might expect.

```
z is 16.
z is 4.
SQUARE(x) is 16.
SQUARE(x+2) is 14.
100/SQUARE(2) is 100.
SQUARE(++x) is 30.
```

The first two lines are predictable. Notice, however, that even the **x** inside the double quotes of **PR**'s definition gets replaced by the corresponding argument. ALL arguments in the *definition* get replaced.

The third line is interesting:

```
PR(SQUARE(x));
```

becomes

```
printf("SQUARE(x) is %d.\n", SQUARE(x));
```

after the first stage of macro expansion. The second **SQUARE(x)** is expanded to **x*x,** but the first is left as it is, for it is now inside double quotes in a program statement and thus is immune to further expansion. The final program line is

```
printf("SQUARE(x) is %d.\n", x*x);
```

and that produces the output

```
SQUARE(x) is 16.
```

when the program is run.

Let's run over that double-quote business one more time. If your macro definition includes an argument within double quotes, that argument will be replaced by the string in the macro call. But after that, it is not expanded any further, even if the string is another macro. In our example, **x** became **SQUARE(x)** and stayed that way.

Now we come to some peculiar results. Recall that **x** has the value **4**. This might lead you to expect that **SQUARE(x+2)** would be **6*6** or **36**. But the printout says it is **14**, which sure doesn't look like a square to us! The simple reason for this misleading output is the one we have already stated: the preprocessor doesn't make calculations, it just substitutes strings. Wherever our definition shows an **x**, the preprocessor will substitute the string **x+2**. Thus

```
x*x    becomes    x+2*x+2
```

The only multiplication is **2*x**. If **x** is **4**, then the value of this expression is:

```
4+2*4+2 = 4 + 8 + 2 = 14
```

This example pinpoints a very important difference between a function call and a macro call. A function call passes the *value* of the argument to the function while the program is running. A macro call passes the argument *string* to the program before compilation; it's a different process at a different time.

Can our definition be fixed to make **SQUARE(x+2)** equal to 36? Sure. We simply need more parentheses:

```
#define SQUARE(x)   (x)*(x)
```

Then **SQUARE(x+2)** becomes **(x+2)*(x+2)**, and we get our desired multiplication as the parentheses carry over in the replacement string.

This doesn't solve all our problems, however. Consider the events leading to the next output line:

```
100/SQUARE(2)    becomes    100/2*2
```

By the laws of precedence, the expression is evaluated from left to right:

```
(100/2)*2   or   50*2   or   100.
```

This mix-up can be cured by defining **SQUARE(x)** this way:

```
#define SQUARE(x)   (x*x)
```

This produces

```
100/(2*2)   which eventually evaluates to   100/4   or   25
```

To handle both of the last two examples, we need the definition

```
#define SQUARE(x)   ((x)*(x))
```

The lesson here is to use as many parentheses as necessary to ensure that operations and associations are done in the right order.

Even these precautions fail to save the final example from grief:

```
SQUARE(++x)   becomes   ++x*++x
```

and **x** gets incremented twice, once before the multiplication and once afterwards:

```
++x*++x = 5*6 = 30
```

(Because the order of operations is left open, some compilers will render the product **6*5,** but the end result is the same.)

The only remedy for this problem is to avoid using **++x** as a macro argument. Note that **++x** *would* work as a *function* argument, for it would be evaluated to **5** and then the value **5** would be sent to the function.

Macro or Function?

Many tasks can be done by using a macro with arguments or by using a function. Which one should you use? There is no hard and fast rule, but here are some considerations.

Macros are somewhat trickier to use than regular functions, for they can have odd side effects if you are unwary. Some compilers limit the macro definition to one line, and it is probably best to observe that limit even if your compiler does not.

The macros-versus-function choice represents a trade-off between time and space. A macro produces "in-line" code; that is, you get a statement in your program. If you use the macro 20 times, then you get 20 lines of code inserted into your program. If you use a function 20 times, you have just one copy of the function statements in your program, so less space is used.

On the other hand, program control must shift to where the function is and then return to the calling program, and this takes longer than in-line code.

Macros have an advantage in that they don't worry about variable types. (This is because they deal with character strings, not with actual values.) Thus, our **SQUARE(x)** macro can be used equally well with **int** or **float.**

Programmers typically use macros for simple functions like the following:

```
#define MAX(X,Y)     ( (X) > (Y) ? (X) : (Y))
#define ABS(X)       ((X) < 0 ? -(X) : (X))
#define ISSIGN(X)    ( (X) == '+' || (X) == '-' ? 1 : 0 )
```

(The last macro has value 1—true—if **x** is an algebraic sign character.) Here are some points to note:

1. Remember that there are no spaces in the macro, but spaces can appear in the replacement string. The preprocessor thinks the macro ends at the first space, so anything after that space is lumped into the replacement string.

Figure 11.2
Faulty spacing in a macro definition

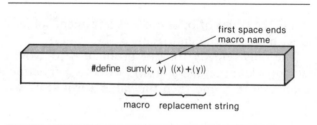

2. Use parentheses around each argument and around the definition as a whole. This ensures that the terms are grouped properly in an expression like `forks = 2 * MAX(guests + 3, last);`
3. Use capital letters for macro function names. This convention is not as widespread as that of using capitals for macro constants, but one good reason for using it is that it reminds you to be alert to possible macro side effects.

Suppose you have developed some macro functions you like. Do you have to retype them each time you write a new program? Not if you remember the **#include** directive. We will review that now.

File Inclusion: *#include*

When the preprocessor spots an **#include** directive, it looks for the following file name and includes it with the current file. The directive comes in two varieties:

```
#include <stdio.h>        file name in angle brackets
#include "mystuff.h"      file name in double quotes
```

On a UNIX system, the angle brackets tell the preprocessor to look for the file in one or more standard system directories. The quotes tell it to first look in your directory (or some other directory, if you specify it in the file name) and then look in the standard places.

```
#include <stdio.h>        searches system directories
#include "hot.h"          searches your current working directory
#include "/usr/biff/p.h"  searches the /usr/biff directory
```

Depending on the microprocessor system, the two forms may be synonymous, and the preprocessor looks through the indicated disk drive.

```
#include "stdio.h"        searches the default disk drive
#include <stdio.h>        searches the default disk drive
#include "a:stdio.h"      searches disk drive a
```

Many newer microcomputer implementations, however, use conventions similar to UNIX's. You will have to consult your compiler manual.

Why include files? Because they have information you need. The **stdio.h** file, for example, typically includes definitions of **EOF, getchar( )**, and **putchar( )**. The last two are defined as macro functions.

The **.h** suffix conventionally is used for *header* files, files with information to go at the head of your program. Header files usually consist of preprocessor statements. Some, like **stdio.h,** come with the system, but you are free to create your own.

Header Files: An Example

Suppose, for instance, that you like using Boolean values. That is, instead of having **1** be true and **0** be false, you would rather use the words **TRUE** and **FALSE.** You could create a file called, say, **bool.h,** which contains these definitions:

```
/* bool.h file */
#define BOOL int
#define TRUE 1
#define FALSE 0
```

Here is an example of a program using this header:

```
/* counts whitespace characters */
#include <stdio.h>
#include "bool.h"
main()
{
    int ch;
    int count = 0;
    BOOL whitesp();

    while ( (ch = getchar()  ) != EOF)
         if ( whitesp(ch) )
                  count++;
    printf("There are %d whitespace characters.\n", count);
}
BOOL whitesp(c)
char c;
{
    if ( c == ' ' || c == '\n'  || c == '\t' )
         return(TRUE);
    else
         return(FALSE);
}
```

Note the following points about this program:

1. If the two functions in this program, **main( )** and **whitesp( )**, were to be compiled separately, you would use the **#include "bool.h"** directive with each.

2. The expression **if (whitesp(ch))** is the same as **if (whitesp(ch) == TRUE)**, since **whitesp(ch)** itself has the value **TRUE** or **FALSE.**

3. We have not created a new type **BOOL**, since **BOOL** is just **int.** The purpose of labeling the function **BOOL** is to remind the user that the function is being used for a logical (as opposed to arithmetic) calculation.

4. Using a function for involved logical comparisons can make a program clearer. It also can save effort if the comparison is made more than one place in a program.

5. We could have used a macro instead of a function to define **whitesp( ).**

Many programmers develop their own standard header files to use with their programs. Some files might be for special purposes; others might be used with almost every program. Since included files can incorporate

#include directives, you can create concise, well-organized header files if you like.

Consider this example:

```
/* header file mystuff.h */

#include <stdio.n>
#include "bool.h"
#include "funct.h"
#define YES 1
#define NO 0
```

First, we'll remind you that the C preprocessor recognizes the comment marks /* and */ so that we can include comments in these files.

Second, we have included three files. Presumably the third one contains some macro functions we use often.

Third, we have defined **YES** to be **1,** whereas in **bool.h** we defined **TRUE** to be **1.** There is no conflict here; we can use **YES** and **TRUE** in the same program. Each will be replaced by a **1.**

There would be a conflict if we added the line

```
#define TRUE 2
```

to the file. The second definition would supersede the first, and some preprocessors would warn you that **TRUE** had been redefined.

The **#include** directive is not restricted to header files. If you had stored a needed function in the file **sort.c,** you could have used

```
#include "sort.c"
```

to get it compiled along with your current program. However, this is considered poor style.

The **#include** and **#define** directives are the most heavily used C preprocessor features. We will treat the other directives in less detail.

Other Directives: *#undef, #if, #ifdef, #ifndef, #else, #elif,* **and** *#endif*

The **#undef, #if, #ifdef, #ifndef, #else, #elif,** and **#endif** directives are typically used with larger blocks of programming. They allow you to suspend earlier definitions and to produce files that can be compiled in more than one way.

The **#undef** directive *undefines* a given macro. That is, suppose we have this definition:

```
#define LIMIT 400
```

Then the directive

```
#undef LIMIT
```

removes that definition. Now, if you like, you can redefine **LIMIT** so that it has a new value. Even if **LIMIT** is not defined in the first place, it still is valid to undefine it. Thus, if you want to use a particular name and if you are unsure whether it has been used previously, you can undefine it to be on the safe side.

Some compilers allow you to redefine a defined name and to nest **#define**s and **#undef**s so that undefining a name causes it to revert to its original value. This is not, however, the standard practice. More typically, you get a warning if you redefine a name. So use **#undef** first if you wish to redefine.

The other directives we mentioned let you set up conditional compilations. Here is an example:

```
#ifdef MAVIS

#include    "horse.h"      /* gets done if MAVIS is #defined */
#define  STABLES     5

#else

#include "cow.h"       /* gets done if MAVIS isn't #defined */
#define  STABLES     15

#endif
```

The **#ifdef** directive says that if the following identifier (**MAVIS**) has been defined by the preprocessor, then follow all the directives up to the next **#else** or **#endif,** whichever comes first. If there is an **#else,** then everything from the **#else** to the **#endif** is done if the identifier isn't defined.

Incidentally, an "empty" definition like

```
#define MAVIS
```

is sufficient to define **MAVIS** for the purposes of **#ifdef**.

The structure is much like that of the C **if-else.** The main difference is that the preprocessor doesn't recognize the { } method of marking a block, so it uses the **#else** (if any) and the **#endif** (which must be present) to mark blocks of directives. These conditional structures can be nested.

The **#ifndef** and **#if** directives can be used with **#else** and **#endif** in the same way. The **#ifndef** asks if the following identifier is *not* defined; it is the negative of **#ifdef.** The **#if** directive is more like the regular C **if.** It is followed by a constant expression that is considered to be true if nonzero:

```
#if SYS == "IBM"
#include "ibm.h"
#endif
```

The **#elif** directive allows you to extend an **if-else** sequence. For example, you could do this:

```
#if SYS == "IBMPC"
#include "ibmpc.h"
#elif SYS == "IBMAT"
#include "ibmat.h"
#elif SYS == "MAC"
#include "mac.h"
#else
#include "general.h"
#endif
```

Many newer implementations have removed the restriction that the preprocessor directive must begin in the left-most column. If that is so, you can use C-style indentation for the **if-else** structure.

Also, many newer implementations offer a second way to test whether a name is defined. Instead of using

```
#ifdef VAX
```

we can use this form:

```
#if defined (VAX)
```

The advantage of this newer form is that it can be used with **#elif.**

One use for these "conditional compilation" features is to make a program more portable. By changing a few key definitions at the beginning of a file, you can set up different values and include different files for different systems.

These brief examples illustrate C's marvelous ability for sophisticated and close control of programs.

What You Should Have Learned

How to **#define** symbolic constants: **#define FINGERS 10**
How to include other files: **#include "albanian.h"**
How to define a macro function: **#define NEG (X) (−(X))**

When to use symbolic constants: often
When to use macro functions: sometimes
The dangers of macro functions: side effects

Review Questions

1. Here are groups of one or more macros followed by a source code line that uses them. What code results in each case? Is it valid code?

   a. ```
   #define FPM 5280   /* feet per mile */
   dist = FPM * miles;
   ```

   b. ```
   #define FEET 4
   #define POD FEET + FEET
   plort = FEET * POD;
   ```

   c. ```
   #define SIX = 6;
   nex = SIX;
   ```

   d. ```
   #define NEW(X) X + 5
   y = NEW(y);
   berg = NEW(berg) * lob;
   est = NEW(berg) / NEW(y);
   nilp = lob * NEW(-berg);
   ```

2. Fix the definition in **1.d.** to make it more reliable.

3. Define a macro function that returns the minimum of two values.

4. Define a macro to take the place of the **whitesp(c)** function in the program to count white-space characters.

5. Define a macro function that prints the representations and the values of two integer expressions.

6. Create **#define** statements to accomplish the following goals:

   a. Create a named constant of value 25.
   b. Have SPACE represent the space character.
   c. Have PS represent printing the space character.
   d. Have BIG(X) represent adding 3 to X.
   e. Have SUMSQ(X,Y) represent the sums of the squares of X and Y.

7. Define a macro that prints out the name, value, and address of an **int** variable in the following format:

   ```
   name: fop;  value: 23;  address: 4016
   ```

Answers

1. **a. dist = 5280 * miles;** valid.

   b. plot = 4 * 4 + 4; This is valid, but if the user really wanted 4 * (4 + 4), he or she should have used **#define POD (FEET + FEET).**

    c. nex = = 6;; This is not valid; apparently the user forgot that he or she was writing for the preprocessor, not writing in C.

    d. y = y + 5; valid.

        berg = berg + 5 * lob; This is valid but is probably not the desired result.

        est = berg + 5 / y + 5; ditto.

        nilp = lob *−berg + 5; ditto.

2. `#define NEW(X) ( (X) + 5 )`

3. `#define MIN(X,Y) ( (X) < (Y) ? (X) : (Y) )`

4. `#define WHITESP(C)  ((C) == ' ' || (C) == '\n' || (C) == '\t')`

5. `#define PR2(X,Y) printf("X is %d and Y is %d.\n", X, Y)` Since X and Y are never exposed to any other operations (such as multiplication) in this macro, we don't have to cocoon everything in parentheses.

6.   **a.** `#define LIMIT 25`
    b. `#define SPACE ' '`
    c. `#define PS putchar(SPACE)`
    d. `#define BIG(X) ( (X) + 3 )`
    e. `#define SUMSQ(X,Y)  ( (X)*(X) + (Y)*(Y) )`

7. Try this:

    `#define PR(X) printf("name: X; value: %d; address: %u\n",X,&X)`

Exercises

1. Start developing a header file of preprocessor definitions that you wish to use.

2. The harmonic mean of two numbers is obtained by taking the inverses of the two numbers, averaging them, and taking the inverse of the result. Use a **#define** directive to define a macro "function" that performs this operation.

12

Arrays and Pointers

Concepts
- Arrays
- Multidimensional arrays
- Initializing arrays
- Pointers and pointer operations
- The array-pointer connection

Operators
- & * (unary)

rrays and pointers have an intimate relationship to each other, so traditionally they are discussed together. Before we explore that relationship, however, we will review and augment our knowledge of arrays. Then we will study the connection with pointers.

Arrays

By now you are familiar with the fact that an array is composed of a series of elements of one data type. We use declarations to tell the compiler when we want an array. The compiler needs to know the same things about an array that it needs to know about an ordinary variable (known as a *scalar* variable in the trade): the type and the storage class. In addition, it needs to know how many elements the array has. Arrays can have the same types and storage classes as ordinary variables, and the same default rules apply. Consider the following example of array declarations:

```
/* some array declarations */
int temp[365];   /* external array of 365 ints  */
main()
{
    float rain[365];  /* automatic array of 365 floats */
    static char code[12]; /*static array of 12 chars */
    extern temp[];    /* external array; size given above */
```

You recall, too, that the brackets (**[ ]**) identify **temp** and the rest as arrays and that the enclosed number indicates the number of elements in the array. We identify an individual element by using its subscript number, also called an *index*. The numbering starts with 0. Hence, **temp[0]** is the first element of **temp**, and **temp[364]** is the 365th and last element.

This is rather old hat; let's learn something new.

Initialization and Storage Classes

Often we use arrays to store data needed for a program. For instance, a 12-element array can store the number of days in each month. In cases such as these, we would like to have a convenient way to initialize the array at the beginning of a program. There is a way, but only for static and external storage classes. Let's see how it is done.

We know that we can initialize scalar variables in a declaration with expressions like

```
int fix = 1;
float flax = PI*2;
```

where, we hope, **PI** was defined earlier as a macro. Can we do something similar with arrays? The answer is that old favorite, yes and no: *external* and *static* arrays *can* be initialized: *automatic* and *register* arrays *cannot* be initialized.

Before trying to initialize an array, let's see what's in it if we don't put anything there.

```
/* arraypeek */
main()
{
    int fuzzy[2];              /* automatic array */
    static int wuzzy[2];       /* static array    */

    printf("%d %d\n", fuzzy[1], wuzzy[1]);
}
```

The output is:

```
525 0
```

This reflects the following rules. If you do nothing, external and static arrays are initialized to zero. Automatic and register arrays get whatever garbage happens to be left over in that part of memory.

Great! We now know how to initialize a static or external array to 0: just do nothing. But what if we want some other values, say the number of days in each month. Then we can do this:

```
/* daysofmonth */
int days[12] = {31,28,31,30,31,30,31,31,30,31,30,31};
```

```
main()
{
  int index;
  extern int days[];  /* optional declaration */

  for ( index = 0; index < 12; index++)
    printf("Month %d has %d days.\n", index + 1,
           days[index]);
}
```

The output:

```
Month 1 has 31 days.
Month 2 has 28 days.
Month 3 has 31 days.
Month 4 has 30 days.
Month 5 has 31 days.
Month 6 has 30 days.
Month 7 has 31 days.
Month 8 has 31 days.
Month 9 has 30 days.
Month 10 has 31 days.
Month 11 has 30 days.
Month 12 has 31 days.
```

Not quite a superb program, but it's wrong only one month in every four years. By defining **days[ ]** outside the function, we made it external. We initialized it with a list enclosed in braces; commas are used to separate the members of the list.

The number of items in the list should match the size of the array. What if we count wrong? Let's try the last example again with a list that is too short (and two short, too):

```
/* daysofmonth */
int days[12] = {31,28,31,30,31,30,31,31,30,31};
main()
{
  int index;
  extern int days[];  /* optional declaration */

  for ( index = 0; index < 12; index++)
    printf("Month %d has %d days,\n", index + 1, days[index]);
}
```

This time the output looks like this:

```
Month 1 has 31 days.
Month 2 has 28 days.
Month 3 has 31 days.
Month 4 has 30 days.
Month 5 has 31 days.
Month 6 has 30 days.
Month 7 has 31 days.
Month 8 has 31 days.
Month 9 has 30 days.
Month 10 has 31 days.
Month 11 has 0 days.
Month 12 has 0 days.
```

As you can see, the compiler had no problem. When it ran out of suggestions from the list, it initialized the rest to 0.

The compiler is not so forgiving if you have too many list members. This overgenerosity is considered an ERROR. There is no need, however, to expose yourself to the ridicule of your compiler. Instead, let the compiler match the array size to the list:

```
/* daysofmonth */
int days[] = {31,28,31,30,31,30,31,31,30,31};
main()
{
  int index;
  extern int days[];   /* optional declaration */

  for ( index = 0; index < sizeof days/(sizeof (int)); index++)
    printf("Month %d has %d days,\n", index + 1, days[index]);
}
```

There are two main points to note in the program:

1. If you use empty brackets when initializing an array, it will count the number of items in the list and make the array that large.

2. Notice what we did in the **for** control statement. Lacking (justifiably) faith in our ability to count correctly, we let the computer give us the size of the array. The **sizeof** operator gives us the size, in bytes, of the object or type following it. (We mentioned this way back in Chapter 3.) On our system, each **int** element occupies 2 bytes, so we divide the total number of bytes by 2 to get the number of elements. But other systems may have a different size **int**. Therefore, to be general, we divide by **sizeof (int)**.

Here is the result of running this program:

```
Month 1 has 31 days.
Month 2 has 28 days.
Month 3 has 31 days.
Month 4 has 30 days.
Month 5 has 31 days.
Month 6 has 30 days.
Month 7 has 31 days.
Month 8 has 31 days.
Month 9 has 30 days.
Month 10 has 31 days.
```

Oops! We put in just ten values. But our method of letting the program find the array size kept us from trying to print past the end of the array.

There is one more short method of initializing arrays, but, since it works only for character strings, we will save it for the next chapter.

Finally, we should point out that you can *assign* values to array members, regardless of storage class. For example, the following fragment assigns even numbers to an automatic array:

```
/* array assignment */
main()
{
    int counter, evens[50];

    for ( counter = 0; counter < 50; counter++)
        evens[counter] = 2 * counter;

    ...
}
```

Pointers to Arrays

Pointers, as you may recall from Chapter 9, give us a symbolic way of using addresses. Since the hardware instructions of computing machines use addresses heavily, pointers allow us to express ourselves in a way that is close to the way the machine expresses itself. This makes programs with pointers efficient. In particular, pointers offer an efficient way to deal with arrays. Indeed, as we shall see, our array notation is simply a disguised use of pointers.

An example of this disguised use is that an array name is also a pointer to the first element of an array. That is, if **flizny[ ]** is an array, then

```
flizny == &flizny[0]
```

h represent the memory address of that first element. (Recall that **&**
ldress operator.) Both are pointer *constants,* for they remain fixed
luration of the program. However, they can be assigned as values to
variable, and we can change the value of a variable, as the next
shows. Notice what happens to the value of a pointer when we add
to it.

```
/* pointer addition */
main()
{
    int dates[4], *pti, index;
    float bills[4], *ptf;

    pti = dates;    /* assign address of array to pointer */
    ptf = bills;
    for (index = 0; index < 4; index ++)
        printf("pointers + %d: %10u %10u\n",
                index, pti + index, ptf + index);
}
```

Here is the output:

```
pointers + 0:      56014      56026
pointers + 1:      56016      56030
pointers + 2:      56018      56034
pointers + 3:      56020      56038
```

The first line prints the beginning addresses of the two arrays, and the
next line gives the result of adding 1 to the address, and so on. What?

```
56014 + 1 = 56016?
56026 + 1 = 56030?
```

Pretty dumb? Like a fox! Our system is addressed by individual bytes, but
type **int** uses 2 bytes and type **float** uses 4 bytes. What is happening here is
that when you say "add 1 to a pointer," C adds one *storage unit.* For arrays,
this means the address is increased to the address of the next *element,* not
just the next byte. This is one reason we have to declare what sort of object
a pointer points to; the address is not enough, for the computer needs to
know how many bytes are used to store the object. (This is true even for
pointers to scalar variables; otherwise, the ***pt** operation to fetch the value
wouldn't work.)

Figure 12.1
An array and pointer addition

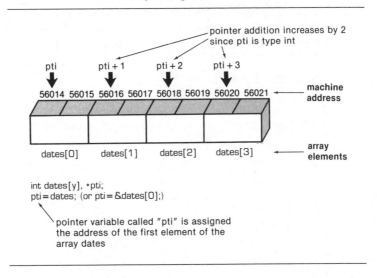

As a result of this cleverness of C, we have the following equalities:

```
dates + 2 == &dates[2]   /* same address */
*(dates + 2) == dates[2]   /* same value */
```

These relationships sum up the close connection between arrays and pointers. They mean we can use a pointer to identify an individual element of an array and to get its value. In essence, we have two different notations for the same thing. Indeed, the compiler converts the array notation to pointers, so the pointer approach is the more basic of the two.

Incidentally, don't confuse ***(dates+2)** with ***dates+2.** The value operator **(*)** binds more tightly (has higher precedence) than **+**, so the latter means **(*dates)+2**:

```
*(dates + 2)   /*  value of the 3rd element of dates */
*dates + 2   /* 2 added to the value of the 1st element */
```

The relationship between arrays and pointers means we can often use either approach when writing a program. One example is when we have a function with an array as an argument.

Functions, Arrays, and Pointers

Arrays can appear in two places in a function. First, they can be declared in the body of the function. Second, they can be arguments of a function. So far, everything we have said in this chapter pertains to arrays of the first kind; we now need to discuss arrays as arguments.

We brought up the matter of array arguments in Chapter 10. Now that we know more about pointers, we can take a deeper look. Let's begin by looking at the skeleton of a program, paying attention to the declarations:

```
/* array argument  */
main()
{
   int ages[50];    /* an array of 50 elements */

   convert(ages);
   ...
}
convert(years)
int years[];      /* how big an array? */
{
   ...
}
```

Clearly, the array **ages** has 50 elements. What about the array **years?** Surprise! There is no array **years!** The declaration

```
int years[];
```

creates not an *array,* but a *pointer.* Let's see why this is so.

This is our function call:

```
convert(ages);
```

The argument is **ages.** And the name **ages,** you may recall, is a *pointer* to the first element of the 50-element array. So the function call passes a pointer, that is, an address, to the function **convert( ).** This means that the argument of **convert( )** is a pointer, and we could have written **convert( )** this way:

```
convert(years)
int *years;
{
}
```

Indeed, these two declarations are synonymous when used for formal arguments to a function:

```
int years[];
int *years;
```

Both declare **year** to be a pointer-to-integer. The chief difference is that the first form reminds us that **year** points to the first element of an array.

How does this relate to the **ages** array? Recall that when we use a pointer for an argument, the function affects the corresponding variable in the calling function. Thus, the operations involving **years** in **convert( )** actually affect the the array **ages** in **main( )**.

Let's see how that works. First, the function call initializes **years** to point to **ages[0]**. Now suppose somewhere in **convert( )** we have the expression **years[3]**. Well, as we saw in the preceding section, that's the same as saying ***(years+3)**. But if **years** points to **ages[0]**, then **years+3** points to **ages[3]**. This makes ***(years+3)** stand for **ages[3]**. Put this chain of relationships together, and we find that changing **years[3]** is the same as changing ***(years+3)**, which is the same as changing **ages[3]**. And this is what we claimed: that operations on **years** wind up as operations on **ages**.

In short, when you use an array name as a function argument, you pass a pointer to the function. The function then uses this pointer to effect changes on the original array in the calling program.

If **years** is a pointer to the **ages** array, how does the **convert( )** function know how many elements are in **ages**? It doesn't, unless we tell it or unless something special about the last element marks it as the end of the array. Usually, functions that work with arrays are passed two items of information: the address of the array and the number of elements. Thus, a more realistic example would be to have this function call:

```
convert(ages, 50);
```

And the function heading would look like this:

```
convert(years, size)
int years[];     /* pointer to an array */
int size;          /* size of array */
```

Let's look at an example.

Using Pointers to Do an Array's Work

Here we are going to write a function that uses arrays. Then we will rewrite it using pointers.

Consider the following simple function, which finds the average (or mean) of an array of integers. The input is an array name and the number of array elements. The output is the mean, which is communicated through **return.** The calling statement could be something like

```
printf("The mean of these values is %d.\n",
mean(numbs,size));
```

```
/* finds the mean of an array of n integers */
int mean(array,n)
int array[], n;
{
    int index;
    long sum;  /* too many ints may sum to a long int */

    if (n > 0 )
        {
        for (index = 0, sum = 0; index < n; index++)
            sum += long array[index];
        return( (int) (sum/n)  ); /* return an int */
        }
    else
            {
            printf("No array.\n");
            return(0);
            }
}
```

It is simple to convert this to a program using pointers. Declare, say, **pa** as a pointer to **int**. Then replace the array element **array[index]** by the corresponding value: ***(pa+index)**.

```
/* uses pointers to find the mean of an array of n integers */

int mean(pa,n)
int *pa, n;
{
    int index;
    long sum;  /* too many ints may sum to a long int */

    if (n > 0 )
        {
        for (index = 0, sum = 0; index < n; index++)
            sum += *(pa + index);
        return( (int) (sum/n) ); /* return an int */
        }
    else
            {
            printf("No array.\n");
            return (0);
            }
}
```

Easy, but do we have to change the function call? After all, **numbs** in

mean(numbs,size) was an array name. No change is needed, for an array name *is* a pointer. As we discussed in the preceding section, the declarations

```
int pa[];
```

and

```
int *pa;
```

are identical in effect; both say that **pa** is a pointer. We could use the first declaration and still use ***(pa+index)** in the program.

Conceptually, how does the pointer version work? A pointer points to the first element, and the value stored there is added to **sum.** Then the next element is pointed to (1 is added to the pointer), and the value stored there is added to **sum,** etc. If you think about it, this is just what the array version does, with the subscript acting as the finger that points to each element in turn.

Another approach, which makes use of the fact that the pointer **pa** is a variable, is to use **pa++** instead of adding **index** to **pa.** (See Question 9.)

Now that we have two ways to do things, which should we use? First, although arrays and pointers are closely related, they do have differences. Pointers are more general and far-reaching in their uses, but many users (initially, at least) find arrays more familiar and obvious. Then, too, there is no simple pointer equivalent for declaring the size of an array. The most typical situation in which you can use either is the one we have just shown: a function that operates on an array defined elsewhere. We suggest you use whichever approach you want. The main advantage of using pointers in these situations is to gain familiarity with them so that they are easier to use when you *have* to use them.

Pointer Operations

Just what can we do with pointers? C offers five basic operations that we can perform on pointers, and the next program shows these possibilities. To show the results of each operation, we will print out the value of the pointer (which is the address it points to), the value stored in the pointed-to address, and the address of the pointer itself.

```
/* pointer operations */
#define PR(X) printf("X = %u, *X =%d, &X = %u\n", X, *X, &X)
/* prints value of pointer (an address), the value stored at */
/* that address, and the address of the pointer itself. */
main()
{
    static int urn[] = {100,200,300};
    int *ptr1, *ptr2;
```

```
    ptr1 =urn;          /* assign an address to a pointer */
    ptr2 = &urn[2];     /* ditto */
    PR(ptr1);   /* see macro definition above */
    ptr1++;          /* increment a pointer */
    PR(ptr1);
    PR(ptr2);
    ++ptr2;     /* going past end of the array */
    PR(ptr2);
    printf("ptr2 - ptr1 = %u\n", ptr2 - ptr1);
}
```

Here is the output:

```
ptr1 = 234, *ptr1 =100, &ptr1 = 3606
ptr1 = 236, *ptr1 =200, &ptr1 = 3606
ptr2 = 238, *ptr2 =300, &ptr2 = 3604
ptr2 = 240, *ptr2 =1910, &ptr2 = 3604
ptr2 - ptr1 = 2
```

This example shows the five basic operations that we can perform with or on pointer variables.

1. *Assignment.* We can assign an address to a pointer. Typically we do this by using an array name or by using the address operator **(&).** In our example, **ptr1** is assigned the address of the beginning of the array **urn**; this address happens to be memory cell number 234. (On our system, static variables are stored in low memory locations.) The variable **ptr2** gets the address of the third and last element, **urn[2].**

2. *Value-finding.* The * operator gives us the value stored in the pointed-to location. Thus, ***ptr1** initially is **100,** the value stored at location 234.

3. *Take a pointer address.* Like all variables, pointer variables have an address and a value. The **&** operator tells us where the pointer itself is stored. In our example, **ptr1** is stored in memory location 3606. The content of that memory cell is **234,** the address of **urn.**

4. *Increment a pointer.* We can do this by regular addition or by using the increment operator. Incrementing a pointer makes it move to the next element of an array. Thus, **ptr1++** increases the numerical value of **ptr1** by **2** (2 bytes per **int**) and makes **ptr1** point to **urn[1].** (See Figure 12.2.) Now **ptr1** has the value **236** (the next array address) and ***ptr1** has the value **200,** the

value of **urn[1].** Note that the address of **ptr1** itself remains **3606.** After all, a variable doesn't move around just because it changes value!

Of course, you can also decrement a pointer. There are some cautions to note, however. The computer does not keep track of whether or not a pointer still points to an array. The operation **++ptr2** caused **ptr2** to move up another 2 bytes, and now it points to whatever happened to be stored after the array.

Also, you can use the increment operator for pointer variables but not for pointer constants, just as you can't use the increment operator on regular constants. You can use simple addition for pointer variables and constants.

Valid	Invalid
ptr1++;	urn++;
x++;	3++;
ptr2 = ptr1 + 2;	ptr2 = urn++;
ptr2 = urn + 1;	x = y + 3++;

5. *Differencing.* You can find the difference between two pointers. Normally you do this for two pointers to elements in the same array to find out how far apart the elements were. Note that the result is in the same units as the type size.

Figure 12.2
Incrementing a type *int* pointer

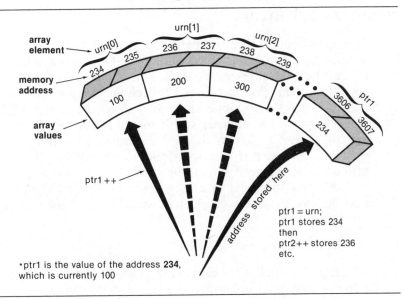

*ptr1 is the value of the address **234**, which is currently 100

These operations open many gateways. C programmers create arrays of pointers, pointers to functions, arrays of pointers to pointers, arrays of pointers to functions, and so on. We will stick to the basic uses we have already unveiled. The first basic use is to communicate information to and from functions. We have seen that we must use pointers if we want a function to affect variables in the calling function. The second basic use is in functions designed to manipulate arrays.

Multidimensional Arrays

Tempest Cloud, a weather person who takes her subject cirrusly, wants to analyze 5 years of monthly rainfall data. One of the first decisions she must make is how to represent the data. One choice is to use 60 variables, one for each data item. (We mentioned this choice once before, and it is as dumb now as it was then.) Using an array with 60 elements would be an improvement, but it would be nicer still if we could keep each year's data separate. We could use 5 arrays, each with 12 elements, but that is clumsy and could get really awkward if Tempest decides to study 50 years' worth of rainfall instead of 5. We need something better.

A good answer is to use an array of arrays. The master array would have 5 elements, and each element would be a 12-element array. This is how it is done:

```
static float rain[5][12];
```

We can also visualize the **rain** array as a two-dimensional array consisting of 5 rows, each of 12 columns.

Figure 12.3
Two-dimensional array

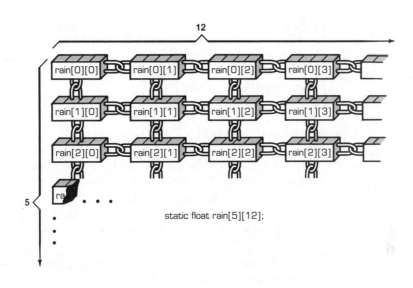

static float rain[5][12];

By changing the second subscript we move along a row, and by changing the first subscript we move vertically along a column. For our example, the second subscript takes us through the months, and the first subscript takes us through the years.

Let's use this two-dimensional array in a weather program. Our program goal will be to find the total rainfall for each year, the average yearly rainfall, and the average rainfall for each month. To find the total rainfall for a year, we have to add all the data in a given row. To find the average rainfall for a given month, we first have to add all the data in a given column. The two-dimensional array makes it easy to visualize and execute these activities. Figure 12.4 shows the program.

Figure 12.4
Weather program

```
/* finds yearly totals, yearly average, and monthly average */
/* for several years of rainfall data */
#define TWLV 12    /* number of months in a year */
#define YRS  5     /* number of years of data    */
main()
{
```

```
static float rain[YRS][TWLV] = {
{10.2, 8.1, 6.8, 4.2, 2.1, 1.8, 0.2, 0.3, 1.1, 2.3, 6.1, 7.4},
{9.2, 9.8, 4.4, 3.3, 2.2, 0.8, 0.4, 0.0, 0.6, 1.7, 4.3, 5.2},
{6.6, 5.5, 3.8, 2.8, 1.6, 0.2, 0.0, 0.0, 0.0, 1.3, 2.6, 4.2},
{4.3, 4.3, 4.3, 3.0, 2.0, 1.0, 0.2, 0.2, 0.4, 2.4, 3.5, 6.6},
{8.5, 8.2, 1.2, 1.6, 2.4, 0.0, 5.2, 0.9, 0.3, 0.9, 1.4, 7.2}
                         };
/* initializing rainfall data for 1970 - 1974 */
int year, month;
float subtot, total;

printf(" YEAR    RAINFALL  (inches)\n");
for ( year = 0, total = 0; year < YRS; year++)
     { /* for each year, sum rainfall for each month */
     for ( month = 0, subtot = 0; month < TWLV; month++)
           subtot += rain[year][month];
     printf("%5d %15.1f\n", 1970 + year, subtot);
     total += subtot;       /* total for all years */
     }
printf("\nThe yearly average is %.1f inches.\n\n", total/YRS);
printf("MONTHLY AVERAGES:\n\n");
printf("Jan  Feb  Mar  Apr  May  Jun  Jul  Aug  Sep  Oct ");
printf(" Nov  Dec\n");

for ( month = 0; month < TWLV; month++ )
     {    /* for each month, sum rainfall over years */
     for ( year = 0, subtot =0; year < YRS; year++)
           subtot += rain[year][month];
     printf("%4.1f ", subtot/YRS);
     }
printf("\n");
}
```

Here is the output for Figure 12.4:

```
YEAR       RAINFALL (inches)
1970          50.6
1971          41.9
1972          28.6
1973          32.2
1974          37.8

The yearly average is 38.2 inches.
```

```
MONTHLY AVERAGES:

Jan  Feb  Mar  Apr  May  Jun  Jul  Aug  Sep  Oct  Nov
7.8  7.2  4.1  3.0  2.1  0.8  1.2  0.3  0.5  1.7  3.6
```

The main points to notice in this program are the initialization and the computation scheme. The initialization is the more involved of the two, so we will look at the computation first.

To find the total for a given year, we kept **year** constant and let **month** go over its full range. This is the inner **for** loop of the first part of the program. Then we repeated the process for the next value of **year.** This is the outer loop of the first part of the program. A nested loop structure like this is natural for handling a two-dimensional array. One loop handles one subscript, and the other loop handles the second subscript.

The second part of the program has the same structure, but now we change **year** with the inner loop and **month** with the outer. Remember, each time the outer loop cycles once, the inner loop cycles its full allotment. Thus, this arrangement cycles through all the years before changing months, and this gives us a five-year total for the first month, then a five-year total for the second month, and so on.

Initializing a Two-Dimensional Array

For the initialization we included five embraced sets of numbers, all enclosed by one more set of braces. The data in the first interior set of braces is assigned to the first row of the array, the data in the second interior set goes to the second row, and so on. The rules we discussed about mismatches between data and array sizes apply to each row. That is, if the first set of braces encloses 10 numbers, only the first 10 elements of the first row are affected. The last two elements in that row would get the standard default initialization to zero. If there are too many numbers, that is an error; they do not get shoved into the next row.

We could have left out the interior braces and just retained the two outermost braces. As long as we have the right number of entries, the effect is the same. If we are short of entries, however, the array is filled sequentially without regard to row until the data runs out. Then the remaining elements are initialized to 0. See Figure 12.5.

Everything we have said about two-dimensional arrays can be generalized to three-dimensional arrays and further. We declare a three-dimensional array this way:

```
int solido[10][20][30];
```

You can visualize this as 10 two-dimensional arrays (each 20 x 30) stacked atop each other. Or you can think of it as an array of arrays of arrays. That

Figure 12.5
Two methods of initializing an array

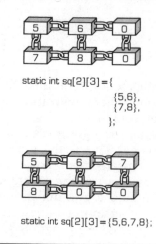

```
static int sq[2][3] = {
                        {5,6},
                        {7,8},
                      };
```

```
static int sq[2][3] = {5,6,7,8};
```

is, it is a 10-element array, each element of which is an array. Each of these arrays has 20 elements, each of which is a 30-element array. The advantage of this second point of view is that it is more easily extended to arrays of more dimensions, unless you happen to be able to visualize four-dimensional objects! We'll stick to two dimensions.

Pointers and Multidimensional Arrays

How do pointers relate to multidimensional arrays? We'll look at some examples now to find the answer.

Suppose we have this declaration:

```
int zippo[4][2];  /* an array of arrays of ints */
```

Then **zippo**, being the name of an array, is a pointer. What, then, does **zippo** point to? An array name points to the first element of the array. In this case, the first element is itself an array of two **int**s, so **zippo** points to the whole array. What can we call the array **zippo** points to? Well, the first element of **zippo** is **zippo[0]**, so we can think of **zippo[0]** as being the name of the first two-**int** array. That makes **zippo[0]** a pointer to its first element, the integer **zippo[0][0]**.

Let's summarize that: **zippo** points to **zippo[0]**, which is an array of **int**s, and **zippo[0]** points to **zippo[0][0]**, which is an **int**. This makes **zippo** a pointer to a pointer.

You may be wondering about the difference between a pointer to an array and a pointer to an integer. Both, of course, are addresses. Is the address of an array somehow different from the address of a single element? Let's see. Here is a program that prints out addresses:

```
main()
{
    int zippo[4][2];

    printf("zippo = %u, zippo[0] = %u, &zippo[0][0] = %u\n",
            zippo, zippo[0], &zippo[0][0] );
}
```

And here is the output:

```
zippo = 3512, zippo[0] = 3512, &zippo[0][0] = 3512
```

This shows that the address of the array (**zippo**) and the address of the **int** (**zippo[0]**) are the same. Each is the address of the first element; that is, each is numerically the same as **&zippo[0][0]**.

Nonetheless, there is a difference. The pointer **zippo[0]** is the address of an **int**, so it points to a 2-byte data object. The pointer **zippo** is the address of an array of two **int**s, so it points to a 4-byte data object. Thus, adding 1 to **zippo** should produce an address 4 bytes larger, while adding 1 to **zippo[0]** should produce an address 2 bytes larger. Let's modify the program to check that:

```
main()
{
    int zippo[4][2];

    printf("zippo = %u, zippo[0] = %u, &zippo[0][0] = %u\n",
            zippo, zippo[0], &zippo[0][0] );
    printf("zippo + 1 = %u, zippo[0] + 1 = %u\n",
            zippo + 1, zippo[0] + 1 );
}
```

Here is the new output:

```
zippo = 3512, zippo[0] = 3512, &zippo[0][0] = 3512
zippo + 1 = 3516, zippo[0] + 1 = 3514
```

It turns out as we predicted. Thus, adding 1 to **zippo** moves us from one array to the next array, while adding 1 to **zippo[0]** moves us from one array element to the next element. Also, note what happens if we add 2 to

zippo[0]. That would take us past the end of the first two-**int** array to the beginning of the next.

Another point to note is that *each* element of **zippo** is an array and hence a pointer to a first element. Thus, we have these relationships:

```
zippo[0] == &zippo[0][0]
zippo[1] == &zippo[1][0]
zippo[2] == &zippo[2][0]
zippo[3] == &zippo[3][0]
```

Now suppose we want to declare a pointer variable **pz** that is compatible with **zippo**. Such a pointer could be used, for example, in writing a function to deal with **zippo**-like arrays. Will the type pointer-to-**int** suffice? No. That type is compatible with **zippo[0]**, which points to a single **int**, but we want **pz** to point to an array of **int**s. Here is what we can do:

```
int (*pz)[2];
```

This says that **pz** is a pointer to an array of two **int**s. Why the parentheses? Well, **[ ]** have a higher precedence than **∗**. Thus, with a declaration like

```
int *pax[2];
```

we apply the brackets first, making **pax** an array of two somethings. After that we apply the **∗**, making **pax** an array of two pointers. Finally, we use the **int**, making **pax** an array of two pointers to **int**. Thus, this declaration creates two pointers. But our original version uses parentheses to apply the **∗** first, creating one pointer to an array of two **int**s.

Functions and Multidimensional Arrays

Suppose we want to write a function to deal with two-dimensional arrays. We have several choices. We can use a function written for one-dimensional arrays on each subarray. Or we can use the same function on the whole array, but treat the whole array as one-dimensional instead of two-dimensional. Or we can write a function that explicitly deals with two-dimensional arrays. To illustrate these three approaches, let's take a small two-dimensional array and apply each of the approaches to double the magnitude of each element.

Applying a One-Dimensional Function to Subarrays—We'll keep things simple. We'll declare **junk** to be a **static** array of arrays so that we can initialize it. We'll write a function that takes an array address and an array size as arguments and doubles the indicated elements. We'll use a **for** loop to apply this function to each subarray of **junk**. And we'll print out the array contents. Here is the program:

```
/* dubarr1.c -- double array elements */
#include <stdio.h>
main()
{
     static junk[3][4] = {
                            {2,4,5,8},
                            {3,5,6,9},
                            {12,10,8,6}
                            };
     int i, j;
     void dub();

     for (i = 0; i < 3 ; i++ )
        dub(junk[i], 4);

     for (i = 0; i < 3; i++ )
        {
        for (j = 0; j < 4; j++)
           printf("%5d", junk[i][j]);
        putchar('\n');
        }
}

void dub (ar, size)
int ar[];    /* or int *ar; */
int size;
{
     int i;

     for ( i = 0; i < size; i++ )
         ar[i] *= 2;
}
```

The first **for** loop in **main( )** uses **dub( )** to process subarray **junk[0]**, then **junk[1]**, and so on. Note that we pass **dub( )** a size parameter of 4, since that is the number of elements in each subarray. Here is the output:

```
   4    8   10   16
   6   10   12   18
  24   20   16   12
```

Applying a One-Dimensional Function to the Whole Array—In the preceding example, we looked at **junk** as being an array of 3 arrays of 4 **int**s. We also can look at **junk** as being an array of 12 **int**s. Suppose, for instance, we pass **dub( )** the value **junk[0]** as an argument. This initializes the pointer **ar** in **dub( )** to the address of **junk[0][0]**. This means **ar[0]** corresponds to **junk[0][0]**, and **ar[3]** corresponds to **junk[0][3]**. What about **ar[4]**? That represents the element following **junk[0][3]**, which is **junk[1][0]**, the first element of the next subarray. In other words, we've finished one row and have gone to the beginning of the next.

The next program continues in this fashion to cover the whole array, with **ar[11]** representing **junk[2][3]**.

```
/* dubarr2.c -- double array elements */
#include <stdio.h>
main()
{
    static junk[3][4] = {
                          {2,4,5,8},
                          {3,5,6,9},
                          {12,10,8,6}
                         };
    int i, j;
    void dub();

    dub(junk[0], 3*4);

    for (i = 0; i < 3; i++ )
       {
       for (j = 0; j < 4; j++)
          printf("%5d", junk[i][j]);
       putchar('\n');
       }
}

void dub (ar, size)
int ar[];     /* or int *ar; */
int size;
{
    int i;

    for ( i = 0; i < size; i++ )
        ar[i] *= 2;
}
```

Note that **dub( )** is unchanged from the example before; we merely changed the limit to **3*4** (or 12) and used one call to **dub( )** instead of three. (We wrote the limit as **3*4** to emphasize that it is the total number of elements calculated by multiplying the number of rows times the number of columns.) Does it work? Here is the output:

```
  4    8   10   16
  6   10   12   18
 24   20   16   12
```

Applying a Two-Dimensional Function—Both of the approaches so far lose track of the column-and-row information. In this application (doubling each element), that information is unimportant. But suppose each row represented a year and each column a month. Then you might want a function to, say, total up individual columns. In that case, the function should have the row and column information available. This can be accomplished by declaring the right kind of formal variable so that the function can pass the array properly. In this case, the array **junk** is an array of three arrays of four **ints**. As our earlier discussion has implied, this means that **junk** is a pointer to an array of four **ints**. And a variable of this type can be declared in this way:

```
int (*pj)[4];
```

Alternatively, if **pj** is a formal argument to a function, we can declare it this way:

```
int pj[][4];
```

Such a variable can then be used in the same way as **junk**. That is what we have done in the next example:

```
/* dubarr3.c -- double array elements */
#include <stdio.h>
main()
{
    static junk[3][4] = {
                    {2,4,5,8},
                    {3,5,6,9},
                    {12,10,8,6}
                    };
    int i, j;
    void dub2();

    dub2(junk,3);

    for (i = 0; i < 3; i++ )
       {
       for (j = 0; j < 4; j++)
          printf("%5d", junk[i][j]);
```

```
                putchar('\n');
                }
    }

    void dub2 (ar, size)
    int ar[][4];      /* or int
    (*ar)[4]; */
    int size;
    {
          int i, j;

          for ( i = 0; i < size; i++ )
                for ( j = 0; j < 4; j++)
                ar[i][j] *= 2;
    }
```

This time we pass as arguments **junk**, which is a pointer to the first array, and **3**, the number of rows. The **dub2( )** function then treats **ar** as an array of arrays of 4 **int**s. The length of the row is built into the function, but the number of rows is left open. The same function will work with, say, a 12-by-4 array if 12 is passed as the number of elements. That's because **size** is the number of elements; but, since each element is an array, or row, **size** becomes the number of rows.

Note that **ar** is used in the same fashion as **junk** is used in **main( )**. That is possible because **ar** and **junk** are the same type: pointer to array-of-four-**int**s.

Here is the output:

```
        4     8    10    16
        6    10    12    18
       24    20    16    12
```

Note that this declaration will not work properly:

```
int ar[][]; /* faulty declaration */
```

Recall that the compiler converts array notation to pointer notation. This means, for example, that **ar[1]** will become **ar+1**. But for the compiler to evaluate this, it needs to know what size object **ar** points to. The declaration

```
int ar[][4];
```

says that **ar** points to an array of 4 **int**s, hence to an object 8 bytes long on our system. So **ar+1** means "add 8 bytes to the address." With the empty-bracket version, the compiler would not know what to do.

We've used **int**-arrays in this discussion, but the same concepts apply to other types. Character strings, however, have many special rules. This stems from the fact that the terminal null character in a string provides a way for functions to detect the end of a string without being passed a size. We will look at character strings in detail in the next chapter.

What You Should Have Learned

How to declare a one-dimensional array: **long id_no[200];**
How to declare a two-dimensional array: **short chess[8][8];**
Which arrays can be initialized: external and static
How to initialize an array: **static int hats[3] = {10,20,15};**
Another way to initialize: **static int caps[ ] = {3,56,2};**
How to get the address of a variable: use the **&** operator
How to get the value a pointer points to: use the ***** operator
The significance of an array name: **hats == &hats[0]**
Array-pointer correspondences: if **ptr = hats;** then **ptr + 2 == & hats[2]** and ***(ptr + 2) == hats[2]**
The five operations you can apply to pointer variables: see text
The pointer approach for functions operating on arrays

Review Questions

1. What printout will this program produce?

```
#define PC(X,Y) printf("%c %c\n", X, Y)
char ref[] = { 'D', 'O', 'L', 'T'};
main()
{
  char *ptr;
  int index;

  for( index = 0, ptr = ref; index < 4; index++, ptr++)
     PC(ref[index], *ptr);
}
```

2. In Question 1, why was **ref** declared before **main( )?**

3. What is the value of ***ptr** and of ***(ptr + 2)** in each case?
   a. int *ptr;
      static int boop[4] = {12,21,121, 212};
      ptr = boop;
   b. float *ptr;

```
       static float awk[2][2] = { {1.0, 2.0}, {3.0, 4.0} };
       ptr = awk[0];
    c. int *ptr;
       static int jirb[4] = { 10023, 7};
        ptr = jirb;
    d. int *ptr;
       static int torf[2][2] = { 12, 14, 16};
       ptr = torf[0];
    e. int *ptr;
       static int fort[2][2] = { {12}, {14,16} };
       ptr = fort[0];
```

4. Suppose we have the declaration **static int grid[30][100];**.
    a. Express the address of **grid[22][56]** one way.
    b. Express the address of **grid[22][0]** two ways.
    c. Express the address of **grid[0][0]** three ways.

5. Create an appropriate declaration for each of the following variables:
    a. **digits** is an array of 10 **int**s.
    b. **rates** is an array of 6 **float**s.
    c. **mat** is an array of 3 arrays of 5 integers.
    d. **pstr** is a pointer to an array of 20 **char**s.
    e. **psa** is an array of 20 pointers to **char**.

6. **a.** Declare a static array of 6 **int**s and initialize it to the values 1,2,4,8,16,32.
    b. Use array notation to represent the 3rd element (the one with the value 4) of the array in part **a**.
    c. Use pointer notation to represent the 3rd element of the array.

7. For a 10-element array, the index range is _____ through _____.

8. Suppose we have these declarations:

```
float   rootbeer[10],
things[10][5], *pf, value = 2.2;
int i = 3;
```

Identify each of the following statements as valid or invalid:

		Valid	Invalid
a.	rootbeer[2] = value;		
b.	scanf("%f", &rootbeer[i]);		
c.	rootbeer = value;		
d.	printf("%f", rootbeer);		
e.	things[4][4] = rootbeer[3];		
f.	things[5] = rootbeer;		
g.	pf = value;		
h.	pf = rootbeer;		
i.	rootbeer = pf;		

9. Rewrite the pointer version of the **mean( )** function so that it applies the increment operator directly to the pointer **pa**. (See Question 1 for an

example.) This illustrates that **pa** is, indeed, a variable, unlike an ordinary array name.

Answers

1. The printout is:

   D D
   O O
   L L
   T T

2. That makes **ref** *storage class* **extern** by default, and that storage class of array can be initialized.

3. **a.** 12 and 121
    b. 1.0 and 3.0
    c. 10023 and 0 (automatic initialization to 0)
    d. 12 and 16
    e. 12 and 14 (just the 12 goes in the first row because of the braces)

4. **a.** **&grid[22][56]**
    b. **&grid[22][0]** and **grid[22]**
    c. **&grid[0][0]** and **grid[0]** and **grid**

5. **a.** **int digits[10];**
    b. **float rates[6];**
    c. **int mat[3][5];**
    d. **char (*pstr)[20];** Note: **char pstr[20];** is incorrect. This would make **pstr** a constant pointer (not a variable) to a single **char**, the first member of the array; **pstr + 1** would point to the next byte. With the correct declaration, **pstr** is a variable, and **pstr + 1** points 20 bytes beyond the initial byte.
    e. **char *pstr[20];** Note: The **[ ]** have higher precedence than *****, so in the absence of parentheses, the array descriptor is applied first, then the pointer descriptor. Hence, this declaration is the same as **char *(pstr[20]);**.

6. **a.** **static int twopow[6]= { 1, 2, 4, 8, 16, 32};**
    b. **twopow[2]**
    c. ***(twopow + 2)**

7. 0 through 9

8. Points to keep in mind are these: Do the types match? Can the indicated term be assigned a value?
    a. **rootbeer[2] = value;** valid. It assigns a **float** value to a **float** element of an array.
    b. **scanf("%f", &rootbeer[i]);** valid. It uses the address of a **float** element.
    c. **rootbeer = value;** invalid. First, **rootbeer**, being the name of an array, is

a constant and cannot be assigned a value. Second, **rootbeer** is a pointer, and **value** is not.

d. **printf("%f", rootbeer);** invalid. The **%f** specification requires a single **float** value, not an array. Using, say, **rootbeer[3]** would be okay.

e. **things[4][4] = rootbeer[3];** valid. It assigns the value of a **float** element to a **float** element.

f. **things[5] = rootbeer;** invalid. First, C does not allow one array to be assigned to another. Also, **things[5]** is a constant.

g. **pf = value;** invalid. It assigns a **float** to a pointer.

h. **pf = rootbeer;** valid. It assigns an address to a pointer variable.

i. **rootbeer = pf;** invalid. It assigns an address to a constant.

9. Here is one method. Note that the notation **∗(pa++)** means: "Use the value **pa** points to; then increment **pa** so that it points to the next value." Actually, the precedence rules make the parentheses unnecessary.

```
/* find array mean using moving pointer */
int mean(pa,n)
int *pa, n;
{
     long sum = 0;
     int index;

     if ( n > 0 )
         {
         for( index = 0; index < n; index++ )
             sum += *(pa++); /* use and move to next int */
         return (int) ( sum/n );
         }
     else
         {
         printf("No array.\n");
         return 0;
         }
}
```

Exercises

1. Modify our rain program so that it does the calculations using pointers instead of subscripts. (You still have to declare and initialize the array.)

2. Write a program that initializes an array and then copies the contents of the array into two other arrays. (All three arrays should be declared in the main program.) To make the first copy, use a function with array notation. To make the second copy, use a function with pointer notation and pointer incrementing. Have each function take as arguments the name of the source array, the name of the target array, and the number of elements to be copied.

3. Write a program that initializes a two-dimensional array and uses one of the copy functions from Exercise 2 to copy it to a second two-dimensional array. (Since a two-dimensional array is an array of arrays, a one-dimensional copy function can be used with each subarray.)

4. Use the same copy function to copy the 3rd through 5th elements of a 7-element array into a 3-element array. The function itself need not be altered; just choose the right actual arguments. (The actual arguments need not be an array name and array size; they just have to be the address of an array element and a number of elements to be processed.)

5. Rewrite our rain program so that the main tasks are performed by functions instead of in **main( )**.

6. Write a program that reads floating-point numbers into an array. Have the program quit reading input when it reaches EOF or when the array is filled, whichever comes first. Have the program sort the array into descending order and calculate the average value of the numbers. Have it print the results. Write functions to handle the four main tasks: input, sorting, finding the average, and output. Have the input function skip over any nonnumeric input (aside from EOF).

Here is a sample skeleton for the program; you need not follow it in detail:

```
#define MAX 100  /* maximum array size */
#define FORMAT "Enter up to %d numbers, else use\
                    EOF to end.\n"
main()
{
     float data[MAX];          /* holds input data */
     double average, mean();
     int size;                 /* number of items read */

     printf(FORMAT,MAX);
     size = readin(data);
          /* function fills array, returns # read */
     if (size == 0 )
         printf("No data.  Bye.\n");
     else
         {
         sort(data,size);
         average = mean(data,size);
         showresults(data,size,average);
         }
}
```

13

Character Strings and String Functions

Concepts
- Character strings
- Initializing character strings
- String I/O
- Using string functions
- Command-line arguments

character strings form one of the most useful and important data types in C. Although we have been using character strings all along, we still have much to learn about them. Of course, we already know the most basic fact: a *character string* is a **char** array terminated with a null character ('\0'). In this chapter we will learn more about the nature of strings, how to declare and initialize strings, how to get them into and out of programs, and how to manipulate strings.

Figure 13.1 presents a busy program that illustrates several ways to set up strings, read them in, and print them out. We use two new functions: **gets( )**, which fetches a string, and **puts( )**, which prints out a string. (You probably notice a family resemblance to **getchar( )** and **putchar( )**.) The rest should look fairly familiar.

Figure 13.1
Program using strings

```
/* stringing the user along */
#include <stdio.h>
#define MSG "You must have many talents. Tell me some."
   /* a symbolic string constant */
#define NULL 0
#define LIM 5
#define LINLEN 81   /* maximum string length + 1 */
char m1[] = "Just limit yourself to one line's worth.";
      /* initializing an external character array */
char *m2 = "If you can't think of anything, fake it.";
      /* initializing an external character pointer */
```

```
    main()
    {
      char name[LINLEN];
      static char talents[LINLEN];
      int i;
      int count = 0;
      char *m3 = "\nEnough about me -- what's your  name?";
            /* initializing a pointer */
      static char *mytal[LIM] = {  "Adding numbers swiftly",
            "Multiplying accurately", "Stashing data",
            "Following instructions to the letter",
            "Understanding the C language"};
            /* initializing an array of strings */

      printf("Hi! I'm Clyde the Computer. I have many talents.\n");
      printf("Let me tell you some of them.\n");
      puts("What were they? Ah, yes, here's a partial list.");
      for ( i = 0; i < LIM; i++)
          puts( mytal[i] );  /* print list of computer talents */
      puts(m3);
      gets(name);
      printf("Well, %s, %s\n", name, MSG);
      printf("%s\n%s\n", m1, m2);
      gets(talents);
      puts("Let's see if I've got that list:");
      puts(talents);
      printf("Thanks for the information, %s.\n", name);
    }
```

To help you see what this program does, here is a sample run.

```
Hi! I'm Clyde the Computer. I have many talents.
Let me tell you some of them.
What were they? Ah, yes, here's a partial list.
Adding numbers swiftly
Multiplying accurately
Stashing data
Following instructions to the letter
Understanding the C language

Enough about me -- what's your name?
Nigel Barntwit
Well, Nigel Barntwit, You must have many talents. Tell me some.
Just limit yourself to one line's worth.
If you can't think of anything, fake it.
```

```
Fencing, yodeling, malingering, cheese tasting, and sighing.
Let's see if I've got that list:
Fencing, yodeling, malingering, cheese tasting, and sighing.
Thanks for the information, Nigel Barntwit.
```

Let's sift through the program. However, rather than go through it line by line, we will take a more organized approach. First, we will look at ways of defining a string within a program. Then we will look at what is involved in reading a string into a program. Finally, we will study ways to output a string.

Defining Strings within a Program

You probably noticed when you read our program that there are many ways to define a string. We are going to look at the principal ways now: using string constants, using **char** arrays, using **char** pointers, and using arrays of character strings. A program should make sure there is a place to store a string, and we will take up that topic, too.

Character String Constants

Whenever the compiler encounters something enclosed in double quotes, it recognizes it as a string constant. The enclosed characters, plus a terminating '\0' character, are stored in adjacent memory locations. The computer counts out the number of characters so it knows how much memory will be needed. Our program uses several such character string constants, most often as arguments for the **printf( )** and **puts( )** functions. Note, too, that we can **#define** character string constants.

If you want to have a double quotation mark *in* a string, precede it with the backslash:

```
printf("\"Run, Spot, run!\" said Dick.\n");
```

This produces the output:

```
"Run, Spot, run!" said Dick.
```

Character string constants are placed in storage class **static**. The entire phrase in quotes acts as a pointer to where the string is stored. This is analogous to the name of an array serving as a pointer to the array's location. If this is true, what kind of output should this line produce?

```
/* strings as pointers */
main()
{
printf(" %s, %u, %c\n", "We", "love", *"figs");
}
```

Well, the %s format prints the string, so that should produce a **We.** The %u format produces an unsigned integer. If the phrase **"love"** is a pointer, then it should produce the value of **"love"** pointer, which is the address of the first character in the string. Finally, *"**figs**" should produce the value of the address pointed to, which should be the first character of the string "figs". Does this really happen? Well, here is our output:

```
We, 34, f
```

Voila! Now let's turn to strings stored in **char** arrays.

Character String Arrays and Initialization

When we define a character string array, we must let the compiler know how much space is needed. One way to do this is to initialize the array with a string constant. Since **auto** arrays cannot be initialized, we need to use **static** or external arrays for this purpose. For example,

```
char m1[] = "Just limit yourself to one line's worth.";
```

initialized the external (by default) array **m1** to the indicated string. This form of initialization is short for the standard array initialization form:

```
char m1[] = { 'J', 'u', 's', 't', ' ', 'l', 'i', 'm', 'i',
't', ' ', 'y', 'o', 'u', 'r', 's', 'e', 'l',
'f', ' ', 't', 'o', ' ', 'o', 'n', 'e', ' ',
'l', 'i', 'n', 'e', '\'', 's', ' ', 'w', 'o', 'r',
't', 'h', '.', '\0'
};
```

(Note the closing null character. Without it, we have a character array, but not a string.) For either form (and we do recommend the first), the compiler counts the characters and sizes the array accordingly.

Just as for other arrays, the array name **m1** is a pointer to the first element of the array:

```
m1 == &m1[0] , *m1 == 'J', and *(m1+1) == m1[1] == 'u'
```

Indeed, we can use pointer notation to set up a string. For example, we used

```
char *m3 = "\nEnough about me -- what's your name?";
```

This is very nearly the same as saying

```
static char m3[] = "\nEnough about me -- what's your name?"
```

Both declarations amount to saying that **m3** is a pointer to the indicated string. In both cases the string itself determines the amount of storage set aside for the string. But the forms are not identical.

Array versus Pointer

What is the difference, then, between an array and a pointer? The array form causes an array of 38 elements (one for each character plus one for the terminating '\0') to be created in static storage. Each element is initialized to the corresponding character. Hereafter, the compiler will recognize the name **m3** as a synomym for the address of the first array element, **&m3[0]**. One important point here is that **m3** is a pointer *constant*. You can't change **m3**, because that would mean changing the location (address) where the array is stored. You can use operations like **m3+1** to identify the next element in an array, but **++m3** is not allowed. The increment operator can be used only with the names of variables, not with constants.

The pointer form also causes 38 elements in static storage to be set aside for the string. In addition, it sets aside one more storage location for the pointer *variable* **m3**. This variable initially points to the beginning of the string, but the value can be changed. Thus, we can use the increment operator; **++m3** would point to the second character (**E**). Note that we did not have to declare ***m3** as static. That is because we are not initializing an array of 38 elements; we are initializing a single pointer variable. There are no storage class restrictions for initializing ordinary, nonarray variables.

Are these differences important? Often they are not, but it depends on what you try to do. See the box for some examples. Meanwhile, we return to the problem of creating storage space for strings.

Array and Pointer: Differences

In the text we discuss the differences between using declarations of these two forms:

```
static char heart[] = "I love Tillie!";
char *head = "I love Millie!";
```

The chief difference is that the pointer **heart** is a constant, while the pointer **head** is a variable. Let's see what practical difference this makes.

First, both can use pointer addition.

```
for (i = 0; i < 6; i++)
    putchar( *(heart + i) );
putchar('\n');
for (i = 0; i < 6; i++)
    putchar( *(head + i) );
putchar('\n');
```

produces the output

```
I love
I love
```

Only the pointer version can use the increment operator:

```
while ( *(head) != '\0' ) /* stop at end of string */
    putchar( *(head++); /* print character, advance pointer */
```

and this produces:

```
I love Millie!
```

Suppose we want **head** to agree with **heart.** We can say

```
head = heart;  /* head now points to the array heart */
```

but we cannot say

```
heart = head;  /* illegal construction */
```

The situation is analogous to **x = 3;** versus **3 = x;.** The left side of the assignment statement must be a variable name. Incidentally, **head = heart;** does not make the **Millie** string vanish; it just changes the address stored by **head.**

There is a way to alter the **heart** message, and that is to go into the array itself:

```
heart[7]= 'M';
```

or

```
*(heart + 7) = 'M';
```

The *elements* of an array are variables, but the *name* is not a variable.

Specifying Storage Explicitly

Another way to set up storage is to be explicit. In the external declaration, we could have said

```
char m1[44] = "Just limit yourself to one line's worth.";
```

instead of

```
char m1[] = "Just limit yourself to one line's worth.";
```

Just be sure that the number of elements is at least one more (that null character again) than the length of the string. As in other static or external arrays, any unused elements are automatically initialized to 0 (which in **char** form is the null character, not the zero digit character).

Figure 13.2
Initializing an array

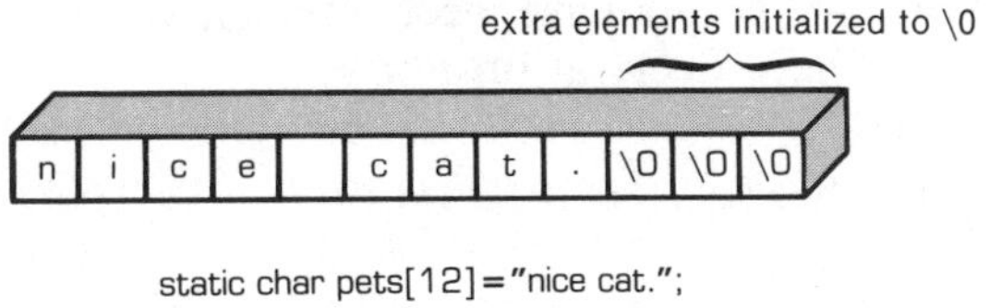

extra elements initialized to \0

| n | i | c | e | | c | a | t | . | \0 | \0 | \0 |

static char pets[12]="nice cat.";

Note that in our program, we had to assign a size for the array **name:**

```
char name[81];
```

Since **name** is to be read in when the program runs, the compiler has no way of knowing in advance how much space to set aside unless we tell it. There is no string constant present whose characters the compiler can count. So we took a gamble that 80 characters will be enough to hold the user's name.

Arrays of Character Strings

Often it is convenient to have an array of character strings. Then you can use a subscript to access several different strings. We used this example:

```
static char *mytal[LIM] = { "Adding numbers swiftly",
        "Multiplying accurately", "Stashing data",
        "Following instructions to the letter",
        "Understanding the C language"};
```

Let's study this declaration. Recalling that **LIM** is **5,** we can say that **mytal** is an array of five pointers to character strings. Each character string, of course, is an array of characters, so we have five pointers to arrays. The first pointer is **mytal[0]** and it points to the first string. The second pointer is **mytal[1]** and it points to the second string. In particular, each pointer points to the first character in each string:

```
*mytal[0] == 'A', *mytal[1] == 'M', mytal[2] == 'S'
```

and so on.

The initialization follows the rules for arrays. The braced portion is equivalent to

```
{{...}, {...},...,{...} };
```

where the dots indicate the stuff we were too lazy to type in. The main point we wish to make is that the first set of double quotes corresponds to a brace-pair and thus is used to initialize the first character string pointer. The next set of double quotes initializes the second pointer, and so on. A comma separates neighboring sets.

Again, we could have been explicit about the size of the character strings by using a declaration like

```
static char mytal[LIM][LINLIM];
```

One difference is that this second choice sets up a "rectangular" array with all the rows the same length. The

```
static char *mytal[LIM];
```

choice, however, sets up a "ragged" array, with each row's length determined by the string it was initialized to. The ragged array doesn't waste any storage space.

Pointers and Strings

Perhaps you noticed an occasional reference to pointers in our discussion of strings. Most C operations for strings actually work with pointers. For example, consider the following useless, yet instructive, program.

```
/* pointers and strings */
#define PX(X) printf("X = %s; value = %u; &X = %u\n", X, X, &X)
main()
{
   static char *mesg = "Don't be a fool!";
   static char *copy;

   copy = mesg;
   printf("%s\n", copy);
   PX(mesg);
   PX(copy);
}
```

Looking at this program, you might think it makes a copy of the string "Don't be a fool!", and your first glance at the output might seem to confirm this guess:

```
Don't be a fool!
mesg = Don't be a fool!; value = 14; &mesg = 32
copy = Dont' be a fool!; value = 14; &copy = 34
```

But study the **PX( )** output. First, **X,** which successively is **mesg** and **copy,** is printed as a string (%s). No surprises here; all the strings are "Don't be a fool!".

Next . . . well, let's come back to that later.

The third item on each line is **&X,** the address of **X.** The two pointers **mesg** and **copy** are stored in locations 32 and 34, respectively.

Now about the second item, the one we called **value.** It is **X** itself. The

Figure 13.3
Rectangular versus ragged array

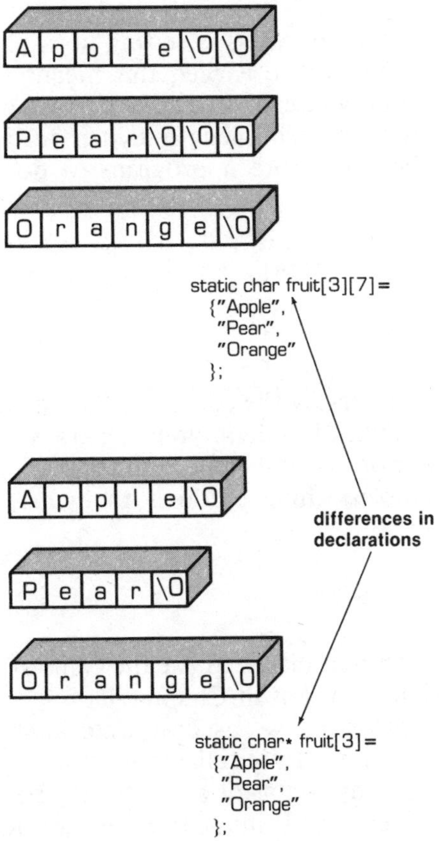
A p p l e \0 \0
P e a r \0 \0 \0
O r a n g e \0
static char fruit[3][7] =
{"Apple",
"Pear",
"Orange"
};
A p p l e \0
P e a r \0
O r a n g e \0
differences in declarations
static char* fruit[3] =
{"Apple",
"Pear",
"Orange"
};

value of the pointer is the address it contains. We see that **mesg** points to location 14, and so does **copy.**

The meaning of this is that the string itself was never copied. All that **copy = mesg;** does is produce a second pointer pointing to the very same string.

Why all this pussyfooting around? Why not just copy the whole string? Well, which is more efficient: copying one address or copying, say, 50 separate elements? Often, the address is all that is needed to get the job done.

Now that we have discussed defining strings within a program, let's turn to strings that are read in.

String Input

Inputting a string has two steps: setting aside space to store the string and using an input function to fetch the string.

Creating Space

The first order of business is setting up a place to put the string once it is read. As we mentioned earlier, this means that we need to allot sufficient storage to hold whatever strings we expect to read. Don't expect the computer to count the string length as it is read and then allot space for it. It won't (unless you write a program to do so). For example, if you try something like this:

```
static char *name;

scanf("%s", name);
```

it probably will get by the compiler. But when the name is read in, it will be written over data or code in your program. Most programmers regard this as highly humorous, but only in other people's programs.

The simplest thing to do is to include an explicit array size in the declaration:

```
char name[81];
```

Another possibility is to use the C library functions that allot memory, and we'll touch on that in Chapter 15.

In our program, we used an **auto** array for **name.** We could do that since we didn't have to initialize the array.

Once you have set aside space for the string, you can read the string in. As we have mentioned, input routines are not part of the definition of C. However, most systems have on tap the two library functions **scanf( )** and gets( ), and both can read in strings. The commonest method is to use **gets( )**, and we will discuss it first.

The *gets( )* Function

The **gets( )** (for **get** string) function is very handy for interactive programs. It gets a string from your system standard input device, which we assume is a keyboard. Since a string has no predetermined length, **gets( )** needs a way to know when to stop. Its method is to read characters until it reaches a newline ('**\n**') character, which you generate by pressing the [enter] key. It takes all the characters before (but not including) the newline, tacks on a null character ('**\0**'), and gives the string to the calling program. Here is a simple means of using it:

```
/* getname1 */
main()
{
  char name[81];  /* allot space */

  printf("Hi, what's your name?\n");
  gets(name);     /* place input in string "name" */
  printf("Nice name, %s.\n", name);
}
```

This will accept any name (including spaces) up to 80 characters long. (Remember to save one space for '**\0**'.)

Note that we want **gets( )** to affect something (**name**) in the calling program. This means we should use a pointer as an argument; and, of course, the name of an array *is* a pointer.

The **gets( )** function is more sophisticated than this last example suggests. Look at this:

```
/* getname2 */
main()
{
  char name[81];
  char *ptr, *gets();

  printf("Hi, what's your name?\n");
  ptr = gets(name);
  printf("%s? Ah! %s!\n", name, ptr);
}
```

Here is a sample interchange:

Hi, what's your name?

Tony de Tuna
Tony de Tuna? Ah! Tony de Tuna!

Gets( ) gets you the input two ways!

1. It uses the pointer method to feed the string to **name.**
2. It uses the **return** keyword to return the address of the string to **ptr.** Notice that **ptr** is a pointer to **char.** This means that **gets( )** must return a value that is a pointer to **char.** And up in the declaration section you can see that we so declared **gets( ).**

The declaration form

```
char *gets();
```

says that **gets( )** is a function (hence the parentheses) of type "pointer-to-char" (hence the * and **char**). We got away without this declaration in **getname1** because we never tried to use the returned value of **gets( ).**

Incidentally, you can also declare something to be a pointer to a function. That would look like this:

```
char (*foop)( );
```

and **foop** would be a pointer to a function whose type is **char.** We'll talk a bit more about such fancy declarations in Chapter 14.

The structure for the **gets( )** function would look something like this:

```
char *gets(s)
char *s;
{
   ...
   return(s);
}
```

Note that **gets( )** returns the same pointer that was passed to it. There is but one copy of the input string, the one placed at the address passed as a function argument.

The actual structure is slightly more complicated, for **gets( )** has two possible returns. If everything goes well, then it returns the read-in string, as we have said. If something goes wrong or if **gets( )** encounters EOF, it returns a null, or zero, address. Thus, **gets( )** incorporates a bit of error-checking.

This makes it convenient to use constructions like this:

```
while ( gets(name) != NULL)
```

where **NULL** is defined in **stdio.h** as **0**. The pointer aspect provides a value for **name**. The **return** aspect provides a value for **gets(name)** as a whole and allows us to check for EOF. This two-pronged approach is more compact than that allowed by **getchar( )**, which has a **return** but no argument.

```
while ( (ch = getchar()) != EOF)
```

The *scanf( )* Function

We've used **scanf( )** with the %s format before to read in a string. The chief difference between **scanf( )** and **gets( )** lies in how they decide they have reached the end of the string; **scanf( )** is more a get word than a get string function. The **gets( )** function, we've seen, takes in all the characters up until the first newline. The **scanf( )** function has two choices. For either choice, the string starts at the first nonwhite-space character encountered. If you use the %s format, the string runs up to (but not including) the next white-space character (blank, tab, or newline). If you specify a field width, as in %10s, then **scanf( )** collects up to 10 characters or to the first white-space character, whichever comes first.

Recall that the **scanf( )** function returns an integer value that equals the number of items read in, if successful, or an EOF character, if that's what it encounters.

```
/* scanf() and counts */
main()
{
    static char name1[40], name2[11];
    int count;

    printf("Please enter 2 names.\n");
    count = scanf("%s %10s",name1, name2);
    printf("I read in the %d names %s and %s.\n",
            count, name1, name2);
}
```

Here are two runs:

```
Please enter 2 names.
    Jessica         Jukes
I read in the 2 names Jessica and Jukes.


Please enter 2 names.
    Liza Applebottham
I read in the 2 names Liza and Applebotth.
```

In the second example, only the first 10 characters of **Applebottham** were read, for we used a %10s format.

If you are obtaining only text from the keyboard, you are best off using **gets( )**. It is easier to use and is a faster, more compact function. The main use for **scanf( )** would be for inputting a mixture of data types in some standard form. For example, if each input line contained the name of a tool, the number in stock, and the cost of the item, you might use **scanf( )**. Or you might throw together a function of your own that did some entry error-checking.

Now let's discuss the output process for strings.

String Output

Again, we must rely upon library functions, which may vary slightly from system to system. The two workhorses for string output are **puts( )** and **printf( )**.

The *puts( )* Function

The **puts( )** function is a very easy one to use; just give it an argument that is a pointer to a string. This next example illustrates some of the many ways to do this.

```
/* puts with ease */
#include <stdio.h>
#define DEF "I am a #defined string."
main()
{
    static char str1[] = "An array was initialized to me.";
    char *str2 = "A pointer was initialized to me.";

    puts("I'm an argument to puts().");
    puts(DEF);
    puts(str1);
    puts(str2);
    puts(&str1[4]);
    puts(str2+4);
}
```

The output:

```
I'm an argument to puts().
I am a #defined string.
An array was initialized to me.
A pointer was initialized to me.
rray was initialized to me.
inter was initialized to me.
```

This example reminds us that phrases in quotes and the names of character array strings are pointers. Note, too, the final two examples. The pointer **&str1[4]** points to the fifth element of the array **str1.** That element contains the character 'r', and that is what **puts( )** uses for its starting point. Similarly, **str2+4** points to the memory cell containing the 'i' of "pointer," and the printing starts there.

How does **puts( )** know when to stop? It stops when it encounters the null character, so there had better be one. Don't try this!

```
/* no! */
main()
{
    static char dont[] = {'H', 'I', '!', '!' };

    puts(dont);    /* dont not a string */
}
```

Because **dont** lacks a closing null character it is not a string. Because it lacks the null character, **puts( )** won't know where to stop. It will just keep going on into the memory cells following **dont** until it finds a null somewhere. If you're lucky it might be the very next cell, but luck may fail you.

Notice that each string outputted by **puts( )** goes on a new line. When **puts( )** finally finds the closing null character, it replaces it with a newline character and then sends the string on.

The *printf( )* Function

We discussed **printf( )** pretty thoroughly elsewhere. Like **puts( )**, it takes a pointer to a string as an argument. The **printf( )** function is slightly less convenient to use than **puts( )**, but it is more versatile.

One difference is that **printf( )** does not put each string on a new line automatically. You have to indicate where you want new lines. Thus

```
printf("%s\n", string);
```

has the same effect as

```
puts(string);
```

As you can see, the first form takes more typing. It also takes longer for the computer to execute. On the other hand, **printf( )** makes it simple to combine strings for one line of printing. For example,

```
printf("Well, %s, %s\n", name, MSG);
```

combines "Well," with the user's name and symbolic character string, all on one line.

The Do-It-Yourself Option

You aren't limited to these library options for input and output. If you don't have them or don't like them, you can prepare your own versions, building upon **getchar( )** and **putchar( ).**

Suppose you lack a **puts( ).** Here is one way to make it:

```
/* put1 -- prints a string */
void put1(string)
char *string;
{
  while(*string != '\0')
    putchar(*string++);
  putchar('\n');
}
```

The **char** pointer **string** initially points to the first element of the called argument. After the contents of that element are printed, the pointer increments and points to the next element. This goes on until the pointer points to an element containing the null character. Then a newline is tagged on at the end.

Many C programmers would use this test for the **while** loop:

```
while ( *string )
```

When **string** points to the null character, ***string** has the value **0**, which value terminates the loop. This approach certainly takes less typing than the previous version. If you are not familiar with C practice, it is less obvious. It may result in more efficient code, depending on the compiler.

Suppose you have a **puts( ),** but you want a function that also tells you how many characters were printed. It's easy to add that feature:

```
/* put2 -- prints a string and counts characters */
int put2(string)
char *string;
{
  int count = 0;
  while(*string != '\0')
    {
    putchar(*string++);
    count++;
    }
  putchar('\n');
  return(count);
}
```

The call

```
put2("pizza");
```

prints the string **pizza,** while the call

```
num = put2("pizza");
```

would also deliver a character count to **num,** in this case, the value **5.** Here is a slightly more elaborate version that shows nested functions:

```
/* nested functions */
#include <stdio.h>
main()
{
  void put1();
  put1("If I'd as much money as I could spend,");
  printf("I count %d characters.\n",
        put2("I never would cry old chairs to mend.") );
}
```

Note that we used **#include stdio.h** because on our system **putchar( )** is defined there, and our new functions use **putchar( ).**

Hmm, we are using **printf( )** to print the value of **put2( ),** but in the act of finding **put2( )**'s value, the computer first must run it, causing the string to be printed. Here's the output:

```
If I'd as much money as I could spend,
I never would cry old chairs to mend.
I count 37 characters.
```

You should be able to build a working version of **gets( )** by now; it would be similar to, but much simpler than, our **getint( )** function of Chapter 10.

String Functions

Most C libraries supply string-handling functions. We'll look at four of the most useful and common ones: **strlen( ), strcat( ), strcmp( ),** and **strcpy( ).**

Already we have used **strlen( ),** which finds the length of a string. We use it in this next example, a function that shortens lengthy strings.

The *strlen( )* Function

```
    /* procrustean function */
void fit(string,size)
char *string;
int size;
{
    if ( strlen(string) > size)
        *(string +size) = '\0';
}
```

Try it in this test program:

```
 /* test */
main()
{
  static char mesg[] = "Hold on to your hats, hackers.";
  void fit();

  puts(mesg);
  fit(mesg,10);
  puts(mesg);
}
```

The output is this:

```
Hold on to your hats, hackers.
Hold on to
```

Our function placed a '\0' character in the eleventh element of the array, replacing a blank. The rest of the array is still there, but **puts( )** stops at the first null character and ignores the rest of the array.

The *strcat( )* Function

Here's what **strcat( )** can do:

```
    /* join two strings */
#include <stdio.h>
main()
{
    static char flower[80];
    static char addon[] = "s smell like old shoes.";
```

```
    puts("What is your favorite flower?");
    gets(flower);
    strcat(flower, addon);
    puts(flower);
    puts(addon);
}
```

The output:

```
What is your favorite flower?
Rose
Roses smell like old shoes.
s smell like old shoes.
```

As you can see, **strcat( )** (for *str*ing con*cat*enation) takes two strings for arguments. A copy of the second string is tacked on to the end of the first, and this combined version becomes the new first string. The second string is not altered.

Caution! This function does not check to see if the second string will fit in the first array. If you fail to allot enough space for the first array, you will run into problems. Of course, you can use **strlen( )** to look before you leap.

```
/* join two strings, check size first */
#include <stdio.h>
#define SIZE 80
main()
{
    static char flower[SIZE];
    static char addon[] = "s smell like old shoes.";

    puts("What is your favorite flower?");
    gets(flower);
    if ( (strlen(addon) + strlen(flower) + 1 ) < SIZE )
        strcat(flower, addon);
    puts(flower);
}
```

We add **1** to the combined lengths to allow space for the null character.

The *strcmp( )* Function

Suppose you wish to compare someone's response to a stored string:

```
/* will this work? */
#include <stdio.h>
#define ANSWER "Grant"
```

```
main()
{
  char try[40];

  puts("Who is buried in Grant's tomb?");
  gets(try);
  while ( try != ANSWER)
      {
      puts("No, that's wrong. Try again.");
      gets(try);
      }
  puts("That's right!");
}
```

As nice as this may look, it will not work correctly. **Try** and **ANSWER** really are pointers, so what the comparison **try != ANSWER** really asks is not if two strings are the same, but if the two addresses pointed to by **try** and **ANSWER** are the same. Since **ANSWER** and **try** are stored in different locations, the two pointers are never the same, and the user is forever told that he or she is wrong. Such programs tend to discourage people.

What we need is a function that compares string contents, not string addresses. We could devise one, but the job has been done for us with **strcmp( )** (for *str*ing *comp*arison).

We now fix up our program:

```
/* this will work */
#include <stdio.h>
#define ANSWER "Grant"
main()
{
  char try[40];

  puts("Who is buried in Grant's tomb?");
  gets(try);
  while (( strcmp(try,ANSWER) != 0 ))
      {
      puts("No, that's wrong. Try again.");
      gets(try);
      }
  puts("That's right!");
}
```

Since nonzero values are interpreted as "true" anyway, we can abbreviate the **while** statement to **while (strcmp(try,ANSWER))**.

From this example you may deduce that **strcmp( )** takes two string pointers as arguments and returns a value of **0** if the two strings are the same. Good for you for so deducing.

One of the nice points is that **strcmp( )** compares strings, not arrays. Thus, although the array **try** occupies 40 memory cells and **"Grant"** only 6 (one for the null character, don't forget), the comparison looks only at the part of **try** up to its first null character. Thus, **strcmp( )** can be used to compare strings stored in arrays of different sizes.

But what if the user answers **"GRANT"** or **"grant"** or **"Ulysses S. Grant"**? Well, that user is told he or she is wrong. To make a friendly program, you have to anticipate other possible correct answers. There are some tricks. You could **#define** the answer as **"GRANT"** and write a function that converts all input to uppercase only. That eliminates the problem of capitalization, but you still have the other forms to worry you.

By the way, what value does **strcmp( )** return if the strings are not the same? Here is a sample:

```
/* strcmp returns */
#include <a:stdio.h>
main()
{

  printf("%d\n", strcmp("A", "A") );
  printf("%d\n", strcmp("A", "B") );
  printf("%d\n", strcmp("B", "A") );
  printf("%d\n", strcmp("C", "A") );
  printf("%d\n", strcmp("apples", "apple") );
}
```

The output:

```
0
-1
1
2
115
```

As promised, comparing **"A"** to itself returns a **0**. Comparing **"A"** to **"B"** gives a **−1**, and reversing the comparison gives a **1**. This suggests that **strcmp( )** returns a negative number if the first string precedes the second alphabetically and that it returns a positive number if the order is the other way. Moreover, comparing **"C"** to **"A"** gives a **2** instead of a **1**. The pattern becomes clearer: the function returns the difference in ASCII code between the two characters. Not all implementations return the ASCII difference, but all will return: a negative number if the first string comes before the second alphabetically, 0 if they are the same, and a positive number if the first string follows the second alphabetically. In general, **strcmp( )** moves along until it finds the first pair of disagreeing characters; it then returns the corresponding code. For instance, in the very last example, **"apples"** and **"apple"** agree until the final **'s'** of the first string. This matches up with the 6th character in **"apple"**, which is the null character, ASCII 0. The value returned is

```
's' - '\0' = 115 - 0 = 115
```

where 115 is ASCII code for 's'.

Usually you don't care about the exact value returned. Typically, you just want to know if it is zero or nonzero; i.e., whether there is a match or not. Or you may be trying to sort the strings alphabetically, in which case you want to know if the comparison is positive, negative, or zero.

We can use this function for checking to see if a program should stop reading input:

```
    /* beginning of some program */
#include <stdio.h>
#define SIZE 81
#define LIM 100
#define STOP ""   /* a null string */
main()
{
   static char  input[LIM][SIZE];
   int ct = 0;
   while( ct < LIM && gets(input[ct]) != NULL &&
          strcmp(input[ct],STOP) != 0)
{
     ...
     ct++;
}
```

This program quits reading input when it encounters an EOF character (**gets( )** returns **NULL** in that case), or when you press the [enter] key at the beginning of a line (you feed in an empty string), or when you reach the limit **LIM.** Entering the empty line gives the user an easy way to terminate the entry phase.

Let's move on to the final string function we will discuss.

The *strcpy( )* Function

We've said that if **pts1** and **pts2** are both pointers to strings, then the expression

```
pts2 = pts1;
```

copies only the address of a string, not the string itself. Suppose, though, you do want to copy a string. Then you can use the **strcpy( )** function. It works like this:

```
/* strcpy() demo */
#include <stdio.h>
#define WORDS  "Please reconsider your last entry."
main()
{
    static char *orig = WORDS;
    static char copy[40];

    puts(orig);
    puts(copy);
    strcpy(copy, orig);
    puts(orig);
    puts(copy);
}
```

Here is the output:

```
Please reconsider your last entry.

Please reconsider your last entry.
Please reconsider your last entry.
```

You can see that the string pointed to by the second argument **(orig)** is copied into the array pointed to by the first argument **(copy)**. You can remember the order of the arguments by noting that it is the same as the order in an assignment statement: the string getting a value is on the left. (The blank line resulted from the first printing of **copy** and reflects the fact that **static** arrays are initialized to zeros, which are null characters in the **char** mode.)

It is your responsibility to ensure that the destination array has enough room for the incoming string. That is why we used the declaration

```
static char copy[40];
```

and not

```
static char *copy;   /* allots no space for string */
```

In short, **strcpy( )** takes two string pointers as arguments. The second pointer, which points to the original string, can be a declared pointer, an array name, or a string constant. But the first pointer, which points to the copy, should point to an array or portion of an array, of sufficient size to hold the string.

Now that we have outlined some string functions, let's look at a full program that handles strings.

A String Example: Sorting Strings

Let's take on the practical problem of sorting strings alphabetically. This task can show up in preparing name lists, in making up an index, and in many other situations. One of the main tools in such a program is **strcmp( )**, since it can be used to determine the order of two strings. Our general plan will be to read in an array of strings, sort them, and print them out. A little while ago we presented a scheme for reading in strings, and we

Figure 13.4
Program to read and sort strings

```
/* reads in strings and sorts them */
#include <stdio.h>
#define SIZE 81      /* size limit for string length with \0 */
#define LIM 20       /* maximum number of lines to be read */
#define HALT ""      /* null string to stop input          */
main()
{
  void stsrt();
  static char input[LIM][SIZE];  /* array to store input */
  char *ptstr[LIM];  /* array of pointer variables */
  int ct = 0;   /* input count */
  int k;        /* output count */

  printf("Input up to %d lines, and I will sort them.\n",LIM);
  printf("To stop, press the [enter] key at a line's start.\n");
  while( ct < LIM && gets(input[ct]) != NULL &&
         strcmp(input[ct],HALT) != 0)
    {
    ptstr[ct] = input[ct];  /* set ptrs to strings */
    ct++;
    }
  stsrt(ptstr, ct);      /* string sorter */
  puts("\nHere's the sorted list:\n");
  for ( k = 0; k < ct; k++)
      puts(ptstr[k]);   /* sorted pointers */
}
/* string-pointer-sorting function */
void stsrt(strings, num)
char *strings[];
int num;
{
  char *temp;
  int top, seek;
```

```
        for ( top = 0; top < num-1; top++)
            for( seek = top + 1; seek < num; seek++)
                if ( strcmp(strings[top],strings[seek]) > 0)
                    {
                     temp = strings[top];
                     strings[top] = strings[seek];
                     strings[seek] = temp;
                    }
    }
```

will start the program that way. Printing the strings out is no problem, and we can use the same sorting algorithm we used earlier for numbers. We will do one slightly tricky thing; see if you can spot it.

We fed it an obscure nursery rhyme to test it.

```
Input up to 20 lines, and I will sort them.
To stop, press the [enter] key at a line's start.
O that I was where I would be,
Then would I be where I am not;
But where I am I must be,
And where I would be I can not.
```

Here's the sorted list:

```
And where I would be I can not.
But where I am I must be,
O that I was where I would be,
Then would I be where I am not;
```

Hmm, the nursery rhyme doesn't seem to suffer much from being alphabetized.

The tricky part is that instead of rearranging the strings themselves, we just rearranged *pointers* to the strings. Let us explain. Originally, **ptrst[0]** points to **input[0],** and so on. Each **input[ ]** is an array of 81 elements, and each **ptrst[ ]** is a single variable. The sorting procedure rearranges **ptrst**, leaving **input** untouched. If, for example, **input[1]** comes before **input[0]** alphabetically, the program switches **ptrst**'s, causing **ptrst[0]** to point at **input[1]** and **ptrst[1]** to point at **input[0].** This is much easier than using, say, **strcpy( )** to interchange the contents of the two **input** strings. See Figure 13.4 for another view of this process.

Finally, let's try to fill an old emptiness in our lives, namely, the void between **main( )**'s parentheses.

Figure 13.5
Sorting string pointers

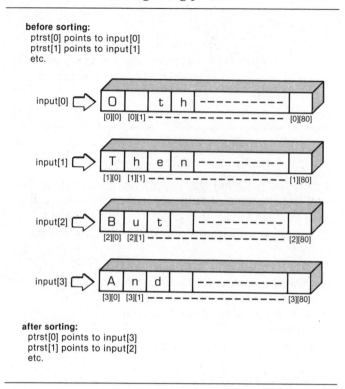

before sorting:
ptrst[0] points to input[0]
ptrst[1] points to input[1]
etc.

input[0] ⇨ | O | | t | h | ----------- | |
[0][0] [0][1] ----------------- [0][80]

input[1] ⇨ | T | h | e | n | ----------- | |
[1][0] [1][1] ----------------- [1][80]

input[2] ⇨ | B | u | t | | ----------- | |
[2][0] [2][1] ----------------- [2][80]

input[3] ⇨ | A | n | d | | ----------- | |
[3][0] [3][1] ----------------- [3][80]

after sorting:
ptrst[0] points to input[3]
ptrst[1] points to input[2]
etc.

Command-Line Arguments

Atten–shun! The command line is the line you type to run your program. At ease! This won't be hard. Suppose we have a program in a file named **fuss**. Then the command line would look like this:

```
% fuss
```

or perhaps

```
A>fuss
```

using two common system prompts.

Command-line arguments are additional items on the same line:

```
% fuss -r Ginger
```

One neat thing about a C program is that it can read in these items for its own use. The mechanism is to use arguments for **main( )**. Here is a typical example:

```
/* main() with arguments */
main(argc,argv)
int argc;
char *argv[];
{
   int count;

   for( count = 1; count < argc; count++)
      printf("%s ", argv[count]);
   printf("\n");
}
```

Put this program in an executable file called **echo,** and this is what happens:

```
A>echo I could use a little help.
   I could use a little help.
```

You probably see why it is called **echo,** but you may still be wondering how it works. Perhaps this explanation will help (we hope so).

C compilers provide for **main( )** having two arguments. The first argument represents the number of strings following the command word. By

tradition (but not necessity) this **int** argument is called **argc** for *argument count*. The system uses spaces to tell when one string ends and the next begins. Thus, our **echo** example has six strings, and our **fuss** example had two. The second argument is an array of string pointers. Each string on the command line is assigned to its own pointer. By convention, this array of pointers is called **argv**, for *argument values*. When possible (some operating systems don't allow this), **argv[0]** is assigned the name of the program itself. Then **argv[1]** is assigned the first following string, etc. For our example, we have

```
argv[0]    points to   echo    (for most systems)
argv[1]    points to   I
argv[2]    points to   could
argv[6]    points to   help.
```

Once you have these identifications, the rest of the program should be easy to follow.

Figure 13.6
Command-line arguments

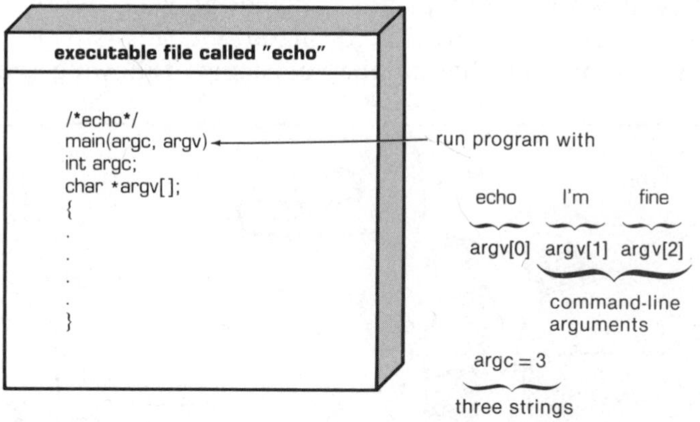

Many programmers use a different declaration for **argv**:

```
main(argc, argv)
int argc;
char **argv;
```

The declaration for **argv** really is equivalent to **char *argv[ ];**. You would read it as saying that **argv** is a pointer to a pointer to **char.** Our example comes down to the same thing. We had an array with seven elements. The name of the array is a pointer to the first element. Thus, **argv** points to **argv[0],** and **argv[0]** is a pointer to **char.** Hence, even with the original definition, **argv** is a pointer to a pointer to **char.** You can use either form, but we feel the first is clearer in meaning.

One very common use for command-line arguments is to indicate options for a program. For example, you might use the combination −**r** to tell a sorting program to work in reverse order. Traditionally, options are indicated using a hyphen and a letter, as in −**r.** These "flags" mean nothing to C; you have to include your own programming to recognize them.

Here is a very modest example showing how a program can check for a flag and make use of it.

```
/* a modest beginning */
#define YES 1
#define NO 0
main(argc, argv)
int argc;
char *argv[];
{
    float array[100];
    int n;
    int flag = NO;

    if ( argv[1][0] == '-' && argv[1][1] == 'r' )
        flag = YES;
    ...

    if flag == NO
        sort1(array,n);
    else
        sort2(array,n);
    ...
}
```

This program checks the first string after the command file name to see if it begins with a hyphen. Then it checks to see if the next character is the code character **r.** If so, it sets a flag to cause a different sorting routine to be used. It ignores strings after the first. (We said it was modest.)

If you have used the UNIX system, you probably have noticed the variety of command-line options and arguments that the UNIX commands offer. These are examples of C command-line arguments, for most of UNIX is written in C.

Command-line arguments also can be file names, and you can use them instead of redirection to tell a program what files to work on. We'll show you how to do that in Chapter 15.

What You Should Have Learned

How to declare a character string: **static char fun[ ]** et al.
How to initialize a character string: **static char *po = "0!"**
How to use **gets( )** and **puts( )**
How to use **strlen( ), strcmp( ), strcpy( ),** and **strcat( )**
How to use command-line arguments
How **char *bliss** and **char bliss[ ]** are similar and different
How to create a string constant: "by using quotes"

Review Questions

1. What's wrong with this attempted declaration of a character string?

```
main()
{
    char   name[] = {'F', 'e', 's', 's' };
```

2. What will this program print?

```
#include <stdio.h>
main()
{
    static char note[] = "See you at the snack bar.";
    char *ptr;

    ptr = note;
    puts(ptr);
    puts(++ptr);
    note[7] = '\0';
    puts(note);
    puts(++ptr);
}
```

3. What will this program print?

```
main()
{
    static char food[] = "Yummy";
    char *ptr;

    ptr = food + strlen(food);
    while ( --ptr >= food)
        puts(ptr);
}
```

4. What will the following program print?

```
main()
```

```
{
static char goldwyn[30] = "art of it all ";
static char samuel[40] = "I read p";
char  *quote = "the way through.";

strcat(goldwyn, quote);
strcat( samuel, goldwyn);
puts(samuel);
}
```

5. Here is an exercise providing practice with strings, loops, pointers, and pointer incrementing. First, suppose we have this function definition:

```
#include <stdio.h>
char *pr (str)
char *str;
{
   char *pc;

   pc = str;
   while (*pc)
      putchar(*pc++);
   do {
      putchar(*--pc);
      } while (pc - str);
   return (pc);
}
```

Consider the following function call:

```
x = pr("Ho Ho Ho!");
```

a. What gets printed?

b. What type should **x** be?

c. What value does **x** get?

d. What does the expression *−−**pc** mean, and how is it different from −−***pc**?

e. What would be printed if *−−**pc** were replaced with ***pc**−−?

f. What do the two **while** expressions test for?

g. What happens if **pr( )** is supplied with a null string as an argument?

h. What must be done in the calling function so that **pr( )** can be used as shown?

6. How many bytes does '$' use? What about "$"?

7. What does the following program print?

```
#include <stdio.h>
#define M1    "How are ya, sweetie? "
char M2[40] = "Beat the clock.";
char *M3  = "chat";
```

```
main()
{
     char words[80];
     printf(M1);
     puts(M1);
     puts(M2);
     puts(M2 + 1);
     strcpy(words,M2);
     strcat(words, " Win a toy.");
     puts(words);
     words[4] = '\0';
     puts(words);
     while(*M3)
         puts(M3++);
     puts(--M3);
     puts(--M3);
     M3 = M1;
     puts(M3);
}
```

8. What does the following program print?

```
main()
{
     static char str[] = "gawsie";
     static char str[] = "bletonism";
     char *ps;
     int i = 0;

     for (ps = str; *ps != '\n'; ps++) {
         if ( *ps == 'a' || *ps == 'e')
                 putchar(*ps);
         else
                 (*ps)--;
         putchar(*ps);
         }

     while (str[i] ) {
         printf("%c", i % 3 ? str[i] : '*');
         ++i;
         }
}
```

9. The **strlen( )** function takes a pointer to a string as an argument and returns the length of the string. Write your own version of this function.

10. Design a function that takes a string pointer as argument and returns a pointer to the first blank in the string on or after the pointed-to position. Have it return a null pointer if it finds no blanks.

Answers

1. Storage class should be **extern** or **static**; initialization should include a '0'.

2. See you at the snack bar.
ee you at the snack bar.
See you
e you

3. y
my
mmy
ummy
Yummy

4. I read part of it all the way through.

5. a. **Ho Ho Ho!!oH oH oH**
   b. pointer-to-**char**
   c. The address of the initial **H**
   d. *−−**pc** means decrement the pointer by 1 and use the value found there.
   −−*****pc** means take the value pointed to by **pc** and decrement that value by 1. (For example, **H** becomes **G**.)
   e. **Ho Ho Ho!!oH oH o**
   Note: a null character comes between ! and !, but it produces no printing effect.
   f. **while(*pc)** does not point to a null character (i.e., to the end of the string). The expression uses the value at the pointed-to location.
   while(pc − str) does not point to the same location that **str** does (the beginning of the string). The expression uses the values of the pointers themselves.
   g. After the first **while** loop, **pc** points to the null character. Upon entering the second loop it is made to point to the storage location before the null character, i.e., to the location just before the one **str** points to. That byte is interpreted as a character and is printed; the pointer then backs up to the preceding byte. The terminating condition (**pc == str**) never occurs, and the process continues until you or the system gets tired.
   h. **pr( )** must be declared in the calling program: **char *pr( );**

6. 1 byte and 2 bytes, respectively.

7. Here is what we get:

How are ya, sweetie? How are ya, sweetie?
Beat the clock.
eat the clock.
Beat the clock. Win a toy.
Beat
chat
hat
at

```
t
t
at
How are ya, sweetie?
```

8. The output is as follows:

```
faavrhee
*le*on*sm
```

9. Here is one solution:

```
int strlen(s)
char *s;
{
  int ct = 0;

  while (*s++)
      ct++;
  return(ct);
}
```

10.
```
char *strblk(string)
char *string;
{
while ( *string != ' ' && *string != '\0' )
   string++;        /* stops at first blank or null */
if ( *string == '\0')
  return(NULL);  /* NULL = 0 */
else
  return(string);
}
```

Exercises

1. Design a function that fetches the next **n** characters from input, including blanks, tabs, and newlines.

2. Modify the last function so that it stops after **n** characters or after the first blank, tab, or newline, whichever comes first. (And don't just use **scanf( )**.)

3. Design a function that fetches the next word from input (define a word as a sequence of characters with no blanks, tabs, or newlines in it).

4. Design a function that searches the specified string for the first occurrence of a specified character. Have the function return a pointer to the character if successful, and a null if the character is not found in the string.

5. The **strncpy(s1,s2,n)** function copies exactly **n** characters from s2 to s1, truncating **s2** or padding it with extra null characters as necessary. The target

string may not be null-terminated if the length of **s2** is **n** or more. The function returns **s1**. Write your own version of this function.

6. Write a program that reads in up to 10 strings or to EOF, whichever come first. Have it offer the user a menu with five choices: print the original list of strings, print the strings in ASCII collating sequence, print the strings in order of increasing length, print the strings in order of the length of the first word in the string, and quit. Have the menu recycle until the user enters the quit request. The program, of course, should actually perform the promised tasks.

14

Structures and Other Data Delights

Concepts
- Data structures
- Structure templates, tags, and variables
- Accessing parts of a structure
- Structure pointers
- Structure arrays
- Functions and structures
- Unions
- Creating new types

Keywords
- *struct, union, typedef*

Operators
- . ->

O ften the success of a program depends on finding a good way to represent the data that the program must work with. C is fortunate in this respect (and not by accident), for it has a very powerful means to represent complex data. This data form, called a *structure,* not only is flexible enough in its basic form to represent a diversity of data, but also allows the user to invent new forms. If you are familiar with the "records" of Pascal, you should be comfortable with structures. Let's study a concrete example to see why a structure might be needed and how to create and use one.

Example Problem: Creating an Inventory of Books

Gwen Glenn wishes to print out an inventory of her books. There is a variety of information she would like for each book: its title, its author, its publisher, its copyright date, the number of pages, the number of copies, and the dollar value. Now some of these items, such as the titles, can be stored in an array of strings. Other items require an array of **int** or an array of **float.** With seven different arrays, keeping track of everything can get hectic, especially if Gwen wishes to have several complete lists—one sorted by title, one sorted by author, one sorted by value, and so on. A much better solution would be to use one array, where each member contained all the information about one book.

But what data form can contain both strings and numbers and somehow keep the information separate? The answer, of course, must be the subject of this chapter, the structure. To see how a structure is set up and how it works, we'll start with a limited example. To simplify the problem, we will impose two restrictions: first, we'll include only title, author, and value; second, we'll limit the inventory to one book. If you have more books than that, don't worry; we'll show you how to extend the program.

Look at the program and its output first; then we will cover the main points.

```
/* one-book inventory */
#include <stdio.h>
#define MAXTIT  41     /* maximum length of title + 1 */
#define MAXAUT  31     /* maximum length of author's name + 1 */
struct book {   /* our first structure template: tag is book */
    char title[MAXTIT];     /* string array for title */
    char author[MAXAUT];    /* string array for author */
    float value;          /* variable to store value of book */
};                    /* end of structure template */
main()
{
    struct book libry;   /* declare variable of book-type */

    printf("Please enter the book title.\n");
    gets(libry.title);      /* access to the title portion */
    printf("Now enter the author.\n");
    gets(libry.author);
    printf("Now enter the value.\n");
    scanf("%f", &libry.value );
    printf("%s by %s: $%.2f\n",libry.title,
        libry.author, libry.value );
    printf("%s: \"%s\" \($%.2f\)\n", libry.author,
        libry.title, libry.value );
}
```

Here is a sample run:

```
Please enter the book title.
Urban Swine Raising
Now enter the author.
Godfrey Porcelot
Now enter the value.
27.50
Urban Swine Raising by Godfrey Porcelot: $27.50
Godfrey Porcelot: "Urban Swine Raising" ($27.50)
```

The structure we created has three parts: one to store the title, one to store the author, and one to store the value. The three main points we will study are:

1. How to set up a format or "template" for a structure.

2. How to declare a variable to fit that template.
3. How to gain access to the individual components of a structure variable.

Setting Up the Structure Template

The *structure template* is the master plan that describes how a structure is put together. Our template looked like this:

```
struct book {
    char title[MAXTIT];
    char author[MAXAUT];
    float value;
    };
```

This template describes a structure made up of two character arrays and one **float** variable. Let's look at the details.

First comes the keyword **struct**; this identifies what comes next as a structure. Next comes an optional "tag," the word **book**. The tag **book** is a shorthand label we can use later to refer to this structure. Thus, later on we have the declaration

```
structure book libry;
```

which declares **libry** to be a structure of the **book** type.

Next we find the list of structure "members" enclosed in a pair of braces. Each member is described by its own declaration. For instance, the **title** portion is a **char** array with **MAXTIT** elements. The members can be any of the data types we have mentioned. That includes other structures!

Finally, we have a semicolon to close off the definition of the template.

You can place this template outside any function (externally), as we have done, or inside a function definition. If the template is defined inside a function, then it can be used only inside that function. If the template is external, it is available to all the functions following the definition in your program. For example, in a second function, you could define

```
struct book dickens;
```

and that function would have a variable **dickens** that followed the form of our template.

We said that the tag name is optional, but you must use one when you set up structures as we did, with the template defined one place, and the actual variables defined elsewhere. We will come back to this point soon, as we look at the business of defining structure variables.

Defining a Structure Variable

The word "structure" is used in two senses. One is the sense "structure template," which is what we just discussed. The template is a plan with no substance; it tells the compiler how to do something, but it doesn't take the next step of actually making the computer do it. The next step is to create a "structure variable"; this is the second sense of the word.

The line in our program that causes a structure variable to be created is

```
struct book libry;
```

Upon receiving this instruction, the computer creates the variable **libry.** Following the plan laid down by **book,** it allots space for a **char** array of **MAXTIT** elements, for a **char** array of **MAXAUT** elements, and for a **float** variable. This storage is lumped together under the single name **libry.** (In the next section we tell how to unlump it as needed.)

Figure 14.1
Memory allocation for a structure

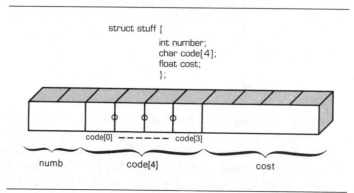

In this declaration, **struct book** plays the same role that **int** or **float** does in a declaration. For example, we could declare two variables of the **struct book** type or even a pointer to that kind of structure:

```
struct book doyle, panshin, *ptbook;
```

The structure variables **doyle** and **panshin** would each have **title, author,** and **value** parts. The pointer **ptbook** could point to **doyle, panshin,** or any other **book** structure.

As far as the computer is concerned,

```
struct book libry;
```

is short for

```
struct book {
    char title[MAXTIT];
    char author[MAXAUT];
    float value;
} libry;      /* tack on variable name to template */
```

In other words, the process of defining a structure template and the process of defining a structure variable can be combined into one step. Combining the template and the variable definitions is the one circumstance in which a tag need not be used:

```
struct  {          /* no tag */
    char title[MAXTIT];
    char author[MAXAUT];
    float value;
} libry;
```

The tag form is much handier if you use a structure template more than once.

There is one aspect of defining a structure variable that did not come up in our example: initialization. We'll take a quick look at that now.

Initializing a Structure

We've seen how to initialize variables and arrays:

```
int count = 0;
static int fibo[] = {0,1,1,2,3,5,8};
```

Can a structure variable be initialized, too? Yes, providing the structure variable is external or static. The point to keep in mind here is that whether or not a structure variable is external depends on where the *variable* is defined, not on where the *template* is defined. In our example, the template **book** is external, but the variable **libry** is not, for it is defined inside the function and is, by default, placed in the automatic storage class. Suppose, though, we had made this declaration:

```
static struct book libry;
```

Then the storage class is static, and we could initialize the structure this way:

```
static struct book libry = {
            "The Pirate and the Damsel",
            "Renee Vivotte",
            1.95
            };
```

To make the associations more obvious, we gave each member its own line of initialization, but all the compiler needs are commas to separate one member's initialization from the next.

Okay, let's continue with our elucidation of structure properties.

Gaining Access to Structure Members

A structure is sort of a superarray in which one element can be **char,** the next element **float,** and the next an **int** array. We can access the individual elements of an array by using a subscript. But how do we access individual members of a structure? We use a ".", the structure member operator. For example, **libry.value** is the **value** portion of **libry.** You can use **libry.value** exactly as you would use any other **float** variable. Similarly, you can use **libry.title** exactly as you would use a **char** array. Thus, we could use expressions like

```
gets(libry.title);
```

and

```
scanf("%f", &libry.value);
```

In essence, **.title, .author,** and **.value** play the role of subscripts for a **book** structure.

Note that although **libry** is a structure, **libry.value** is a **float** type and is used like any other **float** type. For example, **scanf("%f",** . . .) requires the address of a **float** location, and that is what **&libry.float** is. The period has higher precedence here, so the expression is the same as **&(libry.float).**

If you had a second structure variable of the same type, you would use the same system:

```
struct book spiro, gerald;

gets(spiro.title);
gets(gerald.title);
```

The **.title** refers to the first member of **book** structure.

Notice how in our initial program we printed out the contents of the structure **libry** in two different formats; this illustrates the freedom we have in using the members of a structure.

That takes care of the basics. Now we should expand our horizons and look at several ramifications of structures, including arrays of structures, structures of structures, pointers to structures, and functions and structures.

Arrays of Structures

Let's fix up our book program to handle the needs of those with two or three (or perhaps even more!) books. Clearly each book can be described by one structure variable of the **book** type. To describe two books, we need to use two such variables, and so on. To handle several books, we need an array of such structures, and that is what we have created in the next program, shown in Figure 14.2.

Figure 14.2
Multiple book inventory program

```
/* multiple book inventory */
#include <stdio.h>
#define MAXTIT   40
#define MAXAUT   40
#define MAXBKS   100   /* maximum number of books */
#define STOP ""        /* null string, ends input */
struct book {          /* set up book template */
    char title[MAXTIT];
    char author[MAXAUT];
    float value;
    };
main()
{
struct book   libry[MAXBKS];   /* an array of book structures */
int count = 0;
int index;

printf("Please enter the book title.\n");
printf("Press [enter] at the start of a line to stop.\n");
while ( count < MAXBKS &&
        strcmp(gets(libry[count].title),STOP) != 0)
    {
    printf("Now enter the author.\n");
    gets(libry[count].author);
    printf("Now enter the value.\n");
    scanf("%f", &libry[count++].value );
    while ( getchar() != '\n'); /*clear input line */
    if ( count < MAXBKS )
        printf("Enter the next title.\n");
    }
printf("Here is the list of your books:\n");
for( index = 0; index < count; index++)
    printf("%s by %s: $%.2f\n",libry[index].title,
```

```
                           libry[index].author, libry[index].value );
       }
```

Here is a sample program run from Figure 14.2:

```
Please enter the book title.
Press [enter] at the start of a line to stop.
My Life as a Budgie
Now enter the author.
Mack Zackles
Now enter the value.
12.95
Enter the next title.
      ...more entries...
Here is the list of your books:
My Life as a Budgie by Mack Zackles: $12.95
Thought and Unthought by Kindra Schlagmeyer: $33.50
The Anatomy of an Ant by Salome Deschamps: $9.99
Power Tiddlywinks by Jack Deltoids: $13.25
Unix Primer Plus by Waite, Martin, & Prata: $19.95
Coping with Coping by Dr. Rubin Thonkwacker: $0.00
Delicate Frivolity by Neda McFey: $29.99
Fate Wore a Bikini by Mickey Splats: $8.95
A History of Buvania by Prince Nikoli Buvan: $50.00
Mastering Your Digital Watch by Miklos Mysz: $13.95
```

The two main points to note about an array of structures are how to declare them and how to get access to individual members. After explaining that, we will come back to highlight a couple aspects of the program.

Declaring an Array of Structures

The process of declaring a structure array is analogous to declaring any other kind of array:

```
struct book libry[MAXBKS];
```

This declares **libry** to be an array with **MAXBKS** element. Each element of the array is a structure of **book** type. Thus, **libry[0]** is a **book** structure, **libry[1]** is a second **book** structure, and so on. Figure 14.3 may help you visualize this. The name **libry** itself is not a structure name; it is the name of the array holding the structures.

Figure 14.3
An array of structures

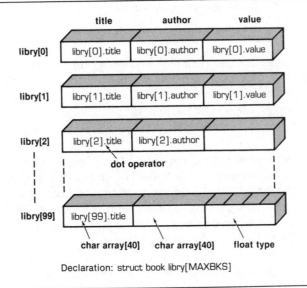

Declaration: struct book libry[MAXBKS]

Identifying Members of a Structure Array

We identify members of an array of structures by applying the same rule we use for individual structures: follow the structure name with the member operator and the member name:

`libry[0].value`   is the value associated with the first   `array element`

`libry[4].title`   is the title associated with the fifth   `array element`

Note that the array subscript is attached to **libry** and not to the end of the name:

```
libry.value[2]    /* WRONG */
libry[2].value    /* RIGHT */
```

The reason we use **libry[2].value** is that **libry[2]** *is* the structure variable name, just as **libry[1]** is another structure variable name and our earlier **doyle** was also a structure variable name.

By the way, what do you suppose

```
libry[2].title[4]
```

would be? It would be the fifth element in the title (that's the **title[4]** part) of the book described by the third structure (that's the **libry[2]** part). In our example, this would be the character **A.** This example points out that subscripts found to the right of the "." operator apply to individual members, while subscripts to the left of the operator apply to arrays of structures.

Let's finish the program now.

Program Details

The main change from our first program is that we put in a loop to read in successive books. We begin the loop with this **while** condition:

```
while ( count < MAXBKS &&
            strcmp(gets(libry[count].title),STOP) != 0)
```

The expression **gets(libry[count].title)** reads an input string for the title of a book. The **strcmp( )** function compares this string to **STOP,** which is just " ", the empty string. If the user presses [enter] at the beginning of a line, the empty string is transmitted, and the loop ends. We also have a check to keep the number of books read in under the size limit of the array.

Then there is the strange line

```
while ( getchar() != '\n'); /*clear input line */
```

This line is included to handle a peculiarity of **scanf( ).** The **scanf( )** function ignores spaces and newlines. When you respond to the request for the book's value, you type something like

```
12.50 [enter]
```

which transmits the sequence of characters

```
12.50\n
```

The **scanf( )** function collects the **1,** the **2,** the **.,** and the **5,** and the **0,** but it leaves the **\n** sitting there, awaiting whatever read statement comes next. If our strange line is missing, the next read statement is **gets(libry[count].title)** in the loop control statement. So it would read the leftover newline character as its *first* character, and the program would think we had sent a stop signal. So we put in our strange line. If you study it, you will see that it eats up characters until it finds and gets the newline. It doesn't do anything with the character except remove it from the input queue. This gives **gets( )** a fresh start.

Now let's return to exploring structures.

Nested Structures

Sometimes it is convenient for one structure to contain, or "nest," another. For example, Shalala Pirosky is building up a structure containing information about her friends. One member of the structure, naturally enough, is the friend's name. The name, however, can be represented by a structure itself, with separate entries for first and last name. Figure 14.4 is a condensed example of Shalala's work.

**Figure 14.4
Nested structure program**

```
    /* example of a nested structure */
#define LEN 20
#define M1 "   Thank you for the wonderful evening, "
#define M2 "You certainly prove that a "
#define M3 "is a special kind of guy. We must get together"
#define M4 "over a delicious "
#define M5 " and have a few laughs."
struct names {                /* first structure template */
            char first[LEN];
            char last[LEN];
            };
struct guy {                  /* second template */
            struct names handle;    /* nested structure */
            char favfood[LEN];
            char job[LEN];
            float income;
            };
main()
{
    static struct guy fellow = {       /* initialized a variable */
            { "Franco", "Wathall" },
            "eggplant",
            "doormat customizer",
            15435.00
            };

    printf("Dear %s, \n\n", fellow.handle.first);
    printf("%s%s.\n", M1, fellow.handle.first);
    printf("%s%s\n", M2, fellow.job);
    printf("%s\n", M3);
    printf("%s%s%s\n\n", M4, fellow.favfood, M5);
    printf("%40s%s\n", " ", "See you soon,");
    printf("%40s%s\n", " ", "Shalala");
}
```

Here is the output:

```
Dear Franco,

    Thank you for the wonderful evening, Franco.
You certainly prove that a doormat customizer
is a special kind of guy. We must get together
over a delicious eggplant and have a few laughs.

                                    See you soon,
                                    Shalala
```

The first point to note is how the nested structure is set up in the template. It is simply declared, just as an **int** variable would be:

```
struct names handle;
```

This says that **handle** is a variable of the **struct names** type. Of course, the file should also include the template for the **names** structure.

The second point to note is how we gain access to a member of a nested structure. We just use the "." operator twice:

```
fellow.handle.first == "Franco"
```

We interpret the construction this way, going from left to right:

```
(fellow.handle).first
```

That is, first find **fellow**, then find the **handle** member of **fellow**, and then find the **first** member of that.

For our next act, we will look at pointers.

Pointers to Structures

Pointer lovers will be glad to know that you can have pointers to structures. This is good for at least three reasons. First, just as pointers to arrays are easier to manipulate (in a sorting problem, say) than the arrays themselves, so are pointers to structures easier to manipulate than structures themselves. Second, in some older implementations, a structure can't be passed as an argument to a function, but a pointer to a structure can be. Third, many wondrous data representations are structures containing pointers to other structures.

The next short example (Figure 14.5) shows how to define a pointer to a structure and how to use it to access the members of a structure.

Figure 14.5
Program with pointer to a structure

```
/*  pointer to a structure */
#define LEN 20
struct names {
            char first[LEN];
            char last[LEN];
    };
struct guy {
            struct names handle;
            char favfood[LEN];
            char job[LEN];
            float income;
    };
main()
{
  static struct guy fellow[2] = {
          {    { "Franco", "Wathall"  },
                "eggplant",
                "doormat customizer",
                15435.00
          },
          {    { "Rodney" , "Swillbelly" },
                "salmon mousse",
                "interior decorator",
                35000.00
          }
    };
  struct guy *him;  /* HERE IT IS -- a pointer to a structure */

  printf("address #1: %u #2: %u\n", &fellow[0], &fellow[1] );
  him = &fellow[0]; /* tell the pointer where to point */
  printf("pointer #1: %u #2: %u\n", him, him + 1);
  printf("him->income is $%.2f: (*him).income is $%.2f\n",
          him->income, (*him).income);
  him++;     /* point to the next structure */
  printf("him->favfood is %s:  him->handle.last is %s\n",
          him->favfood,     him->handle.last);
}
```

The output, please:

```
address #1: 12  #2: 96
pointer #1: 12  #2: 96
him->income is $15435.00: (*him).income is $15435.00
him->favfood is salmon mousse:  him->names.last is Swillbelly
```

Let's look first at how we created a pointer to a **guy** structure. Then we'll study how to specify individual structure members by using the pointer.

Declaring and Initializing a Structure Pointer

Declaration is as easy as can be:

```
struct guy *him;
```

First is the keyword **struct,** then the template tag **guy,** then an * followed by the pointer name. The syntax is the same as for the other pointer declarations we have seen.

The pointer **him** now can be made to point to any structures of the **guy** type. We initialize **him** by making it point to **fellow[0];** note that we use the address operator:

```
him = &fellow[0];
```

The first two output lines show the success of this assignment. Comparing the two lines, we see that **him** points to **fellow[0]** and **him + 1** points to **fellow[1].** Note that adding **1** to **him** adds 84 to the address. This is because each **guy** structure occupies 84 bytes of memory: first name is 20, last name is 20, favfood is 20, job is 20, and income is 4, the size of **float** on our system.

Member Access by Pointer

We have **him** pointing to the *structure* **fellow[0].** How can we use **him** to get a value of a *member* of **fellow[0]?** The third output line shows two methods.

The first method, and the most common, uses a new operator, ->. This operator is formed by typing a hyphen (-) followed by the "greater than" symbol (>). The example helps make the meaning clear:

```
him->income is fellow[0].income if him == &fellow[0]
```

In other words, a structure *pointer* followed by the -> operator works the same as a structure *name* followed by the "." operator. (We can't properly say **him.income** because **him** is not a structure name.)

It is important to note that **him** is a *pointer* but **him->income** is a *member* of the pointed-to structure. Thus, in this case, **him->income** is a **float** variable.

The second method for specifying the value of a structure member follows from this sequence: If **him == &fellow[0],** then ***him == fellow[0].** This is because **&** and ***** are reciprocal operators. Hence

```
fellow[0].income == (*him).income
```

by substitution. The parentheses are required because the "." operator has higher precedence than *****.

In summary, if **him** is a pointer to the structure **fellow[0],** then the following are all equivalent:

```
fellow[0].income == (*him).income == him->income
```

Summary: Structure and Union Operators

The Membership Operator: .
The "." operator is used with a structure or union name to specify a member of that structure or union. If **name** is the name of a structure and **member** is a member specified by the structure template, then

```
name.member
```

identifies that member of the structure. The membership operator can also be used in the same fashion with unions.

Example:

```
struct {
        int code;
        float cost;
      }    item;

item.code = 1265;
```

This assigns a value to the **code** member of the structure **item.**

The Indirect Membership Operator: ->
This operator is used with a pointer to a structure or union to identify a member of that structure or union. Suppose **ptrstr** is a pointer to a structure and that **member** is a member specified by the structure template. Then

---

```
        ptrstr->member
```

identifies that member of the pointed-to structure. The indirect membership operator can be used in the same fashion with unions.

Example:

```
struct {
        int code;
        float cost;
        } item, *ptrst;
ptrst = &item;
ptrst->code = 3451;
```

This assigns a value to the **code** member of **item.** The following three expressions are equivalent:

```
ptrst->code    item.code    (*ptrst).code
```

Now let's see how to handle the interaction between structures and functions.

Telling Functions about Structures

Recall that function arguments pass *values* to the function. Each value is a number, perhaps **int,** perhaps **float,** perhaps ASCII code, or perhaps an address. A structure is a bit more complicated than a single value, so it is not surprising that a structure itself cannot be used as an argument for a function. (This limitation is being removed in newer implementations, however. See Chapter 16.) There are, though, ways to get information about a structure into a function. We'll look at three methods (actually, two with variations) here.

Using Structure Members

As long as a structure member is a variable with a single value (i.e., an **int** or one of its relatives, a **char,** a **float,** a **double,** or a pointer), it can be passed as a function argument. The primitive financial analysis program of Figure 14.6, which adds the client's bank account to his or her savings and loan account, illustrates this point. Note, incidentally, that we combined the template definition, the variable declaration, and the initialization into one statement.

Figure 14.6
Program for passing structure members as function arguments

```
/* passing structure members as function arguments */
struct funds  {
            char *bank;
            float bankfund;
            char *save;
            float savefund;
            }    stan    =    {
                            "Garlic-Melon Bank",
                            1023.43,
                            "Snoopy's Savings and Loan",
                            4239.87
                            };
main()
{
  float total, sum();
  extern struct funds stan;  /* optional declaration */

  printf("Stan has a total of $%.2f.\n",
          sum(stan.bankfund, stan.savefund)  );
}
  /* adds two float numbers */
float sum(x,y)
float x, y;
{
  return(x + y);
}
```

The result of running this program is:

```
Stan has a total of $5263.30.
```

Ah, it works. Notice that the function **sum( )** doesn't know or care whether the actual arguments are members of a structure or not; it just requires that they be type **float.**

Of course if you want a program to affect the value of a member in the calling program, you can transmit the address of the member:

```
modify(&stan.bankfund);
```

and this would be a function that altered Stan's bank account.

The next approach to telling a function about a structure involves letting the summing function know that it is dealing with a structure.

Using the Structure Address

We will solve the same problem as before, but this time we will use the address of the structure as an argument. This is fine, for an address is just a single number. Since the function will have to work with the **funds** structure, it, too, will have to make use of the **funds** template. See Figure 14.7 for the program.

Figure 14.7
Program using address of structure as a function

```
/* passing a structure address to a function */
struct funds {
        char *bank;
        float bankfund;
        char *save;
        float savefund;
    }    stan      = {
                    "Garlic-Melon Bank",
                       1023.43,
                    "Snoopy's Savings and Loan",
                       4239.87
                    };

main()
```

```
{
  float sum();

  printf("Stan has a total of $%.2f.\n", sum( &stan)  );
}
float sum(money)
struct funds *money;
{
  return( money->bankfund + money->savefund );
}
```

This, too, produces the output

```
Stan has a total of $5263.30.
```

The **sum( )** function has a pointer **(money)** to a **fund** structure. Passing the address **&stan** to the function causes the pointer **money** to point to the structure **stan.** We then use the -> operator to gain the values of **stan.bankfund** and of **stan.savefund.**

This function also has access to the institution names, although it doesn't use it. Note that we must use the **&** operator to get the structure address. Unlike the array name, the structure name alone is not a synonym for its address.

Our next method applies to an array of structures and is a variation of this method.

Using an Array

Suppose we have an array of structures. The name of an array *is* a synonym for its address, so it can be passed to a function. Again, the function will need access to the structure template. To show how this works (Figure 14.8), we expand our program to two people, so that we have an array of two **funds** structures.

Figure 14.8
Program passing an array of structures to a function

```
/* passing an array of structures to a function */
struct funds  {
            char *bank;
            float bankfund;
            char *save;
            float savefund;
          }   jones[2] = {
                        {
```

```
                              "Garlic-Melon Bank",
                              1023.43,
                              "Snoopy's Savings and Loan",
                              4239.87
                              },
                              {
                              "Honest Jack's Bank",
                              976.57,
                              "First Draft Savings",
                              1760.13
                              }
                        };
   main()
   {
      float total, sum();

      printf("The Joneses have a total of $%.2f.\n", sum( jones ) );

   float sum(money)
   struct funds *money;
   {
      float total;
      int i;

      for( i = 0, total = 0; i < 2; i++, money++)
         total += money->bankfund + money->savefund;
      return(total);
   }
```

The output:

```
The Joneses have a total of $8000.00.
```

(What an even sum! One would almost think the figures were invented.)

The array name **jones** is a pointer to the array. In particular, it points to the first element of the array, which is the structure **jones[0].** Thus, initially the pointer **money** is given by:

```
money = &jones[0];
```

Then using the -> operator lets us add the two funds for the first Jones. This is really very much like the last example. Next, the **for** loop increments the pointer **money** by 1. Now it points to the next structure, **jones[1],** and the rest of the funds can be added on to **total.**

These are the two main points:

1. We can use the array name to pass a pointer to the first structure in the array to a function.
2. We then can use pointer arithmetic to move the pointer to successive structures in the array. Note that the function call

```
sum(&jones[0])
```

would have the same effect as using the array name, since both refer to the same address. Using the array name is just an indirect way of passing the structure address.

Structures: What Next?

We won't take the explanation of structures any further, but we would like to mention one of the more important uses of structures: creating new data forms. Computer users have developed data forms much more efficient for certain problems than the arrays and simple structures we have presented. These forms have names such as queues, binary trees, heaps, hash tables, and graphs. Many such forms are built from *linked* structures. Typically, each structure will contain one or two items of data plus one or two pointers to other structures of the same type. The pointers serve to link one structure to another and to furnish a path to let you search through the overall structure. For example, Figure 14.9 shows a binary tree structure, with each individual structure (or "node") connected to two below it.

Is such a "branchy" structure more efficient than an array? Well, consider the case of a tree with 10 levels of nodes. If you work it out, you find there are 1023 nodes in which you could store, say, 1023 words. If the words are arranged according to some sensible plan, you can start at the top level and find any word in at most 9 moves as your search moves down one level to the next. If you had the words in an array, you might have to search all 1023 elements before finding the word.

If you are interested in more advanced data structures, consult a book on computing science. With the C structure feature, you will be able to reproduce the forms you read about.

That's our final word on structures. Next, we will take a quick look at two other C features for dealing with data: the union and **typedef**.

Unions—A Quick Look

A *union* is a device that lets you store different data types in the same memory space. A typical use would be creating a table to hold a mixture of types in some order which is neither regular nor known in advance. The

Figure 14.9
A binary tree structure

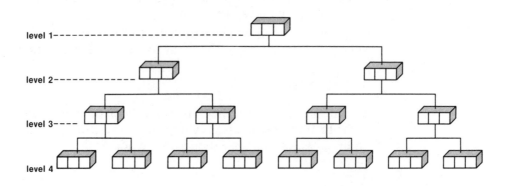

union allows you to create an array of equal-sized units, each of which can hold a variety of data types.

Unions are set up in much the same way as structures. There is a union template and a union variable. They can be defined in one step or, by using a union tag, in two. Here is an example of a template with a tag:

```
union  holdem {
            int digit;
            double bigfl;
            char  letter;
            };
```

Here is an example of defining union variables of the **holdem** type:

```
union holdem fit;  /* union variable of holdem type */
union holdem save[10];  /* array of 10 union variables */
union holdem *pu;  /* pointer to a variable of holdem type */
```

The first declaration creates a single variable **fit.** The compiler allots enough space so that it can hold the largest of the described possibilities. In this case, the biggest possibility listed is **double,** which requires 64 bits, or 8 bytes, on our system. The array **save** would have 10 elements, each 8 bytes big.

Here is how a union is used:

```
fit.digit = 23;  /* 23 is stored in fit; 2 bytes used */
fit.bigfl = 2.0; /* 23 cleared, 2.0 stored; 8 bytes used */
fit.letter = 'h'; /* 2.0 cleared, h stored; 1 byte used */
```

The membership operator shows which data type is being used. Only one value is stored at a time; you can't store a **char** and an **int** at the same time, even though there is enough space to do so.

It is your responsibility to keep track of the data type currently being stored in a union; the next sequence shows what not to do:

```
fit.letter = 'A';
flnum = 3.02*fit.bigfl;    /* ERROR ERROR ERROR */
```

This sequence is wrong because a **char** type is stored, but the next line assumes the content of **fit** is a **double** type.

You can use the -> operator with unions in the same fashion you did with structures:

```
pu = &fit;
x = pu->digit;  /* same as x = fit.digit */
```

Now let's look at another advanced data feature.

typedef—A Quick Look

The **typedef** feature lets you create your own name for a type. It is a lot like **#define** in that respect, but with three differences:

1. Unlike **#define**, **typedef** is limited to giving symbolic names to data types only.
2. The **typedef** function is performed by the compiler, not the preprocessor.
3. Within its limits, **typedef** is more flexible than **#define.**

Let's see how **typedef** works. Suppose you want to use the term **real** for **float** numbers. Then you define **real** as if it were a **float** variable and precede the definition by the keyword **typedef:**

```
typedef float real;
```

From then on, you can use **real** to define variables:

```
real x, y[25], *pr;
```

The scope of this definition depends on the location of the **typedef** statement. If the definition is inside a function, the scope is local, confined to that function. If the definition is outside a function, then the scope is global.

Often, uppercase letters are used for these definitions to remind the user that the type name is really a symbolic abbreviation:

```
typedef float REAL;
```

The last example could have been accomplished with a **#define.** Here is one that couldn't:

```
typedef char *STRING;
```

Without the keyword **typedef,** this example would identify **STRING** itself as a pointer to **char.** With the keyword, it makes **STRING** an *identifier* for pointers to **char.** Thus,

```
STRING name, sign;
```

means

```
char *name, *sign;
```

We can use **typedef** with structures, too. Here is an example:

```
typedef struct COMPLEX {
                        float real;
                        float imag;
                        };
```

We then can use type **COMPLEX** to represent complex numbers.

One reason to use **typedef** is to create convenient, recognizable names for types that turn up often. For instance, many people prefer to use **STRING** or its equivalent as we did above.

A second reason for using **typedef** is that **typedef** names are often used for complicated types. For example, the declaration

```
typedef char *FRPTC () [5];
```

makes **FRPTC** announce a type that is a function that returns a pointer to a five-element array of **char.** (See our box on fancy declarations.)

A third reason for using **typedef** is to make programs more portable. Suppose, for instance, that your program needs to use 16-bit numbers. On some systems, that would be type **short;** on others it might be type **int.** If you used just **short** or **int** in your declarations, you would have to alter all the declarations when you moved from one system to the other. Instead, do this. In an **#include** file have this definition:

```
typedef short TWOBYTE;
```

Use **TWOBYTE** in your programming for those **short** variables that must be 16 bits. Then when you move the program to where type **int** is needed instead, just change the single definition in your **#include** file:

```
typedef int TWOBYTE;
```

This is an example of what makes C such a portable language. When using **typedef,** bear in mind that it does not create new types; it just creates convenient labels.

With structures, unions, and **typedef,** C gives you the tools for efficient and portable data handling.

Fancy Declarations

C allows you to create elaborate data forms. We are sticking to simpler forms, but we feel it is our duty to point out the potentialities. When we make a declaration, the name (or "identifier") we use can be modified by tacking on a modifier:

Modifier	Significance
*	indicates a pointer
( )	indicates a function
[ ]	indicates an array

C lets us use more than one modifier at a time, and that lets us create a variety of types:

```
int board[8][8];  /* an array of arrays of int */
int **ptr;        /* a pointer to a pointer to int */
int *risks[10];   /* a 10-element array of pointers to int */
int (*rusks)[10]; /* a pointer to an array of 10 ints */
int *oof[3][4];   /* a 3 x 4 array of pointers to int */
int (*uuf)[3][4]; /* a pointer to a 3 x 4 array of ints */
int (*uof[3])[4]; /* a 3-element array of pointers to
                     4 element arrays of int */
```

The trick to unravelling these declarations is figuring out the order in which to apply the modifiers. These rules should get you through:

1. The **[ ]** to indicate an array and the **( )** to indicate a function have the same precedence, which is a higher than the precedence of the ***** indirection operator. This means

    ```
    int *risks[10];
    ```

    makes **risks** an array of pointers rather than a pointer to an array.

2. The **[ ]** and **( )** associate from left to right. This means

```
    int goods[12][50];
```

makes **goods** an array of 12 arrays of 50 **int**s, not an array of 50 arrays of 12 **int**s.

3. Parentheses used for grouping have the highest precedence. This means

```
    int (*rusks)[10];
```

makes **rusks** a pointer to an array of 10 **int**s.

Let's apply these rules to

```
int *oof[3][4];
```

The **[3]** has higher precedence than the *, and, because of the left-to-right rule, it has higher precedence than the **[4]**. Hence **oof** is an array with three elements. Next in order is **[4]**, so the elements of **oof** are arrays of four elements. Next, the * tells us these elements are pointers. The **int** completes the picture: **oof** is a three-element array of four-element arrays of pointers to **int**, or, for short, a 3 x 4 array of pointers to **int**.

Now look at this declaration:

```
int (*uuf)[3][4];
```

The parentheses cause the * modifier to have first priority, making **uuf** a pointer to a 3 x 4 array of **int**s.

These rules also yield the following types:

```
char  *fump();        /* function returning pointer to char */
char  (* frump ) (); /* pointer to a function that returns
                             type char */
char  *flump[3] (); /* array of 3 pointers to functions that
                           return type char */
```

When you bring structures into the picture, the possibilities for declarations truly grow baroque. And the applications—well, we'll leave that for non-primers.

What You Should Have Learned

What a structure template is and how to define one
What a structure tag is and how to use one
How to define a structure variable: **struct car honda;**

How to access a member of a structure: **honda.mpg**
How to access a pointer to a structure: **struct car *ptcar;**
How to access a member using a pointer: **ptcar->mpg**
How to feed a member to a function: **eval(honda.mpg)**
How to make a structure known to a function: **rate(&honda)**
How to make a nested structure
How to access a nested member: **honda.civic.cost**
How to make and use arrays of structures: **struct car gm[5];**
How to set up a union: like a structure
How to use **typedef: typedef struct car CRATE;**

Review Questions

1. What's wrong with this template?

```
structure {
        char itable;
        int  num[20];
        char *togs
        }
```

2. Here is a portion of a program. What will it print?

```
struct house {
                float sqft;
                int rooms;
                int stories;
                char *address;
                };
main()
{
   static struct house fruzt = { 1560.0, 6, 1, "22 Spiffo Road"};
   struct house *sign;

   sign = &fruzt;
   printf("%d %d\n", fruzt.rooms, sign->stories);
   printf("%s \n", fruzt.address);
   printf("%c %c\n", sign->address[3], fruzt.address[4]);
}
```

3. Devise a structure template that will hold the name of a month, a three-letter abbreviation for the month, the number of days in the month, and the month number.

4. Define an array of 12 structures of the sort in Question 3 and initialize it for a nonleap year.

5. Write a function that when given the month number, returns the total days in the year up through that month. Assume that the structure template and array of Questions 3 and 4 are declared externally.

6. Given the following **typedef**, declare a 10-element array of the indicated structure. Then, using individual member assignment, let the third element describe a Remarkatar lens of focal length 500 mm and aperture f/2.0.

```
typedef struct {                    /* lens descriptor */
                float foclen;   /* focal length,mm */
                float fstop;    /* aperture */
                char *brand;    /* brand name */
        } LENS;
```

7. Consider the following programming fragment:

```
struct name { char first[20];
              char last[20];
            };
struct bem { int limbs;
             struct name title;
             char type[30];
           };
struct bem *pb;
struct bem deb = { 6,
                   { "Berbnazel", "Gwolkapwolk"},
                   "Arcturan"
                 };

pb = &deb;
```

a. What would each of the following statements print?
```
printf("%d", deb.limbs);
printf("%s", pb->type);
printf("%s", pb->type + 2);
```

b. How could you represent "Gwolkapwolk" in structure notation (two ways)?

c. Write a function that takes the address of a **bem** structure as an argument and prints out the contents of the structure in the form shown below. Assume that the structure definitions are in a file called **starfolk.h**.

```
Berbnazel Gwolkapwolk is a 6-limbed Arcturan.
```

8. Consider the following declarations:

```
struct fullname {
                char fname[20];
                char lname[20];
                };
struct bard      {
                struct fullname name;
```

```
                int born;
                int died;
                };
      struct bard willie;
      struct bard *pt = &willie;
```

  a. Identify the **born** member of the **willie** structure using the **willie** identifier.
  b. Identify the **born** member of the **willie** structure using the **pt** identifier.
  c. Use a **scanf( )** call to read in a value for the **born** member using the **willie** identifier.
  d. Use a **scanf( )** call to read in a value for the **born** member using the **pt** identifier.
  e. Construct an identifier for the third letter of the first name of someone described by the **willie** variable.
  f. Construct an expression representing the total number of letters in the first and last names of someone described by the **willie** variable.

9. Define a structure template suitable for holding the following items: the name of an automobile, its horsepower, its EPA city-driving mpg rating, its wheelbase, and a pointer to another structure of the same type. Use **car** as the template tag.

10. Suppose we have this structure:

```
struct gas {  float distance;
              float gals;
              float mpg;
              };
```

Define a function that takes a pointer to a **gas** structure, computes miles per gallon from the **distance** and **gals** members, places the answer in the **mpg** member and also returns that value.

Answers

1. The key word is **struct**, not **structure**. The template requires either a tag before the opening brace or a variable name after the closing brace. Also, there should be a semicolon after ***togs** and at the end of the template.

2. 6 1
   22 Spiffo Road
   S p

   The member **fruzt.address** is a character string, and **fruzt.address[4]** is the fifth element of that array.

3. struct month {

```
                char name[10];
                char abbrev[4];
                int days;
                int monumb;
            };
```

4.
```
struct month months[12] = {
                        { "January", "Jan", 31, 1},
                        { "February", "Feb", 28, 2},
                                   and so on
                        { "December", "Dec", 31, 12}
                   };
```

5.
```
days(month)
  int month;
  {
     int index, total;

     if ( month < 1 || month > 12 )
        return(-1);  /* error signal */
     else
        for ( index = 0, total = 0; index < month; index ++)
             total += months[index].days;
        return( total);
  }
```

Note that **index** is one less than month number, since arrays start with subscript 0; hence we use **index** < **month** instead of **index** <= **month**.

6.
```
LENS tubby[10];

tubby[2].foclen = 500.0;
tubby[2].fstop = 2.0;
tubby[2].brand = "Remarkatar";
```

7. **a.** 6
```
Arcturan
cturan
```
   b. Use the structure name and use the pointer.

```
deb.title.last
pb->title.last
```
   c. Here is one version:

```
#include "starfolk.h"    /* make the struct defs available */
void prbem ( pbem )
struct bem *pbem;
{
    printf("%s %s is a %d-limbed %s.\n", pbem->title.first,
           pbem->title.last, pbem->limbs, pbem->type);
}
```

8. **a. willie.born**
   b. pt->born
   c. scanf("%d", &willie.born)
   d. scanf("%d", &pt->born)

e. **willie.name.fname[2]** Note that we don't use **willie.fullname.fname[2]**. We use the *member* name, not the *type* identifier. Also, we could use:
pt-> name.fname[2]

f. **strlen(willie.name.fname) + strlen(willie.name.lname)** or
strlen(pt-> name.fname) + strlen(pt-> name.lname)

9. Here is one possibility:

```
struct car {
            char name[20];
            float hp;
            float epampg;
            float wbase;
            struct car *pcar;
          };
```

10. Here is one approach. It returns an error value of -1 if the number of gallons is not a positive number.

```
struct gas { float distance;
             float gals;
             float mpg;
           };

float mpgs (ps)
struct gas *ps;
{
  if (ps->gals > 0)
     return ( ps->mpg = ps->distance / ps->gals) ;
  else
     return (-1.0);
}
```

Note that the **return** statement assigns a value to **ps-> mpg** and also returns that same value to the calling function.

Exercises

1. Redo Question 5, but have the argument be the spelled-out name of the month instead of the month number. (Don't forget about **strcmp( )**.)

2. Write a program that asks the user to input the day, month, and year. The month can be a month number, a month name, or a month abbreviation. The program then returns the total number of days in the year up through the given day.

3. Revise our book-listing program so that it prints out the book descriptions alphabetized by title and so that it prints out the total value of the books.

4. Write a program that fits the following recipe:
  a. Externally define a **name** structure template with two members: a string to hold the first name, and a string to hold the second name.
  b. Externally define a **student** structure template with three members: a **name** structure, a grade array to hold floating-point scores, and a variable to hold the average of the three scores.
  c. Have the **main( )** function declare an array of **CSIZE** (with **CSIZE = 4**) student structures and initialize the name portions to names of your choice.

  Use functions to perform the tasks described in **d.**, **e.**, **f.**, and **g.**
  d. Interactively acquire scores for each student by prompting the user with a student name and a request for scores. Place the scores in the grade array portion of the appropriate structure. The required looping may be done in **main( )** or in the function, as you prefer.
  e. Calculate the average score value for each structure and assign it to the proper location.
  f. Print out the information in each structure.
  g. Print out the class average for each of the numerical structure elements.

15

The C Library and File Input/Output

Concepts

- The C library
- Files in C
- File-handling functions
- Character-checking macros
- Memory allotment functions

Whenever we have used functions such as **printf( )**, **getchar( )**, and **strlen( )**, we have used the C library. The C library contains dozens of functions and macros for you to draw on. Libraries vary from system to system, but there is a core of functions (called the standard library) that most share. We will examine fifteen of the most common of these functions in this chapter, concentrating on input/output functions and on using files.

First, however, let's talk about how to use the library.

Gaining Access to the C Library

How you gain access to the C library depends on your system, so you will have to check to see how our more general statements apply to your system. First, there are often several different places to find library functions. For example, **getchar( )** is usually defined as a macro in the file **stdio.h**, while **strlen( )** is usually kept in a library file. Second, different systems have different ways to reach these functions. Here are three of the possibilities.

Automatic Access

On many UNIX systems, you just compile the program and the more common library functions are made available automatically.

File Inclusion

If a function is defined as a macro, then you can **#include** the file containing the definition. Often, similar functions will be collected together in an appropriately titled "header" file. For example, many systems have a

ctype.h file containing several macros that determine the nature of a character: uppercase, digit, etc.

Library Inclusion

At some stage in compiling or loading a program, you may have to specify a library option. Even a system that checks its standard library automatically may have other libraries of less-frequently-used functions, and these libraries will have to be requested explicitly by using a compile-time option.

Clearly, we can't go through all the specifics for all systems, but these three examples should show you what to look for.

Now let's look at some functions.

Library Functions We Have Used

We're just going to list briefly the library functions to give you the thrill of recollection.

First, there were the I/O functions:

```
getchar()          /* fetch a character     */
putchar()          /* print a character     */
gets()             /* fetch a line          */
puts()             /* print a line          */
scanf()            /* fetch formatted input */
printf()           /* print formatted output */
```

Then there were the string-handling functions:

```
strlen()           /* find the length of a string */
strcmp()           /* compare two strings         */
strcpy()           /* copy a string               */
strcat()           /* combine two strings         */
```

To this list we will add functions to open and close files, functions to communicate with files, functions to test and convert characters, functions to convert strings, an exit function, and functions to allocate memory.

Let's turn first to the problem of communication between a file and a program.

Communicating with Files

Often we need a program to get information from a file or to place results in a file. One method of having a program communicate with files is to use the redirection operators < and >. This method is simple, but it is limited. For instance, suppose you wish to write an interactive program that asks you for book titles (sound familiar?) and you want to save the complete listing in a file. If you use redirection, as in

```
books > bklist
```

your interactive prompts also are redirected to **bklist.** Not only does this put unwanted stuff into **bklist,** it prevents the user from seeing the questions he or she is supposed to answer.

Fortunately, C offers more powerful methods of communicating with files. One approach is to use the **fopen( )** function, which opens a file, then use special I/O functions to read from or write to that file, and then use the **fclose( )** function to close up the file. Before investigating these functions, however, we should look very briefly into the nature of a file.

What Is a File?

To us, a *file* is a section of storage, usually on disk, with a name. We think, for instance, of **stdio.h** as the name of a file containing some useful information. To the operating system, a file is a bit more complicated, but that's the system's problem, not ours. However, we should know what a file is to a C program. For those file functions we will discuss, C represents the file with a structure. Indeed, the file **stdio.h** contains a definition of a file structure. Here is a typical example taken from the IBM version of Lattice C:

```
struct _iobuf
{
char *_ptr;        /* current buffer pointer */
int _cnt;          /* current byte count */
char *_base;       /* base address of I/O buffer */
char _flag;        /* control flags */
char _file;        /* file number */
};

#define FILE struct _iobuf        /* shorthand */
```

Again, we are not going to worry about the details of this definition. The main points are that a file is represented by a structure and that the shorthand name for the file template is **FILE.** (Many systems use **typedef** to set up the same correspondence.) Thus, a program that deals with files will use the **FILE** structure type to do so.

With that in mind, we can better understand file operations.

A Simple File-Reading Program: *fopen( ), fclose( ), getc( ), and putc( )*

To show the rudiments of using files, we have concocted a very limited program that reads the contents of a file called **test** and prints them on the screen. You will find our explanation just after the program.

```
        /* tells us what is in the file "test"   */
        #include <stdio.h>
        main()
        {
            FILE *in;    /* declare a pointer to a file */
            int ch;

            if ( (in = fopen("test", "r")) != NULL)
        /* open test for reading, checking to see if it exists */
        /* the FILE pointer in now identifies to test */
                {
                while ( (ch = getc(in)) != EOF) /* get char from in */
                        putc(ch,stdout); /* send to standard output */
                fclose(in);  /* close the file */
                }
            else
                printf("I couldn't open the file \"test\".\n");
        }
```

The three main points to explain are the workings of **fopen( )**, the workings of **fclose( )**, and the use of the file I/O functions. We take them in turn.

Opening a File: *fopen( )*

Three basic parameters govern **fopen( )**. The first is the name of the file to be opened. This string is **fopen( )**'s first argument; in our case it was **test.**

The second parameter (and the second argument of **fopen( )**) describes the use to be made of the file. There are three basic uses:

"r" : the file is to be read
"w" : the file is to be written
"a" : the file is to be appended to

Many systems offer additional possibilities, but we will stick to these. Note that these "use codes" are strings, not character constants; hence the enclosing double quotes. The "r" choice opens an existing file. The other two choices will open an existing file, and if there is no such file, they will create one. CAUTION: If you do use "w" for an existing file, the old version is erased so that your program starts with a clean slate.

The third parameter is a pointer to the file structure; this value is returned by the **fopen( )** function:

```
FILE *in;

in = fopen("test", "r");
```

Now **in** is a pointer to the file **test.** (More precisely, **in** points to a structure describing the file and the I/O buffers to be used with it.) Henceforth, the program refers to the file by the pointer **in** and not by its name **test.**

If you are sharp-witted right now, you might ask this question: "If **fopen( )** returns a **FILE** pointer for an argument, why didn't we have to declare **fopen( )** as a **FILE** pointer function?" Good question. The answer is that the declaration was made for us in **stdio.h,** which contains the line

```
FILE *fopen();
```

There is one more important fact about **fopen( )** that we used. If **fopen( )** is unable to open the requested file, it returns a null value (defined as 0 in **stdio.h**). Why could it not open a file? You might ask to read a file that doesn't exist. That is why we have the line

```
if ( (in = fopen("test", "r")) != NULL)
```

Or the disk might be full, or the name might be illegal, or some other reason might prevent the opening of the file. So check for trouble: a little error-trapping can go a long way.

Closing the file is simpler.

Closing a File: *fclose( )*

Our example shows how to close a file:

```
fclose(in);
```

Just use the **fclose( )** function. Note that the argument is **in,** the pointer; not **test,** the file name.

For a program less casual than this one, we would check to see if the file was closed successfully. The function **fclose( )** returns a value of **0** if successful, and **−1** if not.

Buffered Text Files

The **fopen( )** and **fclose( )** functions work with *buffered* text files. By buffered, we mean that input and output are stored in a temporary memory area called a *buffer.* When the buffer is filled, the contents are passed on in a block, and the buffering process starts over. One of the main tasks of **fclose( )** is to "flush out" any partially filled buffers when the file is closed.

A *text file* is one in which information is stored as characters using ASCII (or similar) code. This is opposed to a *binary file* such as would be used to store machine language code.

The I/O functions we are about to describe also are designed to work with text files only.

File I/O: *getc( )* and *putc( )*

The two functions **getc( )** and **putc( )** work very much like **getchar( )** and **putchar( )**. The difference is that you must tell the newcomers which file to use. Thus, our old buddy

```
ch = getchar();
```

means get a character from the standard input, but

```
ch = getc(in);
```

means get a character from the file identified by **in**.
Similarly,

```
putc(ch, out);
```

means put the character **ch** into the file identified by the **FILE** pointer **out**. In **putc( )**'s argument list, the character comes first, then the file pointer.
In our example, we used

```
putc(ch,stdout);
```

where **stdout** is a pointer to the standard output. Thus, this statement is equivalent to

```
putchar(ch);
```

Indeed, **putchar(ch)** is **#define**d as **putc(ch,stdout)** in **stdio.h.** That redoubtable file also **#defines stdout** and **stdin** as pointers to the standard output and the standard input of the system.
Does this seem simple enough? Good, let's add a couple of useful wrinkles.

A Simple File-Condensing Program

In our example, the name of the file to be opened was built into the program. We don't have to work under that restriction. By using command line arguments, we can tell our program the name of the file we want read. Our next example (Figure 15.1) does that. It then condenses the contents by the brutal expedient of retaining only every third character. Finally, it places the condensed version in a new file whose name consists of the old name with **.red** (for reduced) appended. The first and last features (command-line argument and file-name appending) are quite useful generally. The condensing feature is of more limited appeal, but it can have its uses, as you will see.

Figure 15.1
File reduction program

```
/* reduce your files by 2/3rds ! */
#include <stdio.h>
main(argc,argv)
int argc;
char *argv[];
{
   FILE  *in, *out;    /* declare two FILE pointers */
   int ch;
   static char name[20];   /* storage for output file name */
   int count = 0;

   if ( argc < 2)     /* check if there is an input file */
      printf("Sorry, I need a file name for an argument.\n");
   else
      {
      if ( (in = fopen(argv[1], "r")) != NULL)
          {
          strcpy(name,argv[1]); /* copy file name into array */
          strcat(name,".red"); /* append .red to name */
          out = fopen(name, "w"); /* open file for writing */
          while ( (ch = getc(in)) != EOF)
                  if ( count++ % 3 == 0 )
                      putc(ch, out); /* print every 3rd char */
          fclose(in);
          fclose(out);
          }
      else
          printf("I couldn't open the file \"%s\". \n", argv[1]);
      }
}
```

We placed the program in a file called **reduce.** We applied this program to a file called **eddy,** which contained a single line:

```
So even Eddy came oven ready.
```

The command was

```
reduce eddy
```

and the output was a file called **eddy.red,** which contained

> Send money

What luck! Our randomly selected file produced an intelligible reduction.

Here are some program notes.

Recall that **argc** is the number of arguments, including the name of the program file. Recall that, operating system permitting, **argv[0]** represents the program name, **reduce** in our case. Then recall that **argv[1]** represents the first argument, **eddy** in our case. Since **argv[1]** is itself a pointer to a string, it should not be placed in double quotes in the function call.

We use **argc** to see if there is an argument. Any surplus arguments are ignored. By putting another loop in the program, you could have the program use the further file name arguments and cycle through each of several files in turn.

To construct the new name for the output file, we used **strcpy( )** to copy the name **eddy** into the array **name**. Then we used the **strcat( )** function to combine that name with **.red**.

This program involves having two files open simultaneously, so we declared two **FILE** pointers. Note that each file is opened and closed independently of the other. There are limits to how many files you can have open at one time. The limit depends on the system but often is in the range of 10 to 20. You can use the same pointer for different files providing the files are not open at the same time.

We are not limited to using just **getc( )** and **putc( )** for file I/O. Next we look at some other possibilities.

File I/O: *fprintf( ), fscanf( ), fgets( ),* and *fputs( )*

The I/O functions we used in the preceding chapters all have file I/O analogues. The main distinction is that you need to use a **FILE** pointer to tell the new functions which file to work with. Like **getc( )** and **putc( )**, these functions are used after **fopen( )** opens a file and before **fclose( )** closes it.

The *fprintf( )* and *fscanf( )* Functions

These two file I/O functions work just like **printf( )** and **scanf( )**, except that they require an additional argument to point to the proper file. This argument is the first in the argument list. Here is an example to illustrate the form:

```
/* form for using fprintf() and fscanf()  */
#include <stdio.h>
main()
{
    FILE *fi;
    int age;
```

```
        fi = fopen("sam", "r");        /* read mode */
        fscanf( fi, "%d", &age );      /* fi identifies sam */
        fclose(fi);
        fi = fopen("data", "a");       /* append mode */
        fprintf( fi, "sam is %d.\n", age); /* fi identifies data */
        fclose(fi);
}
```

Note that we could use **fi** for two different files since we closed the first before opening the second.

Unlike **putc( )**, these two functions take the **FILE** pointer as the first argument. The other two take it as the last argument.

The *fgets( )* Function

This function takes three arguments to **gets( )**'s one. Here is a sample use:

```
/* read a file a line at a time */
#include <stdio.h>
#define MAXLIN 81
main()
{
    FILE *f1;
    char *string[MAXLIN]

    f1 = fopen("story", "r");
    while ( fgets( string, MAXLIN, f1) != NULL)
        puts(string);
}
```

The first of **fgets( )**'s three arguments is a pointer to the destination for the line that is read. Here we are placing the input into the **char** array **string.**

The second argument places a limit on the length of the string being read. The function stops after reading a newline character or **MAXLIN** -1 characters, whichever comes first. In either case, the null character ('\0') is tacked on at the very end.

The third argument is, of course, a pointer to the file being read.

One difference between **gets( )** and **fgets( )** is that **gets( )** replaces the newline character with '\0', while **fgets( )** keeps the newline character.

Like **gets( )**, **fgets( )** returns the value **NULL** when it encounters EOF. This lets you check, as we have done, if you have reached the end of a file.

The *fputs( )* Function

This function is quite similar to **puts( )**. The statement

```
fputs("You did something right.", fileptr);
```

transmits the string "You did something right." to the file identified by the **FILE** pointer **fileptr**. Naturally, the file ought to have been opened by **fopen( )** first. The most general form is

```
status = fputs(string pointer, file pointer);
```

where **status** is an integer that is set to EOF if **fputs( )** encounters an **EOF** or an error.

Like **puts( )**, this function does not copy the closing '\0' of a string into the final destination. Unlike **puts( )**, **fputs( )** does not add a newline character to its output.

The six I/O functions we have just discussed should give you tools aplenty for reading and writing text files. There is one more tool you may find useful, and we discuss it next.

Random Access: *fseek( )*

The **fseek( )** function lets you treat a file like an array and move directly to any particular byte in a file opened by **fopen( )**. Here is a straightforward example to show you how it works. Borrowing from our earlier examples, it uses a command-line argument to obtain the name of the file that it will affect. Note that **fseek( )** has three arguments and returns an **int** value.

```
/* using fseek() to print the contents of a file   */
#include <stdio.h>
```

```
main(number, names)   /* you don't have to use argc and argv */
int number;
char *names[];
{
    FILE *fp;
    long offset = OL; /* note that this is a long type */

    if ( number < 2)
        puts("I need a file name for an argument.");
    else
        {
        if ( (fp = fopen(names[1], "r")) == 0 )
            printf("I can't open %s.\n", names[1]);
        else
            {
            while ( fseek(fp,offset++,0) == 0 )
                    putchar(getc(fp));
            fclose(fp);
            }
        }
}
```

The first of the three arguments of **fseek( )** is a **FILE** pointer to the file being searched. The file should have been opened using **fopen( ).**

The second argument is called the *offset* (which is why we chose that name for the variable). This argument tells us how far to move from the starting point (see below); it must be a **long** value. It can be positive (move forward) or negative (move backward).

The third argument is the *mode,* and it identifies the starting point:

Mode	Measure Offset from
0	beginning of file
1	current position
2	end of file

The value returned by **fseek( )** is **0** if everything is okay, and −1 if there is an error, such as attempting to move past the bounds of the file.

Now we can explain our little loop:

```
while ( fseek(fp,offset++,0) == 0  )
    putchar(getc(fp));
```

Since **offset** is initialized to **0,** the first time through the loop we have the expression

```
fseek(fp,OL,0)
```

which means go to the file pointed to by **fp** and find the byte that is 0 bytes from the beginning. That is, go to the first byte. Then **putchar( )** prints the contents of that byte. Next time through the loop, **offset** has been incremented to **1L**, so the next byte is printed. Essentially, the variable **offset** is acting like a subscript for the file elements. The process continues until **offset** tries to take **fseek( )** past the end of the file. Then **fseek( )** returns a value of −1 and the loop halts.

This last example is purely instructional. We didn't need **fseek( )** because **getc( )** steps through the file byte by byte anyway; **fseek( )** told **getc( )** to look where it was already about to look.

Figure 15.2 is an example that accomplishes something a bit more unusual. (We thank William Shakespeare for suggesting this example in *Twelfth Night*.)

Figure 15.2
Program alternating forward and backward printing

```c
#include <stdio.h>
main(number, names)
int number;
char *names[];
{
  FILE *fp;
  long offset = 0L;
  int ch;

  if ( number < 2)
      puts("I need a file name for an argument.");
  else
      {
      if ( (fp = fopen(names[1], "r")) == 0 )
          printf("I can't open %s.\n", names[1]);
      else
          {
          while ( fseek(fp,offset++,0) == 0 &&
                          (ch = getc(fp)) != EOF)
              {
              putchar(ch);
              if ( fseek(fp,-(offset + 2), 2) == 0 )
                  putchar(getc(fp));
              }
          fclose(fp);
          }
      }
}
```

Applying this program to a file containing the name "Malvolio" produces this pleasing result:

```
MoaillvoovlliaoM
```

Our program prints the first character of the file, then the last character, then the second, then the next to last, and so on. We merely added these lines to the last program:

```
if ( fseek(fp,-(offset + 2), 2) == 0 )
                    putchar(getc(fp));
```

The **2** mode means that we will count positions from the end of the file. The negative sign means that we will count backwards. The **+2** is there so that we start with the last regular character of the file and skip some newlines and **[control-z]**'s at the very end of the file. (The exact value of this adjustment depends on the system.)

So this part of the program alternates printing backward with the part that prints forward. We should mention that some systems may not support the **2** mode for **fseek( )**.

Well, that's enough about files for a while. Let's close the subject and move on to another section of the C library.

Testing and Converting Characters

The header file **ctype.h** defines several macro functions that test characters to see what class they belong to. The function **isalpha(c),** for example, returns a nonzero value (true) if **c** is an alphabetic character, and zero (false) if the character isn't alphabetic. Thus:

```
isalpha('S') != 0,  but   isalpha ('#') == 0
```

Here is a list of the functions most commonly found in this file. In each case the function returns a nonzero value if **c** belongs to the tested class, and zero if it does not.

Function	Tests If c Is
isalpha(c)	alphabetic
isdigit(c)	a digit
islower(c)	lowercase
isspace(c)	white space (blank, tab, or newline)
isupper(c)	uppercase

Your system may have additional functions such as:

Function	Tests If c Is
isalnum(c)	alphanumeric (alphabetic or digit)
isascii(c)	ASCII (0–127)
iscntrl(c)	a control character
ispunct(c)	a punctuation mark

Two more functions make conversions:

toupper(c)	converts c to uppercase
tolower(c)	converts c to lowercase

On some systems the conversion is attempted only if the character is of the opposite case to begin with. It is safer, however, to check the case first.

Figure 15.3 shows a program that uses some of these functions to convert a file to all uppercase or all lowercase, as you request. To provide a little variety, we use an interactive approach instead of command-line arguments to feed information to the program.

Figure 15.3
Case conversion program

```
/* case conversion */
#include <stdio.h>
#include <ctype.h> /* include file of macros */
#define UPPER 1
#define LOWER 0
main()
{
    int crit;   /* to be set to UPPER or LOWER  */
    char file1[14], file2[14]; /* input and output file names */

    crit = choose();  /* choose upper or lowercase */
    getfiles(file1,file2); /* get file names */
    conv(file1,file2, crit);  /* do the conversion */
}
choose()
{
    int ch;

    printf("The program converts a file to all uppercase or \n");
    printf("all lowercase. Enter a U if you want uppercase \n");
    printf("or enter an L if you want lowercase.\n");
    while ( (ch = getchar()) != 'U' && ch != 'u' && ch != 'L' &&
            ch != 'l' )
```

```
            printf("Please enter a U or an L.\n");
        while (getchar() != '\n')
            ; /* clear last \n */
        if ( ch == 'U' || ch == 'u')
            {
            printf("Okay, uppercase it is.\n");
            return(UPPER);
        else
            {
            printf("Okay, lowercase it is.\n");
            return(LOWER);
            }
}
getfiles(name1,name2)
char *name1, *name2;
{
    printf(" What file do you wish to convert?\n");
    gets(name1);
    printf("That was \"%s\".\n", name1);
    printf("What name do you desire for the converted file?\n");
    while ( strcmp(gets(name2), name1) == NULL)
        printf("Choose a different name.\n");
    printf("Your output file is \"%s\".\n", name2);
}
conv(name1, name2, crit)
char *name1, *name2;
int crit;
{
    int ch;
    FILE *f1, *f2;

    if ( (f1 = fopen(name1, "r") ) == NULL)
        printf("Sorry, I can't open %s.  Bye.\n", name1);
    else
        {
        puts("Here we go!");
        f2 = fopen(name2, "w");
        while ( (ch = getc(f1)) != EOF)
            {
            if (crit == UPPER)
                ch = islower(ch) ? toupper(ch) : ch;
            else
                ch = isupper(ch) ? tolower(ch) : ch;
            putc(ch,f2);
            }
        fclose(f2);
        fclose(f1);
```

```
                          puts("Done!");
                          }
          }
```

We broke the program into three parts: getting the user's decision on case, getting names for the input and output files, and doing the conversion. To keep in practice, we developed a separate function for each part.

The **choose( )** function is pretty straightforward, except perhaps for the loop:

```
while( getchar() != '\n')
      ;
```

This loop is included to solve a problem we faced in Chapter 14. When the user responds to the case question with, say, the letter **U**, he or she presses the **U** key, then the [enter] key, which transmits a '**\n**'. The initial **getchar( )** function picks up the **U** but leaves the '**\n**' sitting there for the next input reader. The **gets( )** function coming up in **getfiles( )** would interpret that as an empty line, so we used the little **while** loop to get rid of the newline. Actually, a simple **getchar( );** would do if the user followed the **U** immediately with [enter]; but our version also allows for the possibility that the user presses the space bar a few times before pressing [enter].

The **getfiles( )** function should have no surprises for you. Note that we have prevented the user from using the same name for the output file as for the input file.

The **conv( )** function is a copy function with case conversion added. The value of **crit** is used to determine which conversion to make. The work is done by simple conditional statements such as

```
ch = islower(ch) ? toupper(ch) : ch;
```

This tests if **ch** is lowercase. If it is, it is converted to uppercase. If it isn't, it is left as is.

The macros of **ctype.h** provide convenient, useful tools for your programming. Now let's turn to some conversion functions of a more ambitious nature.

String Conversions: *atoi( ), atof( )*

Using **scanf( )** to read in numeric values is not the safest course to take, for **scanf( )** is easily misled by user errors in keying in numbers. Many programmers prefer to read in even numerical data as strings and convert the string to the appropriate numerical value. Here the two functions **atoi( )** and

atof( ) are useful. The first converts a string to an integer, and the second converts a string to a floating-point number. Figure 15.4 is a sample usage:

Figure 15.4
Program using *atoi( )*

```
    /* include atoi()    */
#include <stdio.h>
#define issign(c)        ( ((c) == '-' | | (c) == '+') ? (1) : (0) )
#define SIZE 10
#define YES 1
#define NO 0
main()
{
    char ch;
    static char number[SIZE];
    int value;
    int digit = YES;
    int count = 0;

    puts("Enter an integer, please.");
    gets(number);
    if ( number[SIZE -1] != '\0' )
       {
       puts("Too many digits; you wiped me out.");
       exit(1);
       }
    while ( (ch =number[count]) != '\0' && digit == YES)
       if( !issign(ch) && !isdigit(ch) && !isspace(ch) )
          digit = NO;
    if ( digit == YES)
       {
       value = atoi(number);
       printf("The number was %d.\n", value );
       }
    else
       printf("That doesn't look like an integer to me.");
}
```

We've put in some error-checking. First we check to see if the input string was too long for the destination array. Because the array **number** is static **char,** it is initialized to nulls. If the last array member isn't a null, something is wrong, and the program bails out. Here we have used the library function **exit( )**, which gets you out of the program. We'll say more about this function shortly.

Then we check to see if the string contains nothing but spaces, digits, and algebraic signs. This rejects strings such as "three" or "1.2E2". It passes mishmash like "3−4+2", but **atoi( )** will do further screening. Recall that **!** is a negation operator, so **!isdigit(c)** means "c is not a digit."

The line

```
value = atoi(number);
```

shows how **atoi( )** is used. Its argument is a pointer to a string; in this case we used the array name **number.** It returns an **int** value for the string. Thus, "**1234**", which is a string of four characters, is translated to **1234,** a single **int** value.

The **atoi( )** function ignores leading blanks, processes a leading algebraic sign, if any, and processes digits up to the first nondigit. Thus, our example of "3−4+2" would be converted to the value **3.** See the questions at the end of the chapter for a possible implementation.

The **atof( )** function performs a similar function for floating-point numbers. It returns type **double,** so it should be declared double in a program that uses it.

Simple versions of **atof( )** will handle numbers of the form **10.2, 46,** and **−124.26.** Higher-powered versions will also convert exponential notation, that is, numbers like **1.25E−13.**

Your system also may have functions that work in the opposite direction. An **itoa( )** function would convert an integer to a string, and an **ftoa( )** function would convert a floating-point number to a string.

The **atoi( )** and **atof( )** functions can be used with command-line arguments, too. These arguments, recall, are passed as strings. If they represent numerical values, they have to be converted. For example, here is a program that prints out command-line arguments in decimal and in hex:

```
/* dec_hex.c -- converts decimal to hex */
main(argc,argv)
int argc;
char *argv[];
{
    int x,i;

    for ( i = 1; i < argc; i++ )
        {
        x = atoi(argv[i]);
        printf("%d is %x in hex\n", x, x);
        }
}
```

Here is a sample run:

```
dec_hex 100 two 5000
100 is 64 in hex
0 is 0 in hex
5000 is 1388 in hex
```

Note that **atoi( )** converts nonnumeric strings to 0.

Getting Out: *exit( )*

The **exit( )** function gives you a convenient way to leave a program. Often it is used to stop a program when an error shows up. If **exit( )** is evoked from a function called by the main program, the whole program stops, not just the function. In our first **atoi( )** example, using **exit( )** let us avoid setting up an extra **else** statement to detour around the rest of the program.

One nice service performed by **exit( )** is that it closes any files that had been opened by **fopen( ).** This makes your exit much tidier.

The argument of **exit( )** is an error code number. On some systems this can be passed to another program when the original is exited. Convention is that **0** indicates a normal termination, while other values indicate a problem.

Before we forget, there is one other matter we wish to discuss.

Memory Allocation: *malloc( )* and *calloc( )*

Your program has to set aside enough memory to store the data it uses. Some of this "memory allocation" is done automatically. For example, we can declare

```
char place[] = "Pork Liver Creek";
```

and enough memory to store that string is set aside.

Or we can be more explicit and ask for a certain amount of memory:

```
int plates[100];
```

This declaration sets aside 100 memory locations, each fit to store an **int** value.

C goes beyond this. It lets you allot more memory as a program runs.

The main tool is the **malloc( )** function. This function takes one argument: the number of bytes of memory desired. Then **malloc( )** finds a suitable block of free memory and returns the address of the first byte of the block. Since **char** represents a byte, **malloc( )** is defined as type pointer-to-**char**.

Here is an unsophisticated program (this is just a primer) showing how **malloc( )** can be used. It creates an array of 100 pointers, and it reads in strings. The **malloc( )** function is used to set aside storage for each string, and the addresses of the strings are stored in the array. Here is the program:

Figure 15.5
Program to add on more memory as needed

```
/* memsym.c -- memorize symphony orchestras */
#include <stdio.h>
#define LINE 81          /* maximum line length for input */
#define MAX  100         /* maximum number of symphonies */
main()
{
     char temp[LINE];      /* temporary input storage */
     char *ps[MAX];        /* array of ptrs to strings */
     int index = 0;        /* number of input lines */
     int count;            /* for loop counter */
     char *malloc();       /* memory allocation function */

     puts("Name some symphony orchestras.");
     puts("Enter them one at a time; [enter] at the start");
     puts("of a line to end your list. Okay, I'm ready.");
     while (index < MAX && gets(temp) != 0 && temp[0] != '\0')
          {
          ps[index] = malloc( strlen(temp) + 1 );
          strcpy (ps[index], temp);
          if ( ++index < MAX )
               printf("That's %d. Continue if you like.\n", index);
          }
     puts("Okay, here is what I've got.");
     for ( count = 0; count < index; count++)
          puts(ps[count]);
}
```

Here is a sample run so you can see the output:

```
Name some symphony orchestras.
Enter them one at a time; press [enter] at the start
```

```
of a line to end your list. Okay, I'm ready.
San Francisco Symphony
That's 1. Continue, if you like.
Chicago Symphony
That's 2. Continue, if you like.
Berlin Philharmonic
That's 3. Continue, if you like.
The Concertgebouw
That's 4. Continue, if you like.
London Symphony
That's 5. Continue, if you like.
Vienna Philharmonic
That's 6. Continue, if you like.
Pittsburgh Symphony
That's 7. Continue, if you like.
[enter]
Okay, here's what I got:
San Francisco Symphony
Chicago Symphony
Berlin Philharmonic
The Concertgebouw
London Symphony
Vienna Philharmonic
Pittsburgh Symphony
```

Let's look at the coding. The input is controlled by this line:

```
while (index < MAX && gets(temp) != 0 && temp[0] != '\0')
```

First, the program checks to see if any more string pointers are left by comparing **index** to **MAX**. Next, it attempts to read the input into a temporary storage area; if the end-of-file is reached, the loop quits. Finally, the program checks to see if the first character in **temp** is the null character. This will occur if the user presses [enter] with no other input; the program responds by quitting the loop.

Next, suppose input has been placed in **temp**. Then the following line allocates enough space to hold the string:

```
ps[index] = malloc( strlen(temp) + 1 );
```

The **strlen( )** function gives the length of the input string, which most likely is significantly less than the length of the **temp** array. The program adds 1 for the null character and stores the beginning address of the still-empty storage block to **ps[index]**.

The next program line copies the contents of **temp** into the allocated storage, freeing **temp** to be reused for the next input string:

```
strcpy (ps[index], temp);
```

What have we gained with this approach? Well, suppose we had not used **malloc( )**. Instead of declaring an array of 100 pointers-to-**char**, we could have declared an array of 100 character arrays, with each character array capable of holding 81 characters. That means we would have allocated 8100 bytes of memory, much of which never would be used, since most of the strings will be smaller than the maximum size. With the **malloc( )** approach we just use the amount of memory that is needed. We pay with the overhead to hold **ps[ ]** and **temp[ ]**, a total of 281 bytes, but that will more than be made up if we have a large number of input values.

We mentioned earlier that the example was unsophisticated. One reason we said that is because we still use an array to store the pointers. Thus, the maximum capacity of the program is limited by the array size. A less limiting approach is to use **malloc( )** to allocate space for the pointers as well as for the strings. To keep track of the pointers, you can define a structure that holds two pointers. Then each structure can hold a pointer to a string and a pointer to the next structure, which holds a pointer to the next string and a pointer to the next structure, and so on. A second example of the program's naïveté is that it fails to check if **malloc( )** succeeds in finding more space. This can be remedied by using an **if** to check **malloc( )**'s return value.

So that is how **malloc( )** is used. But suppose you want **int** memory, not **char**. You still can use **malloc( )**. Here is the procedure:

```
char *malloc();    /* still declare as char pointer    */
int *newmem;

newmem = (int *) malloc(100);  /* use cast operator    */
```

Again, 100 bytes are set aside. The cast operator converts the returned value from a **char** pointer to an **int** pointer. If, as on our system, **int** takes 2 bytes of memory, then this means **newmem + 1** will increment the pointer by 2 bytes, just right to move it to the next integer. It also means that the 100 bytes can be used to store 50 integers.

Another option for memory allotment is to use **calloc( )**. A typical use would look like this:

```
char *calloc();
long *newmem;

newmem = (long *) calloc( 100, sizeof (long)  );
```

Like **malloc( )**, **calloc( )** returns a pointer to **char**. You must use the cast operator if you want to store a different type. This new function has two arguments, both of which should be unsigned integers. The first argument is the number of memory cells desired. The second argument is the size of each cell in bytes. In our case, **long** uses 4 bytes, so this instruction would set up one hundred 4-byte units, using 400 bytes in all for storage.

By using **sizeof (long)** instead of **4,** we made this coding more portable. It will work on systems where **long** is some size other than 4.

The **calloc( )** function throws in one more feature; it sets all the contents of the block to zero.

Another common memory function is **free( )**. It takes as an argument the address of a block of memory previously allocated by **malloc( )** or **calloc( )**. It then returns the block of memory to the "free memory pool" so that it can be used by future calls to **malloc( )** and **calloc( )**. The various assignments expire with the program in any case.

Your C library probably offers several other memory-management functions, and you may wish to check on them.

Other Library Functions

Most libraries will have several more functions in the areas we have covered. Besides functions that allocate memory, there are functions to free up memory when you are done with it. There may be other string functions, perhaps functions that search a string for a particular character or combination of characters.

Other file functions include **open( )**, **close( )**, **create( )**, **lseek( )**, **read( )**, and **write( )**. These accomplish much the same tasks as the functions we discussed, but at a more basic level. Indeed, functions like **fopen( )** typically are written using these more basic functions. They are a little more awkward to use, but they can deal with binary files as well as text files.

Your system may have a math library. Typically, such a library will contain a square root function, a power function, an exponential function, various trig functions, and a random number function.

You will have to take the time to explore what your system has to offer. If it doesn't have what you want, make your own functions. That's part of C. If you think you can do a better job on, say, an input function, do it! And as you refine and polish your programming technique, you will go from C to shining C.

What You Should Have Learned

What a C library is and how to use it
How to open and close text files: **fopen( )** and **fclose( )**
What a **FILE** type is
How to read from and write to files: **getc( )**, **putc( )**, **fgets( )**, **fputs( )**,
    fscanf( ), **fprintf( )**
How to check character classes: **isdigit( )**, **isalpha( )** et al.
How to convert strings to numbers: **atoi( )**, **atof( )**

How to make a quick exit: **exit( )**
How to allot memory: **malloc( )**, **calloc( )**

Review Questions

1. What's wrong with this program?

```
main()
{
    int *fp;
    int k;
    fp = fopen("gelatin");
    for (k = 0; k < 30; k++)
        fputs(fp, "Nanette eats gelatin.");
    fclose("gelatin");
}
```

2. What would the following program do?

```
#include <stdio.h>
#include <ctype.h>
main(argc,argv)
int argc;
char *argv[];
{
int ch;
FILE *fp;

if ( (fp = fopen(argv[1], "r")) == NULL)
    exit(1);
while ( (ch= getc(fp)) != EOF )
    if( isdigit(ch) )
        putchar(ch);
    fclose (fp);
}
```

3. Is there anything wrong with expressions such as **isalpha(c[i])**, where **c** is a **char** array? What about **isalpha (c[i++])**?

4. Use the character classification functions to prepare an implementation of **atoi( )**.

5. How could you allot space to hold an array of structures?

6. Suppose we have these statements in a program:

```
#include <stdio.h>
```

```
FILE *fp1,fp2;
char ch;

fp1 = fopen("terky", "r");
fp2 = fopen("jerky", "w");
```

Also, suppose all files were opened successfully. Supply the missing arguments in the following function calls:

a. **ch = getc(**_____**);**
b. **fprintf(**_____ **,"%c\n",** _____ **);**
c. **putc(**_____ **,** _____ **);**
d. **fclose(**_____ **); /* close the terky file */**

7. Write a program that takes zero command-line arguments or one command-line argument. If there is one argument, it is interpreted as the name of a file. If there is no argument, the standard input (**stdin**) is to be used for input. Assume that the input consists entirely of floating-point numbers. Have the program calculate and report the arithmetic mean (the average) of the input numbers.

8. Write a program that takes two command-line arguments. The first is a character; the second is a file name. The program should print those lines in the file containing the given character. Note: lines in a file are identified by a terminating '**\n**'. Assume that no line is more than 256 characters long. Also, you may wish to use **fgets( )**.

Answers

1. It should **#include** <**stdio.h**> for its file definitions. It should declare **fp** a file pointer: **FILE *fp;**. The function **fopen( )** requires a mode: **fopen("gelatin", "w")**, or perhaps the "a" mode. The order of the arguments to **fputs( )** should be reversed. The **fclose( )** function requires a file pointer, not a file name: **fclose(fp);**.

2. It will open the file given as a command-line argument and print out all the digits in the file. It should check (but doesn't) to see if there is a command-line argument.

3. The first expression is okay, since **c[i]** has a **char** value. The second expression won't choke the computer, but it may yield puzzling results. The reason is that **isalpha( )** is a macro that most likely has its argument appearing twice in the defining expression (checking for lowercase membership, then checking for uppercase membership), and this will produce two increments in **i**. It is best to avoid using the increment operator in the argument of a macro function call.

4. ```
   #include <stdio.h>
   #include <cytpe.h>
   ```
   ```

```
#define issign(c)    ( ((c) == '-' || (c) == '+') ? (1) : (0) )
atoi(s)
char *s;
{
    int i = 0;
    int n, sign;

    while ( isspace( s[i] ) )
        i++;    /* skip whitespace */
    sign = 1;
    if ( issign(s[i]) ) /* handle optional sign */
            sign = ( s[i++]=='+') ? 1 : -1;
    for (n = 0; isdigit( s[i] ); i++)
            n = 10*n + s[i] - '0';
    return( sign * n);
}
```

5. Suppose **wine** is the tag for a structure. These statements, properly placed in a program, will do the job.

```
struct wine *ptrwine;
char *calloc();

ptrwine = (struct wine *) calloc( 100, sizeof (struct wine) );
```

6. **a. ch = getc(fp1);**
   b. fprintf(fp2,"%c\n",ch);
   c. putc(ch,fp2);
   d. fclose(fp1); /* close the terky file */
   Note: **fp1** is used for input operations, since it identifies the file opened in the read mode. Similarly, **fp2** was opened in the write mode, so it is used with output functions.

7. Here is one solution. Notice that it checks for the correct number of arguments and exits if the file cannot be opened.

```
#include <stdio.h>
main(argc, argv)
int argc;
char *argv[];
{
    FILE *fp;
    void mean();

    if (argc > 2) {
        printf("Usage: %s [filename]\n", argv[0]);
        exit(1);
        }
    else if (argc == 2) {
```

```
        if ( (fp = fopen(argv[1], "r") ) == NULL) {
            printf("Can't open %s\n", argv[1]);
            exit(1);
            }
        else {
            mean(fp);
            fclose(fp);
            }
        }
    else    /*  no arguments, use standard input */
        mean(stdin);
}

void mean (fp)
FILE *fp;
{
    double num, sum = 0;
    long ct = 0;

    while ( fscanf(fp, "%lf", &num) > 0 ) {
            sum += num;
            ++ct;
            }
    if (ct)
            printf("The average is %f\n", sum/ct);
    else
            printf("No input\n");
}
```

8. Here is one approach:

```
#include <stdio.h>
#define BUF 256
main(argc,argv)
int argc;
char *argv[];
{
    FILE *fp;
    char ch;
    char line [BUF];
    char *fgets();

    if (argc != 3) {
        printf("Usage: %s character filename\n", argv[0]);
        exit(1);
        }
    ch = argv[1][0];
    if ( (fp = fopen(argv[2], "r")) == NULL){
```

```
                         printf("Can't open %s\n", argv[2]);
                         exit(1);
                         }
            while (fgets(line,BUF,fp) != NULL){
                if (has_ch(ch,line) )
                    fputs(line,stdout);
                }
            fclose(fp);
            }


            int has_ch(ch,line)
            char ch;
            char *line;
            {
               while (*line)
                 if (ch == *line++)
                     return(1);
               return(0);
            }
```

The **fgets( )** and **fputs( )** functions work together, for **fgets( )** leaves the **\n** produced by [enter] in the string, and **fputs( )** does not add in a **\n** the way **puts( )** does.

Exercises

1. Write a file copy program that uses the original file name and the copy file name as command-line arguments.

2. Write a program that will take all files given by a series of command-line arguments and print them one after the other on the screen. Use **argc** to set up a loop.

3. Modify our book inventory program of Chapter 14 so that the information you enter is appended to a file called **mybooks**.

4. Use **gets( )** and **atoi( )** to construct the equivalent of our **getint( )** function of Chapter 10.

5. Rewrite our word count program of Chapter 7 using **ctype.h** macros and using a command-line argument for the file to be processed.

6. Write a program that takes as command-line arguments a character and zero or more file names. If no arguments follow the input character, have the program read standard input. Otherwise, have it open the files in turn. Have the program report on how many times the given character appears in each file; the file name and the character itself should be reported along with the

count. Include error-checking for number of arguments and to see if the files can be opened. If a file can't be opened, have the program report that fact and go on to the next file.

7. Modify Exercise 6 so that it recognizes a −t option that causes it to report the cumulative total for all files read.

16

What Next?

Concepts
- ANSI Standard
- C++

Keywords
- *void, const, volatile, enum, signed*

T wo major developments have affected the C language in the 1980s. First, a committee is working to develop a standard definition of C. Second, an offshoot of C called C++ has been developed at Bell Labs. C++ is not a dialect of C; it is an extension that includes several new features. In this chapter, we will take a brief look at these two developments.

The ANSI C Language Standard

Like English, C is an evolving language. Changes in a language can be good; the vocabulary can expand to accommodate new ideas and needs. But uncontrolled change can lead to problems if different users modify the language differently, and incompatible dialects may develop.

Since 1978, the standard definition of C has been the one given in the reference section of Kernighan and Ritchie's book, *The C Programming Language*. This is just, since Ritchie wrote the language. Compiler vendors often advertise that their products offer a full K & R implementation, meaning that the compiler recognizes all the C features in that document. At that time, C was used primarily in the UNIX environment. Since then, UNIX C has added a few new features, and the use of C has become common in other environments, including the Apple® Macintosh™ and the DOS world of IBM compatibles. This expansion has increased the importance of portability. Developers want to write software in C that will run on many systems. This, in turn, creates a need for an accepted standard for the language, a standard that goes beyond the K & R definition and that more stringently meets the need for portability. (Kernighan and Ritchie, it should be noted, did realize that C would develop further.)

To meet this need, a committee of the American National Standards Institute (ANSI) has been meeting since 1983 to develop a standard for C. The final product is not due until near the end of 1987. Thus, we cannot yet describe the definitive standard. Several features, however, have received wide approval and already are being incorporated into C compilers. We'll look at some of these features next.

An Overview

The expressed goals of the Standard are to promote the portability, reliability, maintainability, and efficient execution of C language programs in a variety of computing environments.

One of the most significant steps towards portability is to develop a standard C library so that the same basic set of functions is available to all systems. There has been, more or less, a de facto standard for C, but not all implementations of, say, the **fopen( )** function have worked exactly the same way. The Standard will detail which library functions are required to meet the standard and how each function should work.

Portability problems are created when different implementations set up types differently. The Standard sets some boundaries; for example, type **short int** must be able to hold at least the value 32767. Also, while implementations still will be allowed to set up **char** as either a signed or an unsigned quantity, the user will be able use the **signed** and **unsigned** modifiers to get the form he or she desires.

C's methods for setting up functions have been a bit loose. One change, which already has been included in many implementations, is to use the keyword **void** to declare functions without return values. Another change is that the Standard will allow type-checking to take place for the arguments in a function call. As it stands now, you can accidentally pass a floating value instead of a pointer without the compiler noticing it. Type-checking will produce more reliable programming.

Some new types (**const, volatile**, and **enum**) serve to enhance program reliability.

We mentioned that many newer implementations allow structures to be passed as arguments. This means that the function works with a copy of the original structure, and this enhances reliability. The Standard includes this feature.

The Standard devotes more attention to floating-point calculations. There is a new type (**long double**), and there are some computational rules that can enhance the speed of calculation.

Then there are various other clarifications and additions to the language. For example, a unary *plus* operator (+) has been added to complement the unary minus operator.

We'll take a closer look at some of these changes now.

The *void* Function Type

In C, a function is assigned a type according to the type of value it returns. A function that returns an integer is type **int,** a function that returns a double precision floating-point number is type **double,** and so on. But some functions don't have a return value at all. They do something, perhaps print output or modify the values of an array, but they have no return value. The older tradition has been to not declare a type at all for these functions. By default, that makes them type **int,** which is logically inconsistent with the fact that they return nothing at all.

The **void** type was invented to handle this situation. Functions without return values should be declared type **void.** For example, suppose we want a function that takes an array name (which, as you will recall, is a pointer to the first element of an array), a multiplier, and an array size as arguments. The function then proceeds to multiply each array member by the multiplier. We could write the function this way:

```
void array_mult( ar, factor, size)
double ar[];
double factor;
int size;
(
    int i;

    for ( i = 0; i < size; i++)
        ar[i] *= factor;
}
```

The calling program could contain lines like these:

```
double costs[20];
void array_mult();
array_mult( costs, 1.20, 20 );
```

The criterion for making a function type **void** is that the function does not use a return statement. Thus, although this function provides new values to the array **costs,** it does not formally return a value; therefore it should be type **void.**

If you really want to be logically consistent, you should use a **void** type cast when you do not make use of a function's return value. For example, suppose you use **printf( )** without checking its return value. (The **printf( )** function is type **int,** and it returns the number of characters printed.) Then, to be absolutely beyond reproach of a rigorous program checker, you should make the call this way:

```
(void) printf("The Black Hole Conspiracy:\n");
```

This is the sort of language used in the ANSI documents, but it is a bit pedantic for everyday use.

An Aside—In a primer, it never hurts to review material, so let's take a quick look at how the **array_mult( )** function works. The function may *look* as if it uses an array, but it really uses a pointer. An array name, you will recall, is a pointer to the first element of an array, so a function call like **array_mult(costs, 1.2, 20)** passes three numbers to the **array_mult( )** function: the address of the first array element, the number **1.2**, and the number **20**. The address is assigned to the pointer **ar**, the **1.2** is assigned to **factor**, and the **20** is assigned to **size**. (The declaration **double ar[ ];** is equivalent to **double *ar;** for formal arguments.) The function then uses the address of the original array to tell which elements to change.

New, Improved Structure Status

Originally, all arguments to a function and all return values had to be single values. That is, you could use integers, characters, pointers, and the like for arguments and for return values, but you couldn't use arrays and structures for that purpose. Instead, structures and arrays were handled by using pointers, as in our last example.

This limitation still holds for arrays, but now structures can be passed as function arguments and returned as function values. (Here the Standard recognizes a C extension already in widespread use.) If, for example, a structure is passed as an argument, then the function creates a new structure, initializing it with the values of the original structure. Then, just as with ordinary variables, the function works with the copy, not the original. This helps protect the integrity of the data. A second consequence is that now a structure type is a valid type for functions. To make the return mechanism workable, the values in one structure can be assigned to another. That is, if **n_data** and **o_data** are both structures of the same type, you can do the following:

```
o_data = n_data;
```

This causes each member of **o_data** to be assigned the value of the corresponding member of **n_data**.

To see how the structure rules work, let's write a simple program handling structures by using pointers; then let's rewrite it to use structure-passing and structure returns. The program itself asks for your first and last names and reports the total number of letters in them. It hardly requires structures, but it provides a simple framework for seeing how they work. Here is the pointer form:

```
/* nameln1.c -- uses pointers to a structure */
#include <stdio.h>
struct namect {
```

```
                char fname[20];
                char lname[20];
                int letters;
               };
    main()
    {
        struct namect person;
        void getinfo(), makeinfo(), showinfo();

        getinfo(&person);
        makeinfo(&person);
        showinfo(&person);
    }


    void getinfo ( pst )
    struct namect *pst;
    {
        printf("Please enter your first name.\n");
        gets(pst->fname);
        printf("Please enter your last name.\n");
        gets(pst->lname);
    }

    void makeinfo ( pst )
    struct namect *pst;
    {
        pst->letters = strlen(pst->fname) +
                        strlen(pst->lname);
    }

    void showinfo ( pst )
    struct namect *pst;
    {
        printf("%s %s, your name contains %d letters.",
            pst->fname, pst->lname, pst->letters);
    }
```

Compiling and running the program produces results like the following:

```
A>nameln1
Please enter your first name:
Nathan
Please enter your last name:
Hale
Nathan Hale, your name contains 10 characters.
```

We've allocated the work of the program to three functions. In each case, we pass the address of the **person** structure to the function.

The **getinfo( )** function transfers information from itself to **main( )**. In particular, it obtains names from the user and places them in the **person** structure, using the **pst** pointer to locate it. Recall that **pst->lname** means the **lname** member of the structure pointed to by **pst**. Note that although **getinfo( )** feeds information to the main program, it does not use the return mechanism, so it is type **void**.

The **makeinfo( )** function performs a two-way transfer of information. By using a pointer to **person**, it locates the two names stored in the structure. It uses the C library function **strlen( )** to calculate the total number of letters and then uses the address of **person** to stow that datum away. Again, the type is **void**.

Finally, the **showinfo( )** function uses a pointer to locate the information to be printed.

In all of these operations, there has been but one structure variable, **person**, and each of the functions used the structure address to access it.

Now let's see how we can program the same task using structure arguments and return values. First, to pass the structure itself, we use the argument **person** rather than **&person**. The corresponding formal argument, then, is declared type **struct namect** instead of being a pointer to that type. Second, when we need to provide structure values to the main program, we can return a structure. Here's what it looks like:

```
/* nameln1.c -- passes and returns structures */
#include <stdio.h>
struct namect  {
                char fname[20];
                char lname[20];
                int letters;
               };
main()
{
    struct namect person;
    struct namect getinfo(), makeinfo();
    void showinfo();

    person = getinfo();
    person = makeinfo(person);
    showinfo(person);
}

struct namect getinfo ( )
{
    struct namect temp;
    printf("Please enter your first name.\n");
    gets(temp.fname);
```

```
      printf("Please enter your last name.\n");
      gets(temp.lname);
      return temp;
}

struct namect makeinfo ( info )
struct namect info;
{
      info.letters = strlen(info.fname) + strlen(info.lname);
      return info;
}

void showinfo ( info )
struct namect info;
{
      printf("%s %s, your name contains %d letters.",
          info.fname, info.lname, info.letters);
}
```

This version produces the same final result as the preceding one, but it proceeds in a different manner. Consider the **makeinfo( )** function, for example. In the first program, the address of **person** was passed, and the function fiddled with the actual **person** values. In the second program, a new structure called **info** is created. The values stored in **person** are copied to **info**, and the function works with the copy. So when the number of letters is calculated, it is stored in **info**, but not in **person**. The return mechanism, however, fixes that. By having the line

```
return info;
```

and the line

```
person = makeinfo(person);
```

we copy the values stored in **info** into **person**. Note that the **makeinfo( )** function had to be declared type **struct namect** because it returns a structure.

Because the second approach uses copies of structure variables instead of manipulating them directly, it is less likely to introduce inadvertent changes to the original structures. Thus, it is a more reliable approach.

The C Library

The original K & R Reference definition of C does not include any library functions. Even input and output functions were left to the discretion of C implementors. The text portion of K & R, however, does discuss several "standard" library functions developed for the UNIX environment. Some of these functions, such as **open( )** and **write( )** are incorporated directly into the UNIX operating system and are called *system calls*. Other functions, such as **printf( ), fopen( )**, and **getchar( )** were developed as convenient programming tools and became part of the UNIX C library. (The **getchar( )** actually is implemented as a macro, but it also is available as a function call.)

Other developers were free to create their own functions, but, in the interests of compatibility, most closely imitated the UNIX models and then supplemented the library with other functions useful for that particular system. For example, the IBM DOS environment requires accessing certain built-in routines called *interrupts,* so C vendors for that environment found it valuable to add functions to access these interrupts. Still, the UNIX family of system calls and library functions has developed as a de facto standard of what library functions a compiler package should provide.

The ANSI Standard will formalize this process. There will be a standard C library, and the Standard will detail how each function will work. (In the past, there have been mild discrepancies between how identically named functions have worked in different compiler-library implementations.) Although UNIX provided the original basis for the library, the Standard is not committed to UNIXizing everything; the final result will represent a compromise agreement worked out between many implementors.

A compiler that meets the ANSI Standard will have to support the entire Standard library or else provide no library at all. Of course, a library can provide additional functions beyond the Standard in order to meet specific needs on a given system or to provide further convenience.

To support the library, there will be a standard set of **#include** files. For example, the **string.h** file will contain all function declarations needed for the string functions. Thus, when you include that file, you won't have to declare the functions explicitly in your program.

Let's look at a couple of changes in the library.

Modes for **fopen( )**—The **fopen( )** function, recall, takes two arguments. The first is the name of the file to be opened, and the second is a mode. We discussed the three basic modes: read, write, and append. Now **fopen( )** also will support the following update modes:

"r+"	Open text file for update; reading and writing are allowed.
"w+"	Create text file for update; reading and writing are allowed. If the file already exists, truncate it to zero length first.
"a+"	Create text file for update; reading and writing are allowed. If the file already exists, writing is allowed only at the end of the file.

In the three update modes you can use the same **FILE** pointer for both reading and writing. However, there should be a call to **fflush( ), fseek( )**, or

rewind( ) between input and output calls. The call ensures that any input or output collected in intermediary buffers is sent on so that the file itself is updated.

There are six more modes. They consist of the previous modes with an appended **b**, for example, **"wb"** and **"r+b"**. These modes open and create *binary* files instead of *text* files. This is a concession to systems such as MS-DOS, which uses two different methods for setting up files. The **b** modifier is not needed for UNIX systems, which have just one form of file structure.

Specifiers for **printf( )**—The **printf( )** function has several extensions and modifications. Here are some of them:

- The **x** specifier for hex uses lowercase letters for the hex digits **a–f**, while the **X** specifier causes uppercase letters to be used.
- Similarly, the **e** and **g** specifiers cause **e** to be used in exponential notation, while **E** and **G** cause an **E** to be used. That is, **%9.2e** produces numbers like **2.34e+012**, while **%9.2E** produces **2.34E+012**.
- A **p** specifier is used for pointers. We used **u** (unsigned) for our examples, but that may not work for all circumstances.
- The **L** modifier can be used with the floating-type specifiers, as in **%20.12Lf**, to indicate that a **long double** is to be printed.
- The **h** modifier can be used with integer specifiers, as in **%hd**, to indicate that a **short int** is to be printed. The **#** modifier provides an alternative form. For example **%#o** causes octal numbers to be printed with a leading **0**, and **%#X** causes hex numbers to be printed with a leading **0X**.

Well, that provides the flavor of some of the changes. The significant point, however, is that there *is* a standard library of functions. This will enhance the portability of C implementations.

Function Prototypes

Now let's look at a feature designed to improve program reliability: function prototypes. First, though, let us develop a bit of background.

Argument-Passing without Type-Checking—Here is a small program that does some sloppy argument-passing:

```
main()
{
    char ch = 'T';
```

```
        float n = 3.0;
        int k, tread();
        k = tread(ch,n);
        printf("k is %d\n", k);
}

int tread(a,b)
int a,b;
{
        printf("a = %d, b = %d\n", a,b);
        return a + b;
}
```

The **tread( )** function expects two **int**s to be passed, but we fed it a **char** and a **float**. What happens? Here is the output we get on our system:

```
a = 84, b = 0
k = 84
```

The ASCII code for 'T' is 84, so apparently that mismatch caused no problems, but 0 is not the integer equivalent of 3.0. Passing the wrong type has caused a problem, and, to understand why, we have to look at how argument-passing takes place.

The details depend on the implementation, but here is a typical scenario. A function call like **tread(ch,n)** causes the value of each argument to be copied into a portion of memory called the *stack*. When this occurs, some "promotions" occur automatically. In particular, each **char** or **short** argument is promoted to **int**. Suppose **int** is 2 bytes in size. Then the ASCII value of 84, which is stored at **ch**, is copied into 2 bytes of stack memory, with the extra byte being set to 0. Similarly, each **float** argument is promoted to **double**. So, say, 8 bytes of stack are used to hold the value 3.0 in floating-point format. The important point is that the compiler allocates space in the stack according to the type of the actual argument; it does not check to see what types **tread( )** expects. Placing the values on the stack is the first step in argument-passing.

The second step is for **tread( )** to use the values it finds on the stack. What **tread( )** expects is two **int**s. So it uses the top 2 bytes (the code for 'T') of the stack for the variable **a**, and it uses the next 2 bytes for the variable **b**. Note that **b** uses just 2 out of the 8 bytes used to store **3.0**, so the **b** value is garbage. It is *not*, for example, an integer conversion of 3.0 to 3. (In our case, those 2 bytes were both 0, which was read as the integer 0.)

What can be done to avoid this problem? We can be careful. Suppose we want to pass a **float** value to a function that wants an **int**. Then we can use a type cast:

```
    k = tread( ch, (int) n);
```

Or, as we will discuss next, we can use function prototypes to inform the compiler what kinds of arguments should be passed.

Argument-Checking—Recall how we normally declare functions before using them so that the compiler will know the proper type for the return value. The Standard refers to these function declarations as *forward declarations*. Function prototypes extend that idea by also providing argument types. This is done with a list of types in the declaration. The preceding example would be rewritten this way:

```
main()
{
    char ch = 'T';
    float n = 3.0;
    int k, tread(int, int);

    k = tread(ch,n);
    printf("k is %d\n", k);
}

int tread(a,b)
int a,b;
{
    printf("a = %d, b = %d\n", a,b);
    return a + b;
}
```

This declaration tells the compiler two things: the **tread( )** function requires two arguments, and both should be type **int**. So what happens if the types don't match? The compiler treats the type list as cast instructions so that each argument is type cast (in this case) to **int**. Now the output looks like this:

```
a = 84, b = 3
k is 87
```

Note that the compiler is not obligated to tell you that it had to make type conversions. It will, however, warn you if you have the wrong number of arguments.

The Standard does not require that you use the type-checking feature. If you declare **tread( )** in the old way **(int tread( );)** in **main( )**, the old method (or lack of method) is used.

Suppose, though, you want to explicitly state that a function has no arguments. Then you can use a forward declaration of this form:

```
char getchoice(void);
```

The **void** keyword indicates **getchoice( )** takes no arguments.

Changes in Types

When we discussed data types in Chapter 3, we mentioned several newer extensions. These are incorporated into the Standard. To summarize, the original categories were **char, short int, int, unsigned int**, and **long int**. The **char** type could be implemented as a signed or as an unsigned type, depending on the implementor's preference. Under the Standard, **unsigned** can be used with all types, so **unsigned char, unsigned short**, and **unsigned long** are valid types. In addition, a new keyword **signed** can be used to make a type signed. This way, if you need a signed **char**, you can use the type **signed char**; then you will get a signed type whether or not the default **char** type is signed.

To support this larger cast of integer types, the Standard introduces the **u** and **U** suffixes for integer constants; they identify the constant as type **unsigned**. Either can be used with **l** or **L** to indicate an **unsigned long** constant, as in **2000UL**.

If a decimal integer constant is given without a suffix, the compiler assumes it is the first of the following types large enough to hold it: **int, long, unsigned long**. If the integer constant is in hex or octal form without a suffix, the compiler assumes it is the first of the following types large enough to hold it: **int, unsigned int, long int**, or **unsigned long int**.

In Chapter 3 we mentioned a hex form of character constant, as in '**\0x41**'. The Standard supports that. It also adds a new escape sequence: \a for the alarm, or bell character (ASCII 7).

The Standard clarifies how character constants are stored; it says they are to be stored as type **int**. As a consequence, a system with a 2-byte **int** can store up to two characters in a character constant. For example, '**ad**' would be a valid character constant. On a 4-byte system, '**abcd**' would be a valid character constant. However, only one character can be assigned to a **char** variable.

The floating-point family has a new addition, **long double**. The minimum range and precision standards for **float, double**, and **long double** are all the same, so all three could be implemented the same way, if necessary. But the possibility of three degrees of precision is there. By default, floating-point constants are type **double**. The **f** or **F** suffix makes the constant type **float**, while an **l** or **L** suffix makes it type **long double**.

When two types, say **int** and **short** or **double** and **long double**, have the same implementation, they are nonetheless considered different types. This preserves logical consistency and supports portability to systems for which the types have distinct implementations.

Arithmetic

One complaint some users have had about C is that it performs floating-point calculations slowly. The reason for this is the automatic promotions that occur with type **float**. For instance, suppose **f**, **m**, and **a** are all type **float** variables and that we have the following statement:

```
f = m * a;
```

Then, under the rules of C, **m** would be converted to type **double, a** would be converted to type **double**, the product would be calculated using **double** values to give a **double** result, and the result would then be converted back to **float**. Typically, **double** calculations are slower than **float** calculations because they involve more bytes.

The new Standard says that these conversions to double precision need not be made as long as the answer comes out the same as if they had been made. Since our example uses type **float** throughout, it could use the more rapid **float** calculations. If, however, **f** had been declared to be type **double**, then the conversions would be made. Note that compilers are not forced to optimize **float** calculations, but that option is open.

Enumerated Types

Enumerated types are another common extension supported by the Standard. By using the **enum** keyword, we can create a new "type" and specify the values it may have. (Actually, **enum** is type **int**, so we really create a new name for an existing type.) The purpose of enumerated types is to enhance the readability of a program. The syntax is similar to that used for structures. For example, we can make these declarations:

```
enum spectrum {red, orange, yellow, green, blue, violet};
enum spectrum color;
```

The first declaration establishes **spectrum** as a type name, and the second declaration makes **color** a variable of that type. The identifiers within the braces enumerate the possible values that a **spectrum** variable can have. Thus, the possible values for **color** are **red, orange, yellow**, and so on. Then, we can use statements like the following:

```
color = blue;
if (color == yellow)
   ...;
```

enum *Constants*—And just what are **blue** and **red**? Technically, they are type **int** constants. For instance, given the preceding enumeration declaration, we can try this:

```
printf("red = %d, orange = %d\n", red, orange);
```

The output is this:

```
red = 0, orange = 1
```

What has happened is that **red** has become a *named constant* representing the integer 0. Similarly, the other identifiers are named constants representing the integers 1 through 5. The process is similar to using defined constants, except that these definitions are set up by the compiler rather than the preprocessor.

Default Values—By default the constants in the enumeration list are assigned the integer values 0, 1, 2, etc. Thus, the declaration

```
enum kids {nippy, slats, skippy, nina, liz};
```

results in **nina** having the value **3**.

Assigned Values—You can choose the integer values you want the constants to have. Just include the desired values in the declaration:

```
enum levels {low = 100, medium = 500, high = 2000};
```

If you assign a value to one constant but not to the following constant, the following constant will be numbered sequentially. For example, suppose we have this declaration:

```
enum feline {cat, lynx = 10, puma, tiger};
```

Then **cat** is **0**, by default, and **lynx, puma,** and **tiger** are **10, 11,** and **12,** respectively.

Usage—As we said earlier, the purpose of enumerated types is to enhance the readability of a program. If you are dealing with colors, using **red** and **blue** is much more obvious than using **0** and **1**. Note that the enumerated types are for internal use. If you want to input a value of **orange** for **color,** you have to read in a **1**, not the word **orange**. Or else you can read in the string **"orange"** and have the program convert it to the value **orange**.

The Standard provides that enumerated variables be considered type **int** variables, so compliance with the Standard implies that **enum** variables can be used in expressions in the same manner as **int** variables.

Other Types

The Standard provides for two new keywords, **const** and **volatile**, that can be used to modify types. Let's look at **const** first.

Suppose you make a declaration like this:

```
const int cut = 40;
```

This establishes an **int** variable called **cut** and initializes it to the value **40**. It also keeps the program from subsequently altering the value of **cut**. As far as the program is concerned, **cut** is a constant.

At first it may seem odd to create a variable that is a constant, but it does have its uses. For example, it usually is desirable that a function work with local variables so that it does not inadvertently alter values in the calling function. For ordinary variables and for structures used as arguments, C automatically creates copies and works with them, protecting the integrity of the original data. But no such mechanism exists for functions that process arrays. In C, a function that uses an array works by passing a pointer to the first element of the array. Working with pointers gives a function the ability to alter the original array. This is fine for, say, a function like **gets( )** which is supposed to place an input string into the array. But it's bad for functions such as **puts( )** that have no need to alter the original array. (If **puts( )** is written correctly, there is no problem. The danger lies in making a subtle programming error that results in an unintentional change in the original array.)

The **const** type provides a method to protect the original array. A function like **puts( )** can be defined this way:

```
int puts(s)
const char *s;
```

The pointer **s** points to the first character of the string, so the function can *use* the string. But the keyword **const** prevents the function from using **s** to *alter* the string. So a programming error that accidentally changes the string will be caught by the compiler. Note: this particular declaration states that what **s** points to is **const**. However, the calling program still can alter the original string, unless it was declared **const** there, too.

The **volatile** modifier indicates that a data object may be modified by means external to the program. For example, it could refer to a memory-mapped port receiving data from a modem. This keyword prevents programming involving a **volatile** object from being altered by an optimizing compiler. Otherwise, for instance, a compiler might note that the variable is used in two places and that the program has done nothing in the intervening code to change the variable. It might then take the short cut of assuming the same value holds both times, not realizing an external action may have changed the variable.

Interestingly enough, a data object may be both **const** and **volatile**. Such an object could not be altered by the program, but it could be altered by, say, hardware. The Standard offers a real-time clock as an example of this sort.

Well, we've seen some of the more interesting aspects of the Standard:

It provides for some new type keywords, including **void, enum, const, volatile, signed**, and **long double**.

It allows for more efficient arithmetic calculations.

It provides for structure assignment, passing structures as arguments, and using structures as return values.

It provides for a standard C library, one that is not tied to any one operating system.

It provides for function prototyping and argument-checking. Again, the main importance of the Standard to most users is that it will increase the portability and reliability of C programs.

C++

The second major topic for this chapter is the C++ language. C++ was developed by Bjarne Stroustrup of Bell Laboratories; it first emerged as C++ in 1983. It is, essentially, a superset of C, adding new features. Some of these features, such as the **const** keyword and function prototype declarations, have made their way into ANSI C. Other, more far-reaching additions, are still exclusive to C++. We'll take a conceptual approach in outlining the nature of these additions.

C++ Goals

One of the primary goals of C was to create an efficient language close enough to the machine that C code could reasonably be used instead of assembly language. C's success in meeting that goal is one reason that it was chosen as the base from which to develop C++. What C++ adds are facilities to make the language closer to many kinds of programming problems, to provide more direct ways to conceptualize and solve a problem.

To accomplish that end, C++ enhances C's facilities for modularizing program design and for representing data and data-related operations. As a result of the improved program structure that this approach provides, Stroustrup (*The C++ Programming Language*) states that large programs can be structured "so that it would not be unreasonable for a single person to cope with 25,000 lines of code."

Classes

The main new tool is the *class*. Indeed, before the language evolved to C++, it was called "C with Classes." The class offers you the means to create user-defined types. At first glance, that may not seem much different from a structure, but the class goes far beyond that. Functions as well as data types can be class members. And a class provides a much more complete definition of what a type is.

Let's pause for a moment to think about what constitutes a type. One aspect, and the one we have emphasized in this book, is the representation of data. An integer type is represented differently from a floating type. A **char** type requires less space than a **long**. A structure lets you store several data types in a single data object. Another, equally important, aspect is the set of operations that can be performed with a given data type. For example, we can use the modulus operator (**%**) with integer types, but not with floating-types or structures. Thus, a complete definition of a type would include a specification of how the type is stored *and* a specification of what operations can be performed on the type.

And that is what the C++ class provides: a means of defining a data type (or set of related data types) and the set of operations that can be performed on them. For example, you could create a **vector** class that included functions for adding and subtracting vectors and for multiplying and dividing a vector by a number. Or you could define a **complex** class to represent complex numbers and operations. Or you could define a **sprite** class to represent a graphic element (such as a game monster) and its actions (movement, eating, etc.).

To provide an example, we will use C++ to create a class for dealing with vectors. You can think of a vector as an array. Indeed, C++ uses the term "vector" where C uses "array." (However, vector is not a C++ keyword, just as array is not a C keyword.) Adding two vectors would consist of adding the two 0-elements to get a new 0-element, adding the two 1-elements to get the new 1-element, and so on. Multiplying a vector by a number would consist of multiplying each element by that number. To deal with vectors we can design a class definition that deals with vector operations. We'll call the class **vector**; in the following explanation, note that **vector** is a user-defined type, not a built-in C++ type. (C++ does call arrays vectors, but it does not use the identifier **vector**.)

Certainly, an operation such as vector addition can be handled in C by writing, say, an **add_vec( )** function. But the class concept goes beyond that. If we define a class called **vector**, we can set things up so that a **vector** data object can be operated on *only* by the functions in that class. This does much to protect the integrity of data; only authorized operations can be performed. Second, we can use C++'s "operator overload" feature so that we can use +, −, *, /, and = with the new data type. That is, suppose **a, force_x, force_y,** and **force_net** are type **vector**, while **m** is **float**. Then a program can contain lines like the following:

```
force_net = force_x + force_y;
a = force_net / m;
```

The first statement will add up the individual elements (or "components") of two vectors and assign them to the corresponding components of **force_net**. The second statement would divide each component of **force_net** by **m** and assign the results to **a**.

As you can see, the class feature can greatly facilitate the ease and clarity with which data can be used. In regular C, we would have had to use functions in the following manner:

```
assign_vec(force_net, add_vec(force_1, force_2) );
assign_vec(a, div_vec(force_net,m));
```

This is much less clear.

Of course, in both approaches you do at some time have to write code to perform the actual operations. But C++ offers a superior way to organize and to use the code.

Operator Overloading

Let's back up and discuss operator overloading. This means assigning an additional meaning to an operator symbol. In this case, we gave new meaning to +, =, etc. The old meanings remain. If **total, toes** and **fingers** are type **int**, and **force_net**, **force_x**, and **force_y** are type **vector**, then we use both forms of addition and assignment in the same program:

```
total = toes + fingers;
force_net = force_x + force_y;
```

How does the program know what to do? It looks at the type of operand and uses the corresponding operation. Since **toes** and **fingers** are **int** operands, integer addition is performed. Since **force_x** and **force_y** are **vector** operands, vector addition is performed.

If this seems strange to you, reflect that ordinary C does the same thing. For example, integer division is a different operation from floating-point division, but both are represented by the / symbol. The difference is that C++ lets you take part in the operator overload game.

Function Overloading

Since we are discussing overloading, it is a good time to mention function overloading. C++ allows you to define two functions having the same name, providing they have different argument lists. This is possible because function declarations include a list of the argument types. (Function prototypes specifying argument types are obligatory.) For example, you could have these three lines:

```
overload pow;
double pow ( double, int );
double pow ( double, double);
```

The **overload** keyword indicates the **pow** identifier is to be overloaded. The first function could evaluate powers for integer exponents, and the second could use the slower algorithm needed to evaluate powers for floating-point exponents. Then a function call like **pow (2.5,2)** would use the first function, while a call like **pow (4.0, 2.5)** would evoke the second function. Thus, when you need the power of a number, you would use **pow( )**, and C++ would then choose the more efficient version, depending on the arguments.

Back to Classes

A class, as we've said, lets you define a data object and the operations that can be performed on it. How do you go about doing that? You use the keyword **class** in much the same way that **struct** is used. Typically, you would set up a template defining a class and use a tag to define variables of that type. For example, we can set up a **vector** class and variables along these lines:

```
class vector {
      double x;   // x component
      double y;   // y component
      double z;   // z component
public:
      vector(double, double, double); // initializer
      vector operator+(vector); // new + operator
      double vec_mag();   // magnitude of vector
      /* more function definitions */
};
/* ...other stuff ...*/
main()
{
      vector force = vector( 1.2, 3.5, 0);
       /* create and initialize a vector variable */
```

Well, this already looks a bit strange. We will have to examine it line by line to understand what's going on, but let's get an overview first. The part before **public** describes the data form, the rest of the class template names the class functions that can be used with a **vector** type, and the declaration in **main( )** creates a **vector** called **force** and initializes it. The // is an alternative way to indicate a comment. Everything from // to the end of the line is a comment. Now let's look at each step more closely.

The Data Form—First, the template establishes that three **double** values are stored in the **x, y,** and **z** members of a class object. This is like a structure definition. Thus, the **x** component of the **force** vector would be expressed as **force.x**. However, these components are protected from tampering. The **main( )** program, for example, cannot use the expression **force.x**. The only places the **x** member can be used are in the functions declared in the class template. This means, in turn, that **force** can be manipulated only by those functions. For instance, in the preceding example, the **vector( )** function is used to initialize **force**. (In C++, the class name is used for functions meant to initialize variables of that class.) As you can see, this provides data integrity.

The **public** keyword separates the inaccessible part of a class from aspects that can be used by a "client" program. The functions are allowed to manipulate the data, and the program is allowed to use those functions.

Class Functions Declarations—In our template we declared a couple functions, but we did not define them. The actual function definitions can be made inside the template, or they can be done elsewhere. We'll see how in a moment, but first let's discuss the three declarations.

The **vector( )** function is one used to initialize a vector. In C++, functions are allowed to return classes, so we declare the **vector( )** function is to be type **vector**. The function needs three **double** values; they are provided by the arguments. By having the declaration here and the actual function definition elsewhere, we give the user of the class the facts that he or she needs to know to use the class while placing the details elsewhere.

The second declaration has a more peculiar appearance:

```
vector operator+(vector); // new + operator
```

The combination **operator+** means that we are defining a function that will be invoked when the + operator is encountered in vector addition, as in our earlier example:

```
force_net = force_x + force_y;
```

The declaration says that the operator will take a type-**vector** operand and yield a type-**vector** result. But addition involves adding two values. How does this function get away with just one argument? We'll answer that when we look at the implementation.

The third declaration says that **vec_mag( )** returns a type **double** value representing the magnitude, or size, of a vector; it takes a **vector** argument.

Class Function Definitions—The next step is to write functions that do the promised tasks. We have declared a **vector( )** function for initializing a **vector** variable, an **operator+( )** function to redefine the + operator for **vector** operands, and a **vec_mag( )** function that provides the magnitude of a **vector** quantity. So let's see how to implement these promises.

In C++, a function used to create and initialize a variable of a particular class is called a *constructor*. A constructor has the same name as the class it services, so our constructor is named **vector( )**. Here is one possible implementation:

```
vector::vector(double a, double b, double c)
{
    x = a;
    y = b;
```

```
        z = c;
  }
```

The **vector::** notation is used to indicate that the following function is part of the definition of the **vector** class. Thus, different classes can use functions of the same name, and the double colon notation will keep straight which definition goes with which class.

Note that the variables are declared *inside* the parentheses: C++ uses this style instead of having a list of declarations coming after the parentheses. So this function takes three double values as arguments and assigns them to **x**, **y**, and **z**. And what are they? They are the **x**, **y**, and **z** members of whatever **vector** variable is being initialized. Perhaps an example will clarify this. Suppose we have this declaration:

```
vector force = vector(2.0, 3.0, 1.0);
```

This creates a **vector**-type variable called **force**. It sets **force.x** to **2.0**, **force.y** to **3.0**, and **force.z** to **1.0**. (Recall that a **vector** has three members.)

You can use a shorter format for the same process:

```
vector torque(10.0, 0, 15.0);
```

This creates a **torque** vector and makes **torque.x 10.0**, etc.

Once you define a constructor, you must use it. That is, don't do this:

```
vector velocity;    // no good, must initialize
```

However, you can set up a default initialization that will take place when a declaration like the preceding appears; we won't go into that. Also, you can initialize a variable by assignment:

```
vector force0 = force; // ok if force defined earlier
```

In short, when a class member name is used in a class function, it is understood to apply to the particular class object being processed. So, in the first initialization, **x** meant **force.x**, and in the second initialization, **x** meant **torque.x**. But what if a function deals with two variables? The next example shows that situation.

Our second function overloaded the + operator. The method for doing that is to name the function **operator+( )**. Similarly, **operator*( )** would be used to overload the * operator. Once again, we will use the double colon notation to indicate the class for which we are defining the function:

```
vector vector::operator+(vector a)
{
      return vector (x + a.x, y + a.y, z + a.z);
}
```

We can assign the value of a particular class of object to another object of the same type, so we declare **operator+( )** to be of type **vector** and let it return a value of that type. We use the **vector( )** initialization function to produce a vector whose **x** component is the sum of two **x** components, and so on. In this function, **x** implicitly stands for the **x** component of the first vector in the sum, and **a.x** explicitly represents the **x** component of the second vector. For example, suppose we have this statement:

```
force_tot = force1 + force2;
```

Then the **x** in the function definition represents the **x** component of **force1**, while **a.x** is the corresponding component for **force2**. Because the definition uses the first vector implicitly, we need to provide just one explicit argument.

The magnitude function could have been implemented in a similar fashion, using one **vector** as an argument. But we will use a slightly different approach that illustrates that class functions are, indeed, members of the class. Here is one possible implementation:

```
extern double sqrt(double);
double vector::vec_mag()
{
    return sqrt (x*x + y*y + z*z);
}
```

This assumes that a **sqrt( )** function is available in a math library. Here **x** is the **x** member of a **vector**, and so on. But of which vector is **x** a member? An example should clarify that question:

```
force_size = force.vec_mag();
```

C++ allows the dot membership operator to refer to member *functions* as well as to data components. Since this invocation of **vec_mag( )** is associated with the **force** variable, then **x** is understood to be **force.x**. Similarly, the call **force_tot.vec_mag( )** would cause **x** to mean **force_tot.x**.

This membership feature also clarifies how the new addition function works. The form

```
force_tot = force1 + force2;
```

is interpreted as this:

```
force_tot = force1.operator+(force2);
```

In other words, the **operator+( )** member of **force1** is used; that is why **x** is understood to be **force1.x**. These two methods for invoking the addition function are equivalent, but the first is easier to read and understand.

We have just scratched the surface of C++, but this is more a conceptual introduction than a tutorial. So let's look at some of the broader points.

C++ Philosophy

One intent of C++ is to let you develop data types that correspond to the needs of a particular problem. In essence, you can create a custom language with data forms and operations that express the concepts of a problem in a natural way. Typically, the most difficult, important, and time-consuming aspect in creating a program would be the design of the classes; here, you create the programming elements that you will use. Once you have done that, two distinct tasks remain. One is implementing the classes by writing the required functions and operators. The second is using the tools you've created to solve a particular programming problem.

Because C++ does let you develop your own programming vocabulary, it is particularly important to document your work thoroughly. Someone else reading through your main program most likely will encounter types and operations he or she has never seen before. Therefore, the header files defining the types should take care to explain the theory and use of the defined classes.

Another C++ emphasis is data integrity. In C, data is protected by having functions work on copies of data. C++ carries that a step further by allowing class data to be accessed only by functions that are members of the class.

C++ emphasizes modularity. Programming concepts are modularized into classes. Tasks are modularized into functions. On a larger scale, C++ encourages you to compartmentalize your work into separate files. A sensible way to organize a C++ program is to place the class definitions in an include file; for instance, our **vector** definition, suitably expanded, could be placed in a **vector.h** file. Then the implementations of the functions could be placed in a second file holding just those functions. Our **vector** functions, for instance, could be placed in a file called **vector.c**. These two files define the programming *tools* that are available. Finally, the programming *problem* would be dealt with in one or more additional files that used these tools. At that level of programming, you would not worry about the various class implementations; instead, you would think in terms of what the operations do. You will have created a high-level language whose concepts correspond to those of the problem.

C++ and C

Programming in C++ tends to be more abstract than programming in standard C. With standard C, one tends to think in terms of what actions the computer should perform. In C++, you should think in terms of what conceptual actions a programming problem requires. Does it move graphic images around the screen? Does it manipulate lists of information? Does it track a set of evolving populations? After clarifying what the concepts are, you should try to devise classes that express the concepts naturally. C++ puts greater demands on planning and creativity. It also, at first thought, may seem to be a more cumbersome, less efficient language than C. But, in fact, it is not. That is because the conversion of abstract concepts to computer instructions occurs during compilation, not during run time. Thus, a C++ compiler has much greater responsibilities than a C compiler, but, being based on C, the C++ compiler produces code of comparable efficiency.

Actually, you may not use a C++ compiler at all. Another approach is to use a C++ "translator" to translate C++ source code to C source code. Then you can use a regular C compiler. Again, the time-consuming work takes place in processing the source code, not during run time.

C++ is intended to be a superset of C; that is, it is meant to be compatible with C but to offer additional features. In fact, since each has evolved somewhat independently, C++ is not completely compatible. But they have influenced each other. C++ has adapted C's **void** addition, and ANSI C is following C++'s lead with **const** and function prototypes. Undoubtedly, once the final ANSI Standard emerges, an effort will be made to make C++ a superset of that Standard.

Is C++ the language for you? If you deal primarily with small programs, it may require more effort than it saves. (But it still can change your way of thinking about programming.) With large programming projects, it can save you effort and produce more reliable code.

Closing Words

We've come a long way since the beginning of this primer. By now, you have encountered most of the main features of the C language. (Appendix F covers the main omission: C bit operations.) You've seen and used C's wealth of operators, its enormous variety of basic and derived data types, its intelligent control structures, and its powerful pointer system. And you have seen some of what the future holds. We hope we've helped prepare you to use C for your own purposes. So good luck, and good programming!

What You Should Have Learned

Reasons for a C Standard: increased portability, reliability
Who is working on a standard: an ANSI committee
New C types: **void, enum, const, volatile, signed**, and **long double**
Numerical benefits of ANSI C: more efficient arithmetic calculations
Enhanced features for structures: structure assignment, passing structures
    as arguments, and using structures as return values
New features for functions: function prototyping and argument-checking
What C++ is: a superset of C

C++'s main addition: classes

C++'s main advantages: increased reliability, creating language elements suited to a particular problem

Review Questions

1. Suppose we have this structure:

```
struct gas {  float distance;
              float gals;
              float mpg;
           };
```

   Define a function that takes a **gas** structure as an argument, computes miles per gallon from the **distance** and **gals** members, and returns a structure having the correct **distance, gals,** and **mpg** values.

2. In our examples, we have used **int** for character input when checking for EOF, since the usual EOF value of −1 is incompatible with some implementations of C. Does ANSI C offer an alternative?

Answers

1. Here is one approach. It sets the **mpg** member to −1 if the number of gallons is not a positive number.

```
struct gas {  float distance;
              float gals;
              float mpg;
           };

struct gas mpgs (gastr)
struct gas gastr;
{
   if (gastr.gals > 0)
       gastr.mpg = gastr.distance / gastr.gals ;
   else
       gastr.mpg = -1.0;
   return gastr;
}
```

2. Yes, we can use a declaration like this:

```
signed char ch;
```

   Then **ch** could be set to −1, even if the default **char** type could not.

Appendices

- A: Additional Reading
- B: Keywords in C
- C: C Operators
- D: Data Types and Storage Classes
- E: Program Flow Control
- F: Bit Fiddling: Operators and Fields
- G: Binary Numbers and Others
- H: IBM PC Music
- I: ASCII Table

A

Additional Reading

If you wish to learn more about C and programming, you will find the following references useful.

The C Language

BYTE, **8 (no. 8): August 1983.**

This issue of *BYTE* magazine is devoted to C. It includes articles discussing the history, philosophy, and uses of C. Twenty C compilers for microprocessors are tested and evaluated. Also included is an extensive, up-to-date bibliography of books and articles on C. Each bibliographic entry includes a short summary of the book or article.

Feuer, Alan R. *The C Puzzle Book.* **Englewood Cliffs, New Jersey: Prentice-Hall, 1982.**

This book contains a large number of programs whose output you are supposed to predict. This gives you a good opportunity to test and expand your understanding of C. The book includes answers and explanations.

Kernighan, Brian W., and Dennis M. Ritchie. *The C Programming Language.* **Englewood Cliffs, New Jersey: Prentice-Hall, 1978.**

This is the first and most authoritative book on C. (Note that the creator of C, Dennis Ritchie, is one of the authors.) It is practically the official definition of C and includes many interesting examples. It does, however, assume that the reader is familiar with systems programming.

Prata, Stephen. *Advanced C Primer++.* **Indianapolis: Howard W. Sams, 1986.**

This book takes a more detailed look at topics such as file I/O, structures, functions, and bit operations. The second half emphasizes the IBM PC interface and shows how to integrate assembly-language modules into a C program.

Ritchie, D. M., S. C. Johnson, M. E. Lesk, and B. W. Kernighan. "The C Programming Language." *The Bell System Technical Journal* **57 (no. 6): July–August 1978.**

This article discusses the history of C and provides an overview of its design features.

Stroustrup, Bjarne. *The C++ Programming Language.* **Reading, Maine: Addison-Wesley, 1986.**

This book, by the creator of C++, presents the C++ language and includes the Reference Manual for C++.

Programming

Kernighan, Brian W., and P. J. Plauger. *The Elements of Programming Style* **2d ed. New York: McGraw-Hill, 1978.**

This slim classic draws on examples from other texts to illustrate the dos and don'ts of clear, effective programming.

———. *Software Tools.* **Reading, Maine: Addison-Wesley, 1976.**

This book develops several useful programs and systems of programs, while emphasizing good program design. It comes in a RATFOR (rationalized FORTRAN) and in a Pascal version. Since RATFOR represents an attempt to make FORTRAN work like C, the first version is the choice of C users.

The UNIX Operating System

Prata, Stephen. *Advanced UNIX—A Programmer's Guide.* **Indianapolis: Howard W. Sams, 1985.**

The first half of the book deals with the UNIX system, and the second half covers the C-UNIX interface.

Waite, Mitchell, Don Martin, and Stephen Prata, *UNIX Primer Plus* **2d ed. Indianapolis: Howard W. Sams, 1987.**

This book provides an easy-to-read introduction to the UNIX operating system, including several powerful Berkeley enhancements.

———. *UNIX System V Primer* **2d ed. Indianapolis: Howard W. Sams, 1987.**

This is the System V version of *UNIX Primer Plus*.

B

Keywords in C

The keywords of a language are the words used to express the actions of that language. The keywords of C are reserved; that is, you can't use them for other purposes, such as for the name of a variable.

Program Flow Keywords

Loops

```
for while do
```

Decision and Choice

```
if else switch case default
```

Jumps

```
break continue goto
```

Data Types

```
char int short long unsigned float enum
double struct union typedef void signed const volatile
```

Storage Classes

```
auto extern register static
```

Miscellaneous

```
return sizeof
```

C

C Operators

C is rich in operators. Here we present a table of operators, indicating the priority ranking of each and how each operator is grouped. Next, we will summarize the operators except for the bit-wise operators, which are discussed in Appendix F.

Operators (from high to low priority)	Grouping
() [] -> .	L–R
! ~ ++ -- - (type) * & sizeof (all unary)	R–L
* / %	L–R
+ -	L–R
<< >>	L–R
< <= > >=	L–R
== !=	L–R
&	L–R
^	L–R
|	L–R
&&	L–R

Operators (from high to low priority)	Grouping
||	| L–R
? :	| L–R
= += −= *= /= %= ^= &= |=	| R–L
,	| L–R

Here is what these operators do:

Arithmetic Operators

+   Adds value at its right to the value at its left.

−   Subtracts value at its right from the value at its left.

−   As a unary operator, changes the sign of the value to its right.

*   Multiplies value at its right by the value at its left.

/   Divides value at its left by the value at its right. Answer is truncated if both operands are integers.

%   Yields the remainder when the value at its left is divided by the value to its right (integers only).

++   Adds 1 to the value of the variable to its left (prefix mode), or adds 1 to the value of the variable to its right (postfix mode).

−−   Like ++, but subtracts 1.

Assignment Operators

=   Assigns value at its right to the variable at its left.

Each of the following operators updates the variable at its left by the value at its right, using the indicated operation. We use r-h for right-hand, l-h for left-hand.

+=   Adds the r-h quantity to the l-h variable.

−=   Subtracts the r-h quantity from the l-h variable.

*=   Multiplies the l-h variable by the r-h quantity.

/=   Divides the l-h variable by the r-h quantity.

%=   Gives the remainder from dividing the l-h variable by the r-h quantity.

Example

```
rabbits *= 1.6;   is the same as   rabbits = rabbits * 1.6;
```

Relational Operators

Each of these operators compares the value at its left to the value at its right. The relational expression formed from an operator and its two operands has the value 1 if the expression is true and the value 0 if the expression is false.

<	Less than.
<=	Less than or equal to.
==	Equal to.
>=	Greater than or equal to.
>	Greater than.
!=	Unequal to.

Logical Operators

Logical operators normally take relational expressions as operands. The ! operator takes one operand, and it is to the right. The rest take two: one to the left, one to the right.

&&	Logical AND: the combined expression is true if both operands are true, and it is false otherwise.
||	Logical OR: the combined expression is true if one or both operands are true, and it is false otherwise.
!	Logical NOT: the expression is true if the operand is false, and vice versa.

Pointer-Related Operators

&	The address operator: when followed by a variable name, it gives the address of that variable. **&nurse** is the address of the variable **nurse.**
*	The indirection operator: when followed by a pointer, it gives the value stored at the pointed-to address:

```
nurse = 22;
ptr = &nurse;   /* pointer to nurse */
val = *ptr;
```

The net effect is to assign the value 22 to **val.**

Structure and Union Operators

The membership operator (the period) is used with a structure or union name to specify a member of that structure or union. If **name** is the name of a structure and **member** is a member specified by the structure template, then

```
name.member
```

identifies that member of the structure. The membership operator can also be used in the same fashion with unions:

```
struct {
     int code;
     float cost;
     } item;
```

```
item.code = 1265;
```

This assigns a value to the **code** member of the structure **item.**

-> The indirect membership operator is used with a pointer to a structure or union to identify a member of that structure or union. Suppose **ptrstr** is a pointer to a structure and that **member** is a member specified by the structure template. Then

```
ptrstr->member
```

identifies that member of the pointed-to structure. The indirect membership operator can be used in the same fashion with unions:

```
struct {
     int code;
     float cost;
     } item, *ptrst;
```

```
ptrst = &item;
ptrst->code = 3451;
```

This assigns a value to the **code** member of **item.** The following three expressions are equivalent:

```
ptrst->code      item.code      (*ptrst).code
```

Miscellaneous Operators

sizeof   Yields the size, in bytes, of the operand to its right. The operand can be a type-specifier in parentheses, as in **sizeof (float),** or it can be the name of a particular variable or array, etc., as in **sizeof foo.**

(type)   Cast operator: converts following value to the type specified by the enclosed keyword(s). For example, **(float) 9** converts the integer 9 to the floating-point number 9.0.

,   The comma operator, like others, links two expressions into one and guarantees that the leftmost expression is evaluated first. A typical use is to include more information in a **for** loop control expression:

```
for ( step = 2, fargo = 0; fargo < 1000; step *= 2)
    fargo += step;
```

The value of a comma expression is the value of the expression to the right of the comma.

?:   The conditional operator takes three operands, each of which is an expression. They are arranged this way:

expression1 ? *expression2* : *expression3*

The value of the whole expression equals the value of *expression2* if *expression1* is true, and equals the value of *expression3* otherwise. Examples:

```
( 5 > 3 ) ? 1 : 2   has the value 1.
( 3 > 5 ) ? 1 : 2   has the value 2.
( a > b ) ? a : b   has the value of the larger of a or b.
```

D

Data Types and Storage Classes

The Basic Data Types

Keywords

The basic data types are set up using the following seven keywords: **int, long, short, signed, unsigned, char, float, double.**

Signed Integers

These can have positive or negative values.

int: the basic integer type for a given system.

long or **long int:** can hold an integer at least as large as the largest **int** and possibly larger.

short or **short int:** the largest **short** integer is no larger than the largest **int** and may be smaller. Typically, **long** will be bigger than **short,** and **int** will be the same as one of the two. For example, IBM C has 16-bit **short** and **int,** and 32-bit **long.** It all depends on the system.

Unsigned Integers

These have zero or positive values only. This extends the range of the largest possible positive number. Use the keyword **unsigned** before the desired type: **unsigned int, unsigned long, unsigned short.** A lone **unsigned** is the same as **unsigned int.**

Characters

These are typographic symbols such as A, &, and +. Typically just 1 byte of memory is used.

char: the keyword for this type.

The **char** type may be implemented either as a **signed** or **unsigned** type. You can use **unsigned char** to guarantee an **unsigned** type and **signed char** to guarantee a **signed** type.

Floating Point

These can have positive or negative values.

float: the basic floating-point size for the system.

double: a (possibly) larger unit for holding floating-point numbers. It may allow more significant figures and perhaps larger exponents.

long double: a (possibly) even larger unit for holding floating-point numbers.

How to Declare a Simple Variable

1. Choose the type you need.
2. Choose a name for the variable.
3. Use this format for a declaration statement:

   type-specifier variable-name;

   The *type-specifier* is formed from one or more of the type keywords. Here are some examples:

   ```
   int erest;
   unsigned short cash;
   ```

4. You may declare more than one variable of the same type by separating the variable names by commas:

   ```
   char ch, init, ans;
   ```

5. You can initialize a variable in a declaration statement:

   ```
   float mass = 6.0E24;
   ```

Storage Classes

Keywords

The keywords for storage classes are: **auto, extern, static, register.**

General Comments

The storage class of a variable determines its scope and how long the variable persists. Storage class is determined by where the variable is defined and by the associated keyword. Variables that are defined outside a function are external and have global scope. Variables that are declared inside a function are automatic and local unless one of the other keywords is used. External variables defined above a function are known to it even if not declared internally.

Properties

Storage Class	Keyword	Duration	Scope
automatic	`auto`	temporary	local
register	`register`	temporary	local
static	`static`	persistent	local
external	`extern*`	persistent	global (all files)
external static	`static`	persistent	global (one file)

Note: The variables above the dotted line are declared inside a function.
Those below the line are defined outside a function.

*The keyword **extern** is used only to redeclare variables that have been defined externally elsewhere; the act of defining the variable outside of a function makes it external.

E

Program Flow Control

C has several control structures for guiding the flow of a program. Here we summarize the looping statements (**while, for,** and **do while**), the branching statements (**if, if-else,** and **switch**), and the jump statements (**goto, break,** and **continue**).

The *while* Statement

Keyword: *while*

General Comments

The **while** statement creates a loop that repeats until the test *expression* becomes false, or zero. The **while** statement is an *entry-condition* loop; the decision to go through one more pass of the loop is made *before* the loop is traversed. Thus, it is possible that the loop is never traversed. The *statement* part of the form can be a simple statement or a compound statement.

Form

```
while ( expression )
        statement
```

The *statement* portion is repeated until the *expression* becomes false or zero.

Examples

```
while ( n++ < 100 )
      printf(" %d %d\n", n, 2*n+1 );


while ( fargo < 1000 )
      {
      fargo = fargo + step;
      step = 2 * step;
      }
```

The *for* Statement

Keyword: *for*

General Comments

The **for** statement uses three control expressions, separated by semicolons, to control a looping process. The *initialize* expression is executed once, before any of the loop statements are executed. If the *test* expression is true (or nonzero), the loop is cycled through once. Then the *update* expression is evaluated, and it is time to check the *test* expression again. The **for** statement is an *entry-condition* loop; the decision to go through one more pass of the loop is made *before* the loop is traversed. Thus, it is possible that the loop is never traversed. The *statement* part of the form can be a simple statement or a compound statement.

Form

```
for ( initialize ; test ; update )
      statement;
```

The loop is repeated until *test* becomes false or zero.

Example

```
for ( n = 0; n < 10 ; n++ )
      printf(" %d %d\n", n, 2*n+1 );
```

The *do while* Statement

Keywords: *do, while*

General Comments

The **do while** statement creates a loop that repeats until the test *expression* becomes false, or zero. The **do while** statement is an *exit-condition* loop; the decision to go through one more pass of the loop is made *after* the loop is traversed. Thus, the loop must be executed at least once. The *statement* part of the form can be a simple statement or a compound statement.

Form

```
do
    statement
    while ( expression );
```

The *statement* portion is repeated until the *expression* becomes false or zero.

Example

```
do
    scanf("%d", &number)
        while( number != 20 );
```

Using *if* Statements for Making Choices

Keywords: *if, else*

General Comments

In each of the following forms, the *statement* can be either a simple statement or a compound statement. A "true" expression, more generally, means one with a nonzero value.

Form 1

```
if ( expression )
    statement
```

The *statement* is executed if the *expression* is true.

Form 2

```
if ( expression )
    statement1
else
    statement2
```

If the *expression* is true, *statement1* is executed. Otherwise, *statement2* is executed.

Form 3

```
if ( expression1 )
    statement1
else if ( expression2 )
    statement2
else
    statement3
```

If *expression1* is true, then *statement1* is executed. If *expression1* is false but *expression2* is true, *statement2* is executed. Otherwise, if both expressions are false, *statement3* is executed.

Example

```
if (legs == 4)
    printf("It might be a horse.\n");
else if (legs > 4)
    printf("It is not a horse.\n");
else      /* done if legs < 4 */
    {
    legs++;
    printf("Now it has one more leg.\n")
    }
```

Multiple Choice with *switch*

Keyword: *switch*

General Comments

Program control jumps to the statement bearing the value of *expression* as a label. Program flow then proceeds through the remaining statements unless redirected again. Both *expression* and labels must have integer values (type **char** is included), and the labels must be constants or expressions formed solely from constants. If no label matches the expression value, control goes to the statement labeled **default,** if present. Otherwise, control passes to the next statement following the **switch** statement.

Form

```
switch ( expression )
     {
     case label1 : statement1
     case label2 : statement2
     default     : statement3
     }
```

There can be more than two labeled statements, and the **default** case is optional.

Example

```
switch ( letter )
     {
     case 'a'   :
     case 'e'   :    printf("%d is a vowel\n", letter);
     case 'c'   :
     case 'n'   :    printf("%d is in \"cane\"\n", letter);
     default    :    printf("Have a nice day.\n");
     }
```

If **letter** has the value 'a' or 'e', all three messages are printed: 'c' and 'n' cause the last two to be printed. Other values print just the last message.

Program Jumps

Keywords: *break, continue, goto*

General Comments

These three instructions cause program flow to jump from one location of a program to another location.

break

The **break** command can be used with any of the three loop forms and with the **switch** statement. It causes program control to skip over the rest of the loop or **switch** containing it and to resume with the next command following the loop or **switch.**

Example

```
switch (number )
    {
    case    4:      printf("Good choice!\n");
                    break;
    case    5:      printf("That's a fair choice.\n");
                    break;
    default:        printf("That's a poor choice.\n");
```

continue

The **continue** command can be used with any of the three loop forms but not with a **switch.** It causes program control to skip the remaining statements in a loop. For a **while** or **for** loop, the next loop cycle is started. For a **do while** loop, the exit condition is tested and then, if necessary, the next loop cycle is started.

Example

```
while ( (ch = getchar()) != EOF)
    {
    if ( ch == ' ' )
        continue;
    putchar(ch);
    chcount++;
    }
```

This fragment echoes and counts nonspace characters.

goto

A **goto** statement causes program control to jump to a statement bearing the indicated label. A colon is used to separate a labeled statement from its label. Label names follow the rules for variable names. The labeled statement can come either before or after the **goto.**

Form

```
goto label;
    ...
label : statement
```

Example

```
top : ch = getchar();
    ...
if ( ch != 'y' )
    goto top;
```

F

Bit Fiddling: Operators and Fields

Some programs need (or, at least, benefit from) an ability to manipulate individual bits in a byte or word. For example, I/O devices often have their options set by a byte in which each bit acts as an on-off flag. C has two facilities to help you manipulate bits. The first is a set of six "bitwise" operators that act on bits. The second is the **field** data form, which gives you access to bits within an **int.** We will outline these C features here.

Operators

C offers bitwise logical operators and shift operators. In the following, we will write out values in binary notation so that you can see the mechanics. In an actual program, you would use integer variables or constants written in the usual forms. For instance, instead of **(00011001)**, you would use **25** or **031** or **0x19.** For our examples, we will use 8-bit numbers, with the bits numbered 7 to 0, left to right.

Bitwise Logical Operators

The four bitwise logical operators work on integer-class data, including **char.** They are termed "bitwise" because they operate on each bit independently of the bit to the left or right.

One's Complement, or Bitwise Negation: ~

This unary operator changes each 1 to a 0 and each 0 to a 1. Thus,

~(10011010) == (01100101)

Bitwise AND: &

This binary operator makes a bit-by-bit comparison between two operands. For each bit position, the resulting bit is 1 only if both corresponding bits in the operands are 1. (In terms of true-false, the result is true only if each of the two bit operands is true.) Thus,

(10010011) & (00111101) == (00010001)

since only bits 4 and 0 are 1 in both operands.

Bitwise OR: ¦

This binary operator makes a bit-by-bit comparison between two operands. For each bit position, the resulting bit is 1 if either of the corresponding bits in the operands is 1. (In terms of true-false, the result is true if one or the other bit operands are true or if both are true.) Thus,

(10010011) ¦ (00111101) == (101111111)

since all bit positions but bit 6 have the value 1 in one or the other operands.

Bitwise EXCLUSIVE OR: ^

This binary operator makes a bit-by-bit comparison between two operands. For each bit position, the resulting bit is 1 if one or the other (but not both) of the corresponding bits in the operands is 1. (In terms of true-false, the result is true if one or the other bit operands—and not both—are true.) Thus,

(10010011) ^ (00111101) == (10101110)

Note that since bit position 0 has the value 1 in both operands, that the resulting 0 bit has value 0.

Usage

The bitwise logical operators often are used to set certain bits while leaving others unchanged. For example, suppose we **#define MASK** to be **2**, i.e., binary 00000010, with only bit number 1 being nonzero. Then the statement

```
flags = flags & MASK;
```

would cause all the bits of flags (except bit 1) to be set to 0, since any bit combined with 0 via the **&** operator yields 0. Bit number 1 will be left unchanged. (If the bit is 1, then **1 & 1** is 1; if the bit is 0, then **0 & 1** is 0.)

Similarly, the statement

```
flags = flags | MASK;
```

will set bit number 1 to 1 and leave all the other bits unchanged. This follows because any bit combined with 0 via the | operator is itself, and any bit combined with 1 via the | operator is 1.

Bitwise Shift Operators

The bitwise shift operators shift bits to the left or right. Again, we will write binary numbers explicitly to show the mechanics.

Left Shift: <<

This operator shifts the bits of the left operand to the left by the number of places given by the right operand. The vacated positions are filled with 0s, and bits moved past the end of the left operand are lost. Thus,

```
(10001010) << 2 == (00101000)
```

where each bit is moved two places to the left.

Right Shift: >>

This operator shifts the bits of the left operand to the right by the number of places given by the right operand. Bits moved past the right end of the left operand are lost. For **unsigned** types, the places vacated at the left end are replaced by 0s. For signed types, the result is machine dependent. The vacated places may be filled with 0s, or they may be filled with copies of the sign (leftmost) bit. For an unsigned value, we have

```
(10001010) >> 2 == (00100010)
```

where each bit is moved two places to the right.

Usage

The bitwise shift operators provide swift, efficient multiplication and division by powers of 2:

number << n   multiplies **number** by 2 to the **n**th power.

number >> n   divides **number** by 2 to the **n**th power if number is not negative.

This is analogous to the decimal system procedure of shifting the decimal point to multiply or divide by 10.

Fields

The second method of manipulating bits is to use a field. A field is just a set of neighboring bits within an **int** or **unsigned int.** A field is set up via a structure definition, which labels each field and determines its width. The following definition sets up four 1-bit fields:

```
struct   {
          unsigned autfd   : 1;
          unsigned bldfc   : 1;
          unsigned undln   : 1;
          unsigned itals   : 1;
          } prnt;
```

The variable **prnt** now contains four 1-bit fields. The usual structure membership operator can be used to assign values to individual fields:

```
prnt.itals = 0;
prnt.undln = 1;
```

Because each field is just 1 bit, 1 and 0 are the only values we can use for assignment.

The variable **prnt** is stored in an **int**-sized memory cell, but only 4 bits are used in this example.

Fields aren't limited to 1-bit sizes. We can do this:

```
struct {
          unsigned code1 : 2;
          unsigned code2 : 2;
          unsigned code3 : 8;
          } prcode;
```

This creates two 2-bit fields and one 8-bit field. We can make assignments such as:

```
prcode.code1 = 0;
prcode.code2 = 3;
prcode.code3 = 102;
```

Just make sure that the value doesn't exceed the capacity of the field.

What if the total number of bits you declare exceeds the size of an **int?** Then the next **int** storage location is used. A single field is not allowed to overlap the boundary between two **int**s; the compiler automatically shifts an overlapping field definition so that the field is aligned with the **int** boundary. If this occurs, it leaves an unnamed hole in the first **int.**

You can "pad" a field structure with unnamed holes by using unnamed field widths. Using an unnamed field width of 0 forces the next field to align with the next integer:

```
struct {
        field1 : 1;
               : 2;
        field2 : 1;
               : 0;
        field3 : 1;
        } stuff;
```

Here, there is a 2-bit gap between **stuff.field1** and **stuff.field2;** and **stuff.field3** is stored in the next **int.**

One important machine dependency is the order in which fields are placed into an **int.** On some machines the order is left to right, and on others it is right to left.

G

Binary Numbers and Others

Binary Numbers

The way we usually write numbers is based on the number 10. Perhaps you were once told that a number like 3652 has a 3 in the thousand's place, a 6 in the hundred's place, a 5 in the ten's place and a 2 in the one's place. This means we can think of 3652 as being

$$3 \times 1000 + 6 \times 100 + 5 \times 10 + 2 \times 1$$

But 1000 is 10 cubed, 100 is 10 squared, 10 is 10 to the first power, and, by convention, 1 is 10 (or any positive number) to the zero power. So we also can write 3652 as

$$3 \times 10^3 + 6 \times 10^2 + 5 \times 10^1 + 2 \times 10^0$$

Because our system of writing numbers is based on powers of ten, we say that 3652 is written in *base 10*.

Presumably, we developed this system because we have ten fingers. A computer bit, in a sense, has only two fingers, for it can be set only to 0 or 1, off or on. This makes a *base 2* system natural for a computer. How does it work? It uses powers of two instead of powers of ten. For instance, a binary number such as 1101 would mean

$$1 \times 2^3 + 1 \times 2^2 + 0 \times 2^1 + 1 \times 2^0$$

In decimal numbers this becomes

$$1 \times 8 + 1 \times 4 + 0 \times 2 + 1 \times 1 = 13$$

The base 2 (or "binary") system lets us express any number (if we have enough bits) as a combination of 1s and 0s. This is very pleasing to a computer, especially since that is its only option. Let's see how this works for a 1-byte integer.

A byte contains 8 bits. We can think of these 8 bits as being numbered from 7 to 0, left to right. This "bit number" corresponds to an exponent of 2. Imagine the byte as looking like this:

bit number	7	6	5	4	3	2	1	0
value	128	64	32	16	8	4	2	1

Here, 128 is 2 to the 7th power, and so on. The largest number this byte can hold is one with all bits set to 1: 11111111. The value of this binary number is

$$128 + 64 + 32 + 16 + 8 + 4 + 2 + 1 = 255$$

The smallest binary number would be 00000000, or a simple 0. A byte can store numbers from 0 to 255 for a total of 256 possible values.

Binary Floating Point

Floating-point numbers are stored in two parts: a binary fraction and a binary exponent. Let's see how this is done.

Binary Fractions

The ordinary fraction .324 represents

$$3/10 + 2/100 + 4/1000$$

with the denominators representing increasing powers of ten. In a binary fraction, we use powers of two for denominators. Thus, the binary fraction .101 represents

$$1/2 + 0/4 + 1/8$$

which in decimal notation is

$$.50 + .00 + .125$$

or .625.

Many fractions, such as 1/3, cannot be represented exactly in decimal notation. Similarly, many fractions cannot be represented exactly in binary notation. Indeed, the only fractions that can be represented exactly are combinations of multiples of powers of 1/2. Thus, 3/4 and 7/8 can be represented exactly as binary fractions, but 1/3 and 2/5 cannot be.

Floating-Point Representation

To represent a floating-point number in a computer, a certain number (system-dependent) of bits are set aside to hold a binary fraction. Additional bits hold an exponent. In general terms, the actual value of the number consists of the binary fraction times 2 to the indicated exponent. Thus, multiplying a floating-point number by, say, 4, increases the exponent by 2 and leaves the binary fraction unchanged. Multiplying by a number that is not a power of 2 will change the binary fraction and, if necessary, the exponent.

Other Bases

Computer workers often use number systems based on 8 and on 16. Since 8 and 16 are powers of 2, these systems are more closely related to a computer's binary system than is the decimal system.

Octal

"Octal" refers to a base 8 system. In this system, the different places in a number represent powers of 8. We use the digits 0 to 7. For example, the octal number 451 (written 0451 in C) represents

$$4 \times 8^2 + 5 \times 8^1 + 1 \times 8^0 = 297 \text{ (base 10)}$$

Hexadecimal

"Hexadecimal" (or "hex") refers to a base 16 system. Here we use powers of 16 and the digits 0 to 15. But since we don't have single digits to represent the values 10 to 15, we use the letters A to F for that purpose. For instance, the hex number A3F (written 0xA3F in C) represents

$$10 \times 16^2 + 3 \times 16^1 + 15 \times 16^0 = 2623 \text{ (base 10)}$$

H

IBM PC Music

The IBM PC's speaker can be controlled by using the PC's I/O ports. In Chapter 6 we discussed how to use port 97 to sound the IBM PC's beeper. We used the special-purpose **inp( )** and **outp( )** I/O functions supplied with some IBM PC C compilers. Most compilers for the IBM PC also allow you to use the assembly language equivalents. We've seen how to use a time delay loop to control the duration of the sound, and in this appendix we will extend our approach to allow us to select the frequency, too. We will design a function **tone( )** whose arguments represent the frequency and duration. Then we will present a sample program using **tone( )** to turn part of the IBM PC keyboard into a simple musical keyboard.

The *tone( )* Function

Here is the heading for our function:

```
tone(freq,time)
int freq, time;
```

The variable **freq** represents the pitch of the tone in hertz (Hz). (Hertz is the same as what once was called cycles per second.) The variable **time** represents the duration of the tone in tenths of a second; a value of 10 for **time** thus implies a duration of 10 tenths, or 1 second. Now we have to develop ways of getting this information to the sound-producing apparatus. First, let's look at duration.

Tone Duration

We can control the duration the same as we did in Chapter 6. The speaker is controlled, recall, by a device called the 8255 Programmable Parallel Interface Controller. Special I/O channels called *ports* connect this and other controllers to the brains of the outfit, the 8088 microprocessor. We use port 97 to turn the speaker on, use a loop to mark time, and then use port 97 to turn the speaker back off. Here's a code fragment that will do the job:

```
#define TIMESCALE 1270   /* number of counts in 0.1 second */
#define BEEPPORT 97       /* port controls speaker    */
#define ON 79             /* signal to turn speaker on */
    count = TIMESCALE * time; /* convert time to timer units */
    port = inp(BEEPPORT); /* save port setting */
    outp(BEEPPORT,ON);    /* turn speaker on    */
    for (i=0; i < count; i++)
    ;                         /* mark time */
    outp(BEEPPORT,port);  /* turn speaker off, restore setting */
```

Here the value of **count** determines how long the speaker remains on. The **TIMESCALE** factor converts tenths of a second to an equivalent number of counts. Of course, we have to set the desired pitch before sounding the speaker, so let's have a look at that next.

Tone Frequency

The frequency of the tone can be set using another device, one known as the 8253 Programmable Interval Timer. This controller, among its other duties, determines how many pulses per second are sent to the speaker. The 8253 generates a base frequency of 1,190,000 Hz, which is far beyond the range of human hearing. But we can send the 8253 a number to divide into this base rate. For example, if we send a divisor of 5000, we get a pulse rate of

$$1,190,000/5000 = 238 \text{ Hz}$$

which is a little below middle C (the note, not a lower-class version of the language). On the other hand, if we know what frequency **freq** we want, we can calculate the divisor we need by saying

```
divisor = 1,190,000 / freq;
```

Our function will do this, so all we need to know now is how to feed the value of **divisor** to the 8253. This requires using two more ports.

The first step is to put the 8253 timer in the correct operating mode for receiving the divisor. This is done by sending the value 182 (0xB6 in hex) out port 67. Once this is done we can use port 66 to send the divisor.

Sending the divisor presents a slight problem. The divisor itself is a 16-bit number, but it must be sent in two parts. First we send the low-order byte, or final 8 bits of the number. Then we send the high-order byte, or initial 8 bits of the number. In the following program we call these two parts **lobyt** and **hibyt,** and we calculate their values from **divisor:**

```
lobyt = divisor % 256;
hibyt = divisor / 256;
```

Alternatively, we could use the bitwise operators:

```
lobyt = divisor & 255;
hibyt = divisor >> 8;
```

The first statement of each pair converts the first 8 bits to 0s, leaving the last 8 bits as a 1-byte number. Check the workings of the modulus operator and of the bitwise **AND** operator to see how that works. The second statement of each pair takes the original value of **divisor** and shifts the bits 8 places to the right (which is equivalent to dividing by 2^8, or 256). The 8 leftmost bits are set to 0, leaving an 8-bit number consisting of the original leftmost 8 bits.

Here now is the complete function:

```
/* tone(freq,time) -- makes tone of given frequency,length */

#define TIMERMODE 182      /* code to put timer in right mode */
#define FREQSCALE 1190000L /* basic time frequency in Hz */
#define TIMESCALE 1230L    /* number of counts in 0.1 second */
#define T_MODEPORT 67      /* port controls timer mode */
#define FREQPORT 66        /* port controls tone frequency */
#define BEEPPORT 97        /* port controls speaker */
#define ON 79              /* signal to turn speaker on */

tone(freq,time)
int freq,time;
{
    int hibyt, lobyt, port;
    long i, count, divisor;

    divisor = FREQSCALE/freq; /* scale frequency to timer units */
    lobyt = divisor % 256;       /* break integer */
    hibyt = divisor / 256;       /* into two bytes */
    count = TIMESCALE * time;   /* convert time to timer units */
    outp(T_MODEPORT,TIMERMODE);   /* prepare timer for input */
    outp(FREQPORT,lobyt);  /* set low byte of timer register */
    outp(FREQPORT,hibyt);  /* set high byte of timer register */
    port = inp(BEEPPORT);  /* save port setting */
    outp(BEEPPORT,ON);       /* turn speaker on    */
    for (i=0; i < count; i++)
```

```
       ;                            /* mark time */
     outp(BEEPPORT,port);   /* turn speaker off, restore setting*/
}
```

We **#define TIMESCALE** as a **long** integer so that the calculation of **TIMESCALE * time** will be done in **long** instead of **int**. Otherwise, the result, if greater than 32767, will be truncated before it is placed in **count**.

Using the *tone( )* Function

Our **tone( )** function pretty much duplicates the action of the IBM PC's BASIC **SOUND** statement. Here we use it to create a rather limited (8-note, 1-octave) keyboard, using eight keys in the A row to sound notes. Here's the program:

```
/* simple musical keyboard   */

#include <stdio.h>
#include <conio.h>    /* use unbuffered I/O */
#include <ctype.h>
#define C 262         /* define frequencies */
#define D 294
#define E 330
#define F 349
#define G 392
#define A 440
#define B 494
#define C2 524

main()
{
    int key, freq, tempo, time;

    puts("Please enter the basic tempo: 10 = 1 second.");
    scanf("%d", &tempo);
    puts("Thank you. Use the key row a-k to play notes. The");
    puts("shift key doubles the duration. A ! halts the show.");

    while ( (key = getch()) != '!')
        {
        time = isupper(key)? 2 * tempo : tempo;
        key = tolower(key);
        switch (key)
            {
            case 'a' : tone( C, time);
                       break;
```

```
            case 's' : tone( D, time);
                           break;
            case 'd' : tone( E, time);
                           break;
            case 'f' : tone( F, time);
                           break;
            case 'g' : tone( G, time);
                           break;
            case 'h' : tone( A, time);
                           break;
            case 'j' : tone( B, time);
                           break;
            case 'k' : tone( C2, time);
                           break;
            default  : break;
            }
        }
    puts("Bye bye!\n\r");
    }
```

The main feature of the design is a **switch** statement that assigns different pitches to the eight keys A–K. In addition, the program doubles the note duration if you use uppercase. This duration (**time**) is set before the **switch:** then uppercase is converted to lowercase to reduce the number of labels we need.

The second main feature is that we used the **conio.h** header file. This file declares the **getch( )** function, which is similar to **getchar( )**, except that input is not echoed and is not buffered. As a result, when you press, say, the [A]-key, the note plays immediately, and you don't have to press [enter]. Also, the keystroke is not shown on the screen. If you want the keys you press to be echoed to the screen, use **getche( )** instead of **getch( )**.

This particular version was written for the Microsoft C Compiler. Other compilers may have different means for providing unbuffered input.

Although the input is not buffered, the keyboard has its own buffer. This allows you to type ahead if you like. The notes themselves will play at their own steady pace. Incidentally, the basic tempo scaling is for a standard IBM PC.

And here is the opening to "Joy to the World":

```
kjhGfdsA
```

We leave it to you to finish the melody.

I

ASCII Table

Decimal-Hexadecimal-Octal-Binary-ASCII Numerical Conversions

DEX X_{10}	HEX X_{16}	OCT X_8	Binary X_2	ASCII	Key
0	00	00	000 0000	NUL	CTRL/1
1	01	01	000 0001	SOH	CTRL/A
2	02	02	000 0010	STX	CTRL/B
3	03	03	000 0011	ETX	CTRL/C
4	04	04	000 0100	EOT	CTRL/D
5	05	05	000 0101	ENQ	CTRL/E
6	06	06	000 0110	ACK	CTRL/F
7	07	07	000 0111	BEL	CTRL/G
8	08	10	000 1000	BS	CTRL/H, BACKSPACE
9	09	11	000 1001	HT	CTRL/I, TAB
10	0A	12	000 1010	LF	CTRL/J, LINE FEED
11	0B	13	000 1011	VT	CTRL/K
12	0C	14	000 1100	FF	CTRL/L
13	0D	15	000 1101	CR	CTRL/M, RETURN
14	0E	16	000 1110	SO	CTRL/N
15	0F	17	000 1111	SI	CTRL/O
16	10	20	001 0000	DLE	CTRL/P
17	11	21	001 0001	DC1	CTRL/Q
18	12	22	001 0010	DC2	CTRL/R
19	13	23	001 0011	DC3	CTRL/S

ASCII Numerical Conversion—*Continued*

DEX X_{10}	HEX X_{16}	OCT X_8	Binary X_2	ASCII	Key
20	14	24	001 0100	DC4	CTRL/T
21	15	25	001 0101	NAK	CTRL/U
22	16	26	001 0110	SYN	CTRL/V
23	17	27	001 0111	ETB	CTRL/W
24	18	30	001 1000	CAN	CTRL/X
25	19	31	001 1001	EM	CTRL/Y
26	1A	32	001 1010	SUB	CTRL/Z
27	1B	33	001 1011	ESC	ESC, ESCAPE
28	1C	34	001 1100	FS	CTRL<
29	1D	35	001 1101	GS	CTRL/
30	1E	36	001 1110	RS	CTRL/=
31	1F	37	001 1111	US	CTRL/-
32	20	40	010 0000	SP	SPACEBAR
33	21	41	010 0001	!	!
34	22	42	010 0010	,,	,,
35	23	43	010 0011	#	#
36	24	44	010 0100	$	$
37	25	45	010 0101	1/2	1/2
38	26	46	010 0110	&	&
39	27	47	010 0111	'	'
40	28	50	010 1000	(	(
41	29	51	010 1001	)	)
42	2A	52	010 1010	*	*
43	2B	53	010 1011	+	+
44	2C	54	010 1100	,	,
45	2D	55	010 1101	-	-
46	2E	56	010 1110	.	.
47	2F	57	010 1111	/	/
48	30	60	011 0000	0	0
49	31	61	011 0001	1	1
50	32	62	011 0010	2	2
51	33	63	011 0011	3	3
52	34	64	011 0100	4	4
53	35	65	011 0101	5	5
54	36	66	011 0110	6	6
55	37	67	011 0111	7	7
56	38	70	011 1000	8	8

ASCII Numerical Conversion—*Continued*

DEX X_{10}	HEX X_{16}	OCT X_8	Binary X_2	ASCII	Key
57	39	71	011 1001	9	9
58	3A	72	011 1010	:	:
59	3B	73	011 1011	;	;
60	3C	74	011 1100	<	<
61	3D	75	011 1101	=	=
62	3E	76	011 1110	>	>
63	3F	77	011 1111	?	?
64	40	100	100 0000	@	@
65	41	101	100 0001	A	A
66	42	102	100 0010	B	B
67	43	103	100 0011	C	C
68	44	104	100 0100	D	D
69	45	105	100 0101	E	E
70	46	106	100 0110	F	F
71	47	107	100 0111	G	G
72	48	110	100 1000	H	H
73	49	111	100 1001	I	I
74	4A	112	100 1010	J	J
75	4B	113	100 1011	K	K
76	4C	114	100 1100	L	L
77	4D	115	100 1101	M	M
78	4E	116	100 1110	N	N
79	4F	117	100 1111	O	O
80	50	120	101 0000	P	P
81	51	121	101 0001	Q	Q
82	52	122	101 0010	R	R
83	53	123	101 0011	S	S
84	54	124	101 0100	T	T
85	55	125	101 0101	U	U
86	56	126	101 0110	V	V
87	57	127	101 0111	W	W
88	58	130	101 1000	X	X
89	59	131	101 1001	Y	Y
90	5A	132	101 1010	Z	Z
91	5B	133	101 1011	[	[
92	5C	134	101 1100	\	\
93	5D	135	101 1101	]	]

ASCII Numerical Conversion—*Continued*

DEX X_{10}	HEX X_{16}	OCT X_8	Binary X_2	ASCII	Key
94	5E	136	101 1110	∧	∧
95	5F	137	101 1111	—	—
96	60	140	110 0000	`	`
97	61	141	110 0001	a	a
98	62	142	110 0010	b	b
99	63	143	110 0011	c	c
100	64	144	110 0100	d	d
101	65	145	110 0101	e	e
102	66	146	110 0110	f	f
103	67	147	110 0111	g	g
104	68	150	110 1000	h	h
105	69	151	110 1001	i	i
106	6A	152	110 1010	j	j
107	6B	153	110 1011	k	k
108	6C	154	110 1100	l	l
109	6D	155	110 1101	m	m
110	6E	156	110 1110	n	n
111	6F	157	110 1111	o	o
112	70	160	111 0000	p	p
113	71	161	111 0001	q	q
114	72	162	111 0010	r	r
115	73	163	111 0011	s	s
116	74	164	111 0100	t	t
117	75	165	111 0101	u	u
118	76	166	111 0110	v	v
119	77	167	111 0111	w	w
120	78	170	111 1000	x	x
121	79	171	111 1001	y	y
122	7A	172	111 1010	z	z
123	7B	173	111 1011	R	R
124	7C	174	111 1100	¦	¦
125	7D	175	111 1101	T	T
126	7E	176	111 1110	~	~
127	7F	177	111 1111	DEL	DEL,RUBOUT

Index

A

A mode, with **fopen( )** function, 450
A+ mode, in ANSI C, 486
Absolute value function, 259–261
Actual arguments, 257–258, 277
Addition operation, 97–98, 102–104
   array and pointer, 348–349
Additive assignment operation, 214, 218,
      220
Addresses and address operation, 262–263,
      513
   and pointers, 265–272, 354
   and **scanf( )** function, 37, 66, 84
   structure, as arguments, 430–431
   of variables, and names, 271–272
Alarm, escape sequence for, 490
Algorithms, and pseudocode, 208
Alphabetic characters, testing for, 459
Alphanumeric characters, testing for, 460
American National Standards Institute, and
      C language standards, 479–494
And operation
   bitwise, 528
   logical, 180–181, 513
Angle brackets, and **#include**, 333
Animal names program, 192–197
ANSI C language standards, 479–494
Argc, and **main( )** function, 402
Arguments
   arrays as, 349–351
   arrays of structures as, 431–433
   command-line, 400–403
   with **#define**, 328–331
   for **fgets( )** function, 455
   for **fopen( )** function, 450

Arguments—cont
   for **fprintf( )** function, 454–455
   for **fscanf( )** function, 454–455
   for **fseek( )** function, 457
   and function overloading, in C++,
      496–497
   and functions, 24–25, 255–259, 277
   and increment operation, 111–112
   with macros, 328–331
   for **printf( )** function, 75, 77
   for **scanf( )** function, 83–84
   structure, and ANSI C, 482–485
   structure addresses as, 430–431
   structure members as, 428–430
   type-checking of, in ANSI C, 487–490
Argv, and **main( )** function, 402
Arithmetic operations, 95–112, 121, 512
   in ANSI C, 491
Arrays, 233–241, 343–347
   of character strings, 66–67, 381–382
   compared to pointers, 379–380
   and functions and pointers, 349–367
   input for, 311–314
   multidimensional, 356–367
   and pointers, 347–367
   protection of, with **const**, 492–493
   of structures, 419–424, 431–433
ASCII codes and characters, 49
   conversion of, to integer, 307
   and **printf( )** function, 82–83
   table of, 543–546
   testing for, 460
Assembly code files, 12
Assembly language, and ports, 155

Assignment operations, 96–97, 121, 214–215, 218, 220, 512–513
 compared to equality operators, 173–174
 in expressions, 112–113
 pointer, 354
Assignment statements, 20, 24–25, 114
Associativity, of operators, 103–104, 511–512
Asterisk modifier
 in **printf( )** function, 85
 in **scanf( )** function, 85–86
 in type declarations, 437–438
Atof( ) function, 462–464
Atoi( ) function, 307, 462–465
Auto and automatic variables, 289, 295, 519
Automatic arrays, initialization of, 344

B

Backslash character
 for double quotes, 377
 escape sequence for, 26, 51
 with macro definitions, 325–326
 for nonprinting characters, 50–52
Backspace, 26
 escape sequence for, 51
Base 2 numbers, 533–535
Base 8 numbers, 535. *See also* Octal numbers
Base 10 numbers, 533
Base 16 numbers, 535. *See also* Hexadecimal numbers
Base conversions, and **printf( )** function, 45
BASIC language
 assignment and equality operators in, 173
 compared to C, 3, 12
Bell Labs, and C, 3
Binary files
 end of file in, 141
 and **fopen( )** modes, 487
 library functions for, 469
Binary numbers, 533–535
Binary operations, 98–99
Binary tree structures, 433–434
Bit operations, 527–531
Bits, 40
Black box concept, of functions, 252, 258–259
Blank lines, for readability, 27

Blanks
 for output spacing, 87
 and **scanf( )** function, 68
Blocks, 115–118
Body, of functions, 26–27
Braces
 for array initialization, 344–345
 and functions, 21, 26
 for statements, 19–20, 115–116
 for structure members, 415
 in **while** loops, 95
Brackets
 as array indicator, 67
 in type declarations, 437–438
Break statement, 227–228, 232, 525
 avoiding **goto** statements with, 231
 with **switch,** 194–197
Buffers
 input, 136–137
 for text files, 451
Bytes, 40

C

C language, 3
 and C++, 501–502
 sources of information for, 507–508
 standards for, 479–494
 virtues of, 4–6
C preprocessor. *See* Preprocessor, C
C Programming Language, The (Kernighan and Ritchie), 223, 479
C++, 494–502
C++ Programming Language, The (Stroustrup), 494
C suffix, for program files, 21
Calloc( ) function, 468–469
Calls
 function, 25, 253
 macro, 330–331
Carriage return, escape sequence for, 51
Case conversion program, 460–462
Cast operations, 120–121, 515
Cat, UNIX command, 146
Cc compile command, 9
Char. *See* Characters and **char** data type
Character strings, 65–70, 375–376
 and arrays, 234–235, 378–379, 381–382
 and command-line arguments, 401–404
 compared to characters, 68–69
 control. *See* Control strings
 conversions involving, 304–307, 462–465

Character strings—cont
defining, 377–384
input of, 84, 384–388
library functions for, 391–397
output of, 81, 388–391
and pointers, 382–384
replacement, and macros, 326
sorting, program for, 398–400
Characters and **char** data type, 36, 39,
49–52, 56, 66–67, 518
compared to character strings, 68–69
conversion of, 459–462
in **for** statements, 214
pointers to, 386
ranking of, 117
sketch program using, 184–191
testing of, 459–462
variables, 36
Classes, storage. *See* Storage classes
Closing, file, 451
Colons
:: notation, in C++ classes, 499
in bit structures, 530
with labels, 193–195, 229–230, 524–525
Combined redirection, 146–147
Comma operation, 217–220, 515
Command-line arguments, 400–403
Commas
in array initialization, 344–345
for multiple arguments, 259
as operator, 217–220, 515
as variable separator, 28, 43, 219, 518
Comments, 18–19, 21, 335
Compare function, string, 393–396
Compile time substitution, 71
Compiled languages, 5, 8
Compiling C
on IBM PC, 10–12, 279
and speed, 12
on UNIX systems, 9–10, 279
Compound statements, 115–118
Concatenation function, 392–393
Conditional compilation, and portability,
337
Conditional loops, 207
Conditional operation, 191–192, 515
Const modifiers, 492–493
Constants
capitalization of, 72
character, 49–50
character string, 68, 377–378

Constants—cont
compared to variables, 37
enumerated, 491–492
floating point, 54
integer, 44, 48
named, 492
pointer, 266, 348
symbolic, and preprocessor, 66, 70–75,
325–328
Constructors, in C++, 498–499
Continue statement, 229, 231–232, 525
Control characters, testing for, 460
Control strings
for **printf( )** function, 75–77
for **scanf( )** function, 83
Control structures
break statement, 227–228
continue statement, 229, 231–232, 525
do while loops, 222–225, 523
for loops, 212–220, 522
goto statement, 229–233
if statements. *See* **If** statements
jumps, 227–233, 525–526
switch and **break,** 192–197, 524–525
while loops. *See* **While** statements
Control-d, as end-of-file indicator, 143
Control-z, as end-of-file indicator, 141, 143
Conversion specifications, and **printf( )**
function, 77, 83
%c, 36, 52, 75, 84
%d, 20, 26, 45, 75, 82
%e, 55, 75
%f, 36, 55, 72, 75
%g, 75
%ld, 48
%lu, 48
%o, 45, 75, 82
%s, 66, 68, 75
%u, 48, 75, 82
%x, 45, 75, 82
Conversions
base, 45
of character strings, 304–307, 462–465
of characters, 459–462
type, 82–83, 117–121
Copy function, string, 396–397
Copying, of files, using redirection, 146–147
Cypher program, 148–149, 165–166

D

Data identifiers, 45, 66, 77, 82–83

Data integrity, and C++, 501
Data types 37–42, 56–59
  in ANSI C, 490–494
  char. *See* Characters and **char** data type
  checking of, 480, 487–489
  choosing, 310
  conversions, 82–83, 117–121
  double, 53–54, 117, 491, 518
  enumerated, 491–492
  float. *See* Floating-point numbers and
      float data type
  int. *See* Integers and **int** data type
  keywords for, 517
  specifiers, 518
  unsigned. *See* **Unsigned types**
  user-defined, 435–438, 494–501
DEC systems, data type sizes in, 57
Declarations, 22–23, 114
  of arrays of structures, 420–424
  of array of type **char,** 67
  of character variables, 49
  of class functions, in C++, 498
  compared to definitions, 290
  of enumerated types, 492
  of external variables, 289–290, 295
  of floating-point constants, 54
  of floating-point variables, 53–54
  forward, 275, 489
  of function types, 274–277
  of integer variables, 43, 47
  of pointers, 267–268
  of simple variables, 57, 518
  of structure pointer, 426
  of types, 437–438
Decrement operation, 109–112
  in **for** statements, 214
  and pointers, 355
Default, in **switch** statements, 194, 524–525
Default options, and **printf( )** function,
    80–81
Default values, in enumerated data type,
    492
Defensive programming, 313
#define directive
  and C preprocessor, 325–331
  compared to **typedef,** 435
  and symbolic constants, 71–74
Definitions
  character string, 377–384
  of class functions, in C++, 498–500
  compared to declarations, 290

Definitions—cont
  function, 254
  macro, 326
  simple variable, 43–44
  structure variable, 417–418
Demotion, and type conversions, 117–119
Dice-rolling simulation, 298–301
Differencing operation, for pointers, 355
Digits, testing for, 459
Direct input, 136–137
Directives, preprocessor
  #define, 71–74, 325–331
  #elif, 337
  #else, 336–337
  #endif, 336–337
  #if, 336–337
  #ifdef, 336–337
  #ifndef, 336–337
  #include, 333–335
  #undef, 335–336
Division operations, 101–104
  by powers of two, 529
Divisional assignment operation, 218, 220
Do while loops, 222–225, 523
Documentation, and C++, 501
Double data type, 53–54, 518
  ranking of, 117
  speed of calculations with, 491
Double quotes
  and character strings, 66, 377
  and constant substitution, 74
  escape sequence for, 51
  and **#include,** 333
  and macros, 327, 329–330
Driver programs, 259
Dyadic operators, 98–99

E

Echo, and input, 136
Editors, for program preparation, 7–9
Electric bill program, 167–169
Elements, array, 234–235, 380
  and pointers, 347–349
#elif directive, 337
Else, 165–172, 523–524
#else directive, 336–337
Else-if, 167–172
End-of-file indicators, for text files, 141–143
#endif directive, 336–337
Entry-condition loops. *See* **For** statements;
    While statements

Enum and enumerated types, 491–492
EOF (end of file), 142–143
  and **scanf( )** function, 240
Equal to operator, 164
  compared to assignment operations,
    173–174
Equality, testing for with floating-point
    numbers, 174
Error checking
  of input, 190–191, 310–311
  and program design, 318
Errors, roundoff. *See* Roundoff errors
Escape sequences, 25–26, 50–51
Exclusive OR, bitwise, 528–529
Executable files, 9, 12
Execution time substitution, 71
Exit( ) function, 465
Exit-condition loops, 222–225, 523
Exponentiation program, 272–275
Exponents and exponential notation, 53–55
Expression tree, for precedence, 102–103
Expressions, 112–113, 118
  relational, 173–178
Extensions, file, 8–9
Extern and external variables, 289–291,
    293, 295, 519
External arrays, initialization of, 344–346
External **static** variables, 292–293, 295
External storage class, 287–288, 295

F
False value, and relational expressions, 113,
    175–178
Fclose( ) function, 451
Fflush( ) function, and **fopen( )**, 486–487
Fgets( ) function, 455
Field width
  and asterisk, in **printf( )** function, 85
  and columns, 86–87
  for print formatting, 79–80
Fields, and bit manipulation, 530–531
File pointer, and **fseek( )**, 457
File reduction program, 452–454
Files
  copying, 146–147
  description of, 449
  executable, 9, 12
  inclusion of, with **#include,** 333–335
  input-output of, 141–143, 447–459
  program, 8
  redirection of, 144–150

Files—cont
  source, 9
Floating-point numbers and **float** data type,
    39–42, 53–56, 518
  binary, 534–535
  compared to integers, 41–42
  conversions with, 462–464
  division of, 101
  precision of, and **printf( )** function, 79
  printing of, 80–81
  ranking of, 117
  testing for equality with, 174
  variables for, 36–37
Fopen( ) function, 450–451
  in ANSI C, 486–487
For loops, 212–220, 522
  and arrays, 235
  compared to **while** loops, 223–225
Form feed, escape sequence for, 51
Formal arguments, 257–258, 277
Formatting, with **printf( )** function, 79–87
FORTRAN, assignment and equality
    operators in, 173
Forward declarations, of functions, 275,
    489
Fprintf( ) function, 454–455
Fputs( ) function, 455–456
Fractions, binary, 534–535
Free( ) function, 469
Fscanf( ) function, 454–455
Fseek( ) function, 456–459, 486–487
Ftoa( ) function, 464
Functions, 18, 273–275, 278–280
  arguments for, 255–259
  and arrays and pointers, 349–367
  and braces, 21
  calling, 25, 253
  compared to macros, 330–332
  definition, 254
  description of, 26–27
  macro, 328–331
  and multidimensional arrays, 362–367
  overloading of, in C++, 496–497
  and parentheses, 21
  and pointers, 268–272, 386
  purpose of, 251–252
  returning values from, 259–263, 277
  standard. *See* Standard library functions
  statements for, 115
  and structures, 428–433
  types, 274–277, 481

Functions—cont
    user-defined, 29–30
    and variables, calling program, 263–265
    void, 276, 481

G

Getarray( ) function, creation of, 311–314
Getc( ) function, 452
Getchar( ) function, 134–144
Getche( ) function, 136
Getint( ) function, creation of, 301–308
Gets( ) function
    and character strings, 385–387
    compared to **scanf( )** function, 387–388
Global variables, 287–288, 295, 519
Goto statement, 229–233, 295, 525
Graphics program, using characters,
        151–152, 184–191
Greater than operator, 110, 173

H

H suffix, for header files, 73, 333
Header files, 73, 333–335
Headers, 20
    for functions, 26–27
Hexadecimal numbers, 525
    conversions of, and **printf( )** function,
        82
    prefix for, 44–45
    representation of ASCII codes by, 50

I

IBM PC
    compiling C on, 10–12, 280
    data type sizes in, 57
    music on, 537–541
    ports in, 152–156, 538
Identifiers, for **printf( )** function, 75
#if directive, 336–337
If statements, 163–172, 523–524
    avoiding **goto** statements in, 230–231
    compared to **while** loops, 207
#ifdef directive, 336–337
If-else statements, 165–167, 191–192
#ifndef directive, 336–337
#include directive, 18
    and file input-output, 333–335, 447–448
Increment operation, 106–112
    and macros, 331
    and pointers, 354–355

Indices, array, 234–235, 344
Indirect membership operation, 426–428,
        514
Indirection operation, 266–267, 271, 513
Infinite loops, 108, 207
Initialization
    of arrays, and storage classes, 344–347
    of character constants, 49–50
    of character string arrays, 378–379, 381
    expression, in **for** loops, 212–220, 522
    of multidimensional arrays, 359–360
    of structure pointer, 426
    of structures, 417–418
    of variables, 43–44, 518
Inp( ) function, and ports, 155
Input
    of array data, 237–241
    buffered, 136–137
    error checking of, 190–191
    getchar( ) function, 134–144
    integer, and **getint( )** function, 301–308
    of numeric data, 310–314
    with **scanf( )** function. *See* **Scanf( )**
        function
    standard, 144
    stop signal for, 310
Input-output 133, 157–158
    character string, 81, 84, 376–377,
        384–391
    file, 141–143, 452–459
    using ports, 152–156, 538
    redirection, 144–150
    and **stdio.h** file, 20–21, 135
    See also Input; Output
Instructions, compared to statements,
        113–114
Integers and **int** data type, 20, 22, 39–41,
        43–48, 517
    compared to floating-point numbers,
        41–42
    conversions involving, 304–307, 462–465
    declaration of, 22
    division of, 101
    input of, and **getint( )** function, 301–308
    and modulus operator, 105
    overflow of, 47
    printing of, 79–80
    ranking of, 117
Intel systems
    8086/8088, ports for, 152–156
    80386, data type sizes in, 57

Interaction, programs with, 37
Interpreted languages, 5, 8
Inventory program, 413-415
Isalnum( ) function, 460
Isalpha( ) function, 459
Isascii( ) function, 460
Iscntrl( ) function, 460
Isdigit( ) function, 459
Islower( ) function, 459
Ispunct( ) function, 460
Isspace( ) function, 459
Isupper( ) function, 459
Iteration, 207
Itoa( ) function, 464

J

Jumps, 227-233, 525-526

K

Kernighan, Brian, *The C Programming
    Language,* 223, 479-480
  on **goto** statement, 229
Keyboard, musical, 537-541
Keywords, 22
  data type, 56, 517
  program flow, 509
  storage class, 519

L

L suffix, for **long,** 48
  and **printf( )** function, 79
Labels
  for **goto** statement, 229-230, 525
  with **switch,** 195-197, 524-525
Left shift operation, 529
Length, of character strings, 66, 68-70, 392
Less than operator, 95, 173
Letterhead program, 256-257
Library routines. *See* Standard library
    routines
Lines, input of, 140-141
Link command, 10-11
Linked structures, 433
Local variables, 262, 289, 295, 519
Logical operations, 179-183, 513
  bitwise, 527-529
Logo, assignment and equality operators
    in, 173
Long, 46-48, 79, 457, 480, 517-518
Loops

Loops—cont
  do while, 222-225, 523
  for. *See* **For** statements
  infinite, 108, 207
  nesting of, 225-227
  while. *See* **While** statements
Lowercase, conversion function for, 460
Lowercase characters, testing for, 459
Ls list command, 9, 146

M

Machine language code, 9-10, 12
Macro expansion, 326
Macros
  compared to functions, 330-332
  and preprocessor, 326-338
Main( ) function, 18, 21, 26, 251, 278
  and command-line arguments, 400-403
Malloc( ) function, 465-468
Masking, with bitwise logical operations,
    528-529
Members and membership operations, 514
  and bit operations, 530
  as function arguments, 428-430
  structure, 415, 418
  structure array, 421-422, 426-428
Memory, units of, 40
Memory allocation
  and arrays, 235
  and **calloc,** 468-469
  and character strings, 384-385
  for data types, 46-47, 57
  and declarations, 22, 114
  and **malloc,** 465-468
  and storage classes, 289-290, 295
  and structures, 416-417
  and variable definitions, 43
Microprocessors, Intel
  8086/8088, ports for, 152-156
  80386 data sizes, 57
Microsoft C, compilation with, 10-12, 279
Mixed types, division with, 101
Modes
  for **fopen( ),** 450-451, 486-487
  with **fseek( ),** 457
Modification, program, and modularity,
    237
Modifiers
  conversion specification, and **printf( )**
    function, 79-81, 85
  for **scanf( )** function, 85-86

Modifiers—cont
   and type declarations, 437–438, 492–493
Modularity
   and C, 4
   and C++, 501
   and program design, 318
   and program modification, 237
Modulo assignment operation, 218, 220
Modulus operation, 105
   and overflow, 83
Msc compiler command, 10
MS-DOS 2
   files, 141
   redirection in, 149–150
Multidimensional arrays, 356–367
Multiplication operation, 28, 98, 102–104
   by powers of two, 529
Multiplicative assignment operation, 215,
      218, 220
Music, on IBM PC, 537–541

N

Named constants, 492
Names
   array, 347–348, 380
   macro, 326, 332
   for program files, 8
   of variables, 23, 271–272
Negation, bitwise, 528
Negative numbers, representation of, 82
Nesting
   and **break** statement, 228
   of **#define**, 336
   and **goto** statement, 231–232
   of **if** statements, 169–171
   of loops, 225–227
   of macros, 327
   of structures, 422–424
   of **while** loops, 157
Newline character, 20, 25–26
   escape sequence for, 51
   and **scanf( )** function, 68
Nonprinting characters, 50–52
Not, logical, 181, 513
Not equal to operator, 138
Null address, and **gets( )** function, 386–387
Null characters, in character strings, 66–67
Null statements, 156, 213
Number-crunching program, 157–158
Number-guessing program, 209–210

O

O prefix for octal number, 44–45
Object code, 9–10, 12
Octal numbers, 535
   conversions of, and **printf( )** function,
      82
   prefix for, 44–45
   representation of ASCII codes by, 50
Offset, with **fseek( )**, 457
One's complement operation, 528
Opening, file, 450–451, 486–487
Operands, 97–98
Operators
   address. *See* addresses and address
      operations
   arithmetic, 95–112, 121, 491, 512–513
   assignment. *See* Assignment operations
   bit, 527–531
   cast, 120–121, 515
   comma, 217–220, 515
   conditional, 191–192, 515
   decrement. *See* Decrement operation
   equal to, 164, 173–174
   increment. *See* Increment operation
   indirect membership, 426–428, 514
   indirection, 266–267, 271, 513
   logical, 179–183, 513, 527–529
   membership, 418, 427, 514, 530
   modulus, 105
   or, 181, 513, 528
   overloading of, in C++, 496
   pipe, 148
   pointer, 353–356, 513
   redirection, 145–147
   relational, 173–180, 513
   shift, 529–530
   sizeof, 58–59, 69–70, 121, 515
   symbols for, 511–515
   union, 433–435, 514
Options, program, and command-line
      arguments, 403
Or
   bitwise, 528
   logical, 181, 513
Order of evaluation
   for comma operations, 219
   of logical operations, 182
   of subexpressions, 113
Outp( ) function, and ports, 155
Output, 316
   character string, 376–377, 388–391

Output—cont
    and ports, 155
    with **printf( )**. *See* **Printf( )** function
    putchar( ) function, 134–144
    redirection of, 145–147
    See also Input-output;
Overflow
    floating-point, 55
    integer, 47
    and modulo arithmetic, 83
Overload and overloading, in C++,
    496–497
Ox prefix hexadecimal numbers, 44–45

P

Padding, of field structures, 531
Parentheses
    with arguments, 24–25
    with cast operations, 120
    with **for** statements, 212
    with functions, 18, 21, 26
    and macros, 328, 330–332
    for operation precedence, 102–104
    with **sizeof**, 70
    with **switch** statements, 194
    in type declarations, 437–438
Pascal
    assignment and equality operators in,
      173
    compared to C, 3
Pipe operator, 148
PL/I, assignment and equality operators
    in, 173
Pointers, 265–272
    and arrays, 344–367, 379–380
    and character strings, 382–384, 386
    to characters, 386
    constants, 266, 348
    to functions, 386
    and functions and arrays, 349–367
    operations with, 353–356, 513
    and structures, 424–428
    variables, 266, 348
Portability, 4
    and C standards, 479–480
    and conditional compilation, 327
    and input-output functions, 133
    and **typedef**, 436
Ports, input-output, 152–156, 538
Postfix mode, for increment operation,
    106–109

Precedence
    of arithmetic operations, 102–104
    of increment operation, 111
    of logical operations, 181–182
    of modifiers, 437–438
    of operator symbols, list of, 511–512
    of relational operations, 178–179
    of value operation, 349
Precision
    of floating-point numbers, 42, 53
    in **printf( )** function, 79, 85
Prefix mode, for increment operation,
    106–109
Preprocessor, C, 21
    and symbolic constants, 66, 70–75,
      325–338
Prime number program, 225–227
Printf( ) function, 20, 26, 36–38, 52
    in ANSI C, 487
    and character strings, 68, 81
    of characters, 52
    compared to **puts( )** function, 389
    compared to **scanf( )** function, 84
    of floating-point numbers, 55, 80–81
    formatting with, 72, 75–83, 85–87
    of integer values, 45, 48, 79–80
    and newline character, 25–26
    and unsigned integer types, 48
Program control. *See* Control structures
Program files, names for, 8
Programmable Parallel Interface Controller
    (8255), 153–154, 538
Programming
    in C, overview of, 7–12
    opportunities in, and C, 5
Programming techniques
    algorithms and pseudocode, 208
    for braces in **while** loops, 116
    and column printing, 86–87
    for data types, 59
    defensive programming, 313
    design, 317–318
    for **getint( )** function, 301–308
    and **goto** statements, 230–232
    and interaction, 37
    keyboard input, 235
    modularity, 237
    protective programming, 294
    and readability, 27–28, 491
    for sorting program, 308–317
    and storage classes, 294

Programming techniques—cont
and symbolic constants, 71–72, 328
and type names, 435–436
and variable names, 23
Programs
and statements, 113
structure of, 26–27
Promotions, and type conversions, 117–118, 488
Protective programming, 294
Pseudocode, and algorithms, 208
Punctuation characters, testing for, 460
Putc( ) function, 452
Putchar( ) function, 134–144
Puts( ) function
and character strings, 388–389
compared to **printf( )** function, 389
creation of, 390–391

Q

Quotation marks. *See* Double quotes;
Single quotes

R

R mode, with **fopen( )** function, 450
R+ mode, in ANSI C, 486
Ragged arrays, 382–383
Random access file input-output, 456–459
Random number function, 294–301
Range
of floating-point numbers, 53
of signed integers, 43
of unsigned integers, 46
Ranking, of data types, 117
Readability, program
and enumerated types, 491
techniques for, 27–28
Real numbers. *See* Floating-point numbers
Rectangular arrays, 382–383
Recursion, 280
Redirection, of files, 144–150
Register and register variables, 293–295, 519
Registers, microprocessor, 153
Relational expressions, 173–178
Relational operations, 173–180, 513
Remainder operation, 105, 512
Replacement strings, and macros, 326
Return, and functions, 259–262, 265, 277
and **void** function type, 481

Return value, of **scanf( )** function, 239–241
Rewind( ) function, and **fopen( )**, 487
Right shift operation, 529
Ritchie, Dennis, 3
The C Programming Language, 223, 479–480
on **goto** statement, 229
Roundoff errors
and **double,** 119
and floating-point numbers, 42, 174
Runners, program for, 122–123

S

Scalar variables, 343
Scanf( ) function, 36–38, 83–86, 85–86
and character strings, 66
compared to **gets( )** function, 387–388
compared to **printf( )** function, 84
return value of, 239–241
and static storage class, 67–68
Scientific notation, 53
Scope, and storage classes, 287–295, 519
Scoreread program, 235–237
Seeds, for random number generation, 294–295
Semicolons
and **#define,** 71
with **for,** 212–213
in statements, 22, 26, 28, 113–114
for structure templates, 415
Shift operations, 529–530
Short, 46–47, 117, 517
Side effects, and local variables, 263
Sign operator, 98
Signed data types, 43, 49, 56
Single quote
for characters, 49–50
escape sequence for, 51
Single-character input-output, 134–144
Sizeof operation, 58–59, 121, 515
compared to **strlen( )** function, 69–70
Sketch program, character, 184–191
Skipping facility, for **scanf( )** function, 85–86
Sorting programs
for character strings, 398–400
for numbers, 308–317
Source code, 9
Source files, 9
Spacing, in macro definitions, 332
Speaker, port for, in IBM PC, 153–154

Speed
  and compilation, 12
  computation, and **long int** data types,
    46
  and **double**, 491
Stack, and argument-passing, 488
Standard input, 144
Standard library functions
  accessing, 447–448
  and ANSI C, 485–486
  character string, 385–397, 459–465
  file 448–459, 469
  for memory allocation, 465–469
  and portability, 480
  and underscore symbol, 23
  See also specific functions
Standard systems directories, and **#include**,
    333
Standards, ANSI, 479–494
Statements, 113–117
  assignment, 20, 24–25, 114
  braces for, 19
  declaration, 22–23
Static and static variables, 67, 291–292,
    295, 519
  and character strings, 377–378
Static arrays, initialization of, 344–346, 378
Stdio.h file, 20–21, 135
Stoi( ) function, creation of, 304–307
Stop signals, for array input, 238–239, 310
Storage, memory. *See* Memory allocation
Storage classes, 519
  C++, 494–500
  and initialization of arrays, 344–347
  and scope, 287–295
Storage units, 347–349
Strcat( ) function, 392–393
Strcmp( ) function, 393–396
Strcpy( ) function, 396–397
Strings. *See* Character strings
Strlen( ) function, 66, 68–70, 392
  compared to **sizeof**, 69–70
Stroustrup, Bjarne, *The C++*
    Programming Language, 494
Struct and structures, 413–415
  and ANSI C, 482–485
  arrays of, 419–424, 431–433
  bit, 529–531
  and functions, 428–433
  operators for, 514

Struct and structures—cont
  and pointers, 424–428
  templates for, 415, 417
  variables, 416–418
Structured programming, and C, 4. *See*
    also Control structures
Structured statements, 115
Subexpressions, 112–113
Subscripts, array, 234–235, 344
Subtraction operation, 98, 102–104
Subtractive assignment operation, 218, 220
Switch statements, 192–197, 524–525
Symbol groups, in print statements, 26
Symbolic constants, and C preprocessor,
    66, 70–75, 325–328
Symbols,
  operator, 511–514, 527–531
  for syntax. *See* specific symbol names
    (e.g., Braces; Brackets;)
System calls, and UNIX, 486

T

Tabs, 26
  escape sequence for, 26, 51
  and **scanf( )** function, 68
Tags
  in structure templates, 415, 417
  union, 434
Templates
  structure, 415, 417
  union, 434
Test condition
  in **for** loops, 212–217, 522
  in **while** loops, 115
Testing, of characters, 459–462
Text files, 145
  buffered, 451
  end-of-file indicators for, 141–143
Thompson, Ken, 3
Tolower( ) function, 460
Tone( ) function, creation of, 537–541
Toupper( ) function, 460
Translators, C++, 502
True value, and relational expressions, 113,
    175–178
Truncation, and integer division, 101
Two's complement notation, 82
Typedef, 435–438
Types. *See* Data types

U

Unary operations, 98–99, 103
Unbuffered input, 136–137
#undef directive, 335–336
Underflow, floating-point, 55
Underscore symbol, and library routines, 23
Unions, and union operations, 433–435, 514
UNIX operating system
   accessing library functions in, 447
   and C, 3–5, 479
   command-line arguments in, 403
   compiling C on, 9–10, 12, 279
   editors for, 7–8
   files, 141
   #include on, 333
   redirection of files in, 145–149
   sources of information for, 508
   and standard library functions, 485–486
UNIX Primer Plus, 148
Unsigned types, 46–48, 56, 517–518
   in ANSI C, 490
   conversions with, 82
   ranking of, 117
Update expression, in **for** loops, 212–220, 522
Uppercase, conversion function for, 460
Uppercase characters, testing for, 459
User-defined data types, 435–438, 494–501
User-defined functions, 29–30

V

Value operator, and pointers, 349, 354
Variables
   addresses of, 271–272
   in assignment operations, 96
   automatic, 289, 295
   calling program, and pointers, 263–267
   character, 36, 39, 49
   compared to constants, 37
   constant, 492–493
   declaration of, 22–23, 57, 518
   definitions of, 43–44
   external, 289–291, 293, 295

Variables—cont
   external static, 292–293, 295
   floating-point, 36–37, 53–54
   global, 287–288, 295, 519
   initialization of, 43–44, 518
   integer, declaring, 43
   local, 262, 289, 519
   names of, 23, 271–272
   pointer, 266, 348
   register, 293–295
   scalar, 343
   scope of, 287–295, 519
   static, 291–292, 295
   storage classes of, 288, 295
   structure, 416–418
   union, 434
Vector functions, class for, in C++, 495–500
Void, and arguments, 490
Void function type, 276
   and ANSI C, 481
Volatile modifiers, 493–494

W

W mode with **fopen( )** function, 450
W+ mode, in ANSI C, 486
Weather program, 357–359
While statements, 93–95, 115–117, 205–207, 211, 521–522
   and avoiding **goto** statements, 231
   compared to **for** statements, 223–225
   and **if** statements, 163–165
   and increment operation, 107
   nesting of, 157
White space
   and **scanf( )** function, 68, 84
   testing for, 459
Width, field. *See* Field width
Word-count program, 182–184
Words, 40

X

X, for hexadecimal numbers, 50, 487